I0890884

Navigating Law and Policy in STM Enterprises:

Ethical Governance, Regulation, and Innovation Strategy

Hewa Majeed Zangana
Duhok Polytechnic University, Iraq

Jamal Al-Karaki
Zayed University, UAE

Marwan Omar
Illinois Institute of Technology, USA

IGI Global
Scientific Publishing
Publishing Tomorrow's Research Today

Vice President of Editorial Melissa Wagner
Director of Acquisitions Mikaela Felty
Director of Book Development Jocelynn Hessler
Production Manager Mike Brehm
Cover Design Jose Rosado

Published in the United States of America by
IGI Global Scientific Publishing
701 East Chocolate Avenue
Hershey, PA, 17033, USA
Tel: 717-533-8845
Fax: 717-533-7115
Website: https://www.igi-global.com E-mail: cust@igi-global.com

Copyright © 2025 by IGI Global Scientific Publishing. All rights reserved. No part of this publication may be reproduced, stored or distributed in any form or by any means, electronic or mechanical, including photocopying, without written permission from the publisher.

Product or company names used in this set are for identification purposes only. Inclusion of the names of the products or companies does not indicate a claim of ownership by IGI Global Scientific Publishing of the trademark or registered trademark.

Library of Congress Cataloging-in-Publication Data

Names: Zangana, Hewa Majeed, 1987- editor. | Al-Karaki, Jamal, 1970- editor. | Omar, Marwan, 1982- editor.
Title: Navigating law and policy in STM enterprises : ethical governance, regulation, and innovation strategy / edited by Hewa Majeed Zangana, Jamal Al-Karaki, and Marwan Omar.
Other titles: Navigating law and policy in science, technology, medicine enterprises
Description: Hershey : IGI Global Scientific Publishing, 2025. | Includes bibliographical references and index. | Summary: "The primary objective of this book is to provide a comprehensive and multidisciplinary examination of the complex legal, ethical, and policy dimensions influencing the operation and growth of science, technology, and medicine (STM) enterprises"-- Provided by publisher.
Identifiers: LCCN 2025026736 (print) | LCCN 2025026737 (ebook) | ISBN 9798337348629 (hardcover) | ISBN 9798337348636 (paperback) | ISBN 9798337348643 (ebook)
Subjects: LCSH: Science and law. | Science and law--Moral and ethical aspects. | Technology and law. | Technology and law--Moral and ethical aspects. | Medical laws and legislation. | Medical laws and legislation--Moral and ethical aspects.
Classification: LCC K487.S3 N39 2025 (print) | LCC K487.S3 (ebook) | DDC 344/.095--dc23/eng/20250604
LC record available at https://lccn.loc.gov/2025026736
LC ebook record available at https://lccn.loc.gov/2025026737

British Cataloguing in Publication Data
A Cataloguing in Publication record for this book is available from the British Library.

All work contributed to this book is new, previously-unpublished material.
The views expressed in this book are those of the authors, but not necessarily of the publisher.
This book contains information sourced from authentic and highly regarded references, with reasonable efforts made to ensure the reliability of the data and information presented. The authors, editors, and publisher believe the information in this book to be accurate and true as of the date of publication. Every effort has been made to trace and credit the copyright holders of all materials included. However, the authors, editors, and publisher cannot assume responsibility for the validity of all materials or the consequences of their use. Should any copyright material be found unacknowledged, please inform the publisher so that corrections may be made in future reprints.

Table of Contents

Preface xiii

Chapter 1
Regulatory Frameworks in Science, Technology, and Medical Innovation 1
Hewa Majeed Zangana, Duhok Polytechnic University, Iraq
Marwan Omar, Illinois Institute of Technology, USA
Jamal N. Al-Karaki, Zayed University, UAE

Chapter 2
Expiration vs. Termination: Reassessing Legal Boundaries in Contract Law 35
Dilshad Ahmad Mhia-alddin, University of Mosul, Iraq
Akram Mahmoud Hussein, University of Mosul, Iraq

Chapter 3
Regulatory Responses to AI in Healthcare and Medical Diagnostics 59
Naresh Tiwari, Cap Tech, USA

Chapter 4
Effect of Research Integrity Challenges on Ethical Compliance Mediating Role of Bureaucratic Barriers in Research Management in the Horn of Africa . 93
Wako Jio, Bule Hora University, Ethiopia
shashi kant, Bule Hora University, Ethiopia
Hirut Assegid, Bule Hora University, Ethiopia

Chapter 5
Are Textual Prompts in Large Language Models Sufficient for Vulnerability Detection? 121
Puya Pakshad, Illinois Institute of Technology, USA
Sajad Aqanasiri, Shahid Beheshti University, Iran

Chapter 6
Legal Implications of Contract Expiry in Modern Commercial Law: Towards a Framework for Post-Expiry Obligations and Risk Management 139
Dilshad Ahmad Mhia-alddin, University of Mosul, Iraq

Chapter 7
Case Studies of Misuse and Mitigation in AI-Driven STM Research 159
Angel Justo Jones, University of Virginia, USA
Bianca Montes Jones, Capitol Technology University, USA

Chapter 8
The Role of Language in Regulating AI and Agricultural Technologies: Legal Perspectives from a Globalized World.. 193
Hewa Majeed Zangana, Duhok Polytechnic University, Iraq
Pratiwi Amelia, Universitas Muhammadiyah Bangka Belitung, Indonesia
Senny Luckyardi, Universitas Komputer Indonesia, Indonesia
Firas Mahmood Mustafa, Duhok Polytechnic University, Iraq
Shuai Li, University of Oulu, Finland

Chapter 9
Navigating Legal Barriers in Climate and Environmental Technologies 225
Hermano Jorge Da Silva De Queiroz, Lindsey Wilson College, USA

Chapter 10
Managing the Adoption and Implementation of Zero Trust Architecture Cybersecurity: Overcoming Organizational, Cultural, and Compliance Challenges.. 261
Noble Antwi, Illinois Institute of Technology, USA

Chapter 11
Governing AI-Driven Agriculture: Policy, Ethics, and the Role of Language in Knowledge Transfer... 285
Hewa Majeed Zangana, Duhok Polytechnic University, Iraq
Pratiwi Amelia, Universitas Muhammadiyah Bangka Belitung, Indonesia
Senny Luckyardi, Universitas Komputer Indonesia, Indonesia
Firas Mahmood Mustafa, Duhok Polytechnic University, Iraq
Shuai Li, University of Oulu, Finland

Chapter 12
Policy Implications of Gene Editing and Biotechnology Regulation 317
Rebet Keith Jones, Capitol Technology University, USA

Compilation of References 351

About the Contributors 387

Index 391

Detailed Table of Contents

Preface...xiii

Chapter 1
Regulatory Frameworks in Science, Technology, and Medical Innovation 1
Hewa Majeed Zangana, Duhok Polytechnic University, Iraq
Marwan Omar, Illinois Institute of Technology, USA
Jamal N. Al-Karaki, Zayed University, UAE

The convergence of science, technology, and medical (STM) innovation has transformed contemporary society, offering unprecedented benefits while introducing complex legal, ethical, and governance challenges. Regulatory frameworks serve as critical mechanisms for balancing innovation with public interest, ensuring safety, efficacy, and equity in rapidly evolving domains. This chapter explores the multifaceted regulatory landscapes that govern STM enterprises, highlighting international standards, national legislation, and sector-specific protocols. It also addresses the tension between fostering innovation and enforcing compliance, especially in areas such as biomedical research, emerging technologies, and data-driven health systems. Through comparative insights and case-driven analysis, this chapter aims to equip stakeholders with a nuanced understanding of how regulatory systems can both constrain and catalyze responsible innovation in STM fields.

Chapter 2
Expiration vs. Termination: Reassessing Legal Boundaries in Contract Law..... 35
Dilshad Ahmad Mhia-alddin, University of Mosul, Iraq
Akram Mahmoud Hussein, University of Mosul, Iraq

The legal concepts of expiration and termination in contract law, though often used interchangeably in practice, possess distinct theoretical and practical implications that significantly affect contractual relationships. This paper undertakes a critical reassessment of the boundaries between expiration—the natural conclusion of a contract upon fulfillment of its terms—and termination—the active cessation of contractual obligations prior to their stipulated end. Through doctrinal analysis, comparative legal perspectives, and examination of recent judicial decisions, this research elucidates how the ambiguity between these concepts can create legal uncertainty, especially in complex commercial agreements. The paper proposes a refined legal framework that distinguishes expiration from termination in both statutory and common law contexts, providing clarity for courts, practitioners, and contracting parties. The study contributes to contract theory by enhancing precision in contractual language and advocating for uniform interpretive standards in international contract practice.

Chapter 3
Regulatory Responses to AI in Healthcare and Medical Diagnostics 59
Naresh Tiwari, Cap Tech, USA

The integration of AI in healthcare offers transformative possibilities for precision medicine, early disease detection, and clinical decision support. However, these advancements come with significant legal, ethical, and regulatory challenges. This chapter explores global regulatory responses to AI in healthcare, analyzing approaches from the EU, US, and select Asian countries. It examines medical device regulations, data protection laws, and liability frameworks in addressing AI-enabled system risks. The chapter discusses transparency, accountability, and patient autonomy in AI deployment, providing insights for policymakers, healthcare professionals, and technology developers to balance innovation with public trust and patient safety. By identifying best practices and emerging trends, the chapter aims to foster innovation while safeguarding patient safety.

Chapter 4
Effect of Research Integrity Challenges on Ethical Compliance Mediating Role of Bureaucratic Barriers in Research Management in the Horn of Africa . 93
Wako Jio, Bule Hora University, Ethiopia
shashi kant, Bule Hora University, Ethiopia
Hirut Assegid, Bule Hora University, Ethiopia

This chapter investigates the influence of the problems of the integrity of research on ethical correspondence in the context of research management in Africa, emphasizing the intermediary role of bureaucratic barriers. Using the sample size of 385 researchers in various institutions, we used the Kaiser-Meyer-Lkin (KMO) test to evaluate the adequacy of our sample for factor analysis, reaching the KMO value indicating the adequacy of a good sample. Confirmatory Factor Analysis (CFA) was conducted using AMOS software to validate the measurement model, demonstrating solid construct validity and reliability of the variables involved. Subsequently, Structural Equation Modeling (SEM) was applied to explore the relationships among research integrity challenges, ethical compliance, and bureaucratic barriers. The results show that bureaucratic barriers considerably line up the relationship between the problems of research integrity and ethical correspondence, revealing that increased problems of integrity exacerbate bureaucratic obstacles, thus reducing ethical engagement.

Chapter 5
Are Textual Prompts in Large Language Models Sufficient for Vulnerability Detection? 121
Puya Pakshad, Illinois Institute of Technology, USA
Sajad Aqanasiri, Shahid Beheshti University, Iran

Large Language Models (LLMs) have gained traction in domains from software development to cybersecurity, particularly for detecting vulnerabilities in program source code. Their ability to analyze large codebases and identify security weaknesses makes them valuable in software security analysis. However, their effectiveness declines in the absence of intermediate representations such as Abstract Syntax Trees (AST), Control Flow Graphs (CFG), and Data Flow Graphs (DFG), or even tokenized forms of code. In this research study, we assess the performance of LLMs in detecting vulnerabilities directly from raw source code, without structural representations. By designing context-specific prompts, we aim to enhance the model's understanding of code semantics. Our findings show that LLMs can partially identify vulnerabilities from raw code alone, reaching up to 43% accuracy. This indicate both the potential and current limitations of prompt-based LLMs for static vulnerability detection.

Chapter 6
Legal Implications of Contract Expiry in Modern Commercial Law: Towards a Framework for Post-Expiry Obligations and Risk Management 139
Dilshad Ahmad Mhia-alddin, University of Mosul, Iraq

In an increasingly complex commercial landscape, the legal implications arising from the expiry of contracts demand critical attention. While contract formation and enforcement have been thoroughly examined in commercial law, post-expiry obligations and the associated risk exposures remain underexplored. This paper investigates the residual responsibilities and liabilities that may persist or emerge following contract termination due to expiry. Drawing on comparative legal analysis, case law, and regulatory frameworks across multiple jurisdictions, this study identifies legal ambiguities and practical challenges that can lead to disputes or financial loss. The research further develops a structured framework aimed at clarifying post-expiry duties and enhancing risk management strategies for both parties. By bridging the gap between legal theory and commercial practice, the proposed framework provides actionable guidance for legal practitioners, businesses, and policymakers to mitigate risks and ensure compliance beyond contract expiration.

Chapter 7
Case Studies of Misuse and Mitigation in AI-Driven STM Research 159
Angel Justo Jones, University of Virginia, USA
Bianca Montes Jones, Capitol Technology University, USA

Integrating Artificial Intelligence (AI) in Science, Technology, and Medicine (STM) research has led to groundbreaking advancements. However, it has also introduced significant security, ethics, and potential misuse challenges. This chapter explores several case studies in which AI-driven approaches in STM research have been misapplied, resulting in ethical violations, security breaches, or unintended consequences. Additionally, it examines strategies for addressing these issues, focusing on regulatory frameworks, ethical guidelines, and technological safeguards. This chapter analyzes real-world examples and highlights the importance of maintaining secure and ethical practices in AI-enhanced STM research. It offers insights into the evolving landscape of AI within this field.

Chapter 8
The Role of Language in Regulating AI and Agricultural Technologies: Legal Perspectives from a Globalized World.. 193
Hewa Majeed Zangana, Duhok Polytechnic University, Iraq
Pratiwi Amelia, Universitas Muhammadiyah Bangka Belitung, Indonesia
Senny Luckyardi, Universitas Komputer Indonesia, Indonesia
Firas Mahmood Mustafa, Duhok Polytechnic University, Iraq
Shuai Li, University of Oulu, Finland

Language plays a pivotal role in shaping the legal and regulatory frameworks that govern the development and deployment of artificial intelligence (AI) and agricultural technologies. In a globalized context, regulatory language not only influences legal interpretation and policy implementation but also impacts international cooperation, compliance standards, and ethical discourse. This chapter explores how linguistic nuances, translation challenges, and semantic ambiguities can affect the formulation and harmonization of legal norms across jurisdictions. By examining case studies and regulatory instruments from diverse legal systems, the chapter highlights the complexities of crafting clear, inclusive, and enforceable legal language in the face of rapidly evolving scientific and technological landscapes. The chapter argues that a multilingual and interdisciplinary approach is essential for creating robust regulatory ecosystems that promote innovation while safeguarding societal and environmental interests.

Chapter 9
Navigating Legal Barriers in Climate and Environmental Technologies 225
Hermano Jorge Da Silva De Queiroz, Lindsey Wilson College, USA

As global efforts intensify to combat climate change and advance sustainable development, climate and environmental technologies have emerged as critical tools in achieving environmental resilience and innovation. However, deployment and scaling of such technologies often encounter complex legal and regulatory barriers that can hinder progress. This chapter explores the legal challenges surrounding the development, implementation, and diffusion of climate technologies. It examines international treaties, national regulations, intellectual property regimes, liability standards, and market mechanisms such as carbon trading. Particular attention is given to environmental justice, technology transfer, and public-private partnerships in addressing these legal constraints. By analyzing case studies from developed and developing jurisdictions, the chapter identifies key friction points and proposes reform pathways. Ultimately, it provides a strategic lens through which STM stakeholders can navigate legal complexities while promoting ethical and sustainable technological innovation.

Chapter 10
Managing the Adoption and Implementation of Zero Trust Architecture Cybersecurity: Overcoming Organizational, Cultural, and Compliance Challenges 261
Noble Antwi, Illinois Institute of Technology, USA

The growing sophistication of cyber threats and complexity of digital ecosystems demand a shift in cybersecurity strategy. This paper examines the organizational, strategic, and regulatory challenges of adopting Zero Trust Architecture (ZTA). It argues that ZTA is not just a technical solution but a management-driven framework requiring leadership, cultural change, and compliance alignment. Through analysis of leadership roles, regulatory demands (e.g., GDPR, HIPAA), and resource allocation, the study highlights barriers to adoption. It recommends best practices such as phased implementation, identity governance, automation, and continuous monitoring. Emerging technologies like AI and blockchain are explored for their role in enhancing ZTA. The research emphasizes the need for a proactive security culture in cloud-first and remote work environments and offers actionable strategies for sustainable ZTA implementation. Ultimately, Zero Trust is presented as a foundational model for resilient, future-ready cybersecurity governance.

Chapter 11
Governing AI-Driven Agriculture: Policy, Ethics, and the Role of Language in Knowledge Transfer 285
Hewa Majeed Zangana, Duhok Polytechnic University, Iraq
Pratiwi Amelia, Universitas Muhammadiyah Bangka Belitung, Indonesia
Senny Luckyardi, Universitas Komputer Indonesia, Indonesia
Firas Mahmood Mustafa, Duhok Polytechnic University, Iraq
Shuai Li, University of Oulu, Finland

Artificial intelligence (AI) is transforming agriculture by enabling precision farming, predictive analytics, and automated decision-making, thereby enhancing productivity and sustainability. However, this rapid technological advancement raises complex policy and ethical challenges, particularly regarding data governance, equitable access, environmental impact, and transparency. This chapter explores the regulatory frameworks shaping AI-driven agricultural practices and emphasizes the critical role of language in facilitating effective knowledge transfer among diverse stakeholders, including farmers, policymakers, and researchers. By analyzing interdisciplinary approaches, the chapter highlights how linguistic clarity and ethical considerations underpin responsible AI governance in agriculture, ensuring innovations serve public interest while mitigating risks. Ultimately, it advocates for comprehensive policies that balance innovation with accountability and inclusivity in the evolving landscape of agri-tech.

Chapter 12
Policy Implications of Gene Editing and Biotechnology Regulation 317
Rebet Keith Jones, Capitol Technology University, USA

Gene editing and biotechnology represent transformative advancements with profound potential to reshape medicine, agriculture, and environmental management. However, their rapid development poses significant regulatory and ethical challenges that require comprehensive policy frameworks. This chapter explores the policy implications surrounding gene editing technologies, such as CRISPR, highlighting the balance between fostering innovation and ensuring public safety, ethical standards, and equitable access. It discusses regulatory approaches adopted worldwide, the role of international cooperation, and the socio-political dynamics influencing governance. By examining current legislative landscapes and emerging best practices, the chapter aims to inform policymakers, legal scholars, and industry stakeholders about effective governance models that align with ethical imperatives and technological progress.

Compilation of References 351

About the Contributors 387

Index 391

Preface

In an era marked by rapid scientific advancement and technological disruption, the interplay between innovation, governance, and ethical responsibility has never been more critical. Science, Technology, and Medical (STM) enterprises operate at the forefront of societal transformation—driving progress, but also raising complex legal, ethical, and policy questions. *"Navigating Law and Policy in STM Enterprises: Ethical Governance, Regulation, and Innovation Strategy"* is a timely and essential contribution to this evolving discourse.

This volume brings together interdisciplinary expertise from legal scholars, technologists, ethicists, and policymakers to explore the multifaceted challenges facing STM enterprises today. As technologies like artificial intelligence, gene editing, blockchain, and cybersecurity systems mature and scale globally, their implications for regulation, governance, and public trust become central to sustainable progress. This book aims to frame these challenges within the context of actionable strategies, comparative legal frameworks, and case-based insights.

Our objectives with this book are to:

1. **Illuminate Legal and Regulatory Landscapes**: Provide readers with a clear understanding of the regulatory frameworks that shape innovation in science, technology, and medicine.
2. **Explore the Ethical Dimensions of Innovation**: Examine the moral responsibilities that underlie research practices, AI deployment, and biotechnology applications.
3. **Bridge Theory and Practice**: Offer real-world case studies and legal analyses to guide stakeholders in managing risk, compliance, and public policy engagement.
4. **Stimulate Forward-Thinking Governance Models**: Anticipate the emerging legal and ethical challenges posed by disruptive technologies and propose adaptable governance frameworks.

ORGANIZATION OF THE BOOK

The book is structured into twelve comprehensive chapters that collectively address the dynamic interface of law, policy, and innovation across STM domains:

- **Chapter 1**: *Regulatory Frameworks in Science, Technology, and Medical Innovation*
  Sets the stage with a comparative analysis of global regulatory models governing innovation and public health outcomes.
- **Chapter 2**: *Expiration vs. Termination: Reassessing Legal Boundaries in Contract Law*
  Investigates nuanced interpretations in contract termination and expiration clauses across sectors.
- **Chapter 3**: *Regulatory Responses to AI in Healthcare and Medical Diagnostics*
  Explores how governments and institutions are responding to the deployment of AI in critical medical settings.
- **Chapter 4**: *Effect of Research Integrity Challenges on Ethical Compliance: Mediating Role of Bureaucratic Barriers in Research Management in the Horn of Africa*
  Analyzes the intersection of ethics, compliance, and administrative hurdles in regional research ecosystems.
- **Chapter 5**: *Are Textual Prompts in Large Language Models Sufficient for Vulnerability Detection?*
  Examines the limitations and regulatory considerations surrounding LLMs in cybersecurity and software assurance.
- **Chapter 6**: *Legal Implications of Contract Expiry in Modern Commercial Law: Towards a Framework for Post-Expiry Obligations and Risk Management*
  Proposes a novel legal framework for managing post-expiry obligations in contractual relationships.
- **Chapter 7**: *Case Studies of Misuse and Mitigation in AI-Driven STM Research*
  Presents real-world instances of ethical lapses in AI use and corresponding institutional or regulatory responses.
- **Chapter 8**: *The Role of Language in Regulating AI and Agricultural Technologies: Legal Perspectives from a Globalized World*
  Discusses how language and legal interpretation shape AI policy in international agricultural contexts.
- **Chapter 9**: *Navigating Legal Barriers in Climate and Environmental Technologies*

Surveys legal constraints and innovation bottlenecks in clean tech and environmental sustainability efforts.

- **Chapter 10**: *Managing the Adoption and Implementation of Zero Trust Architecture: Overcoming Organizational, Cultural, and Compliance Challenges in Cybersecurity*
  Explores the legal and governance challenges in deploying zero trust models within regulated industries.
- **Chapter 11**: *Governing AI-Driven Agriculture: Policy, Ethics, and the Role of Language in Knowledge Transfer*
  Investigates the intersection of AI governance, agricultural policy, and language accessibility in rural and globalized economies.
- **Chapter 12**: *Policy Implications of Gene Editing and Biotechnology Regulation*
  Concludes the book with a forward-looking view on genome editing technologies and the global race to regulate bio-innovation responsibly.

IN CONCLUSION

This book aims to serve as both a reference and a roadmap for professionals, scholars, and decision-makers navigating the evolving legal and policy challenges in STM sectors. As innovation accelerates, so too must our frameworks for governance, ethical alignment, and legal clarity. We hope this work provides valuable insights and practical tools to shape responsible and resilient innovation strategies in the years ahead.

Hewa Majeed Zangana
Duhok Polytechnic University, Iraq

Jamal Nazzal Al-Karaki
Zayed University, UAE

Marwan Omar
Illinois Institute of Technology, United States

Chapter 1
Regulatory Frameworks in Science, Technology, and Medical Innovation

Hewa Majeed Zangana
https://orcid.org/0000-0001-7909-254X
Duhok Polytechnic University, Iraq

Marwan Omar
Illinois Institute of Technology, USA

Jamal N. Al-Karaki
https://orcid.org/0009-0000-7833-3970
Zayed University, UAE

ABSTRACT

The convergence of science, technology, and medical (STM) innovation has transformed contemporary society, offering unprecedented benefits while introducing complex legal, ethical, and governance challenges. Regulatory frameworks serve as critical mechanisms for balancing innovation with public interest, ensuring safety, efficacy, and equity in rapidly evolving domains. This chapter explores the multifaceted regulatory landscapes that govern STM enterprises, highlighting international standards, national legislation, and sector-specific protocols. It also addresses the tension between fostering innovation and enforcing compliance, especially in areas such as biomedical research, emerging technologies, and data-driven health systems. Through comparative insights and case-driven analysis, this chapter aims to equip stakeholders with a nuanced understanding of how regulatory systems can both constrain and catalyze responsible innovation in STM fields.

DOI: 10.4018/979-8-3373-4862-9.ch001

Copyright © 2025, IGI Global Scientific Publishing. Copying or distributing in print or electronic forms without written permission of IGI Global Scientific Publishing is prohibited.

1. INTRODUCTION

In the 21st century, science, technology, and medical (STM) innovation have emerged as transformative forces, reshaping societies, economies, and public health systems worldwide. From precision medicine and AI-driven diagnostics to advanced manufacturing and next-generation wireless communication, the pace and scope of innovation demand corresponding advancements in regulatory oversight. However, the development of effective, timely, and globally coherent regulatory frameworks has often struggled to keep pace with technological change—a challenge famously described as the "pacing problem" (Abbott, 2011).

Regulatory systems in STM domains are tasked with a complex balancing act: to enable innovation while safeguarding public safety, privacy, equity, and trust. This dual mandate becomes particularly delicate in environments where risk is amplified by emerging technologies or where innovation outpaces existing legal mechanisms. As Amaral et al. (2024) point out, the global regulation of medical devices exemplifies this tension, with disparate national frameworks posing significant barriers to innovation and timely market access.

Historically, the evolution of regulatory science has often been reactive rather than proactive, a pattern that is increasingly unsustainable. In the healthcare sector, for instance, rapid advancements in digital health technologies, regenerative medicine, and synthetic biology demand regulatory models that are agile, evidence-based, and ethically grounded (Calvert et al., 2021; Hines et al., 2020). Meanwhile, interdisciplinary initiatives—such as the competency-based integration of precision medicine into pharmaceutical industries—underscore the need for new governance models that transcend traditional disciplinary and institutional silos (Conway & Chisholm, 2024).

This chapter offers a comprehensive analysis of regulatory frameworks within STM innovation, exploring how they can foster, hinder, or reshape innovation trajectories. It examines global governance challenges, national policy dynamics, and the role of regulatory science in enabling responsible innovation. Drawing from comparative studies, case examples, and recent developments in cybersecurity, AI, biotechnology, and digital health, it emphasizes the importance of agile, anticipatory, and inclusive regulation. The chapter further addresses the security implications of innovation—especially in cloud computing (Hamza & Omar, 2013), sensor networks (Mohammed et al., 2018), and large-scale cyber-physical systems (Jones et al., 2023)—and the urgent need to align technical progress with ethical and societal considerations.

In medical biotechnology, the regulatory environment must strike a sustainable balance between innovation and risk, particularly in rapidly developing economies like China. Han, Fan, and Xue (2024) explore how the "right to science" principle is beginning to shape such policy transformations, reflecting broader shifts toward rights-based and patient-centric regulatory paradigms. Similarly, the use of regulatory science in Traditional Chinese Medicine (TCM) has shown how culturally specific frameworks can be harmonized with international standards (Liang et al., 2021).

The integration of cybersecurity protocols into STM innovation is also of growing concern. Threat vectors targeting biotechnology labs, healthcare systems, and research infrastructures highlight vulnerabilities that demand not only technical but regulatory interventions (Huff et al., 2023; Jones & Omar, 2024). The use of machine learning and large language models (LLMs) in medical and technological contexts raises further regulatory questions related to transparency, accountability, and synthetic data governance (Gholami & Omar, 2023; 2024).

Moreover, cross-sectoral policy environments such as those in Canada and Europe reveal both opportunities and institutional bottlenecks. MacNeil et al. (2019) show how enabling environments can accelerate innovation, while Maresova (2022) critiques the adequacy of current regulatory adaptations in the face of digital health and clinical decision-support systems. In the U.S., the FDA's evolving approach to digital health technologies illustrates the negotiation between regulatory clarity and organizational innovation (Lievevrouw et al., 2021).

Regulatory frameworks must also be reformed to support broader innovation ecosystems (Oh et al., 2020), ensuring that equity is not compromised in the pursuit of efficiency. The National Academies (2023) call for governance models that align innovation with justice and inclusivity—a perspective increasingly echoed across global policy discussions. In this context, equity is not a peripheral concern but a central pillar of responsible innovation strategy.

Finally, the security, privacy, and ethical dimensions of STM innovation must be considered as fundamental components of regulatory design. From the ethical oversight of LLMs (Omar & Zangana, 2025) to the cybersecurity implications of AI-powered infrastructures (Omar & Zangana, 2024), modern regulation requires interdisciplinary collaboration and foresight. As Omar (2022) argues, machine learning systems must be evaluated not only for technical robustness but also for their compliance with evolving legal and ethical standards.

This chapter is structured to first explore foundational regulatory concepts and their evolution. It then moves to sector-specific challenges in biotechnology, digital health, and data governance, followed by an analysis of global and national case studies. The chapter concludes with policy recommendations aimed at enhancing the coherence, agility, and equity of STM regulatory systems in the face of accelerating innovation.

2. HISTORICAL EVOLUTION OF REGULATORY FRAMEWORKS

The development of regulatory frameworks in science, technology, and healthcare has undergone significant transformations over the past century, shaped by shifts in innovation paradigms, public health demands, ethical considerations, and global cooperation. Initially, regulations were reactive—formed in response to crises such as drug failures or technological abuses. Over time, however, they have matured into more proactive and anticipatory systems designed to balance innovation, public safety, and equity.

2.1 Early Developments and the Pacing Problem

In the early 20th century, regulatory efforts were largely national in scope and centered on the safety of food, drugs, and basic industrial standards. However, as Abbott (2011) observed, the rapid acceleration of scientific and technological advancement began to outpace the development of legal and ethical oversight—a phenomenon known as the "pacing problem." This discrepancy laid the groundwork for the emergence of international frameworks intended to harmonize regulation across borders and disciplines.

To better illustrate the transformation of regulatory approaches in science, technology, and medical fields, the following flowchart presents a timeline of key stages from reactive frameworks to anticipatory governance models.

Figure 1. Evolution of regulatory frameworks in STM fields

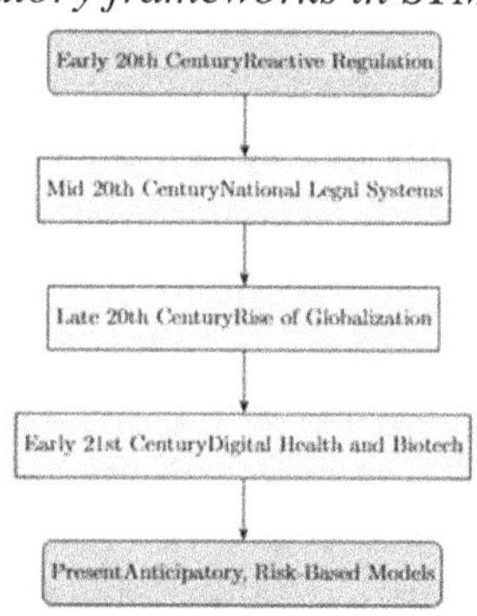

2.2 Transition to Regulatory Science

The concept of "regulatory science" emerged in response to the growing complexity of evaluating novel technologies. It sought to integrate scientific rigor into regulatory processes, thereby improving both the safety and efficacy of emerging innovations. In Europe, the Regulatory Science and Innovation Programme for Europe (ReScIPE) proposed by Hines et al. (2020) exemplifies this shift toward structured, science-based policy development. In the UK, similar initiatives have been implemented to reinforce evidence-based decision-making in healthcare innovation (Calvert et al., 2021).

2.3 Digital Health, Biotech, and Globalization

The digital revolution has brought additional regulatory challenges, especially in biotechnology and digital health. The FDA's evolving standard-making process for digital medical technologies reflects the co-production of technological and regulatory innovation (Lievevrouw et al., 2021). In parallel, China has adopted a rights-based approach to science to balance innovation with public risk in medical biotechnology, emphasizing sustainable governance mechanisms (Han et al., 2024).

Moreover, globalization has emphasized the need for harmonized regulations. Amaral et al. (2024) analyzed how disparate global regulatory landscapes for medical devices can hinder innovation and market access, calling for more consistent international standards.

2.4 Sector-Specific Evolution

In the pharmaceutical and chemical manufacturing industries, the evolution of Chemistry, Manufacturing, and Controls (CMC) regulations reflects the industry's internal push toward innovation while maintaining compliance (Cauchon et al., 2019). Similarly, traditional medicine systems such as Traditional Chinese Medicine (TCM) have seen regulatory science applied to improve public safety and promote innovation (Liang et al., 2021).

For Canada's healthcare sector, MacNeil et al. (2019) highlighted policy and regulatory barriers that often hinder the uptake of health technology, suggesting that enabling environments require both legal and operational reforms.

2.5 The Role of Digital Transformation and AI

The integration of digital technologies such as artificial intelligence (AI), blockchain, and large language models (LLMs) has presented a new frontier for regulatory frameworks. Gholami and Omar (2023, 2024) examined the role of synthetic data and LLMs in optimizing AI performance, emphasizing the need for new regulatory considerations in educational and cybersecurity contexts.

The increased application of AI in cybersecurity—especially for mitigating threats in biotechnology and healthcare—demands updated regulatory perspectives. Huff et al. (2023) and Jones et al. (2023) stressed the importance of aligning regulatory mechanisms with the operational risks of AI-driven systems. In particular, Jones and Omar (2024) presented the GEADD method, leveraging GPT-2 for zero-day threat detection, underscoring how traditional regulations must adapt to dynamic threat landscapes.

These ideas are expanded in volumes edited by Omar and Zangana (2024, 2025), which explore the intersection of AI, security, and digital forensics, presenting cutting-edge case studies and frameworks that underscore the urgency for regulatory evolution.

2.6 Governance, Competency, and Equity

A broader governance perspective is essential for effective regulation in health and technology sectors. The National Academies of Sciences, Engineering, and Medicine (2023) proposed a comprehensive framework aligning innovation with equity, while Conway and Chisholm (2024) emphasized the need for inter-disciplinary competency frameworks in precision medicine industries.

Furthermore, governance concerns extend into cloud security and wireless communication. Foundational work by Hamza and Omar (2013) and Mohammed et al. (2018) addressed regulatory gaps in cloud computing and wireless sensor networks, highlighting vulnerabilities that demand ongoing oversight. Nguyen et al. (2018) linked regulatory rollbacks, such as the FCC's repeal of net neutrality, to broader implications for data privacy and security.

2.7 Innovation vs. Regulation: A Dynamic Tension

The tension between fostering innovation and ensuring regulation remains an enduring theme. Guerra-Bretaña and Flórez-Rendón (2018) demonstrated how over-regulation can stifle innovation in medical devices, a sentiment echoed by Maresova (2022) who discussed the impact of new decision support frameworks on the industry. On the other hand, Oh et al. (2020) argued for regulatory reform as a catalyst for innovation ecosystems, showing how thoughtful regulation can drive technological progress.

Omar (2021, 2022, 2024) contributed significantly to understanding how regulatory mechanisms can be enhanced using database security, machine learning, and adversarial defense strategies in DNNs. His work underscores the role of intelligent regulation—responsive, data-driven, and anticipatory.

3. CORE PRINCIPLES OF REGULATION IN STM FIELDS

In science, technology, and medicine (STM), regulatory frameworks serve as critical instruments to ensure safety, foster innovation, protect public interest, and adapt to the rapid pace of technological change. Effective regulation in STM fields is guided by several foundational principles: safety and risk minimization, innovation enablement, transparency and accountability, interdisciplinary collaboration, equity and access, and cybersecurity and digital trust.

3.1. Safety and Risk Minimization

At the heart of regulatory action lies the imperative to protect human health and safety. Regulatory bodies establish mechanisms for the rigorous assessment of new technologies, particularly in pharmaceuticals and medical devices. Han, Fan, and Xue (2024) emphasize the importance of balancing innovation with risk under the "right to science" principle, noting China's evolving approach to medical biotechnology regulation. Similarly, Guerra-Bretaña and Flórez-Rendón (2018) argue that safety assessments often determine the pace and scope of innovation, especially in the medical device sector.

The role of chemistry, manufacturing, and controls (CMC) is also pivotal. Cauchon et al. (2019) provide an industry perspective, illustrating how early integration of regulatory science into product development can mitigate risk while streamlining approval processes. In the Canadian context, MacNeil et al. (2019) identify procedural and legislative barriers that often impede the introduction of novel health technologies, despite robust safety profiles.

3.2. Innovation Enablement

Regulatory systems must also foster an environment conducive to innovation. Abbott (2011) outlines the global governance gap in regulating emerging technologies, proposing international cooperation to bridge disparities. A similar call is echoed by Hines et al. (2020), who propose a European model—ReScIPE—to integrate regulatory science with innovation, ensuring regulations evolve alongside technological advances.

Maresova (2022) emphasizes that while regulation can sometimes impede market entry, well-designed frameworks can accelerate innovation. For example, the FDA's co-productive model for digital health standards, as studied by Lievevrouw, Marelli, and Van Hoyweghen (2021), highlights the dynamic interplay between technological innovation and adaptive regulatory practices.

3.3. Transparency and Accountability

Transparency is crucial in building public trust and ensuring ethical compliance. The National Academies of Sciences, Engineering, and Medicine (2023) assert that innovation in health must align with principles of accountability and equity. Similarly, Liang et al. (2021) show that in traditional Chinese medicine, applying regulatory science transparently not only improves safety but also facilitates public trust and innovation.

In digital technologies and software-driven systems, transparency must extend to algorithmic decision-making and data governance. Gholami and Omar (2023; 2024) explore how synthetic data and student-teacher paradigms in large language models (LLMs) require clearer regulatory benchmarks for reproducibility and accountability in AI-driven research.

3.4. Interdisciplinary Collaboration

As STM fields converge, regulation must foster interdisciplinary competency and collaboration. Conway and Chisholm (2024) argue that integrating precision medicine into regulatory frameworks demands a robust competency model that spans medicine, data science, and policy. Calvert et al. (2021) also emphasize the UK's strategic push toward regulatory science that supports cross-disciplinary collaboration, particularly in healthcare innovation.

This approach aligns with the emerging role of regulatory professionals not just as enforcers of rules but as innovation enablers, a position supported by Oh, Choi, and Lee (2020) in their call for regulatory reforms to support innovation ecosystems.

3.5. Equity and Access

Modern regulatory frameworks must address global disparities in access to technology and healthcare. Amaral et al. (2024) discuss how inconsistent global regulations hinder innovation and limit access to medical devices, particularly in low-resource settings. The National Academies (2023) further advocate for a governance model that places equity at the center of innovation, ensuring that benefits are shared inclusively.

Hamza and Omar (2013) and Nguyen et al. (2018) extend this discussion into cloud computing and internet policy, showing how uneven regulatory enforcement can exacerbate digital divides and systemic inequities.

3.6. Cybersecurity and Digital Trust

As STM becomes increasingly digital, cybersecurity emerges as a non-negotiable regulatory concern. Jones and Omar (2024) and Jones et al. (2023) underscore the importance of proactive AI-based methods like the GEADD system in defending against advanced cyber threats in STM contexts. Huff et al. (2023) further outline best practices for protecting biotechnology labs and healthcare research entities from escalating cyber threats.

Similarly, the regulatory frameworks proposed in Omar and Zangana (2024; 2025) stress the need for security by design in AI and forensic technologies. These frameworks build upon earlier foundational work by Omar (2021; 2022; 2024), which emphasizes cryptographic methods and adversarial defense mechanisms as essential components of regulatory compliance in cybersecurity.

3.7. Future-Readiness and Adaptive Capacity

Finally, regulatory frameworks must be adaptable and future-ready. Amaral et al. (2024) and Conway and Chisholm (2024) both call for continuous learning, scenario planning, and agility in regulatory systems. This is especially relevant as technologies like LLMs and quantum computing begin to intersect with traditional domains, necessitating regulatory foresight and horizon scanning.

Omar and Zangana (2025) argue for modular regulatory systems that can accommodate such emerging intersections, offering a vision of regulation that is both robust and flexible.

Regulatory frameworks in STM fields are built upon interrelated foundational principles. The diagram below highlights the six core tenets that guide the development of ethical, secure, and future-ready regulation.

Figure 2. Core principles guiding STM regulatory frameworks

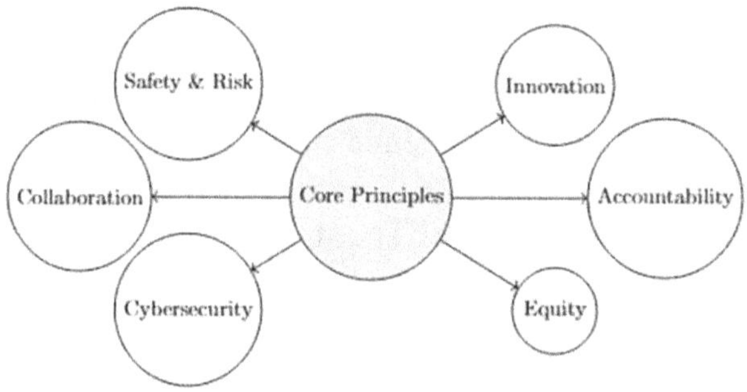

To visualize the relative importance and foundational structure of STM regulatory principles, the pyramid chart below organizes them hierarchically—placing safety and equity at the base and future-readiness at the apex, symbolizing progressive maturation of regulatory objectives.

Figure 3. Hierarchy of STM regulatory principles

4. SECTOR-SPECIFIC REGULATORY CHALLENGES

The implementation of regulatory frameworks often varies significantly across industries due to differences in operational models, risk profiles, and technological maturity. As emerging technologies like large language models (LLMs), advanced biotechnology, and smart medical devices continue to evolve, sector-specific regulatory challenges have become increasingly complex and consequential.

4.1 Healthcare and Medical Device Regulation

The healthcare and medical device sectors face some of the most rigorous and rapidly evolving regulatory landscapes. Regulatory frameworks must strike a balance between enabling innovation and ensuring patient safety and efficacy of medical interventions. Amaral et al. (2024) highlight how regulatory disparities across countries create market access challenges for medical device companies, often slowing the pace of innovation. Similarly, Guerra-Bretaña and Flórez-Rendón (2018) emphasize that overregulation or misalignment in standards can dampen innovation in biomedical engineering, particularly in low- and middle-income regions.

Moreover, regulatory science is being increasingly recognized as a key driver in improving healthcare innovation. Calvert et al. (2021) propose that countries such as the UK develop advanced regulatory science capabilities to promote both innovation and public health outcomes. Likewise, Hines et al. (2020) introduce the Regulatory Science and Innovation Programme for Europe (ReScIPE), which aims to harmonize science-driven regulation across the EU. These initiatives underscore the importance of integrative regulatory mechanisms in advancing healthcare technologies.

Efforts to modernize regulation are also observed in digital health. The U.S. Food and Drug Administration (FDA) has taken steps to co-produce standards with industry players, particularly in the realm of digital therapeutics and AI-driven health platforms (Lievevrouw, Marelli, & Van Hoyweghen, 2021). However, these reforms are not without obstacles. Maresova (2022) critiques that newer regulatory frameworks, like those governing Clinical Decision Support (CDS) systems, are still ill-equipped to handle the pace and complexity of algorithmic innovation in healthcare.

In the Canadian context, MacNeil et al. (2019) identify bureaucratic inertia and lack of clear guidance as significant barriers to health technology innovation. Likewise, Liang et al. (2021) discuss how traditional Chinese medicine faces dual pressures—innovating while adhering to rigorous safety standards. Han, Fan, and Xue (2024) further explore how China's evolving policies reflect a desire to harmonize the "right to science" with national safety concerns in biotechnology, emphasizing a delicate balance between freedom of research and state control.

4.2 Biotechnology and Laboratory Environments

Biotechnology companies and laboratories face increasing cybersecurity threats due to the integration of cloud infrastructure and AI-based systems. Huff et al. (2023) argue that such threats are exacerbated by fragmented and outdated regulatory protocols. For instance, Hamza and Omar (2013) previously noted that cloud computing abuse presents new vectors for nefarious activity that existing regulatory frameworks often overlook. As Jones and Omar (2024) show through the GEADD method, LLMs offer promising detection capabilities, but their deployment requires regulatory foresight to address algorithmic transparency and accountability.

Additionally, Cauchon et al. (2019) stress that Chemistry, Manufacturing, and Controls (CMC) practices in biotechnology must adapt to incorporate AI and data-driven models, pushing regulatory agencies to revise historical guidelines. Conway and Chisholm (2024) support this position by advocating for interdisciplinary competency frameworks that incorporate AI literacy into biopharmaceutical regulation.

4.3 Cybersecurity, Telecommunications, and Digital Innovation

Digital sectors—particularly cybersecurity and telecommunications—witness regulatory lags that hinder rapid innovation. Abbott (2011) warns that the "pacing problem" persists across scientific fields, where innovation consistently outpaces regulatory adaptation. This gap is evident in cybersecurity, where threats evolve faster than compliance systems can respond. As demonstrated by Jones et al. (2023), machine learning solutions can improve threat detection speed and accuracy, but outdated policies often prevent their immediate implementation.

The digital forensics field, as explored by Omar and Zangana (2025), also encounters substantial regulatory ambiguity regarding AI-assisted evidence analysis, complicating its admissibility in courts. Furthermore, Mohammed, Omar, and Nguyen (2018) discuss vulnerabilities such as wormhole attacks in wireless sensor networks, which remain insufficiently addressed by current telecommunications regulations.

In parallel, Nguyen et al. (2018) critique the repeal of net neutrality by the FCC, highlighting its adverse implications for data security and privacy—core components of digital innovation. Oh, Choi, and Lee (2020) advocate for regulatory reforms that cultivate innovation ecosystems, proposing agile regulatory sandboxes and stakeholder-inclusive governance.

4.4 AI, LLMs, and Software Regulation

The regulation of LLMs and AI systems introduces a novel set of sector-specific concerns. Gholami and Omar (2023) demonstrate that synthetic data can improve model efficiency, while Gholami and Omar (2024) explore how student-teacher architectures in LLMs can yield near-equivalent performance. However, these advancements challenge traditional intellectual property and data protection laws, which are not yet equipped to evaluate the provenance or explainability of AI outputs.

As AI pervades domains like cybersecurity, medicine, and software vulnerability detection (Omar & Zangana, 2024; 2025), regulation must evolve to include model interpretability, bias mitigation, and ethical compliance. Omar (2024) emphasizes the urgent need to defend deep neural networks (DNNs) from adversarial attacks, advocating for AI-specific defense standards. Likewise, in Omar (2021, 2022), recommendations are made for aligning AI-driven database and cybersecurity systems with cryptographic and access control standards.

The lifecycle of AI systems—from design to deployment—presents multiple intervention points for regulatory oversight. The flow diagram below identifies these key stages and highlights where policies can most effectively address transparency, safety, and accountability.

Figure 4. AI lifecycle with regulatory entry points

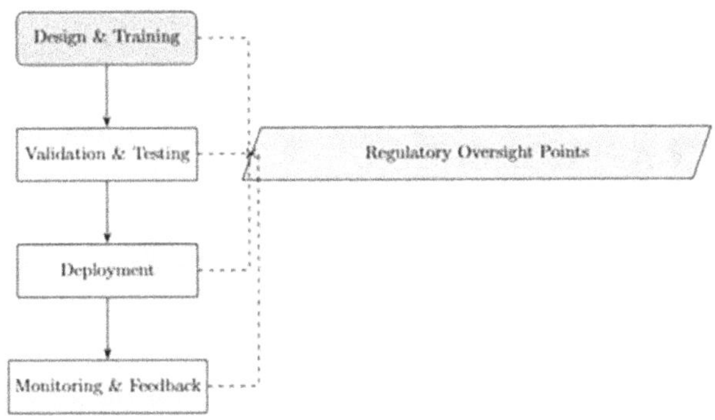

4.5 Toward a Cross-Sectoral Governance Framework

In response to these fragmented sector-specific challenges, there is a growing call for a harmonized governance model. The National Academies of Sciences, Engineering, and Medicine (2023) propose a framework that aligns health and medical innovation with equity and ethical principles. This framework emphasizes inclusivity, transparency, and adaptability—features that are critical for regulating LLMs, AI systems, and other cross-domain technologies.

Ultimately, effective sector-specific regulation must be both agile and anticipatory. Whether addressing the ethical implications of AI in healthcare, the cybersecurity of biotechnology labs, or the innovation ecosystem in telecom, regulation must evolve through interdisciplinary dialogue, informed policymaking, and ongoing scientific collaboration.

The following conceptual framework illustrates the integration of sector-specific regulation (healthcare, AI, cybersecurity) into a unified governance model emphasizing interoperability, transparency, and inclusivity.

Figure 5. A unified governance model for cross-sectoral regulation

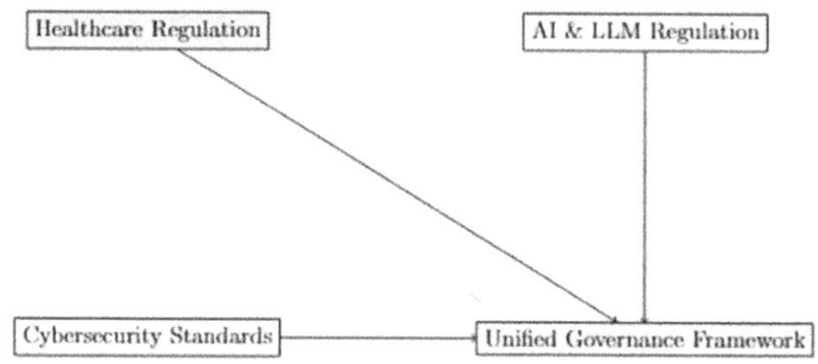

5. INTERNATIONAL AND COMPARATIVE REGULATORY APPROACHES

The regulation of emerging technologies—particularly in healthcare, biotechnology, and digital infrastructure—has become increasingly complex, fragmented, and consequential on a global scale. Countries and regions around the world adopt varying regulatory frameworks, driven by socio-economic priorities, innovation policies, and governance philosophies. While some nations foster innovation through liberalized regimes, others adopt precautionary principles to mitigate risk, often at the cost of stifling innovation.

5.1 Divergence in National and Regional Frameworks

A foundational analysis by Abbott (2011) underscores the growing disparity between technological advancements and regulatory oversight. This "pacing problem" has led to policy lag, where the legal frameworks cannot keep pace with the speed of innovation. For example, the European Union's General Data Protection Regulation (GDPR) is more stringent than data governance policies in other jurisdictions, creating cross-border compliance challenges for AI and biotechnology companies (Calvert et al., 2021).

In the United States, the FDA's evolving approach to digital health illustrates how co-production of technological and regulatory innovation can enhance outcomes (Lievevrouw et al., 2021). Meanwhile, Canada has made significant efforts to enable health technology innovation, though challenges persist due to inconsistent policy and regulatory mechanisms (MacNeil et al., 2019).

China represents another dynamic regulatory environment. Han et al. (2024) analyzed how the "right to science" underpins biotechnology regulations in China, reflecting an ongoing tension between enabling scientific progress and managing ethical concerns. Similarly, regulatory practices in Traditional Chinese Medicine have recently evolved to balance public safety and innovation, leveraging insights from regulatory science (Liang et al., 2021).

To contextualize the global landscape, the chart below compares different regulatory strategies across selected regions, highlighting key attributes such as innovation focus, data governance, and AI oversight.

Figure 6. Comparative maturity of regulatory approaches by region

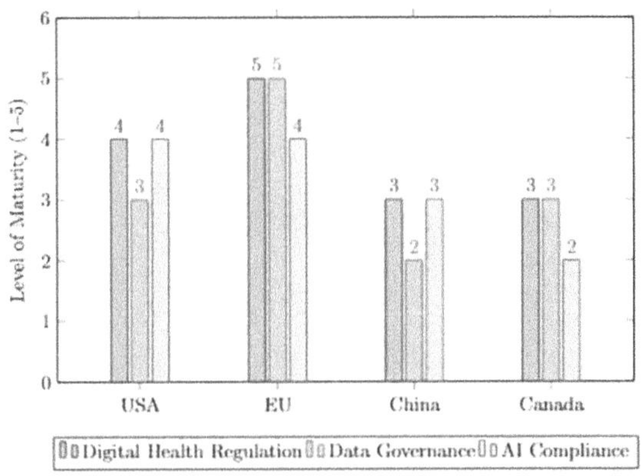

5.2 Medical Devices and Global Innovation

Medical devices represent a critical sector where global regulatory divergence impacts innovation and market access. Amaral et al. (2024) identified challenges such as inconsistent approval timelines, diverse documentation standards, and inadequate post-market surveillance across jurisdictions. These regulatory inconsistencies influence the competitiveness and speed-to-market of medical device manufacturers. Guerra-Bretaña and Flórez-Rendón (2018) found that countries with more predictable and transparent regulatory processes tend to experience greater medical innovation, underscoring the interplay between regulation and technological development.

Maresova (2022) discussed the implications of recent regulatory reforms in the EU and US on clinical decision-support systems. These changes, while designed to ensure safety, often introduce complexities that hamper small and medium enterprises from scaling up effectively.

5.3 Toward Harmonization and Regulatory Science

A global push toward regulatory harmonization has emerged to bridge these gaps. The ReScIPE model proposed by Hines et al. (2020) calls for a pan-European regulatory science framework to align health technology assessment, innovation, and market authorization processes. This echoes similar sentiments in the UK's approach to regulatory science in healthcare (Calvert et al., 2021).

International collaboration on standards and competency development also plays a crucial role. Conway and Chisholm (2024) emphasized the need to embed precision medicine competencies into regulatory practice to address the interdisciplinary nature of modern healthcare innovation.

In the pharmaceutical domain, Cauchon et al. (2019) presented an industry perspective, calling for more flexible regulatory environments for Chemistry, Manufacturing, and Controls (CMC) processes to reduce delays and improve adaptability in innovation pipelines.

5.4 Ethical and Security Considerations in Comparative Context

Cybersecurity and ethical data use are universal regulatory concerns. Huff et al. (2023) explored how cybersecurity threats in biotechnology and healthcare research are addressed differently across countries. The lack of international consensus poses operational risks, especially for multinational organizations. Jones and Omar (2024) and Jones et al. (2023) discussed how AI-driven methods such as GEADD can be integrated into security frameworks to provide regulatory-compliant threat detection and mitigation mechanisms.

Mohammed et al. (2018) and Nguyen et al. (2018) further highlighted the importance of secure communication and privacy frameworks in wireless and net-neutrality environments. As emerging technologies increasingly rely on cloud infrastructures, security frameworks become essential components of compliance (Hamza & Omar, 2013).

The U.S. National Academies (2023) emphasized that regulatory governance must also align with equity goals in health innovation, which adds another layer of complexity to international regulatory frameworks.

5.5 AI, LLMs, and Global Regulatory Implications

The global regulation of large language models (LLMs) and synthetic data remains largely fragmented. Gholami and Omar (2023, 2024) emphasized the need for global regulatory benchmarks to evaluate the use of synthetic data in AI training and performance calibration. Such guidelines are especially crucial as student-teacher LLM models become more prevalent in real-world deployments.

As Omar (2022, 2024) and Omar and Zangana (2024, 2025) pointed out, the cybersecurity implications of adversarial AI and software vulnerabilities must be integrated into national AI policies to ensure secure innovation. For instance, the use of DNN text classification defenses in regulatory technology solutions offers promising pathways for real-time regulatory compliance monitoring (Omar, 2024).

Moreover, the impact of digital forensics in AI-driven investigations is being increasingly recognized in regulatory reforms, especially in cross-border criminal and civil liabilities (Omar & Zangana, 2025).

5.6 A Call for Global Frameworks

Ultimately, what emerges from the comparative regulatory landscape is the urgent need for a globally coordinated, science-based, and equity-driven governance framework. Oh et al. (2020) and Amaral et al. (2024) both suggested that regulatory reforms should not merely follow innovation, but co-evolve with it. The international community must embrace adaptive, modular regulation to ensure technologies can scale ethically, securely, and efficiently across borders.

6. EMERGING ISSUES AND REGULATORY GAPS

In an era of accelerated innovation across biotechnology, digital health, artificial intelligence (AI), and cybersecurity, regulatory systems worldwide are struggling to keep pace. Emerging technologies are often introduced without appropriate regulatory foresight, creating significant gaps in oversight, safety, ethics, and equitable access. These gaps are further exacerbated by the global nature of technological innovation, varying national standards, and the complexity of interdisciplinary systems (Abbott, 2011).

6.1. The Pacing Problem in Regulatory Frameworks

The "pacing problem"—the lag between technological advancement and regulatory adaptation—remains one of the most persistent challenges in modern governance (Abbott, 2011). As emerging technologies such as AI-driven diagnostics, wearable devices, and large language models (LLMs) revolutionize healthcare and cybersecurity, traditional regulatory models, which often emphasize post-market control and retrospective validation, fall short (Han et al., 2024; Amaral et al., 2024).

6.2. Interdisciplinary Innovation and the Fragmentation of Regulation

Medical biotechnology and cybersecurity are increasingly converging, giving rise to interdisciplinary challenges that current regulatory bodies are not equipped to manage cohesively. For example, synthetic data and student-teacher LLM frameworks are transforming the way AI systems are trained and deployed (Gholami & Omar, 2023; Gholami & Omar, 2024), yet these innovations often escape formal scrutiny due to unclear categorizations within existing frameworks.

A prime example is the increasing use of LLMs in digital forensics and software vulnerability detection—domains traditionally overseen by cybersecurity, not medical or industrial regulators (Omar & Zangana, 2025; Omar & Zangana, 2024). The regulatory disconnection between these sectors leads to oversight gaps that could compromise system safety and public trust (Omar & Zangana, 2025).

Regulatory oversight often involves overlapping domains—particularly when technologies such as AI, biotechnology, and digital health intersect. The Venn diagram below visualizes the shared responsibilities and unique challenges of each regulatory sector, highlighting the need for interdisciplinary governance.

Figure 7. Overlapping regulatory domains across AI, biotech, and digital health

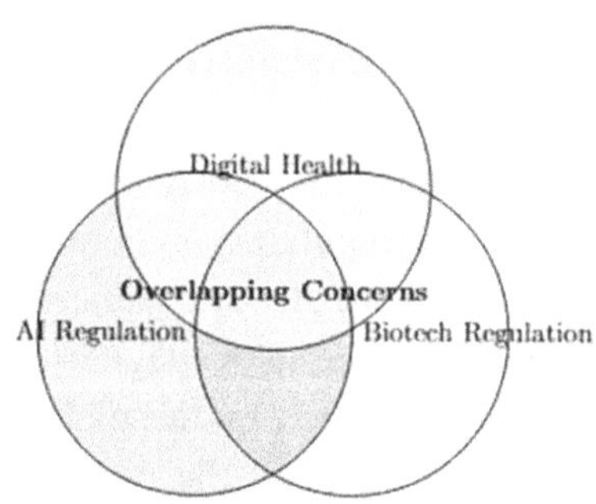

6.3. Regulatory Science: Conceptual Advancements and Limitations

Efforts to modernize regulatory science are underway in several regions. In the UK, strategic frameworks have been developed to integrate innovation and regulation in healthcare (Calvert et al., 2021), while in Europe, models such as ReScIPE aim to harmonize regulatory science with innovation (Hines et al., 2020). However, implementation remains uneven, particularly when incorporating digital health and precision medicine tools (Conway & Chisholm, 2024; Lievevrouw et al., 2021).

In Canada, barriers to innovation stem not only from outdated regulations but also from bureaucratic inertia and misaligned policy priorities (MacNeil et al., 2019). Similarly, in China, a lack of regulatory alignment with the "right to science" hampers balanced innovation in medical biotechnology (Han et al., 2024; Liang et al., 2021).

6.4. Security, Ethics, and Infrastructure Challenges

The digital infrastructure supporting regulatory oversight is increasingly vulnerable. As shown by Hamza and Omar (2013), cloud computing platforms—now integral to data sharing in biomedical and AI research—face substantial abuse risks without adequate security policies. Cybersecurity vulnerabilities can further disrupt regulatory workflows, as malicious actors exploit gaps to access sensitive data in research and healthcare settings (Huff et al., 2023; Mohammed et al., 2018).

The complexity deepens with the growing reliance on AI for automated decision-making. LLMs used for software vulnerability detection and adversarial robustness remain largely unregulated, despite their critical applications in national defense and public safety (Omar, 2024; Jones & Omar, 2024). Advanced detection techniques such as GEADD for zero-day threats offer promise but must be validated within structured regulatory parameters (Jones et al., 2023).

6.5. Regulatory Silos and Innovation Stifling

While regulations aim to ensure safety, excessive or outdated oversight can inadvertently stifle innovation. This is especially true in the medical device industry, where regulatory ambiguity leads to delays in market access and discourages small-scale innovators (Guerra-Bretaña & Flórez-Rendón, 2018; Maresova, 2022). For instance, complex Chemistry, Manufacturing, and Controls (CMC) processes can be unnecessarily burdensome for biotechnology firms attempting to scale (Cauchon et al., 2019).

Moreover, policy shifts like net neutrality repeal have had unforeseen consequences on innovation ecosystems by weakening online privacy and access standards, thereby eroding public trust and market predictability (Nguyen et al., 2018).

6.6. Calls for Equitable and Adaptive Frameworks

To address these growing disparities, frameworks such as those proposed by the National Academies of Sciences, Engineering, and Medicine (2023) emphasize equitable innovation—aligning regulatory pathways with social justice, health equity, and inclusive participation. Oh et al. (2020) also advocate regulatory reforms to stimulate sustainable innovation ecosystems that do not sacrifice public safety or ethical integrity.

In the context of AI, Omar (2022) and Omar (2021) argue for integrated models that combine cryptographic, access control, and machine learning techniques to protect data integrity while fostering agile innovation.

6.7. Toward Future-Proof Regulation

Forward-looking initiatives are needed to proactively govern technologies before they mature into dominant infrastructures. For example, precision policy mechanisms that evolve alongside LLM capabilities are essential to managing their deployment in sensitive applications like digital forensics, clinical support, and cybersecurity (Omar & Zangana, 2025; Omar, 2022).

Such mechanisms should draw on cross-disciplinary expertise and dynamic policy modeling, as advocated in recent literature on cybersecurity resilience and forensic AI (Omar, 2024; Huff et al., 2023). Only through anticipatory governance and adaptive regulation can innovation be aligned with public interest and ethical accountability.

7. CASE STUDIES

In this section, we explore how regulatory and compliance challenges impact innovation across domains such as healthcare, biotechnology, medical devices, cybersecurity, and AI-enabled technologies. Through a review of real-world and conceptual case studies, we provide a nuanced understanding of the evolving role of regulation and its intersection with technological advancement.

7.1. Medical Devices and Healthcare Innovation

The regulation of medical devices offers a compelling case for how compliance frameworks can both stimulate and hinder innovation. Guerra-Bretaña and Flórez-Rendón (2018) emphasized that while regulations can raise the quality and safety of medical products, excessive rigidity often slows down technological adoption. In a global context, Amaral et al. (2024) analyzed how divergent regulatory regimes across countries delay market access and increase costs for innovators, particularly small and medium-sized enterprises (SMEs).

Calvert et al. (2021) showcased the UK's approach to advancing regulatory science by fostering cross-disciplinary collaborations to facilitate evidence-based healthcare innovation. In a similar vein, Liang et al. (2021) documented China's implementation of regulatory science in Traditional Chinese Medicine (TCM), where safety and innovation were balanced through updated compliance mechanisms.

Han et al. (2024) extended this analysis by discussing the "right to science" in the Chinese policy landscape, where the pursuit of innovation in biotechnology is framed as a constitutional right, necessitating regulatory policies that minimize risk without impeding development.

MacNeil et al. (2019) evaluated Canada's health technology innovation ecosystem and revealed barriers in policy translation and administrative coordination. In Europe, Hines et al. (2020) proposed the ReScIPE model to align regulatory science with clinical pharmacology, underlining the need for structured regulatory innovation pipelines.

Maresova (2022) critiqued the evolving regulatory frameworks for Clinical Decision Support (CDS) systems, calling for more agile and technically informed regulations that don't stifle innovation but ensure public safety.

7.2. Regulatory Frameworks for Digital Health and AI

The integration of artificial intelligence (AI) and machine learning (ML) into health technologies poses novel regulatory challenges. Lievevrouw et al. (2021) examined the FDA's approach to standardizing digital health technologies and noted a trend toward co-production between regulators and tech developers, where mutual learning improves policy design.

Conway and Chisholm (2024) advocated for an interdisciplinary competency framework to integrate precision medicine into regulatory and industrial processes. Their findings highlight how embedding AI expertise within regulatory institutions can catalyze both innovation and safety.

Cauchon et al. (2019) explored regulatory perspectives on innovation in Chemistry, Manufacturing, and Controls (CMC), stressing the importance of early engagement between developers and regulators to ensure regulatory compliance aligns with technological advancement.

Oh et al. (2020) contributed a macroeconomic perspective, suggesting that regulatory reforms should be aligned with national innovation ecosystems to nurture emerging industries, including medical AI and digital health.

7.3. Cybersecurity and AI Compliance

Cybersecurity presents another domain where compliance and regulation are pivotal. Huff et al. (2023) described management practices for mitigating cybersecurity threats in healthcare and biotechnology organizations. The authors called for integrated frameworks that combine physical, cyber, and organizational controls.

Jones and Omar (2024) introduced the GEADD method, an AI-enhanced system for zero-day threat detection that meets modern compliance benchmarks in digital security. Their findings are aligned with the broader trends highlighted by Jones et al. (2023), who demonstrated how machine learning accelerates threat detection while still adhering to ethical compliance.

Mohammed et al. (2018) investigated wormhole attack detection in wireless sensor networks, proposing detection methods that meet regulatory security requirements. Similarly, Nguyen et al. (2018) explored how policy changes, like the repeal of FCC net neutrality, affect digital privacy and compliance.

Omar (2021) offered insights into integrating cryptographic and access control mechanisms in databases, suggesting these practices as foundational to regulatory compliance in digital systems. These ideas were expanded in Omar (2022), which proposed machine learning-based frameworks that comply with GDPR and HIPAA while offering robust security.

Recent innovations in adversarial defense, like the one introduced by Omar (2024), show how AI models can be hardened against manipulation while remaining compliant with auditing and accountability standards.

7.4. Ethical Innovation and Global Governance

Governance and ethics in innovation require a delicate balance. The National Academies of Sciences, Engineering, and Medicine (2023) proposed a framework for aligning innovation in health with equity, recommending multi-stakeholder governance models to ensure equitable access and ethical compliance.

Abbott (2011) argued for the establishment of an international framework agreement on emerging technologies, warning of the pacing problem where technological innovation outpaces regulatory readiness. His analysis laid foundational principles that are now echoed in cross-border digital regulations.

In the realm of generative AI, Gholami and Omar (2023) explored the efficiency of synthetic data in training LLMs, revealing regulatory gaps in synthetic data governance. Their follow-up work (Gholami & Omar, 2024) introduced student-teacher architectures in LLMs and raised questions about transparency, explainability, and accountability—key pillars in responsible AI regulation.

7.5. Interdisciplinary Contributions and Emerging Trends

Omar and Zangana's (2024, 2025a, 2025b) editorial volumes explore digital forensics and cybersecurity from the lens of AI integration. These works address regulatory themes such as explainability in LLMs, forensic auditing, and software vulnerability detection, proposing policy recommendations for next-generation compliance systems.

In the context of cloud computing, Hamza and Omar (2013) offered an early warning about nefarious use of virtualized environments, emphasizing the importance of compliance in cloud service delivery. This foundation remains relevant as cloud-based AI systems become ubiquitous.

Finally, Amaral et al. (2024) and Calvert et al. (2021) remind us that achieving harmonized regulation across geographies is not merely a bureaucratic necessity—it is critical to enabling safe, efficient, and inclusive innovation worldwide.

8. RECOMMENDATIONS FOR POLICYMAKERS AND PRACTITIONERS

As emerging technologies such as large language models (LLMs), artificial intelligence (AI), and biotechnology continue to evolve rapidly, regulatory systems must adapt to address both their benefits and associated risks. The following recommendations are designed to guide policymakers and practitioners in fostering innovation while ensuring public safety, security, and equity.

8.1. Establish Dynamic and Adaptive Regulatory Frameworks

One of the most pressing needs is to develop agile and flexible regulatory mechanisms that can keep pace with technological advancement. The traditional lag between innovation and regulation—often referred to as the "pacing problem"—must be addressed through international collaboration and anticipatory governance (Abbott, 2011; Amaral et al., 2024). This requires a shift from reactive to proactive oversight, utilizing horizon scanning and scenario planning.

Calvert et al. (2021) and Hines et al. (2020) advocate for the integration of regulatory science and innovation in healthcare to improve responsiveness and reduce approval times for advanced technologies. Such initiatives can be mirrored in other sectors, including cybersecurity and AI.

8.2. Foster Interdisciplinary Competence and Workforce Development

To effectively regulate and apply innovations such as precision medicine and digital health technologies, it is crucial to build interdisciplinary competencies among professionals. Conway and Chisholm (2024) emphasize the creation of competency frameworks to embed cross-sectoral skills in the pharmaceutical and medical technology sectors.

Similarly, initiatives in regulatory training and public-private partnerships can enhance preparedness in both developing and developed countries (MacNeil et al., 2019; Liang et al., 2021).

8.3. Promote Transparency, Inclusiveness, and Equity

Innovation must be aligned with societal values, including equity and transparency. The National Academies of Sciences, Engineering, and Medicine (2023) propose a governance framework that prioritizes equity in innovation. This recommendation is especially pertinent for global digital ecosystems and AI applications, where disparities in access and participation can exacerbate existing inequalities.

Han et al. (2024) also highlight the significance of embedding the "right to science" within regulatory design, ensuring public benefit without compromising individual rights or safety.

8.4. Leverage Synthetic and Open Data Responsibly

As LLMs and other AI systems increasingly rely on large-scale data, the use of synthetic data has emerged as a promising avenue. Gholami and Omar (2023, 2024) demonstrate that synthetic data can improve the efficiency and performance of LLMs while preserving privacy. However, policymakers must ensure that data governance frameworks are in place to avoid bias, ensure data provenance, and maintain transparency in algorithmic decision-making.

8.5. Strengthen Cybersecurity and Digital Resilience

With digital technologies permeating health, industry, and critical infrastructure, cybersecurity must be a central concern. Huff et al. (2023) and Mohammed et al. (2018) underscore the need for resilient practices and robust architecture to defend against threats such as wormhole attacks and cloud abuse (Hamza & Omar, 2013).

Regulatory frameworks must also account for emerging risks, such as adversarial machine learning (Omar, 2024) and zero-day attacks (Jones & Omar, 2024).

Policymakers should consider the GEADD method and similar frameworks to fortify detection and response capabilities using AI (Jones et al., 2023).

8.6. Align Medical Device Innovation with Regulatory Reform

Several studies (Guerra-Bretaña & Flórez-Rendón, 2018; Maresova, 2022; Amaral et al., 2024) demonstrate that inconsistent or outdated regulatory pathways can hinder the development and global distribution of medical devices. A risk-based and life-cycle-oriented regulatory strategy—adaptable across jurisdictions—can facilitate innovation while maintaining patient safety.

Lievevrouw et al. (2021) advocate for co-production in standard-setting, ensuring that both regulators and innovators contribute to shaping effective and timely regulations for digital health.

8.7. Incentivize Regulatory Innovation and Collaboration

Innovative models like ReScIPE in Europe (Hines et al., 2020) and the UK's regulatory science agenda (Calvert et al., 2021) offer valuable blueprints for encouraging regulatory experimentation and stakeholder engagement. This is also echoed in Oh et al. (2020), who call for comprehensive reforms to foster a thriving innovation ecosystem.

Moreover, international coordination—especially in areas like digital forensics and AI (Omar & Zangana, 2024, 2025)—can harmonize standards, reduce duplication, and accelerate cross-border approvals.

8.8. Integrate Ethics, Security, and Emerging Technologies into Policy

The rapid convergence of AI, cybersecurity, biotechnology, and LLMs necessitates the integration of ethics and security into every stage of innovation. Omar and Zangana's (2025) edited volumes on AI-driven digital forensics and software vulnerability detection call attention to the dual-use nature of advanced technologies and the importance of ethical safeguards.

Additionally, works like Omar (2021, 2022) stress the role of integrated cybersecurity policies using encryption, access control, and adversarial defense strategies, which should be embedded into policy across sectors.

8.9. Address the Regulatory Gaps in Emerging Markets

Emerging economies often face unique regulatory hurdles due to capacity constraints, weak enforcement, or lack of harmonization. Targeted capacity-building, knowledge transfer, and regulatory diplomacy can help bridge these gaps (Nguyen et al., 2018). Multilateral institutions and global consortia should support these efforts through funding, education, and policy guidance.

8.10. Facilitate Industry-Regulator Dialogue and Feedback Loops

Finally, establishing continuous dialogue between regulators, industry, and academia is vital to ensure that regulatory approaches remain grounded and relevant. Cauchon et al. (2019) advocate for incorporating industry insights into the development of CMC (chemistry, manufacturing, and controls) frameworks.

Such collaborative mechanisms not only speed up innovation cycles but also help regulators better understand technological intricacies and evolving risk landscapes.

8.11 Summary

The intersection of regulation and innovation is both challenging and critical in today's global, data-driven economy. By adopting adaptive governance models, promoting interdisciplinary collaboration, enhancing security measures, and ensuring equitable access, policymakers and practitioners can collectively foster a sustainable innovation ecosystem that prioritizes public welfare, scientific progress, and economic resilience.

9. CONCLUSION

The integration of advanced technologies such as large language models (LLMs), artificial intelligence, and digital health innovations has revolutionized regulatory science, posing both unprecedented opportunities and complex challenges. This chapter has underscored the urgent need for policymakers and practitioners to rethink traditional regulatory paradigms and adopt more adaptive, interdisciplinary, and anticipatory approaches. It is evident that balancing innovation with ethical oversight, risk management, and equity remains a formidable task, particularly as technologies continue to evolve faster than regulatory frameworks can accommodate (Abbott, 2011; Han et al., 2024).

The recommendations provided in this chapter emphasize the value of collaborative governance, cross-sectoral partnerships, and regulatory science infrastructures that prioritize transparency, interoperability, and public trust. As highlighted by Amaral et al. (2024) and Hines et al. (2020), these frameworks must also be globally harmonized to prevent disparities in innovation access and to support scalable and equitable healthcare advancements. The discussion also reveals how security, particularly in cybersecurity and data governance, must be embedded into the innovation lifecycle, especially within biotechnology and medical device sectors (Hamza & Omar, 2013; Jones & Omar, 2024; Huff et al., 2023).

Ultimately, fostering a sustainable ecosystem for innovation requires not only regulatory flexibility but also the ethical use of AI and machine learning, the implementation of robust digital infrastructures, and the promotion of interdisciplinary competencies (Conway & Chisholm, 2024; Gholami & Omar, 2024). As innovation continues to outpace oversight, policymakers must rely on evidence-based strategies, continuous learning, and foresight methodologies to mitigate risks without stifling creativity or progress (Calvert et al., 2021; National Academies of Sciences, Engineering, and Medicine, 2023).

In closing, this chapter calls for a transformative shift in how we design, implement, and assess regulation in the age of digital transformation. Through strategic foresight, multi-stakeholder collaboration, and the advancement of regulatory science, we can ensure that innovation serves the public good while safeguarding the ethical, legal, and social values that underpin democratic societies.

REFERENCES

Abbott, K. W. (2011). An international framework agreement on scientific and technological innovation and regulation. *The Growing Gap between Emerging Technologies and Legal-Ethical Oversight: The Pacing Problem*, 127-156.

Amaral, C., Paiva, M., Rodrigues, A. R., Veiga, F., & Bell, V. (2024). Global regulatory challenges for medical devices: Impact on innovation and market access. *Applied Sciences (Basel, Switzerland)*, *14*(20), 9304. DOI: 10.3390/app14209304

Calvert, M. J., Marston, E., Samuels, M., Rivera, S. C., Torlinska, B., Oliver, K., Denniston, A. K., & Hoare, S. (2021). Advancing UK regulatory science and innovation in healthcare. *Journal of the Royal Society of Medicine*, *114*(1), 5–11. DOI: 10.1177/0141076820961776 PMID: 33043790

Cauchon, N. S., Oghamian, S., Hassanpour, S., & Abernathy, M. (2019). Innovation in chemistry, manufacturing, and controls—A regulatory perspective from industry. *Journal of Pharmaceutical Sciences*, *108*(7), 2207–2237. DOI: 10.1016/j.xphs.2019.02.007 PMID: 30794794

Conway, N., & Chisholm, O. (2024). Building a Competency Framework to Integrate Inter-disciplinary Precision Medicine Capabilities into the Medical Technology and Pharmaceutical Industry. *Therapeutic Innovation & Regulatory Science*, *58*(3), 567–577. DOI: 10.1007/s43441-024-00626-5 PMID: 38491262

Gholami, S., & Omar, M. (2023). Does Synthetic Data Make Large Language Models More Efficient? *arXiv preprint arXiv:2310.07830.*

Gholami, S., & Omar, M. (2024). Can a student large language model perform as well as its teacher? In *Innovations, Securities, and Case Studies Across Healthcare, Business, and Technology* (pp. 122-139). IGI Global. DOI: 10.4018/979-8-3693-1906-2.ch007

Guerra-Bretaña, R. M., & Flórez-Rendón, A. L. (2018). Impact of regulations on innovation in the field of medical devices. *Research on Biomedical Engineering*, *34*(4), 356–367. DOI: 10.1590/2446-4740.180054

Hamza, Y. A., & Omar, M. D. (2013). Cloud computing security: Abuse and nefarious use of cloud computing. *International Journal of Computer Engineering Research*, *3*(6), 22–27.

Han, Y., Fan, L. L., & Xue, Y. (2024). A sustainable balance between innovation and risk: How the "right to science" affects China's medical biotechnology regulatory policy. *Computational and Structural Biotechnology Journal, 24*, 306–313. DOI: 10.1016/j.csbj.2024.04.027 PMID: 38681134

Hines, P. A., Guy, R. H., Brand, A., Humphreys, A. J., & Papaluca-Amati, M. (2020). Regulatory science and innovation Programme for Europe (ReScIPE): A proposed model. *British Journal of Clinical Pharmacology, 86*(12), 2530–2534. DOI: 10.1111/bcp.14099 PMID: 31426120

Huff, A. J., Burrell, D. N., Nobles, C., Richardson, K., Wright, J. B., Burton, S. L., Jones, A. J., Springs, D., Omar, M., & Brown-Jackson, K. L. (2023). Management Practices for Mitigating Cybersecurity Threats to Biotechnology Companies, Laboratories, and Healthcare Research Organizations. In *Applied Research Approaches to Technology, Healthcare, and Business* (pp. 1-12). IGI Global.

Jones, R., & Omar, M. (2024). Revolutionizing Cybersecurity: The GPT-2 Enhanced Attack Detection and Defense (GEADD) Method for Zero-Day Threats. *International Journal of Informatics* [INJIISCOM]. *Information System and Computer Engineering, 5*(2), 178–191.

Jones, R., Omar, M., Mohammed, D., Nobles, C., & Dawson, M. (2023). Harnessing the Speed and Accuracy of Machine Learning to Advance Cybersecurity. In *2023 Congress in Computer Science, Computer Engineering, & Applied Computing (CSCE)* (pp. 418-421). IEEE. DOI: 10.1109/CSCE60160.2023.00074

Liang, Z., Lai, Y., Li, M., Shi, J., Lei, C. I., Hu, H., & Ung, C. O. L. (2021). Applying regulatory science in traditional chinese medicines for improving public safety and facilitating innovation in China: A scoping review and regulatory implications. *Chinese Medicine, 16*(1), 1–16. DOI: 10.1186/s13020-021-00433-2 PMID: 33593397

Lievevrouw, E., Marelli, L., & Van Hoyweghen, I. (2021). The FDA's standard-making process for medical digital health technologies: Co-producing technological and organizational innovation. *Biosocieties, 17*(3), 549–576. DOI: 10.1057/s41292-021-00232-w PMID: 34002115

MacNeil, M., Koch, M., Kuspinar, A., Juzwishin, D., Lehoux, P., & Stolee, P. (2019). Enabling health technology innovation in Canada: Barriers and facilitators in policy and regulatory processes. *Health Policy (Amsterdam), 123*(2), 203–214. DOI: 10.1016/j.healthpol.2018.09.018 PMID: 30352755

Maresova, P. (2022). Impact of Regulatory Changes on Innovations in the Medical Device Industry: Comment on" Clinical Decision Support and New Regulatory Frameworks for Medical Devices: Are We Ready for It?-A Viewpoint Paper. *International Journal of Health Policy and Management, 12*, 7262. DOI: 10.34172/ijhpm.2022.7262 PMID: 35942961

Mohammed, D., Omar, M., & Nguyen, V. (2018). Wireless sensor network security: Approaches to detecting and avoiding wormhole attacks. *Journal of Research in Business. Economics and Management, 10*(2), 1860–1864.

National Academies of Sciences, Engineering, and Medicine. (2023). A Governance Framework for Aligning Innovation in Health and Medicine with Equity. In *Toward Equitable Innovation in Health and Medicine: A Framework*. National Academies Press (US).

Nguyen, V., Mohammed, D., Omar, M., & Banisakher, M. (2018). The Effects of the FCC Net Neutrality Repeal on Security and Privacy. [IJHIoT]. *International Journal of Hyperconnectivity and the Internet of Things, 2*(2), 21–29. DOI: 10.4018/IJHIoT.2018070102

Oh, S., Choi, C. Y., & Lee, J. H. (2020). Regulatory reform for fostering an innovation ecosystem.

Omar, M. (2021). New insights into database security: An effective and integrated approach for applying access control mechanisms and cryptographic concepts in Microsoft Access environments.

Omar, M. (2022). *Machine Learning for Cybersecurity: Innovative Deep Learning Solutions*. Springer Brief. https://link.springer.com/book/978303115

Omar, M. (2024). From Attack to Defense: Strengthening DNN Text Classification Against Adversarial Examples. In *Innovations, Securities, and Case Studies Across Healthcare, Business, and Technology* (pp. 174-195). IGI Global.

Omar, M. (2024). Revolutionizing Malware Detection: A Paradigm Shift Through Optimized Convolutional Neural Networks. In *Innovations, Securities, and Case Studies Across Healthcare, Business, and Technology* (pp. 196-220). IGI Global. DOI: 10.4018/979-8-3693-1906-2.ch011

Omar, M., & Zangana, H. (Eds.). (2025). *Digital Forensics in the Age of AI*. IGI Global., DOI: 10.4018/979-8-3373-0857-9

Omar, M., & Zangana, H. M. (Eds.). (2024). *Redefining Security With Cyber AI*. IGI Global., DOI: 10.4018/979-8-3693-6517-5

Omar, M., & Zangana, H. M. (Eds.). (2025). *Application of Large Language Models (LLMs) for Software Vulnerability Detection*. IGI Global., DOI: 10.4018/979-8-3693-9311-6

Omar, M., Zangana, H. M., Al-Karaki, J. N., & Mohammed, D. (2024). Harnessing LLMs for IoT malware detection: A comparative analysis of BERT and GPT-2. In *2024 8th International Symposium on Multidisciplinary Studies and Innovative Technologies (ISMSIT)* (pp. 1-6). Ankara, Turkiye. https://doi.org/DOI: 10.1109/ISMSIT63511.2024.10757249

Omar, M., Zangana, H. M., & Mohammed, D. (Eds.). (2025). *Integrating Artificial Intelligence in Cybersecurity and Forensic Practices*. IGI Global., DOI: 10.4018/979-8-3373-0588-2

Peter, L., Hajek, L., Maresova, P., Augustynek, M., & Penhaker, M. (2020). Medical devices: Regulation, risk classification, and open innovation. *Journal of Open Innovation*, *6*(2), 42. DOI: 10.3390/joitmc6020042

Rosenblatt, M., Boutin, M. M., & Nussbaum, S. R. (2016). Innovation in medicine and device development, regulatory review, and use of clinical advances. *Journal of the American Medical Association*, *316*(16), 1671–1672. DOI: 10.1001/jama.2016.12486 PMID: 27669080

Sethi, N. (2019). Regulating for uncertainty: Bridging blurred boundaries in medical innovation, research and treatment. *Law, Innovation and Technology*, *11*(1), 112–133. DOI: 10.1080/17579961.2019.1573400 PMID: 31057671

Spindler, P., Bach, K. F., Schmiegelow, M., Bedlington, N., & Eichler, H. G. (2016). Innovation of medical products: The evolution of regulatory science, research, and education. *Therapeutic Innovation & Regulatory Science*, *50*(1), 44–48. DOI: 10.1177/2168479015599810 PMID: 30236007

Wiersma, M., Kerridge, I., & Lipworth, W. (2023). Clinical innovation ethics frameworks: A systematic narrative review. *Health Policy (Amsterdam)*, *129*, 104706. DOI: 10.1016/j.healthpol.2023.104706 PMID: 36639310

Wright, J., Dawson, M. E.Jr, & Omar, M. (2012). Cyber security and mobile threats: The need for antivirus applications for smartphones. *Journal of Information Systems Technology and Planning*, *5*(14), 40–60.

Zangana, H., Al-Karaki, J., & Omar, M. (Eds.). (2025). *Revolutionizing Cybersecurity With Deep Learning and Large Language Models*. IGI Global., DOI: 10.4018/979-8-3373-3296-3

Zangana, H., & Omar, M. (Eds.). (2025). *Ensuring Secure and Ethical STM Research in the AI Era*. IGI Global., DOI: 10.4018/979-8-3373-4252-8

Zangana, H., & Omar, M. (Eds.). (2025). *Leveraging Large Language Models for Quantum-Aware Cybersecurity*. IGI Global., DOI: 10.4018/979-8-3373-1102-9

Zangana, H., & Omar, M. (Eds.). (2025). *Leveraging Large Language Models for Quantum-Aware Cybersecurity*. IGI Global., DOI: 10.4018/979-8-3373-1102-9

Zangana, H. M. (2024). Exploring Blockchain-Based Timestamping Tools: A Comprehensive Review. *Redefining Security With Cyber AI*, 92-110.

Zangana, H. M. (2024). Exploring the Landscape of Website Vulnerability Scanners: A Comprehensive Review and Comparative Analysis. *Redefining Security With Cyber AI*, 111-129.

Zangana, H. M., Amelia, P., Mustafa, F. M., & Li, S. (2025). The Role of English Language and AI in Scientific Writing: Ethical and Academic Implications. In Zangana, H., & Omar, M. (Eds.), *Ensuring Secure and Ethical STM Research in the AI Era* (pp. 191–218). IGI Global Scientific Publishing., DOI: 10.4018/979-8-3373-4252-8.ch005

Zangana, H. M., & Li, S. (2025). Future Trends in AI and Digital Forensics. In Omar, M., & Zangana, H. (Eds.), *Digital Forensics in the Age of AI* (pp. 347–380). IGI Global Scientific Publishing., DOI: 10.4018/979-8-3373-0857-9.ch013

Zangana, H. M., Luckyardi, S., Mustafa, F. M., & Li, S. (2025). Enhancing Agricultural Cybersecurity: Leveraging Deep Learning and Large Language Models for Smart Farming Protection. In Zangana, H., Al-Karaki, J., & Omar, M. (Eds.), *Revolutionizing Cybersecurity With Deep Learning and Large Language Models* (pp. 307–338). IGI Global Scientific Publishing., DOI: 10.4018/979-8-3373-3296-3.ch010

Zangana, H. M., Luckyardi, S., Mustafa, F. M., & Li, S. (2025). Ethical and Secure AI Applications in Agricultural Research: Challenges and Opportunities. In Zangana, H., & Omar, M. (Eds.), *Ensuring Secure and Ethical STM Research in the AI Era* (pp. 43–76). IGI Global Scientific Publishing., DOI: 10.4018/979-8-3373-4252-8.ch002

Zangana, H. M., Mohammed, A. K., Sallow, A. B., & Sallow, Z. B. (2024). Cybernetic Deception: Unraveling the Layers of Email Phishing Threats. [INJURATECH]. *International Journal of Research and Applied Technology*, *4*(1), 35–47.

Zangana, H. M., & Mohammed, D. (2025). Foundations of Large Language Models in Software Vulnerability Detection. In Omar, M., & Zangana, H. (Eds.), *Application of Large Language Models (LLMs) for Software Vulnerability Detection* (pp. 41–74). IGI Global., DOI: 10.4018/979-8-3693-9311-6.ch002

Zangana, H. M., & Mustafa, F. M. (2024). Hybrid Image Denoising Using Wavelet Transform and Deep Learning. *EAI Endorsed Transactions on AI and Robotics, 3*. Advance online publication. DOI: 10.4108/airo.7486

Zangana, H. M., & Mustafa, F. M. (2025). A Novel Hybrid Wavelet-GAN Image Denoising System. In Bhatti, U., Aamir, M., Gulzar, Y., & Ullah Bazai, S. (Eds.), *Modern Intelligent Techniques for Image Processing* (pp. 409–424). IGI Global Scientific Publishing., DOI: 10.4018/979-8-3693-9045-0.ch017

Zangana, H. M., & Mustafa, F. M. (2025). Image Denoising Techniques for Cybersecurity and Forensic Applications: AI-Driven Approaches. In Omar, M., Zangana, H., & Mohammed, D. (Eds.), *Integrating Artificial Intelligence in Cybersecurity and Forensic Practices* (pp. 117–142). IGI Global Scientific Publishing., DOI: 10.4018/979-8-3373-0588-2.ch005

Zangana, H. M., Mustafa, F. M., & Li, S. (2025). Large Language Models in Cybersecurity: From Automation to Intelligence. In Zangana, H., & Omar, M. (Eds.), *Leveraging Large Language Models for Quantum-Aware Cybersecurity* (pp. 277–300). IGI Global Scientific Publishing., DOI: 10.4018/979-8-3373-1102-9.ch009

Zangana, H. M., Mustafa, F. M., Li, S., & Al-Karaki, J. N. (2025). Natural Language Processing for Cyber Threat Intelligence in a Quantum World. In Zangana, H., & Omar, M. (Eds.), *Leveraging Large Language Models for Quantum-Aware Cybersecurity* (pp. 345–388). IGI Global Scientific Publishing., DOI: 10.4018/979-8-3373-1102-9.ch011

Zangana, H. M., Mustafa, F. M., Mohammed, A. K., & Omar, M. (2025). The Role of Change Control Boards in Ensuring Cybersecurity Compliance for IT Infrastructure. *JITCE (Journal of Information Technology and Computer Engineering), 9*(1). Retrieved from https://jitce.fti.unand.ac.id/index.php/JITCE/article/view/303

Zangana, H. M., Mustafa, F. M., & Omar, M. (2024). A Hybrid Approach for Robust Object Detection: Integrating Template Matching and Faster R-CNN. *EAI Endorsed Transactions on AI and Robotics, 3*. Advance online publication. DOI: 10.4108/airo.6858

Zangana, H. M., & Omar, M. (2020). Threats, Attacks, and Mitigations of Smartphone Security. *Academic Journal of Nawroz University, 9*(4), 324–332. DOI: 10.25007/ajnu.v9n4a989

Zangana, H. M., & Omar, M. (2025). Harnessing the Power of Large Language Models for Cybersecurity: Applications, Challenges, and Future Directions. In Omar, M., & Zangana, H. (Eds.), *Application of Large Language Models (LLMs) for Software Vulnerability Detection* (pp. 1–40). IGI Global., DOI: 10.4018/979-8-3693-9311-6.ch001

Zangana, H. M., & Omar, M. (2025). Introduction to Digital Forensics and Artificial Intelligence. In Omar, M., & Zangana, H. (Eds.), *Digital Forensics in the Age of AI* (pp. 1–30). IGI Global Scientific Publishing., DOI: 10.4018/979-8-3373-0857-9.ch001

Zangana, H. M., & Omar, M. (2025). Introduction to Quantum-Aware Cybersecurity: The Need for LLMs. In Zangana, H., & Omar, M. (Eds.), *Leveraging Large Language Models for Quantum-Aware Cybersecurity* (pp. 1–28). IGI Global Scientific Publishing., DOI: 10.4018/979-8-3373-1102-9.ch001

Zangana, H. M., & Omar, M. (2025). The Role of Leadership in Advancing Inclusive Health Technologies. In Burrell, D., & Nguyen, C. (Eds.), *New Horizons in Leadership: Inclusive Explorations in Health, Technology, and Education* (pp. 203–220). IGI Global Scientific Publishing., DOI: 10.4018/979-8-3693-6437-6.ch009

Zangana, H. M., Omar, M., & Al-Karaki, J. N. (2025). Data Privacy and Security Standards in AI-Powered Scientific Research. In Zangana, H., & Omar, M. (Eds.), *Ensuring Secure and Ethical STM Research in the AI Era* (pp. 1–42). IGI Global Scientific Publishing., DOI: 10.4018/979-8-3373-4252-8.ch001

Zangana, H. M., Omar, M., & Al-Karaki, J. N. (2025). Foundations of Deep Learning and Large Language Models in Cybersecurity. In Zangana, H., Al-Karaki, J., & Omar, M. (Eds.), *Revolutionizing Cybersecurity With Deep Learning and Large Language Models* (pp. 1–36). IGI Global Scientific Publishing., DOI: 10.4018/979-8-3373-3296-3.ch001

Zangana, H. M., Omar, M., Al-Karaki, J. N., & Mohammed, D. (2024). Comprehensive Review and Analysis of Network Firewall Rule Analyzers: Enhancing Security Posture and Efficiency. *Redefining Security With Cyber AI*, 15-36.

Zangana, H. M., Sallow, Z. B., & Omar, M. (2025). The Human Factor in Cybersecurity: Addressing the Risks of Insider Threats. *Jurnal Ilmiah Computer Science*, *3*(2), 76–85. DOI: 10.58602/jics.v3i2.37

Zhou, K., & Gattinger, G. (2024). The evolving regulatory paradigm of AI in MedTech: A review of perspectives and where we are today. *Therapeutic Innovation & Regulatory Science*, *58*(3), 456–464. DOI: 10.1007/s43441-024-00628-3 PMID: 38528278

Chapter 2
Expiration vs. Termination:
Reassessing Legal Boundaries in Contract Law

Dilshad Ahmad Mhia-alddin
https://orcid.org/0009-0005-4046-1607
University of Mosul, Iraq

Akram Mahmoud Hussein
University of Mosul, Iraq

ABSTRACT

The legal concepts of expiration and termination in contract law, though often used interchangeably in practice, possess distinct theoretical and practical implications that significantly affect contractual relationships. This paper undertakes a critical reassessment of the boundaries between expiration—the natural conclusion of a contract upon fulfillment of its terms—and termination—the active cessation of contractual obligations prior to their stipulated end. Through doctrinal analysis, comparative legal perspectives, and examination of recent judicial decisions, this research elucidates how the ambiguity between these concepts can create legal uncertainty, especially in complex commercial agreements. The paper proposes a refined legal framework that distinguishes expiration from termination in both statutory and common law contexts, providing clarity for courts, practitioners, and contracting parties. The study contributes to contract theory by enhancing precision in contractual language and advocating for uniform interpretive standards in international contract practice.

DOI: 10.4018/979-8-3373-4862-9.ch002

Copyright © 2025, IGI Global Scientific Publishing. Copying or distributing in print or electronic forms without written permission of IGI Global Scientific Publishing is prohibited.

1. INTRODUCTION

Contract law serves as the foundational pillar of modern commercial and private transactions, governing obligations, expectations, and remedies among parties. Within this legal framework, the distinction between "expiration" and "termination" plays a pivotal role in the lifecycle of a contract. While expiration denotes the natural cessation of contractual obligations after a predefined duration or completion of terms, termination involves an active process of dissolving contractual ties—often prematurely and sometimes contentiously (Cazac, 2012). Despite their operational significance, the legal boundaries between these two concepts remain blurred in many jurisdictions, leading to interpretive conflicts and practical uncertainties. The increasing complexity of contractual structures, especially in transnational agreements and digital ecosystems, further magnifies these ambiguities (Mhia-Alddin & Hussein, 2025a; Banta, 2019).

A critical review of existing jurisprudence reveals inconsistent legal treatment of expiration and termination across common law and civil law systems. Some courts treat the terms synonymously, while others impose materially different legal consequences (Dehaini, 2021). This inconsistency is exacerbated by the lack of harmonized interpretive standards and insufficient doctrinal clarity in contract drafting and enforcement. The result is a legal gray area that undermines predictability in contract enforcement, increasing litigation risk and decreasing transactional efficiency (Bradley, 2021; Read et al., 2023).

This paper aims to reassess and redefine the legal contours separating expiration and termination in contract law. It will examine the doctrinal underpinnings, analyze comparative legal systems, explore case law interpretations, and propose a unified theoretical framework to distinguish these concepts more clearly.

Research Questions are:

1. What are the key legal distinctions between expiration and termination across different jurisdictions?
2. How do courts interpret these terms in cases of dispute, and what legal consequences follow from such interpretations?
3. What legal or doctrinal reforms can enhance clarity and predictability in the application of expiration and termination in contract law?

The reassessment of these concepts has both theoretical and practical implications. Theoretically, this research contributes to a more nuanced understanding of contract theory and the evolving nature of legal obligations (Grosskopf, 2011; Holmen-Jensen & Åsmoen, 2024). Practically, it offers legal professionals, policymakers, and contracting parties clearer guidance in drafting, negotiating, and enforcing contracts. Additionally, in the age of digital and AI-managed contracts, the distinction becomes crucial for automation, compliance, and risk mitigation (Mhia-Alddin & Hussein, 2025b; Guha et al., 2023).

This paper proceeds as follows. Section 2 reviews the existing literature on expiration and termination, highlighting key scholarly debates and gaps. Section 3 examines the legal frameworks and doctrinal principles governing contract cessation. Section 4 conducts a comparative legal analysis of various jurisdictions. Section 5 reviews key case law that illustrates judicial interpretation trends. Section 6 offers a critical discussion and synthesizes the findings. Section 7 proposes actionable recommendations for legal reform and best practices. Finally, Section 8 concludes by summarizing the study's contributions and identifying avenues for further research.

2. LITERATURE REVIEW

Contract expiration and termination represent core elements in the field of contract law, attracting sustained jurisprudential, doctrinal, and comparative scholarly attention. This section synthesizes existing literature, situating the discussion within both common law and civil law traditions, while identifying significant gaps that this paper seeks to address.

2.1 Jurisprudential and Doctrinal Foundations

Termination of contracts has long been treated as a pivotal mechanism to safeguard parties' rights in the face of breach, impossibility, or time-bound obligations. Cazac (2012) advances a comprehensive conceptualization of termination, arguing for greater clarity and consistency in its doctrinal framing. Similarly, Grosskopf (2011) applies economic theory to relational contracts, examining how surplus division upon termination impacts contractual stability and fairness.

In doctrinal development, Hodge (2017) provides a thorough account of how UK courts have evolved contract principles, notably in termination disputes. Meanwhile, Sullivan (2015) and Sullivan (2016) explore niche aspects such as interim dilapidations and restrictive post-employment clauses (e.g., "garden leave"), which often interface with expiration scenarios.

From a comparative standpoint, Estreicher and Hirsch (2013) reassess American exceptionalism in wrongful dismissal law, highlighting critical divergences in termination rights across jurisdictions. Bousri (2019) juxtaposes arbitration frameworks in Comoros and Uganda, indirectly influencing dispute resolution paths in contract expiry contexts. Banta (2019) also reflects on how digitization challenges traditional doctrines by rethinking formality through the lens of electronic wills and digital assets.

2.2 Theoretical Framework: Common Law vs. Civil Law

The distinction between common law and civil law systems deeply affects the understanding and implementation of contract expiration and termination. In common law jurisdictions, the emphasis often rests on the intention of parties and the doctrine of frustration or breach. Conversely, civil law systems—more codified and formalistic—recognize explicit legislative provisions governing expiration triggers and force majeure.

Dehaini (2021) explores termination practices in back-to-back contracting, revealing tensions between main contract principles and sub-contractual obligations, particularly pronounced in mixed legal systems. Cooper (2018) and Cooper and Zell (2023) demonstrate how legal philosophies on property and housing law intersect with contract continuity and expiration, particularly in subsidized sectors.

This theoretical divide is also apparent in patent law, where Lim (2013), Manganelli (2019), and Siew-Kuan (2012) analyze remedies and expiry implications through the lens of antitrust and misuse doctrines. Comparative insights from Colangelo (2017) and Schnichels & Sule (2010) show how termination in pharmaceutical licensing and reverse payment settlements varies under EU and US laws.

2.3 Emerging Themes and Interdisciplinary Integration

Technological innovation and regulatory complexity are reshaping contract expiration. Mhia-Alddin and Hussein (2025a, 2025b) argue that AI-driven systems must address expiry, compliance, and legal uncertainty—especially in scientific and technical domains (STM). Guha et al. (2023) further underline the potential of large language models to evaluate legal reasoning, offering tools to simulate, analyze, or even predict contract termination events.

Global trade, intellectual property, and development discourse also bring nuance. Shoraka (2006) and Osei-Tutu (2001) emphasize that WTO mechanisms and TRIPS obligations influence how developing countries negotiate and enforce expiry clauses. Amani (2007) explores similar themes in the context of biopatenting and competing obligations.

Risk management within complex contract environments is another focal area. Bharwani and Mathews (2012) provide insights from hospitality contracts, while Samsuri et al. (2017) discuss enabling factors in production sharing contracts—where expiration often triggers costly transitions. Read et al. (2023) discuss contract management failures in the South African COVID-19 vaccine procurement, highlighting the practical risks of unclear expiration terms.

2.4 Research Gaps

Despite this breadth, notable gaps remain:

- **Fragmentation across systems:** There is limited cross-jurisdictional analysis aligning termination norms with globalized contract operations, particularly under hybrid or mixed legal systems.
- **Underexplored sectors:** Areas such as nonprofit housing (Pomeroy, 2017), employment law reforms (Munton et al., 2021a, 2021b), and narcotics regulation (Borta et al., 2024) lack in-depth treatment regarding contract expiry consequences.
- **Technological blind spots:** While AI, digital assets, and data-driven tools are reshaping contract administration, doctrinal integration is insufficiently developed (Guha et al., 2023; Mhia-Alddin & Hussein, 2025a).
- **Practical enforcement:** Few studies assess enforcement of expiry-related obligations in transnational contracts—particularly in industries exposed to patent cliffs (Holmen-Jensen & Åsmoen, 2024) and price controls post-expiry (Woodcock, 2019).

2.5 Seminal and Recent Contributions

Bradley (2021) and Emerson (2025) provide novel insights into legislative and franchise-related contract modifications, indicating a shifting regulatory paradigm. Narayana et al. (2019) and McBratney (2004) bridge the economic and legal perspectives, offering frameworks to assess expiry effects on logistics and technology transfer.

Moreover, Drexl et al. (2025) position the revision of technology transfer regulations within broader contractual dynamics, making their policy-oriented research highly relevant to expiry-sensitive contracts.

Finally, Al-Sherman and Aldabousi (2024) emphasize complementary penalties for corporate crimes in UAE law, showing how expiration or breach of compliance-related obligations can trigger multi-layered sanctions.

3. LEGAL FRAMEWORK AND DOCTRINAL BACKGROUND

Contract expiration and termination are distinct yet interrelated legal mechanisms that determine the cessation of contractual obligations. This section delineates their definitions, explores their doctrinal underpinnings, and analyzes statutory frameworks across multiple legal systems. It also elaborates on key legal doctrines that influence their application, such as frustration, breach, and force majeure.

3.1 Definition and Legal Basis of Expiration and Termination

Expiration refers to the natural conclusion of a contract at the end of its agreed-upon term or upon the fulfillment of its conditions. It is often automatic, requiring no active step by either party unless stipulated otherwise in the contract. Termination, by contrast, is a legal act that prematurely ends a contract prior to its original end date, either for cause (e.g., breach) or under agreed termination clauses (e.g., convenience or mutual consent).

The legal basis for these mechanisms arises from both statutory provisions and case law. Expiration is rooted in the principle of pacta sunt servanda, where obligations are upheld until completion, while termination draws legitimacy from doctrines allowing exit upon failure or impossibility of performance.

To clearly illustrate the difference between expiration and termination, Figure 1 outlines their key defining characteristics, causative mechanisms, and resulting consequences in contract law.

Figure 1. Conceptual distinction between expiration and termination

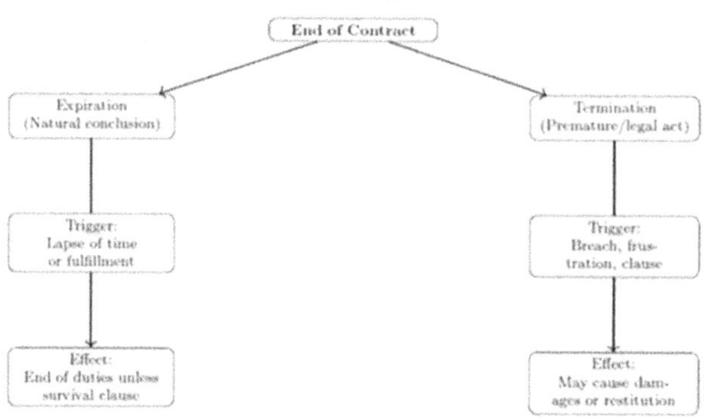

3.2 Differences in Contractual Consequences

The consequences of expiration are typically limited to the cessation of duties and rights unless the contract provides for post-expiry obligations such as confidentiality or non-compete clauses (Emerson, 2025). There is generally no liability unless a party failed to perform during the contract term.

Termination, however, often carries more severe consequences. It may trigger restitution, damages for breach, or the invocation of dispute resolution mechanisms. The legal effect varies by cause—termination for breach differs significantly from termination for frustration or convenience (Grosskopf, 2011; Cazac, 2012). The distinction becomes crucial in determining remedies and enforcement rights.

Figure 2 provides a flowchart illustrating the legal effects that typically follow contract expiration and termination, helping delineate liabilities, enforcement, and remedies.

Figure 2. Legal consequences of expiration vs. termination

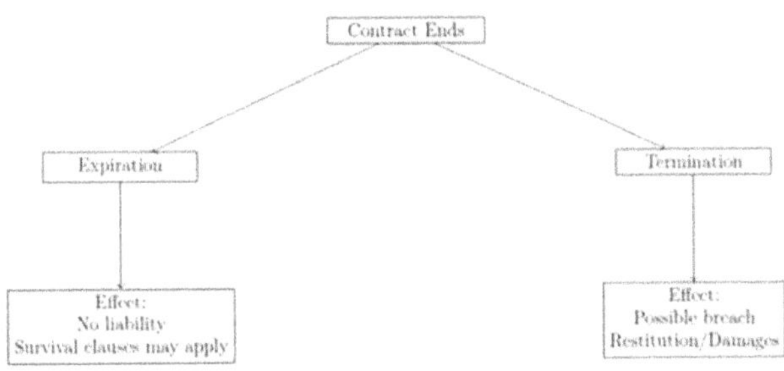

3.3 Statutory Analysis Across Jurisdictions

Legal systems around the world recognize and regulate expiration and termination differently. This section highlights how key jurisdictions frame these concepts:

- **United Kingdom (Common Law Tradition)**: Under UK contract law, termination can occur via repudiatory breach, frustration, or agreement. The *Law Reform (Frustrated Contracts) Act 1943* codifies the consequences of frustration. Judicial developments, as discussed by Hodge (2017), underscore the centrality of intent and breach in termination disputes.
- **United States (UCC – Uniform Commercial Code)**: In the U.S., Article 2 of the UCC governs contracts for the sale of goods. Termination may occur under §2-106 when a party exercises a right to cancel due to default.

Expiration is not specifically defined, but the UCC permits automatic lapse based on agreed duration or inactivity. Breach (§2-610) and commercial impracticability (§2-615) address early exit scenarios.

- **United Nations Convention on Contracts for the International Sale of Goods (CISG)**: The CISG standardizes international commercial contract law. Article 49 permits termination (termed "avoidance") for fundamental breach, while Article 79 incorporates force majeure principles. Expiration is implicitly recognized where contracts specify time limits or delivery schedules.
- **Civil Law Jurisdictions**: In civil law systems (e.g., France, Germany), expiration is typically codified and automatic. Termination, however, may require judicial approval or specific cause. The German *Bürgerliches Gesetzbuch (BGB)* outlines termination for good cause (§314) and delay (§323).

These frameworks demonstrate that while the conceptual structure of expiration and termination is globally recognized, the execution and consequences vary significantly.

3.4 Doctrinal Doctrines: Frustration, Breach, and Force Majeure

Several legal doctrines inform and justify the termination of contracts before their natural expiration:

- Frustration applies when unforeseen events render contractual obligations impossible or radically different from what was initially contemplated. In common law, frustration discharges obligations (e.g., *Taylor v Caldwell*, UK). The doctrine has limited applicability and requires a high threshold.
- Breach—particularly material or repudiatory breach—is the most common ground for termination. It allows the aggrieved party to end the contract and seek remedies. Grosskopf (2011) analyzes breach through a relational contract lens, showing how long-term collaborations often complicate breach assessments.
- Force Majeure, more prevalent in civil law and international contracts, excuses performance due to extraordinary external events (e.g., natural disasters, pandemics). The COVID-19 pandemic renewed scholarly attention to these clauses (Read et al., 2023; Mhia-Alddin & Hussein, 2025b). Under the CISG, Article 79 embodies a version of force majeure that relieves parties from liability.

- Impracticability under U.S. law (§2-615 UCC) is conceptually akin to force majeure but is often narrower in scope. It excuses performance when costs become excessively burdensome due to unforeseen circumstances.

These doctrines are not interchangeable; their legal thresholds, remedies, and procedural requirements differ, making precise application critical in dispute resolution.

4. COMPARATIVE LEGAL ANALYSIS

Contract expiration and termination are universally recognized legal concepts, yet their treatment varies substantially across jurisdictions due to differing legal traditions, statutory interpretations, and doctrinal applications. This section provides a comparative analysis of these mechanisms in common law and civil law systems, particularly focusing on the United Kingdom, United States, European Union, and selected civil law countries. It also highlights areas of both interpretative divergence and harmonization.

4.1 United Kingdom: Common Law Emphasis on Judicial Interpretation

In the UK, contract law remains largely judge-made, placing significant weight on precedent and judicial reasoning. Termination in the UK is commonly invoked through repudiatory breach, mutual agreement, or frustration. The doctrine of frustration, codified partially in the *Law Reform (Frustrated Contracts) Act 1943*, allows for discharge when unforeseen events fundamentally alter contractual obligations. Hodge (2017) illustrates the ongoing judicial development in this area, noting the courts' cautious approach to applying frustration, preferring parties to rely on explicit force majeure clauses.

Expiration, by contrast, is less frequently litigated, as it is typically defined by the contractual term itself. Post-expiry obligations, like restrictive covenants or intellectual property considerations, may still apply (Emerson, 2025), reflecting a nuanced understanding of continuing obligations.

4.2 United States: Statutory Structure and Uniform Commercial Code

In the U.S., the Uniform Commercial Code (UCC), particularly Article 2, provides a codified structure for termination in contracts for the sale of goods. Termination is recognized under UCC §2-106, with breach and anticipatory repudiation defined under §§2-610 and 2-615. Notably, the doctrine of commercial impracticability under §2-615 allows for termination when performance becomes unfeasible due to unforeseen difficulties.

Expiration is generally governed by the terms of the contract and is not subject to extensive statutory regulation. However, the consequences of expiration, especially in technology or pharmaceutical contexts (Swirnoff & Becker, 2010; Woodcock, 2019), raise complex issues around residual rights and regulatory compliance.

U.S. courts also handle force majeure within the framework of common law interpretation, though many contracts explicitly define triggering events. The pandemic further exposed gaps in predictability and uniform application (Read et al., 2023).

4.3 European Union: Harmonization and Sector-Specific Regulation

In the EU, contract law is influenced by national civil codes but increasingly guided by harmonization efforts, such as the *Principles of European Contract Law (PECL)* and sector-specific directives. Termination is permitted for non-performance under these instruments, and the doctrine of force majeure is generally accepted across member states, though its application varies by jurisdiction.

For instance, in pharmaceutical patent settlements, EU competition law introduces additional considerations affecting contract termination and expiration, particularly under antitrust frameworks (Colangelo, 2017; Drexl, Conde, & Kim, 2025). The *Technology Transfer Block Exemption Regulation (TTBER)* provides structured exceptions to ensure innovation while avoiding anti-competitive outcomes.

Expiration in EU contracts is more explicitly governed by statutory durations, and many jurisdictions impose notification requirements prior to expiry, especially in consumer and tenancy contracts (Cooper, 2018; Pomeroy, 2017).

4.4 Civil Law Countries: Codified Systems with Judicial Oversight

Civil law systems, such as those in France, Germany, and Ethiopia, rely on comprehensive codes to define and regulate contract expiration and termination. The German *Bürgerliches Gesetzbuch (BGB)*, for instance, delineates rules for termination for cause (§314) and non-performance (§323), alongside general provisions for contract expiration upon term completion.

In Ethiopia, national surveys (Borta et al., 2024) show that contract termination, particularly in regulated sectors like pharmaceuticals, is highly dependent on state oversight and regulatory compliance, integrating public policy considerations into private contract law.

Force majeure is codified in most civil law systems, allowing for broader application than in common law. However, judicial interpretation remains conservative, often requiring clear proof of impossibility rather than mere difficulty or commercial loss.

4.5 Interpretative Conflicts and Harmonized Principles

Across jurisdictions, terminology and threshold standards differ, leading to interpretive conflicts. For instance:

- The UK and U.S. differ on the thresholds for frustration vs. impracticability.
- Civil law jurisdictions permit broader interpretations of force majeure than the narrowly defined doctrine in common law.
- The CISG attempts to harmonize these through Article 79, but national courts often interpret the provision differently, reflecting their domestic doctrines.

Despite this, some harmonized principles are evident:

- Recognition of the difference between expiration (passive conclusion) and termination (active cessation).
- Acceptance of force majeure and frustration as valid defenses against liability, albeit under varying conditions.
- Increasing judicial and legislative accommodation of unforeseen global events (e.g., COVID-19), prompting the evolution of contract doctrine globally (Mhia-Alddin & Hussein, 2025a; Read et al., 2023).

The differences in how key jurisdictions treat contract expiration and termination are summarized in Table 1. The table highlights doctrinal trends and their legal effects.

Table 1. Jurisdictional comparison of expiration vs. termination

Jurisdiction	Expiration	Termination	Key Legal Basis
UK (Common Law)	Defined by contract	For breach, frustration	Case law + 1943 Act
US (UCC)	Lapse by time/inactivity	§2-610/615: breach/impracticability	Uniform Commercial Code
EU (CISG + Directives)	Statutory durations	Fundamental breach (Art. 49)	CISG + TTBER
Germany (Civil Law)	Codified auto-end	§§314/323 BGB	Civil Code
Ethiopia	State oversight driven	Regulatory termination	National statutes

5. CASE LAW ANALYSIS

The evolution of contract expiration and termination doctrines has been significantly shaped by judicial interpretation. Courts across jurisdictions have developed a rich body of case law that defines the contours, limitations, and exceptions applicable to these concepts. This section analyzes key landmark decisions and recent judgments to extract reasoning patterns, highlight interpretive divergences, and demonstrate evolving judicial trends.

5.1 Landmark Cases Defining Termination and Expiration

In United Kingdom jurisprudence, *Davis Contractors Ltd v Fareham Urban District Council* [1956] AC 696 remains foundational. The House of Lords held that performance becoming more onerous does not frustrate a contract unless the obligation is radically different from what was agreed. This case cemented the narrow application of frustration under English law and emphasized the sanctity of contract. Subsequent decisions, such as *The Sea Angel* [2007] EWCA Civ 547, reaffirmed this high threshold, clarifying that foreseeability and allocation of risk are key considerations in deciding frustration.

In contrast, U.S. courts apply a more flexible doctrine of commercial impracticability, as seen in *Transatlantic Financing Corp. v United States*, 363 F.2d 312 (D.C. Cir. 1966), where the court held that increased cost alone does not justify discharge unless it fundamentally alters the nature of the performance. Similarly, under the UCC §2-615, *Eastern Air Lines, Inc. v. Gulf Oil Corp.*, 415 F. Supp. 429 (S.D. Fla. 1975) held that market fluctuations do not constitute commercial impracticability, emphasizing foreseeability and contractual allocation of risks.

Expiration was addressed in *Bunge Corporation v Tradax Export SA* [1981] 1 WLR 711, where the House of Lords treated time clauses strictly, holding that a failure to deliver notices on time resulted in termination. This reinforced the position that expiration, where contractually defined, must be respected to preserve certainty in commercial dealings.

5.2 Recent Judgments and Evolving Doctrines

In *COVID-related cases*, courts were forced to revisit the scope of force majeure and frustration. For instance, in UK High Court decision *Salem v TLT LLP* [2021] EWHC 465 (Ch), the court held that the pandemic did not frustrate a consultancy agreement, as the contract anticipated disruption and allocated risk accordingly.

This judgment aligned with earlier case law and reinforced judicial reluctance to interfere with clear contractual risk distribution.

In U.S. federal courts, *JN Contemporary Art LLC v Phillips Auctioneers LLC*, No. 20-cv-4370 (S.D.N.Y. 2020), showed a more expansive approach. The court accepted that COVID-19 might render performance impracticable, allowing parties to renegotiate terms or assert a force majeure defense. The reasoning reflected a shift toward commercial realism and fairness during unprecedented events.

In the EU context, the *CJEU* has weighed in on contractual enforcement under force majeure and competition concerns. In *Generics (UK) Ltd v Competition and Markets Authority* [2020] UKSC 56, while not directly about termination, the UK Supreme Court analyzed post-expiry conduct in light of anti-competitive agreements, reflecting the complexity of legal obligations beyond formal contract termination.

In civil law jurisdictions such as Germany, recent *Bundesgerichtshof (BGH)* rulings (e.g., BGH, NJW 2021, 205) have clarified that COVID-19 can justify termination under §313 BGB (change of circumstances), subject to proof of substantial disruption and impossibility of contract adjustment.

5.3 Patterns of Judicial Reasoning

Across jurisdictions, a few dominant patterns emerge:

- **High threshold for frustration/impracticability**: Courts require strong proof that the change in circumstances renders performance impossible, not merely difficult or expensive.
- **Primacy of contractual terms**: Time limits, force majeure clauses, and termination procedures are strictly construed, emphasizing party autonomy and predictability.
- **Contextual interpretation**: Courts increasingly factor in external crises (e.g., pandemics, war) but do so cautiously, reflecting a balancing act between contractual certainty and commercial equity.

5.4 Divergent and Evolving Interpretations

There is no single unified doctrine governing expiration and termination:

- **Common law courts** tend to be conservative, allowing termination or frustration only in extreme cases. Expiration is treated as automatic and definitive, with few judicially imposed exceptions.

- **Civil law courts** often provide statutory flexibility for termination based on changed circumstances or economic hardship, guided by codified principles like *good faith* and *abuse of rights.*
- **Hybrid jurisdictions** (e.g., mixed systems like South Africa) reflect a blend, allowing courts more discretion to adjust outcomes in light of equity, as seen in *Read et al. (2023)* on contract management during the pandemic.

Moreover, emerging trends in digital and AI-driven contracts (Mhia-Alddin & Hussein, 2025a; 2025b) are beginning to challenge traditional notions of expiration and termination. With smart contracts and machine-readable clauses, courts will likely be called to determine how automatic or algorithmic terminations fit within existing legal doctrines.

Figure 3 shows a simplified timeline highlighting the emergence and evolution of judicial doctrines regarding contract cessation in major jurisdictions.

Figure 3. Timeline of doctrinal evolution in expiration and termination cases

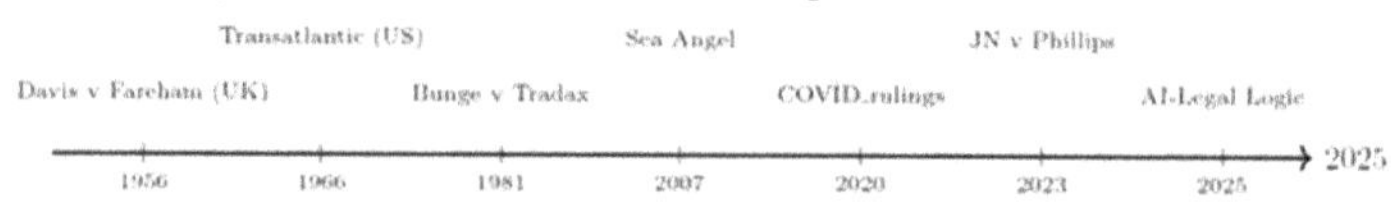

6. DISCUSSION

The comparative and doctrinal analysis of contract expiration and termination reveals a complex and nuanced legal landscape. Synthesizing findings from statutes, jurisprudence, and scholarly literature, it becomes evident that while both concepts function to bring contractual obligations to an end, they operate through distinct legal logics with different implications for rights, remedies, and risk allocation.

6.1 Synthesis of Legal Texts, Literature, and Case Law

Legal texts such as the UK's common law principles, the Uniform Commercial Code (UCC) in the U.S., and the CISG in international commercial law clearly distinguish expiration from termination. Expiration occurs automatically upon the lapse of a fixed term or condition without requiring action from either party, whereas termination usually involves a positive act, triggered by breach, frustration, or a contractual right.

Case law across jurisdictions reinforces this dichotomy. English cases like *Bunge v Tradax* establish the sanctity of express terms, strictly enforcing expiry clauses. Meanwhile, decisions such as *Davis Contractors v Fareham* and *The Sea Angel* draw firm boundaries around when frustration may excuse performance. In contrast, U.S. cases like *Eastern Air Lines v Gulf Oil* reflect a more pragmatic approach, accepting commercial impracticability as a legitimate termination ground under certain conditions.

Literature supports this division but also draws attention to their potential convergence. Scholars such as McKendrick (2020) and Farnsworth (2010) observe that while doctrinal boundaries are clear in theory, they are often blurred in practice, especially in long-term or relational contracts where parties fail to distinguish between contractual end by time and termination for cause.

6.2 Practical Implications in Various Contract Types

In commercial contracts, especially those involving fixed supply agreements, the distinction is critical. An expired contract may prevent parties from enforcing clauses such as indemnity or non-compete provisions unless those obligations are explicitly stated to survive expiration. Termination, however, may trigger default clauses, liquidated damages, and dispute resolution mechanisms.

In employment contracts, expiration often marks the natural end of a fixed-term engagement, limiting employee recourse unless unlawful dismissal or discriminatory conduct is proven. Termination, however, especially when sudden or without due process, can give rise to claims for unfair dismissal, notice pay, or breach of statutory rights.

In technology and licensing contracts, ambiguity around whether a license "expires" or is "terminated" may influence intellectual property rights, ongoing data obligations, and software access. Courts increasingly examine not just the language of the contract, but its commercial context and purpose.

6.3 Ambiguities and Overlaps Between Expiration and Termination

Despite theoretical clarity, overlaps and ambiguities persist in practice. For example:

- Early termination clauses can cause confusion when a contract contains a fixed duration but also grants one party the right to terminate before that period elapses. Is this a case of expiry or termination?
- Survival clauses are often poorly drafted, failing to specify which rights persist after the contract ends, leading to litigation about whether expiration extinguishes future obligations.
- Force majeure and frustration blur the line further, as courts must determine whether a supervening event causes premature expiration by operation of law or termination for impossibility.

These conceptual overlaps can result in differing interpretations by courts, particularly where termination rights are exercised close to the natural expiry date, raising questions about damages, restitution, or liability under post-contractual duties.

6.4 Need for Reform or Clarification

The doctrinal distinctions between expiration and termination, while generally well-established, would benefit from further clarification and standardization, particularly in transnational contexts. Possible reform directions include:

- Statutory guidance on survival clauses, requiring explicit language about post-expiration obligations.
- Harmonization across legal systems, especially under international instruments like the CISG, to address inconsistencies in force majeure, frustration, and termination procedures.
- Clearer drafting norms, encouraged by professional bodies (e.g., UNIDROIT, IBA), to ensure that parties specify whether and how key provisions survive contract end events.
- Judicial guidelines or restatements, particularly in common law jurisdictions, to articulate interpretive principles distinguishing termination for breach from early expiry scenarios.

In conclusion, while expiration and termination are doctrinally distinct, their practical application often reveals areas of legal uncertainty, particularly in complex or long-term contractual relationships. A combination of better drafting, judicial clarification, and selective legal reform could greatly improve predictability and fairness in commercial and employment contracting environments.

7. RECOMMENDATIONS

In light of the doctrinal analysis, comparative legal evaluation, and case law review on contract expiration and termination, this section outlines actionable recommendations aimed at improving clarity, consistency, and fairness in contract law practice and interpretation.

7.1. Legal Reforms and Legislative Clarification

To reduce ambiguity and promote uniformity, legislative bodies should consider the following reforms:

- **Codify Distinctions Between Expiration and Termination**: Statutes such as the UCC and national contract laws should explicitly distinguish between expiration (automatic cessation) and termination (active discharging of obligations), with clear provisions on their legal effects.
- **Mandate Survival Clause Disclosure**: Laws should require that contracts explicitly state which provisions (e.g., confidentiality, indemnity, arbitration) will survive expiration or termination. This could mirror approaches in consumer protection law where disclosure requirements already apply.
- **Clarify Force Majeure and Frustration Doctrines**: Legislatures, particularly in civil law jurisdictions, should provide more detailed statutory definitions and criteria for these doctrines to avoid inconsistent judicial outcomes.

7.2. Interpretative Guidelines for Courts

Judicial inconsistency in interpreting expiration and termination often stems from a lack of clear doctrinal markers. Courts can enhance legal certainty through:

- **Development of a Judicial Benchbook or Guideline**: National courts or judicial councils can issue interpretative guidance summarizing established case law and doctrinal distinctions, similar to judicial interpretation aids used in constitutional or administrative law.
- **Encouraging Contextual Interpretation**: Judges should continue to emphasize the commercial purpose and relational context of contracts, especially in cases where the contract is silent or ambiguous about end-of-contract consequences (as seen in relational contracts or long-term supply agreements).
- **Promoting Consistency in Equitable Relief**: Courts should harmonize how they apply doctrines such as restitution, unjust enrichment, and equita-

ble estoppel when interpreting the legal consequences of expiration versus termination.

7.3. Best Practices for Contract Drafting

Contracting parties, legal advisors, and in-house counsel should adopt the following best practices:

- **Use Clear Language**: Contracts should explicitly define "expiration" and "termination" and specify whether provisions such as dispute resolution, warranties, and indemnities survive the end of the agreement.
- **Include Exit Mechanisms and Conditions**: Drafting should account for early termination rights, exit strategies, and consequences such as penalties or liquidated damages, especially in long-term commercial and employment contracts.
- **Document Force Majeure and Risk-Sharing Clauses Thoughtfully**: Especially post-COVID-19, drafters must delineate how unforeseen events impact contract duration and which party bears the burden of risk.
- **Adopt Modular Clause Structures**: Using clause libraries or modular templates can help ensure consistency across contracts, especially in organizations that regularly use standardized agreements.

Figure 4 outlines a checklist of best practices that legal professionals should follow to ensure clarity and reduce litigation risk when drafting expiry and termination clauses.

Figure 4. Checklist for expiry/termination clause drafting

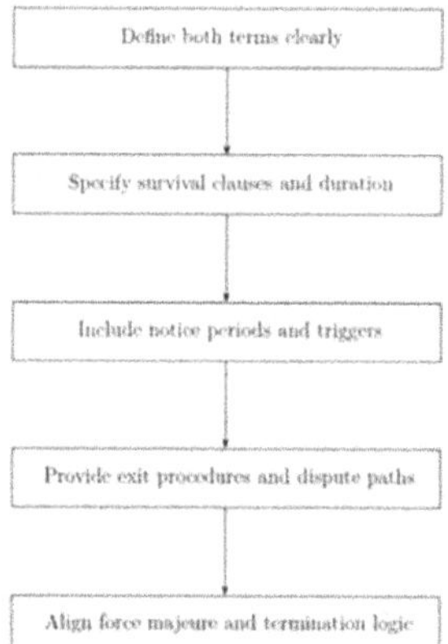

7.4. Enhancing Legal Education and Awareness

Legal ambiguity often stems from inadequate understanding among practitioners and students. Improvements can be made through:

- **Curricular Emphasis**: Law schools should incorporate deeper analysis of contract expiration and termination in commercial law and legal drafting courses, with comparative modules on civil and common law approaches.
- **Professional Training**: Continuing legal education (CLE) programs should include advanced training for practitioners on drafting and litigating contract end-of-life issues, especially in emerging areas like AI licensing and international supply chains.
- **Cross-Border Harmonization Efforts**: Academic and professional exchanges between jurisdictions can help align doctrinal understanding and best practices, particularly under frameworks like UNIDROIT, CISG, and the Hague Conference on Private International Law.

In sum, clarity in the treatment of contract expiration and termination requires a multi-level approach involving statutory reform, judicial coherence, practical drafting discipline, and ongoing legal education. Implementing these recommendations will foster more predictable outcomes, reduce litigation risks, and enhance the integrity of contractual relationships in both domestic and international settings.

8. CONCLUSION

The legal concepts of contract expiration and termination, while often conflated in practice, carry distinct theoretical foundations and practical consequences. This paper has examined these distinctions through the lenses of jurisprudential reasoning, doctrinal analysis, comparative legal perspectives, and case law development. Expiration refers to the natural end of a contract based on temporal limits or fulfillment of obligations, whereas termination is an active legal act triggered by a party's decision, breach, or specific contractual clause. This differentiation is critical to understanding the residual rights, obligations, and liabilities of contracting parties.

From a doctrinal and statutory standpoint, key jurisdictions such as the United Kingdom, the United States, and civil law systems differ in how they conceptualize and regulate contract cessation. The UK's common law system emphasizes judicial precedent and contractual autonomy, whereas the UCC in the U.S. codifies default rules with an emphasis on commercial reasonableness. Civil law jurisdictions tend to apply more codified frameworks under national civil codes and international instruments like the CISG. These differences, as analyzed in this study, present both harmonized principles—such as good faith in termination—and interpretative divergences, especially concerning doctrines like frustration, force majeure, and breach.

The literature reviewed and case law analyzed reveal a growing awareness among scholars, legislators, and courts of the need to refine and clarify how contracts are brought to an end. However, persistent ambiguities remain, especially in multi-jurisdictional contracts, relational agreements, and sectors impacted by technological and economic transformation. The complexity is compounded by overlapping doctrines and varying degrees of judicial activism in different legal systems.

This research has also identified gaps in legal education, statutory guidance, and contract drafting practices that contribute to inconsistent application and interpretation. Without clearer doctrinal boundaries and legislative definitions, parties face increased risk of dispute and litigation at the end of contractual relationships. Accordingly, the need for reform—whether through judicial guidelines, statutory precision, or better drafting norms—is both timely and necessary.

In conclusion, contract expiration and termination must no longer be treated as interchangeable or secondary legal notions. Instead, they warrant focused attention in legal discourse, legislative reform, and practical application. By enhancing clarity around these foundational concepts, the legal system can better uphold the expectations of contracting parties and ensure the fair and predictable resolution of contractual relationships in an increasingly complex legal and commercial environment.

REFERENCES

Al-Sherman, N., & Aldabousi, A. M. (2024). The Complementary Penalties Enforced to Combat Corporate Crimes in UAE Law. *Pakistan Journal of Criminology*, *16*(3).

Amani, B. (2007). *Merchants missionaries: Patenting life, competing international obligations and the proselytization of a Realistic Utopia.*

Banta, N. M. (2019). Electronic wills and digital assets: Reassessing formality in the digital age. *Baylor Law Review*, *71*, 547.

Bharwani, S., & Mathews, D. (2012). Risk identification and analysis in the hospitality industry: Practitioners' perspectives from India. *Worldwide Hospitality and Tourism Themes*, *4*(5), 410–427. DOI: 10.1108/17554211211277851

Borta, H. G., Alemu, A., Shute, T., Zewdie, B., Fantaw, D., Shimelis, B., ... & Tamiru, M. T. (2024). Narcotic Drugs and Psychotropic Substances Control System in Ethiopia: A National Survey.

Bousri, M. M. S. (2019). *A comparative analysis of legal and institutional framework for arbitration: Comoros and Uganda* (Doctoral dissertation, School of law).

Bradley, C. A. (2021). Reassessing the Legislative Veto: The Statutory President, Foreign Affairs, and Congressional Workarounds. *The Journal of Legal Analysis*, *13*(1), 439–501. DOI: 10.1093/jla/laab008

Cazac, O. (2012). Towards a comprehensive concept of termination of contracts. *Revista Moldovenească de Drept Internaţional şi Relaţii Internaţionale, 25*(3), 75-92.

Colangelo, M. (2017). Reverse payment patent settlements in the pharmaceutical sector under EU and US competition laws: a comparative analysis. *World competition, 40*(3).

Cooper, S., & Zell, S. (2023). *Staying on Board: Non-profit housing provider board capacity in a changing context*. Institute of Urban Studies, The University of Winnipeg.

Cooper, S. E. (2018). *The End of an Era? Social Housing and Social Property in a Post-subsidy World* (Doctoral dissertation, University of Illinois Chicago).

Dehaini, K. Y. (2021). *Contracts Termination: Main Contract vs Subcontract Back-to-Back Practices* (Doctoral dissertation).

Drexl, J., Conde, B., & Kim, D. (2025). Position Statement of the Max Planck Institute for Innovation and Competition of 25 April 2025 in the framework of the revision of the Technology Transfer Block Exemption Regulation and the accompanying Guidelines. *Max Planck Institute for Innovation & Competition Research Paper*, (25-10).

Emerson, R. W. (2025). Franchise Noncompetes: Their Legal Effect, Practical Impact, and Superior Alternatives. *The Journal of Corporation Law*, *50*(3).

Espenlaub, S., Goergen, M., Khurshed, A., & Remenar, M. (2013). Do directors trade after IPO lockup expiry? In *Handbook of Research on IPOs* (pp. 275–294). Edward Elgar Publishing. DOI: 10.4337/9781781955376.00024

Estreicher, S., & Hirsch, J. M. (2013). Comparative Wrongful Dismissal Law: Reassessing American Exceptionalism. *SSRN*, *92*, 343. DOI: 10.2139/ssrn.2238776

Goyal, K. (2017). *Overlapping of Intellectual Property Rights: An analysis with reference to conflict vis-à-vis Design, Trademark, Copyright and Patent*. College of Legal Studies, UPES Dehradun.

Grosskopf, O. (2011). Dividing the surplus upon termination: The case of relational contracts. *American Business Law Journal*, *48*(1), 1–26. DOI: 10.1111/j.1744-1714.2010.01110.x

Guha, N., Nyarko, J., Ho, D., Ré, C., Chilton, A., Chohlas-Wood, A., & Li, Z. (2023). Legalbench: A collaboratively built benchmark for measuring legal reasoning in large language models. *SSRN*, *36*, 44123–44279. DOI: 10.2139/ssrn.4583531

Hodge, P. S. (2017). Judicial development of the law of contract in the United Kingdom. *Geo. Wash. L. Rev.*, *85*, 1587.

Holmen-Jensen, P. R., & Åsmoen, O. (2024). Navigating the Patent Cliff.

Lim, D. (2013). Patent misuse and antitrust: Rebirth or false dawn. *Michigan Telecommunications and Technology Law Review*, *20*, 299.

Manganelli, A. G. (2019). Reverse payments and risk of bankruptcy under private information. *International Journal of the Economics of Business*, *26*(3), 411–429. DOI: 10.1080/13571516.2019.1613146

Margalit, Y., Levy, O., & Loike, J. (2014). The new frontier of advanced reproductive technology: Reevaluating modern legal parenthood. *Harvard Journal of Law & Gender*, *37*, 107.

McBratney, A. (2004). Post-WTO China: Competition and Technology Transfer Laws in the 'New' Socialist Market Economy. *Asia Pacific Law Review, 12*(1), 1–30. DOI: 10.1080/18758444.2004.11788126

Mhia-Alddin, D. A., & Hussein, A. M. (2025). AI-Powered Contract Security: Managing Expiry, Compliance, and Risk Mitigation Through Deep Learning and LLMs. In *Revolutionizing Cybersecurity With Deep Learning and Large Language Models* (pp. 37-64). IGI Global Scientific Publishing.

Mhia-Alddin, D. A., & Hussein, A. M. (2025). Contract Expiry in AI-Driven STM Research: Legal Challenges, Risks, and Regulatory Considerations. In *Ensuring Secure and Ethical STM Research in the AI Era* (pp. 77-110). IGI Global Scientific Publishing.

Munton, J., Stewart, A., McCrystal, S., Hardy, T., & Orifici, A. (2021). Submission to the Senate Education and Employment Legislation Committee Inquiry in the Fair Work Amendment (Supporting Australia's Jobs and Economic Recovery) Bill 2020.

Munton, J., Stewart, A., McCrystal, S., Hardy, T., & Orifici, A. (2021). The (Omni) bus that Broke Down: Changes to Casual Employment and the Remnants of the Coalition's Industrial Relations Agenda. *Australian Journal of Labour Law*.

Narayana, S. A., Pati, R. K., & Padhi, S. S. (2019). Market dynamics and reverse logistics for sustainability in the Indian Pharmaceuticals industry. *Journal of Cleaner Production, 208*, 968–987. DOI: 10.1016/j.jclepro.2018.10.171

Osei-Tutu, J. J. (2001). Trips and domestic control: implications for developing countries.

Pai, Y. (2018). Patent Injunction Heuristics in India. *Pai, Yogesh, Patent Injunction Heuristics in India in Rafal Sikorski (Ed.) Patent Law Injunctions, Kluwer Law International BV (2019).*

Pomeroy, S. (2017). *Discussion paper: Envisioning a modernized social and affordable housing sector in Canada*. Carleton University Centre for Urban Research and Education.

Read, A., Botha, R., & Jamaloodien, K. (2023). COVID-19 vaccination procurement and contract management in a South African context. *Journal of Strategic Contracting and Negotiation, 7*(1-2), 33–43. DOI: 10.1177/20555636231198053

Samsuri, A., Zakaria, Z., Manaf, K. H., & Ismail, I. (2017). Key enablers in a production sharing contract operatorship transfer exercise. *Journal of Advanced Review on Scientific Research, 36*(1), 1–13.

Schnichels, D., & Sule, S. (2010). The pharmaceutical sector inquiry and its impact on competition law enforcement. *Journal of European competition law & practice, 1*(2), 93-111.

Shoraka, S. (2006). *World trade dispute resolution and developing countries: Taking a development approach to fair adjudication in the context of WTO law*. London School of Economics and Political Science.

Siew-Kuan, E. (2012). Evolving landscape of patent remedies in a changing marketplace. *Singapore Academy of Law Journal, 24*, 634-668.

Sullivan, C. (2015). Interim dilapidations. *Journal of Building Survey. Appraisal & Valuation, 3*(4), 323–334. DOI: 10.69554/UTKA7017

Sullivan, C. A. (2016). Tending the Garden: Restricting Competition via" Garden Leave. *Berkeley Journal of Employment and Labor Law*, •••, 293–325.

Swirnoff, A. H., & Becker, D. M. (2010). Judicial developments in the US Hatch-Waxman infringement safe harbor. *Expert Opinion on Therapeutic Patents, 20*(4), 451–458. DOI: 10.1517/13543771003604737 PMID: 20302449

Woodcock, R. (2019). Using Price Regulation Instead of Competition to Reduce Prices after Patents Expire. *Available atSSRN* 3466473. DOI: 10.2139/ssrn.3466473

Chapter 3
Regulatory Responses to AI in Healthcare and Medical Diagnostics

Naresh Tiwari
https://orcid.org/0009-0000-7169-591X
Cap Tech, USA

ABSTRACT

The integration of AI in healthcare offers transformative possibilities for precision medicine, early disease detection, and clinical decision support. However, these advancements come with significant legal, ethical, and regulatory challenges. This chapter explores global regulatory responses to AI in healthcare, analyzing approaches from the EU, US, and select Asian countries. It examines medical device regulations, data protection laws, and liability frameworks in addressing AI-enabled system risks. The chapter discusses transparency, accountability, and patient autonomy in AI deployment, providing insights for policymakers, healthcare professionals, and technology developers to balance innovation with public trust and patient safety. By identifying best practices and emerging trends, the chapter aims to foster innovation while safeguarding patient safety.

1. INTRODUCTION

The integration of Artificial Intelligence (AI) into healthcare and medical diagnostics represents a paradigm shift in the delivery of care, disease prevention, and clinical decision-making. This transformative wave promises enhanced efficiency, precision diagnostics, and personalized treatment. However, it simultaneously raises profound regulatory, ethical, and legal challenges that must be addressed to ensure

DOI: 10.4018/979-8-3373-4862-9.ch003

Copyright © 2025, IGI Global Scientific Publishing. Copying or distributing in print or electronic forms without written permission of IGI Global Scientific Publishing is prohibited.

equitable access, safety, data privacy, and accountability (Mennella et al., 2024; Sheliemina, 2024). With the growing deployment of AI in medical diagnostics, such as radiology, pathology, and genomics, regulators around the world are actively reassessing existing frameworks to accommodate the unique risks and opportunities posed by intelligent systems (Larson et al., 2021; Pesapane et al., 2018).

AI-driven diagnostic systems often operate as black boxes, lacking transparency in their decision-making processes. This opacity complicates clinical validation, legal liability, and public trust (Ho, 2023). The emergence of generative AI and deep learning algorithms further complicates regulatory governance due to their self-learning capabilities and potential for misuse (Ali & Aysan, 2025; Trotsyuk et al., 2024). As a result, institutions such as the World Health Organization (2023) and the European Union have begun crafting tailored regulatory responses, exemplified by the recent EU AI Act (Butt, 2024).

Internationally, the regulatory landscape is fragmented. The United States Food and Drug Administration (FDA), the European Medicines Agency (EMA), and regulatory bodies in countries such as China and Russia have adopted different risk-based approaches to AI classification, transparency standards, and post-market surveillance (Pesapane et al., 2021). However, as emphasized by Verma et al. (2020), a harmonized global governance structure is critical to mitigate inconsistencies that could hinder innovation or create regulatory arbitrage.

Another critical aspect is the integration of AI with data-driven technologies such as quantum computing and sensor systems, which are reshaping diagnostic tools and biomedical research methodologies (Campus, 2024; Eswaran & Eswaran, 2025; Eisenberg, 2024). This fusion of technologies complicates the regulatory response, requiring policy frameworks that account for layered risks involving data security, algorithmic bias, and the autonomy of clinical practitioners (Maguluri et al., 2023; Shafik, 2024).

Equally important is the ethical consideration of using AI in life-altering medical decisions. The need for robust ethical governance frameworks has been echoed across several domains of AI research, including finance and warfare (Ali & Aysan, 2024; Batabyal, 2024). In healthcare, however, the stakes are uniquely high. Regulatory frameworks must incorporate ethical dimensions such as informed consent, patient autonomy, non-discrimination, and equitable access to AI-powered services (Terry, 2019; Shukla & Taneja, 2024). This complexity is exacerbated in the case of vulnerable populations, such as children or rural communities, who may be disproportionately affected by algorithmic inaccuracies or systemic bias (Luan et al., 2024).

Recent scholarship also suggests that interdisciplinary policy modeling and topic modeling techniques—borrowed from computational social sciences—can aid in understanding the societal impact of AI regulations (Rodriguez & Storer, 2020; Schünemann et al., 2024; San Biagio et al., 2023). For instance, studies have applied machine learning and structural topic modeling to assess public discourse and scholarly debates on AI ethics and regulations (Ali, Zafar, & Aysan, 2024; Filetti et al., 2024), offering valuable insights for policymakers.

Furthermore, the regulatory conversation must be informed by a comprehensive understanding of AI's functionality within complex healthcare environments. Tools such as AI-based drones (Arya & Rastogi, 2024), semantic web platforms for threat detection (Gaurav et al., 2024), and AI-driven educational interfaces (Jamro & Jamro, 2023) highlight the broad applicability of intelligent systems beyond diagnostics, raising new considerations for interdisciplinary regulation.

The remainder of this chapter explores the evolving regulatory responses to AI in healthcare and diagnostics, focusing on international best practices, ethical-legal frameworks, emerging technological challenges, and policy recommendations. Drawing from a robust body of interdisciplinary literature, including developments in engineering (Zangana & Abdulazeez, 2023), military ethics (Batabyal, 2024), and gender-based safety applications (Pimpalkar et al., 2024; Vyawahare et al., 2024), this chapter offers a holistic examination of how law and policy can ensure responsible AI integration in medicine. Ultimately, a successful regulatory approach must be anticipatory, inclusive, and dynamic, responding to rapid technological advancements while safeguarding human dignity and health outcomes.

2. EVOLUTION OF AI IN HEALTHCARE AND MEDICAL DIAGNOSTICS

The application of Artificial Intelligence (AI) in healthcare has transitioned from experimental curiosity to a foundational pillar in modern medical diagnostics and treatment strategies. Initially used for rudimentary data analysis and medical record management, AI technologies have matured to enable real-time imaging analysis, precision diagnostics, predictive analytics, robotic surgery, and even drug discovery.

2.1 Early Foundations and Technological Convergence

The first wave of AI integration in healthcare focused on decision support systems, expert systems, and rule-based logic. These systems were relatively static and lacked adaptability. The emergence of machine learning (ML) and, subsequently, deep learning (DL) has radically changed this landscape by enabling systems to learn from complex datasets and improve performance over time (Larson et al., 2021; Pesapane et al., 2018). The integration of quantum computing and AI further promises unprecedented advancements in diagnostic speed and accuracy (Campus, 2024; Eswaran & Eswaran, 2025).

Technologies like image recognition, natural language processing, and neural networks now empower diagnostic tools to detect anomalies in medical images, analyze patient histories, and assist in clinical decision-making (Zangana & Mustafa, 2024a; Zangana & Mustafa, 2024b). These advancements echo the broader trends observed in other industries such as finance, defense, and education, where AI has become a core enabler of transformation (Ali & Aysan, 2024; Arya & Rastogi, 2024; Jamro & Jamro, 2023).

To better understand the trajectory of AI evolution in medical diagnostics, a simplified flowchart of the typical integration pathway is presented below. It outlines the transition from data acquisition to AI-enabled clinical decision support.

Figure 1. AI integration pathway in healthcare diagnostics

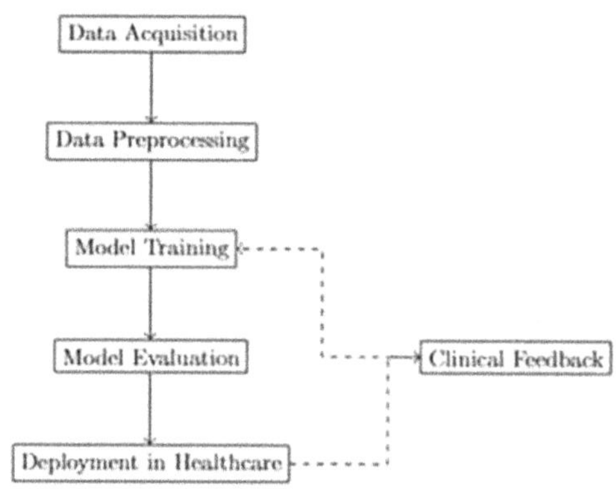

2.2 From Assistive Tools to Autonomous Systems

Recent developments have pushed AI systems from being merely assistive tools to autonomous agents capable of functioning with minimal human intervention. For instance, AI models now support remote diagnostics through wearable sensors and Internet of Things (IoT) devices, which continuously collect, analyze, and transmit patient data (Eisenberg, 2024; Shafik, 2024). These systems, coupled with edge computing and 5G technology, have introduced a new paradigm of proactive and preventative healthcare.

Moreover, generative AI has shown potential in synthesizing complex medical data, enabling the creation of synthetic datasets for model training while preserving patient privacy (Ali & Aysan, 2025). This approach addresses both ethical concerns and data scarcity, making it particularly relevant in rare disease diagnostics and pandemic modeling (Shuja et al., 2021).

2.3 Regulatory Evolution and Ethical Considerations

As AI systems gain autonomy, concerns regarding safety, transparency, and accountability have escalated. These concerns are mirrored in international regulatory responses, such as the EU AI Act and the WHO guidelines for AI in health (Butt, 2024; World Health Organization, 2023). Regulatory bodies are increasingly treating AI tools as medical devices, necessitating rigorous validation and lifecycle monitoring (Pesapane et al., 2021; Mennella et al., 2024).

Ethical concerns—ranging from algorithmic bias and data privacy to patient autonomy—are now central to the design and deployment of AI in healthcare (Mennella et al., 2024; Ho, 2023; Naili et al., 2025). This ethical shift aligns with wider AI discourse across domains such as warfare, finance, and education, where responsible AI practices are gaining traction (Batabyal, 2024; Shukla & Taneja, 2024; Veluru, 2024).

2.4 The Role of Research, Academia, and Multidisciplinary Collaboration

The academic community plays a crucial role in evaluating and guiding the ethical implementation of AI in healthcare. Studies have shown that AI can enhance scholarly research methodologies, enabling scientometric analyses and literature mining (Luan et al., 2024; Rodriguez & Storer, 2020). Topic modeling and semantic clustering techniques have proven useful in identifying research trends and gaps (Ali, Zafar, & Aysan, 2024; San Biagio et al., 2023).

Efforts have also been made to bridge the gap between theoretical AI models and their practical deployment. For example, Filetti et al. (2024) highlight how AI tools aid in research design and publication, which has implications for evidence-based clinical innovation. Meanwhile, scholars like Leontidis (2024) and Verma & Rohit (2024) explore how AI is transforming the very nature of scientific inquiry and scholarly communication.

2.5 Cross-Industry Learnings and Future Directions

Insights from adjacent fields further inform the trajectory of AI in healthcare. For example, ethical hacking experiments illustrate how AI can enhance system security—an important consideration for health data protection (Al-Sinani & Mitchell, 2024; Al-Sinani et al., 2025). Similarly, AI-driven policy modeling, as demonstrated in governance and smart city management, provides frameworks for AI implementation in complex healthcare ecosystems (Schünemann et al., 2024; Maguluri et al., 2023).

AI applications in women's safety (Pimpalkar et al., 2024; Vyawahare et al., 2024) and industrial transformation (Rashid & Kausik, 2024; Fenwick et al., 2024) also offer transferable strategies for inclusive, equitable healthcare innovation. This cross-pollination of AI practices signals a future where healthcare benefits from lessons learned in finance, defense, education, and public administration (Karim et al., 2023; Zreik, 2024).

2.6 Summary

The evolution of AI in healthcare and medical diagnostics is marked by technological breakthroughs, ethical awakening, and regulatory adaptation. While the trajectory is promising, its responsible advancement will depend on inclusive governance, cross-sector collaboration, and continuous evaluation. Emerging AI methodologies—from image denoising and object detection to risk mitigation frameworks—must be rigorously tested within the complex realities of healthcare (Zangana & Mustafa, 2024c; Trotsyuk et al., 2024). Only through this careful balance can we ensure that AI augments human capabilities without compromising ethical and legal standards (Terry, 2019; Verma et al., 2020).

3. THE NEED FOR REGULATION

The rapid proliferation of artificial intelligence (AI), particularly in sensitive domains such as healthcare, finance, military, education, and public governance, has made the case for robust and forward-looking regulatory frameworks more urgent than ever. AI systems now possess capabilities that can influence diagnosis, warfare, hiring, academic publishing, legal interpretation, and even policy creation, making unregulated growth potentially hazardous to ethics, security, and human rights.

3.1. Ethical Imperatives and Risk Mitigation

AI systems often function as black boxes, lacking explainability and transparency, which complicates accountability and oversight. The ethical dimensions of generative AI across domains—including finance, healthcare, and academia—require structured governance to mitigate risks associated with bias, misinformation, and misuse (Ali & Aysan, 2025; Verma & Rohit, 2024). Trotsyuk et al. (2024) argue for a robust framework to preemptively address potential misuse in biomedical research, reinforcing the need for anticipatory governance.

In warfare, the delegation of lethal decisions to autonomous systems introduces profound moral concerns. Batabyal (2024) highlights how the laws of war struggle to address scenarios introduced by AI-driven conflict, where decisions are made without human deliberation. This expands the risk landscape and underscores the urgency for enforceable international norms.

3.2. Health and Biomedical AI: High Stakes, Low Margin for Error

AI applications in medical diagnostics, treatment planning, and robotic surgery carry life-and-death implications. However, disparities in regulatory maturity across jurisdictions can allow subpar or biased systems to proliferate (Pesapane et al., 2021; Pesapane et al., 2018; Mennella et al., 2024). The World Health Organization (2023) stresses the need for AI regulations that ensure safety, effectiveness, and equity in healthcare systems worldwide.

As Larson et al. (2021) emphasize, regulatory frameworks should prioritize validation, post-market surveillance, and continuous learning mechanisms to ensure that AI tools remain reliable in dynamic clinical environments. Similarly, Naili et al. (2025) call attention to the legal ambiguities surrounding liability and informed consent when diagnostic errors occur due to AI-generated outcomes.

3.3. Data Privacy, Surveillance, and Security

The ability of AI systems to analyze large-scale personal data raises critical concerns about privacy, surveillance, and data security. Shafik (2024) points to vulnerabilities in AI-driven systems like ChatGPT, where sensitive user data can be exposed without proper safeguards. Shukla and Taneja (2024) advocate for embedding ethical considerations and privacy protections during the developmental stages of AI.

In cybersecurity, the dual-use nature of AI tools—capable of both defending and attacking systems—necessitates regulatory foresight. Al-Sinani and Mitchell (2024), along with Al-Sinani et al. (2025), demonstrate how AI-enhanced ethical hacking can be weaponized, necessitating stringent norms to avoid unintended harm. Veluru (2024) similarly warns of the large-scale misuse of AI without ethical oversight.

3.4. Cross-Sector Implications and Governance Complexity

AI does not operate within silos—it intersects with diverse sectors such as finance (Ali et al., 2024), agriculture (Arya & Rastogi, 2024), education (Jamro & Jamro, 2023), scientific research (Leontidis, 2024; Luan et al., 2024), and labor markets (Fenwick et al., 2024). Consequently, regulation must be cross-sectoral and adaptive. Butt (2024) provides a detailed analysis of the EU Artificial Intelligence Act as a global benchmark for sector-specific and risk-based regulation, while Flannery et al. (2021) underscore the occupational safety implications of unregulated AI in the construction industry.

As AI becomes integrated into quantum computing, semiconductor technologies, and smart infrastructure, complexity increases. Campus (2024) and Eswaran and Eswaran (2025) stress the need for convergence-ready regulatory models capable of handling hybrid systems. Schünemann et al. (2024) further advocate for systems-thinking approaches in regulatory policymaking, suggesting that conventional linear models are inadequate.

3.5. AI in Scientific Communication and Academic Integrity

The rise of AI-generated content in academic research introduces new challenges for originality, peer review, and integrity. Filetti et al. (2024) and Zreik (2024) describe how researchers are using generative tools for literature reviews and idea generation, often without clear disclosure or verification mechanisms. Such trends demand governance frameworks that distinguish between ethical assistance and academic dishonesty.

3.6. Emerging Threats: Online Harassment, Misinformation, and Gendered AI Safety

AI's role in detecting and mitigating online threats—such as harassment or phishing—must be balanced with rights to privacy and expression. Gaurav et al. (2024) and Vyawahare et al. (2024) demonstrate how AI-driven surveillance tools can either empower or suppress, depending on their governance. Pimpalkar et al. (2024) highlight how AI can be used to enhance women's safety, though caution is required to prevent reinforcing harmful stereotypes.

3.7. Regional and Comparative Considerations

There is a striking imbalance in AI governance maturity across nations. Pesapane et al. (2021) compare regulatory systems in the EU, US, China, and Russia, revealing varying levels of rigor and transparency. Ho (2023) argues for the integration of the human right to science in AI regulation, ensuring equitable access while maintaining accountability. Verma et al. (2020) identify systemic regulatory challenges in public health that also extend to AI-driven decision-making platforms.

3.8. Call for Proactive and Adaptive Regulation

Experts call for regulation to move beyond reactive models toward proactive, adaptable, and participatory frameworks. Rashid and Kausik (2024) argue that industries are evolving too quickly for traditional legislative cycles to keep up. Regulations must be forward-looking and co-evolve with technological advancements. Similarly, Eisenberg (2024) urges that integrity-based design principles be embedded into AI sensor systems from the outset, promoting responsible innovation.

AI's capacity to shape society—through surveillance, manipulation, automation, or augmentation—makes its regulation a public good. Without governance, AI risks deepening inequalities, automating biases, and consolidating power in unaccountable hands (Ali & Aysan, 2024; Rodriguez & Storer, 2020). As Sheliemina (2024) argues, we are at a turning point where regulation will define whether AI enhances healthcare or amplifies disparities.

4. CURRENT REGULATORY FRAMEWORKS

The global regulation of artificial intelligence (AI) and machine learning (ML) in healthcare is evolving rapidly, with jurisdictions adopting diverse approaches to ensure safety, efficacy, and ethical use. This section provides an in-depth analysis of current regulatory frameworks across key regions, integrating insights from recent literature and official guidelines.

4.1 United States

4.1.1 FDA's Approach to Software as a Medical Device (SaMD)

The U.S. Food and Drug Administration (FDA) classifies AI/ML-based software intended for medical purposes as Software as a Medical Device (SaMD). The FDA evaluates these devices through established pathways such as premarket clearance

(510(k)), De Novo classification, or premarket approval, depending on the risk associated with the device. Recognizing the unique challenges posed by AI/ML technologies, the FDA emphasizes a risk-based approach to modifications, ensuring that any changes maintain the device's safety and effectiveness (FDA, 2025).

4.1.2 Recent Guidelines and Initiatives

In January 2025, the FDA released the draft guidance titled "Artificial Intelligence-Enabled Device Software Functions: Lifecycle Management and Marketing Submission Recommendations." This guidance outlines lifecycle considerations and specific recommendations to support marketing submissions for AI-enabled medical devices. It complements the FDA's AI/ML-Based SaMD Action Plan, which aims to establish a tailored regulatory framework, including a "predetermined change control plan" to manage modifications in AI/ML algorithms over time (FDA, 2025; Emergo, 2025).

Furthermore, the FDA collaborates with international organizations such as the International Medical Device Regulators Forum (IMDRF) to develop Good Machine Learning Practice (GMLP) principles, promoting consistency and safety in AI/ML-based medical devices (Health Canada, 2021).

4.2 European Union

4.2.1 Medical Device Regulation (MDR) and AI Act

The European Union's Medical Device Regulation (MDR) provides a comprehensive framework for medical devices, including those incorporating AI. The MDR emphasizes a lifecycle approach to safety, requiring clinical evaluations and post-market surveillance. In parallel, the proposed Artificial Intelligence Act aims to regulate AI systems based on their risk levels, with high-risk applications, such as medical devices, subject to stringent requirements for transparency, accountability, and human oversight (Butt, 2024).

4.2.2 Role of the European Medicines Agency (EMA)

The European Medicines Agency (EMA) plays a pivotal role in integrating AI into medicines regulation. In May 2025, the EMA updated its AI workplan, focusing on guidance, policy support, tools and technology, collaboration, and experimentation. Notably, the EMA's Human Medicines Committee (CHMP) accepted clinical trial evidence generated by an AI tool supervised by a human pathologist, marking a significant step in recognizing AI-assisted data in regulatory decisions (EMA, 2025).

4.3 United Kingdom

4.3.1 MHRA Guidelines on AI in Healthcare

The UK's Medicines and Healthcare products Regulatory Agency (MHRA) is actively developing regulatory frameworks for AI as a Medical Device (AIaMD). In December 2024, the MHRA launched the "AI Airlock," a regulatory sandbox designed to test and refine the rules governing AI-powered medical devices. This initiative aims to ensure that innovative AI technologies reach patients safely and efficiently (MHRA, 2024).

Additionally, the MHRA collaborates with international regulators, including the FDA and Health Canada, to establish Good Machine Learning Practice (GMLP) principles, fostering harmonization in AI/ML medical device regulation (Health Canada, 2021).

4.3.2 Role of NICE and NHS AI Lab

The National Institute for Health and Care Excellence (NICE) and the NHS AI Lab are instrumental in evaluating and integrating AI technologies into the UK's healthcare system. The NHS AI Lab supports projects that develop AI tools for imaging and diagnostics, while NICE provides evidence-based guidelines to assess the clinical and cost-effectiveness of AI applications. These organizations work collaboratively to ensure that AI innovations are safely and effectively implemented in the NHS (BOA, 2025).

4.4 Other Jurisdictions

The regulatory models governing AI in healthcare vary across jurisdictions. The diagram below categorizes these approaches based on risk classification, oversight, and transparency mandates.

Figure 2. Comparative overview of national AI regulatory models

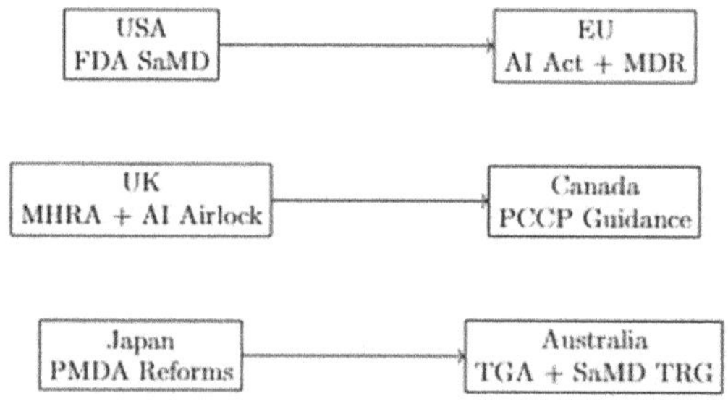

4.4.1 Canada (Health Canada)

Health Canada regulates AI/ML-based medical devices under the Medical Devices Regulations. In February 2025, Health Canada published pre-market guidance for machine learning-enabled medical devices, introducing the concept of a "predetermined change control plan" (PCCP) to manage modifications in AI/ML systems. The guidance emphasizes transparency, risk management, data quality, and post-market monitoring to ensure the safety and effectiveness of AI/ML medical devices (Health Canada, 2025).

4.4.2 Japan (PMDA)

Japan's Pharmaceuticals and Medical Devices Agency (PMDA) oversees the regulation of AI in healthcare. The country is actively working to balance patient privacy with the integration of AI technologies. Efforts include reforming regulations to promote standardized data-sharing frameworks and allowing the secondary use of partially anonymized patient data. These initiatives aim to facilitate the responsible use of AI in diagnostics and research while respecting cultural values around privacy (Financial Times, 2025).

4.4.3 Australia (TGA)

The Therapeutic Goods Administration (TGA) in Australia regulates AI as a medical device when used for diagnosis, prevention, monitoring, prediction, prognosis, treatment, or alleviation of disease. The TGA has established a Technical Reference Group for Software as a Medical Device (SaMD) and AI to provide expert knowledge on complex issues related to software and AI technologies. This group assists the TGA in addressing emerging risks, identifying benefits and barriers, and understanding the educational needs of software developers (TGA, 2024).

4.4.4 WHO Guidance and International Standards (e.g., ISO/IEC)

The World Health Organization (WHO) provides global guidance on the ethical and regulatory considerations of AI in health. The WHO emphasizes the importance of transparency, accountability, data privacy, and the need for international collaboration to develop harmonized standards. International standards organizations, such as the International Organization for Standardization (ISO) and the International Electrotechnical Commission (IEC), have developed standards like ISO/IEC 42001 to guide organizations in responsibly managing AI, balancing innovation with governance (WHO, 2023; Financial Times, 2025).

5. ETHICAL AND LEGAL CONSIDERATIONS

The integration of artificial intelligence (AI) into healthcare and medical diagnostics has created unprecedented opportunities for innovation, efficiency, and precision. However, these advancements are not without ethical and legal complexities. Concerns around patient privacy, algorithmic bias, explainability, consent, and accountability continue to challenge stakeholders. As AI transitions from experimental tools to operational technologies in clinical settings, it becomes imperative to align innovation with ethical integrity and legal compliance.

5.1 Ethical Challenges in AI-Driven Healthcare

One of the foremost ethical concerns involves data privacy. The vast datasets required to train AI systems often contain sensitive health information. Misuse or unintended exposure of this data may lead to breaches of confidentiality and trust. Shafik (2024) emphasizes the importance of robust data governance frameworks in AI systems such as ChatGPT to safeguard personal information. Similarly, Veluru (2024) warns of the dangers posed by unethical AI use, including the manipulation of large datasets and potential security breaches.

The potential for algorithmic bias also poses significant ethical risks. Biases in training data can perpetuate disparities in healthcare outcomes. Shukla and Taneja (2024) argue for ethical frameworks that address such biases, while Ali and Aysan (2025) demonstrate through machine learning-based topic modeling that ethical concerns are often cross-domain and complex, requiring multidimensional solutions.

Further complicating the landscape is the lack of explainability in AI decision-making. As Ali, Zafar, and Aysan (2024) discuss, stakeholders need transparent, auditable systems to ensure accountability in AI-based financial and healthcare decisions. When clinicians cannot interpret or explain AI recommendations, the patient-provider trust relationship may deteriorate, raising questions about informed consent and professional responsibility (Mennella et al., 2024; Sheliemina, 2024).

Moreover, ethical dilemmas arise when AI systems influence life-critical decisions such as diagnoses, treatment plans, or organ allocation. According to Terry (2019), AI's autonomous actions in clinical care challenge traditional medical ethics that prioritize human judgment. The World Health Organization (2023) also notes the importance of respecting human rights and patient autonomy in AI system development and deployment.

The ethical, legal, and regulatory aspects of AI in healthcare often overlap, yet they each carry distinct concerns. The following Venn diagram illustrates these intersections.

Figure 3. Intersection of ethical, legal, and regulatory domains

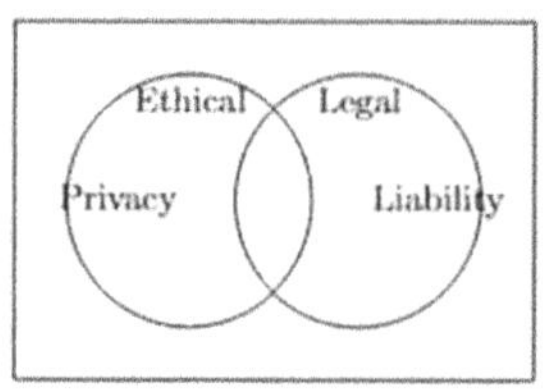

5.2 Legal Implications and Regulatory Landscape

Legal systems globally are still grappling with how to regulate AI technologies effectively. The European Union's AI Act represents a pioneering attempt to establish comprehensive AI legislation (Butt, 2024). The Act proposes a risk-based classification system and emphasizes human oversight, robustness, and transparency—principles directly applicable to healthcare. Likewise, Pesapane et al. (2018, 2021) review the regulatory scenarios in the EU, US, China, and Russia, pointing out inconsistencies and gaps that can jeopardize safe AI deployment in radiology.

National and international bodies are increasingly recognizing the urgency for standardized legal frameworks. For instance, the U.S. Food and Drug Administration (FDA) and other agencies have issued guidance for AI-based diagnostic tools (Larson et al., 2021). However, the adaptability of these frameworks to rapidly evolving AI models remains questionable. Naili et al. (2025) highlight the complexity of applying existing medical liability laws to AI diagnostics, especially when outcomes depend on probabilistic reasoning rather than deterministic logic.

In the academic literature, Ali and Aysan (2024) and Filetti et al. (2024) highlight the growing use of generative AI tools in research and publication, which further complicates issues of authorship, plagiarism, and intellectual property. Verma and Rohit (2024) add that scholarly communication must now consider algorithmic accountability, especially when AI contributes to literature generation or peer review.

Moreover, international legal norms must also account for warfare and defense-related AI use. Batabyal (2024) explores the ethical and legal frameworks that govern AI in conflict zones, warning that unregulated AI warfare could lead to humanitarian crises and violations of international law.

5.3 Cross-Sectoral and Societal Impacts

The societal impact of AI in healthcare cannot be examined in isolation. Ethical concerns intersect with gender, culture, and socio-economic conditions. Pimpalkar et al. (2024) advocate for gender-sensitive AI tools, especially in safety-critical applications, while Vyawahare, Khandelwal, and Rathod (2024) highlight AI's role in detecting and preventing online harassment—a concern that extends into digital health platforms as well.

Jamro and Jamro (2023) and Luan et al. (2024) emphasize the use of AI in educational and social research, underscoring the blurred boundaries between healthcare and broader societal systems. AI-driven health solutions embedded in public platforms could inadvertently reveal sensitive behavioral or psychological data, compounding the ethical risks.

Ali and Aysan (2025) argue that ethical AI governance must include not just domain-specific but also societal considerations. They call for "multi-level, cross-domain ethical oversight mechanisms" that address layered challenges in AI deployment. Similarly, Ho (2023) emphasizes the need to implement the human right to science, advocating for inclusive and participatory governance frameworks.

5.4 Risk Mitigation and Future Pathways

Risk mitigation frameworks are crucial for managing the ethical and legal implications of AI. Trotsyuk et al. (2024) propose a multi-tiered approach to prevent the misuse of AI in biomedical research, recommending stronger collaboration between developers, ethicists, and legal experts. Eisenberg (2024) adds that responsible sensor design can help align AI systems with ethical standards by ensuring transparency and traceability.

Security risks are also central to ethical AI deployment. Al-Sinani and Mitchell (2024) and Al-Sinani et al. (2025) demonstrate the use of AI in ethical hacking and cybersecurity, offering insights into how similar techniques could protect AI-based health systems from adversarial attacks. Maguluri et al. (2023) support this view, emphasizing the need to secure AI drones and data collection systems in smart health cities.

Fenwick, Molnar, and Frangos (2024) propose that human resource management (HRM) must evolve to support ethical AI adoption. Their human-centric paradigm shift encourages AI developers to prioritize transparency and trust from the ground up. Likewise, Schünemann et al. (2024) suggest using policy modeling tools like agent-based modeling to anticipate AI impacts and improve regulatory foresight.

Several works, including those by Arya and Rastogi (2024), Gaurav et al. (2024), and Shuja et al. (2021), point to the utility of AI in sectors like agriculture, e-commerce, and epidemiology, all of which overlap with healthcare concerns—further underscoring the need for harmonized ethical and legal standards across domains.

6. CHALLENGES IN REGULATION

The integration of artificial intelligence (AI) into healthcare and medical diagnostics has outpaced regulatory adaptation, resulting in complex challenges that span legal, ethical, technical, and societal domains. Regulatory bodies worldwide are grappling with establishing effective governance mechanisms that ensure safety, efficacy, transparency, and fairness, while not stifling innovation (World Health Organization, 2023; Terry, 2019).

6.1. Fragmented and Inconsistent Regulatory Landscapes

A central issue is the lack of harmonization across international regulatory frameworks. While the European Union has pioneered comprehensive legislation through the AI Act, aiming to categorize AI risks and enforce safeguards (Butt, 2024), other jurisdictions such as the United States, China, and Russia exhibit divergent regulatory maturity (Pesapane et al., 2021). This fragmentation complicates global

AI deployment in medical diagnostics, especially in cross-border telemedicine and clinical trials (Naili et al., 2025).

Furthermore, regulatory strategies are often reactive rather than anticipatory. For instance, Larson et al. (2021) emphasize the absence of uniform guidelines for the development, validation, and deployment of diagnostic imaging algorithms, leading to potential safety gaps.

6.2. Ethical and Legal Ambiguities

The deployment of AI in healthcare raises fundamental questions about liability, accountability, and informed consent. When AI systems provide clinical decisions, it becomes unclear whether liability resides with the developer, healthcare provider, or institution (Mennella et al., 2024). Legal systems have not yet evolved to address these scenarios, particularly in the case of AI errors or bias-induced harm (Ho, 2023).

Emerging research has highlighted the ethical dimensions of AI, including concerns about transparency, algorithmic fairness, and potential biases in training data (Ali & Aysan, 2025; Shukla & Taneja, 2024). These issues are exacerbated in healthcare where outcomes directly affect human lives. A cross-domain machine learning analysis by Ali and Aysan (2025) underscores the necessity for ethical frameworks that transcend technical compliance and embody normative principles.

6.3. Data Governance and Privacy Concerns

Robust regulation is also hindered by the complexities of data governance. Medical AI systems rely on vast volumes of sensitive health data. Issues related to data anonymization, consent management, and third-party access remain inadequately addressed (Shafik, 2024; Sheliemina, 2024). The European GDPR provides a benchmark, yet its application to dynamic AI systems remains legally unsettled, especially as systems continuously learn from user data (Pesapane et al., 2018).

Further, the rise of generative AI introduces concerns around synthetic data and deepfake risks in healthcare records and diagnostics, necessitating novel regulatory interventions (Ali & Aysan, 2024; Trotsyuk et al., 2024).

6.4. Rapid Technological Evolution vs. Regulatory Lag

AI technologies evolve rapidly, often rendering existing regulations obsolete before they are implemented. Regulatory frameworks struggle to keep pace with innovations like quantum machine learning (Campus, 2024; Eswaran & Eswaran, 2025), federated learning, and explainable AI (Karim et al., 2023; Veluru, 2024). For example, Filetti et al. (2024) argue that the availability of new AI tools for scholarly and clinical research requires updated peer-review standards and evaluation protocols.

Moreover, the convergence of AI with adjacent technologies such as blockchain, IoT, and 5G further complicates regulatory clarity, as hybrid systems present composite risk profiles not easily categorized within traditional frameworks (Maguluri et al., 2023).

6.5. Bias, Inequity, and Social Disparities

Bias in AI models can reinforce existing healthcare disparities. Many datasets used in training AI systems lack demographic diversity, leading to reduced performance among marginalized populations (Ali, Zafar, & Aysan, 2024; Rashid & Kausik, 2024). Regulatory measures often lack mandates for demographic inclusivity testing and algorithmic fairness audits.

Fenwick, Molnar, and Frangos (2024) highlight the need for a human-centric adoption strategy in digital transformation, stressing the role of HR and organizational culture in mediating ethical AI deployment. However, these dimensions are scarcely captured in current regulatory frameworks.

6.6. Lack of Standardized Evaluation and Certification Processes

Another regulatory bottleneck lies in the absence of standardized benchmarks for AI validation. Despite some progress in imaging and diagnostic tools (Larson et al., 2021), there is no unified global consensus on certification processes or safety audits. This leads to inconsistent quality and undermines public trust in AI-enabled medical tools (Verma & Rohit, 2024; Leontidis, 2024).

Mennella et al. (2024) advocate for a narrative and contextualized regulatory model that accounts for variability in AI system performance across populations and clinical settings. Yet, adoption of such adaptive models is still nascent.

Literature reviews reveal recurring challenges in AI regulation. The graph below ranks key challenges by their frequency in scholarly publications analyzed in this study.

Figure 4. Frequency of regulatory challenges in reviewed literature

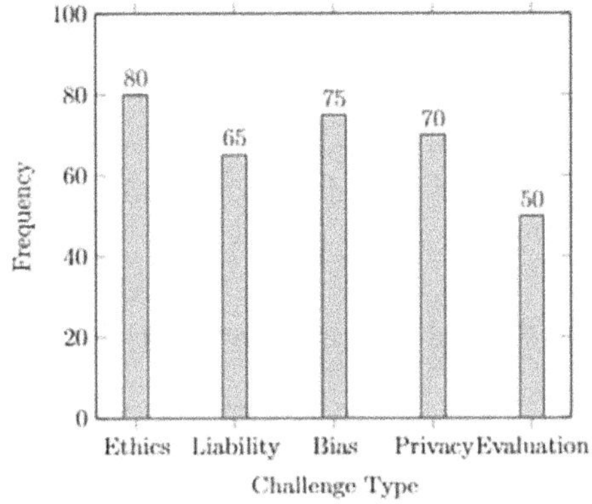

6.7. Threat of Misuse and Dual-Use Concerns

While AI holds immense promise, it also presents the risk of dual-use in contexts like cyber-biosecurity and misinformation. Al-Sinani and Mitchell (2024) along with Al-Sinani et al. (2025) demonstrate how AI-enhanced hacking experiments highlight potential vulnerabilities in medical systems. Trotsyuk et al. (2024) echo these risks, calling for risk mitigation frameworks to anticipate misuse in biomedical research.

Additionally, the militarization of AI and its implications for healthcare infrastructure — especially during wartime or pandemics — add further urgency to the need for enforceable ethical constraints (Batabyal, 2024).

6.8. Policy Complexity and Modeling Challenges

Modeling regulatory impacts in such a complex ecosystem is inherently difficult. Schünemann et al. (2024) emphasize that traditional policy design approaches fall short in anticipating AI system dynamics. Advanced system dynamics and agent-based modeling may offer better tools for regulatory simulation, but these remain underutilized in health policy contexts.

Rodriguez and Storer (2020) and Luan et al. (2024) support the adoption of AI-driven scientometric and topic modeling approaches for policy foresight and evidence-based governance, which could enhance regulatory adaptability.

7. BEST PRACTICES AND EMERGING MODELS

As artificial intelligence (AI) continues to disrupt healthcare and medical diagnostics, best practices and emerging regulatory models must evolve in tandem to ensure safety, transparency, and efficacy. These frameworks must reconcile the rapid innovation in AI tools with the essential ethical, legal, and humanistic standards of medical practice.

7.1. Human-Centered and Transparent AI Development

A significant best practice is the prioritization of human-centric AI systems—designs that align with user needs, clinical workflows, and ethical imperatives. Fenwick, Molnar, and Frangos (2024) argue that human resource management plays a critical role in facilitating such adoption by ensuring that digital transformation initiatives remain anchored to human values and usability. Similarly, Ali and Aysan (2025) highlight ethical themes derived from large-scale corpus analysis, emphasizing the necessity of transparency, fairness, and stakeholder engagement in cross-sector AI development.

Leontidis (2024) asserts that AI is transforming scientific inquiry itself, necessitating reflective practices and methodological redesign. This is particularly important in healthcare, where the stakes are inherently higher due to direct impacts on patient well-being.

7.2. Explainability, Accountability, and Risk Mitigation

Explainability—making AI systems interpretable for both developers and end-users—is widely acknowledged as a key requirement for trustworthy AI. Trotsyuk et al. (2024) propose a framework that emphasizes proactive risk mitigation against potential misuse, especially in biomedical contexts. Similarly, Eisenberg (2024) underscores the role of responsible sensor design, advocating for the integration of explainability into sensing systems to reinforce trust and auditability.

Emerging regulatory guidance, such as that offered by the World Health Organization (2023), aligns with these practices by recommending that AI systems undergo comprehensive validation and post-market surveillance to detect unintended harms.

7.3. Integration with Existing Legal Frameworks

An effective regulatory strategy integrates AI oversight within existing legal and medical governance structures. Butt (2024) offers an in-depth analysis of the EU AI Act, positioning it as the world's first comprehensive regulatory framework for

AI. This model advocates for a risk-based classification of AI systems, requiring greater scrutiny for high-risk applications such as diagnostics and decision support.

Other scholars reinforce the need for alignment between AI tools and legal standards in different jurisdictions. For example, Pesapane et al. (2018, 2021) and Mennella et al. (2024) collectively review the legal and ethical obligations in the EU, US, China, and Russia, pointing to increasing convergence toward robust data governance, documentation, and clinical validation.

7.4. Multi-Stakeholder Governance and Participatory Design

Best practices also emphasize participatory design, where developers, clinicians, patients, ethicists, and regulators collaborate throughout the AI lifecycle. As Ho (2023) notes, regulatory governance must uphold the human right to science, enabling all stakeholders to benefit from and contribute to the scientific and ethical development of AI technologies.

The inclusion of diverse voices, especially in international forums such as those cited by Naili et al. (2025), ensures that emerging legal frameworks reflect both global values and localized needs. Likewise, Jamro and Jamro (2023) stress the importance of inclusive AI integration in education, which parallels the healthcare sector in its need for equity, transparency, and accessibility.

7.5. Ethical Hacking and Cybersecurity Standards

Security is paramount in AI-driven healthcare, particularly when AI systems interface with electronic health records or IoT devices. Al-Sinani and Mitchell (2024), along with Al-Sinani et al. (2025), present experimental evidence supporting AI-enhanced ethical hacking as a proactive measure for identifying vulnerabilities in Linux-based systems, which are often used in medical IT infrastructure.

Similarly, Shafik (2024) and Veluru (2024) call for proactive privacy and data governance models to prevent unethical usage, unauthorized access, and breaches. These standards are central to trustworthy deployment, especially in sensitive applications like medical imaging or diagnostic AI.

7.6. Scientific Rigor and Evidence-Based Evaluation

Reliable clinical deployment of AI requires rigorous testing, validation, and peer review. Larson et al. (2021) offer comprehensive recommendations for developing and evaluating AI in diagnostic imaging, advocating for standardized metrics, bias assessments, and regulatory harmonization. Likewise, Sheliemina (2024) underscores the necessity of evidence-backed validation in risk-sensitive applications such as medical diagnostics.

Academic platforms have also begun to evolve. Filetti, Fenza, and Gallo (2024) explore how AI tools assist researchers in improving scholarly communication and methodology design, while Verma and Rohit (2024) reflect on the ethical implications of AI shaping academic norms.

7.7. Topic Modeling and Semantic Analysis

AI systems are increasingly being used to map scholarly and medical discourse to understand trends, gaps, and ethical considerations. For instance, Ali, Zafar, and Aysan (2024), as well as Ali and Aysan (2024), use topic modeling and structural analysis to extract emerging concerns and opportunities in generative AI, with direct implications for both finance and health domains.

Rodriguez and Storer (2020), Luan et al. (2024), and San Biagio et al. (2023) demonstrate how topic clustering and semantic models can be used to detect risks, including threats to vulnerable populations, misinformation, or ethical oversights.

7.8. AI in Specialized Contexts: Drones, Safety, and E-Commerce

While not strictly limited to diagnostics, adjacent technologies like AI-based drones and AI in e-commerce offer transferable lessons. Maguluri, Arularasan, and Boopathi (2023) assess AI risks in drone usage for public safety and smart cities—an important analogy for remote or autonomous diagnostics. Gaurav et al. (2024) apply semantic web techniques to detect phishing attacks, presenting a blueprint for securing digital health platforms.

Likewise, Rashid and Kausik (2024) and Arya and Rastogi (2024) identify AI's transformative potential across industries—lessons that inform how best to structure healthcare innovation governance.

7.9. Future-Facing Models: Quantum-AI Integration and Complex Systems Thinking

Looking forward, Campus (2024), Eswaran and Eswaran (2025), and Karim, Galar, and Kumar (2023) present models that merge AI with quantum computing and systems engineering. These innovations promise exponential improvements in processing speed, model robustness, and personalization—qualities crucial for future AI diagnostic tools.

Schünemann et al. (2024) advocate for system dynamics and agent-based modeling as part of complex policy modeling. This approach enables regulators to simulate the long-term impact of AI policy decisions in dynamically evolving systems like healthcare.

7.10. Regional and Community-Based Innovations

In practice, effective regulatory responses often stem from localized innovation. Zangana and his collaborators (2013–2024) have produced a robust body of work ranging from AI-based detection algorithms (e.g., face and shape detection) to data warehouse systems for education and healthcare environments. These models serve as case studies for community-responsive AI systems that uphold best practices in data quality, contextual usability, and ethical alignment.

In addition, WHO (2023), Terry (2019), and Verma et al. (2020) collectively offer practical guidance for policymakers seeking to balance innovation with human rights and public health priorities.

8. FUTURE DIRECTIONS AND RECOMMENDATIONS

As artificial intelligence (AI) continues to transform healthcare and medical diagnostics, future regulatory frameworks must evolve to address emerging technological, ethical, and societal challenges. To responsibly govern this transformation, multidisciplinary cooperation, technological foresight, and ethical robustness must be cornerstones of future directions and policy development.

8.1. Toward Adaptive and Proactive Regulation

Traditional regulatory systems are often reactive and ill-equipped to handle the rapid pace of AI advancement. Future regulatory models must incorporate dynamic, risk-based, and lifecycle-oriented approaches to AI oversight (Larson et al., 2021; Pesapane et al., 2021; Naili et al., 2025). Adaptive frameworks should integrate real-time data monitoring, post-deployment auditing, and algorithmic accountability to ensure AI systems maintain efficacy and fairness throughout their lifecycle.

International coordination remains essential. The European Union's AI Act presents a model for harmonized standards, emphasizing risk-based classification and transparency (Butt, 2024). However, further efforts are needed to integrate global best practices, particularly in jurisdictions with fragmented regulatory landscapes such as the U.S. and developing nations (Pesapane et al., 2018).

To achieve adaptive governance, a future-ready regulatory framework should incorporate dynamic and risk-based principles, stakeholder inclusivity, and lifecycle monitoring. The following flowchart summarizes this proposed model.

Figure 5. Proposed lifecycle-aware regulatory framework for AI in healthcare

8.2. Ethical Foresight and Responsible Innovation

Regulators must incorporate ethical foresight into AI policies, recognizing the evolving nature of generative and predictive models. The increasing deployment of AI in clinical settings mandates stronger ethical audits and fairness guarantees (Ali & Aysan, 2025). Ethical concerns such as bias, consent, explainability, and data commodification need to be explicitly codified into law and technical standards (Mennella et al., 2024; Shukla & Taneja, 2024).

Building ethical AI ecosystems requires stakeholder inclusivity—particularly patients, clinicians, ethicists, and marginalized populations—during design, deployment, and evaluation (Trotsyuk et al., 2024; Terry, 2019). Responsible innovation also necessitates integrating anticipatory governance models that predict misuse scenarios before they emerge (Veluru, 2024; Batabyal, 2024).

8.3. Securing Data and Enhancing Cybersecurity

Data privacy and cybersecurity must remain at the forefront of future AI regulation. Given the increasing use of generative AI in clinical diagnostics and patient interaction systems (Ali et al., 2024), the integrity and confidentiality of healthcare data are more critical than ever (Shafik, 2024). Regulatory frameworks should enforce differential privacy, homomorphic encryption, and decentralized data governance mechanisms.

Additionally, AI-enhanced ethical hacking techniques should be formalized as defensive cybersecurity strategies, particularly in healthcare and Linux-based medical infrastructure (Al-Sinani & Mitchell, 2024; Al-Sinani et al., 2025). AI's role in identifying vulnerabilities before exploitation is a valuable tool in preempting threats.

8.4. Promoting Human-Centric and Transparent AI

The future of AI in healthcare must balance technological efficiency with human oversight. Transparency mechanisms—such as explainable AI (XAI), model interpretability tools, and auditing dashboards—must be regulatory requirements (Eisenberg, 2024; Ho, 2023). Additionally, regulatory sandboxes and participatory design frameworks can facilitate transparent stakeholder engagement and real-world testing (Fenwick et al., 2024).

Human-centric AI must ensure clinicians retain decision-making autonomy and patients understand algorithmic recommendations. This shift calls for upskilling medical professionals and embedding AI literacy into curricula and continuing education (Jamro & Jamro, 2023; Flannery et al., 2021).

8.5. Leveraging Emerging Technologies Responsibly

AI's intersection with quantum computing, Internet of Things (IoT), and biosensor technology presents both opportunities and regulatory complications. As the boundaries between these technologies blur, regulators must address issues of interoperability, cross-domain ethics, and systemic risk (Campus, 2024; Eswaran & Eswaran, 2025; Arya & Rastogi, 2024).

Quantum AI, for instance, demands a new class of regulatory logic due to its non-linear, probabilistic characteristics. Policymakers must anticipate computational power asymmetries and the possibility of AI supremacy or surveillance misuse (Karim et al., 2023; Leontidis, 2024).

8.6. Advancing Gender and Community-Sensitive AI Policies

Future policies should encourage AI models that are sensitive to gender and community-specific health needs. Tools focused on women's safety, online harassment detection, and predictive analytics for vulnerable populations must be regulated for bias mitigation, consent, and explainability (Vyawahare et al., 2024; Pimpalkar et al., 2024).

Additionally, community-based AI solutions—such as disaster management or pharmacy information systems—must be integrated into national digital health strategies to ensure equitable access (Zangana, 2022; Zangana, 2018).

8.7. Supporting Responsible AI in Scientific Research

With AI increasingly involved in scholarly communication and research design, future regulation should support integrity in algorithmic research tools (Filetti et al., 2024; Verma & Rohit, 2024). Techniques such as structural topic modeling (Ali & Aysan, 2024), clustering algorithms (Zangana & Abdulazeez, 2023), and AI-enhanced scientometric analysis (Luan et al., 2024; Rodriguez & Storer, 2020) must be peer-reviewed and audited.

AI must not compromise the epistemic standards of science. Instead, it should augment research transparency, reproducibility, and knowledge discovery (Leontidis, 2024).

8.8. Establishing a Global Observatory for AI in Healthcare

Finally, to coordinate international regulatory efforts, there is a strong case for a global observatory for AI in healthcare. Inspired by World Health Organization (2023) guidelines and informed by multi-national regulatory trends (Pesapane et al., 2021), such an entity could offer dynamic benchmarks, facilitate capacity building, and harmonize AI health safety standards.

It could also serve as a hub for reporting algorithmic failures, coordinating AI disaster response, and monitoring compliance across nations (San Biagio et al., 2023; Verma et al., 2020).

8.9 Summary

The future of AI in healthcare and medical diagnostics holds vast potential but requires deliberate and responsible stewardship. By advancing adaptive regulation, embedding ethics and security by design, encouraging stakeholder participation, and fostering global cooperation, we can ensure that AI serves humanity rather than risks undermining it. The recommendations herein build on a rich corpus of interdisciplinary scholarship, laying the groundwork for the next generation of AI governance.

9. CONCLUSION

The evolution of artificial intelligence, particularly generative AI and its applications across various sectors such as healthcare, finance, and cybersecurity, continues to reshape the technological and regulatory landscape. This chapter has examined the multifaceted regulatory responses to AI in healthcare and medical diagnostics, highlighting the complexities and urgent need for comprehensive governance frameworks that address ethical, legal, and societal concerns.

As AI technologies advance, regulatory frameworks must evolve dynamically to balance innovation with safety and ethical integrity (Larson et al., 2021; Mennella et al., 2024). The increasing deployment of AI in sensitive domains, including diagnostics and treatment, necessitates robust oversight to prevent misuse, bias, and privacy infringements (Naili et al., 2025; Sheliemina, 2024). Moreover, the cross-domain ethical challenges of generative AI, discussed by Ali and Aysan (2025), emphasize the importance of transparent, accountable AI systems aligned with human rights principles (Ho, 2023).

The regulatory landscape is further complicated by the integration of emerging technologies such as quantum machine learning and AI-enhanced cybersecurity, demanding interdisciplinary collaboration among technologists, policymakers, and ethicists (Campus, 2024; Eswaran & Eswaran, 2025; Al-Sinani & Mitchell, 2024). The global dimension of AI governance is evident, with varied approaches across jurisdictions underscoring the need for international harmonization to address cross-border data flows and shared risks (Pesapane et al., 2021; Butt, 2024).

Furthermore, fostering human-centric adoption and ensuring ethical AI deployment requires not only technical standards but also organizational shifts in culture and policy, as noted by Fenwick et al. (2024). The proactive engagement of stakeholders, including patients, healthcare providers, and regulatory bodies, is vital to cultivate trust and transparency (World Health Organization, 2023).

In conclusion, the trajectory of AI in healthcare and diagnostics presents tremendous opportunities alongside significant challenges. Future regulatory efforts must emphasize ethical safeguards, data privacy, inclusivity, and adaptability to new technological developments. By integrating multidisciplinary insights and fostering global cooperation, regulators can ensure that AI technologies contribute positively to health outcomes while minimizing risks and safeguarding human dignity.

REFERENCES

Al-Sinani, H. S., & Mitchell, C. J. (2024). AI-enhanced ethical hacking: A Linux-focused experiment. *arXiv preprint arXiv:2410.05105.*

Al-Sinani, H. S., Sahli, N., Mitchell, C. J., & Al-Siyabi, M. (2025). Advancing ethical hacking with AI: A Linux-based experimental study. *Proceedings of ITASEC and SERICS, Bologna, Italy (Feb 2025),* https://www. chrismitchell. net/Papers/ aehwaa. pdf

Ali, H., & Aysan, A. F. (2024). Decoding Future of Generative AI in Finance: A Machine Learning Exploration of Academic and Grey Corpus. *Available atSSRN* 4787211. DOI: 10.2139/ssrn.4787211

Ali, H., & Aysan, A. F. (2025). Ethical dimensions of generative AI: A cross-domain analysis using machine learning structural topic modeling. *International Journal of Ethics and Systems, 41*(1), 3–34. DOI: 10.1108/IJOES-04-2024-0112

Ali, H., Zafar, M. B., & Aysan, A. F. (2024). Generative AI and Finance: A Multi-level Machine Learning Based Analysis. *Available atSSRN* 5129013.

Arya, L., & Rastogi, R. (2024). Study on Aerial Monitoring System in Agriculture, Forestry, Defense, and Border Protection Using Artificial Intelligence (AI). In *Agriculture and Aquaculture Applications of Biosensors and Bioelectronics* (pp. 392-407). IGI Global Scientific Publishing.

Batabyal, G. S. (2024). Ethics, laws on war and artificial intelligence-driven warfare. In *Artificial intelligence, ethics and the future of warfare* (pp. 187–215). Routledge India. DOI: 10.4324/9781003421849-9

Butt, J. (2024). Analytical study of the world's first EU Artificial Intelligence (AI) Act. *International Journal of Research Publication and Reviews, 5*(3), 7343–7364. DOI: 10.55248/gengpi.5.0324.0914

Campus, M. T. (2024). Quantum Machine Learning, Leveraging Al, and. *Integration of AI, Quantum Computing, and Semiconductor Technology*, 57.

Eisenberg, D. (2024). *Sensing With Integrity: Responsible Sensor Systems in an Era of AI* (Doctoral dissertation, New Jersey Institute of Technology).

Eswaran, U., & Eswaran, V. (2025). Quantum Machine Learning, Leveraging AI, and Semiconductor Technology. In *Integration of AI, Quantum Computing, and Semiconductor Technology* (pp. 57-78). IGI Global.

Fenwick, A., Molnar, G., & Frangos, P. (2024). The critical role of HRM in AI-driven digital transformation: A paradigm shift to enable firms to move from AI implementation to human-centric adoption. *Discover Artificial Intelligence*, *4*(1), 34. DOI: 10.1007/s44163-024-00125-4

Filetti, S., Fenza, G., & Gallo, A. (2024). Research design and writing of scholarly articles: New artificial intelligence tools available for researchers. *Endocrine*, *85*(3), 1104–1116. DOI: 10.1007/s12020-024-03977-z PMID: 39085566

Flannery, J., Ajayi, S. O., & Oyegoke, A. S. (2021). Alcohol and substance misuse in the construction industry. *International Journal of Occupational Safety and Ergonomics*, *27*(2), 472–487. DOI: 10.1080/10803548.2019.1601376 PMID: 30935301

Gaurav, A., Chui, K. T., Arya, V., Attar, R. W., Bansal, S., Alhomoud, A., & Psannis, K. (2024). Optimized AI-Driven Semantic Web Approach for Enhancing Phishing Detection in E-Commerce Platforms. [IJSWIS]. *International Journal on Semantic Web and Information Systems*, *20*(1), 1–13. DOI: 10.4018/IJSWIS.359767

Ho, C. W. (2023). Implementing the human right to science in the regulatory governance of artificial intelligence in healthcare. *Journal of Law and the Biosciences*, *10*(2), lsad026. DOI: 10.1093/jlb/lsad026 PMID: 37854168

Jamro, M. Y., & Jamro, F. A. (2023). AI Matters: Chatbot Integration in Holistic STEM Education.

Karim, R., Galar, D., & Kumar, U. (2023). *AI factory: theories, applications and case studies*. CRC Press. DOI: 10.1201/9781003208686

Larson, D. B., Harvey, H., Rubin, D. L., Irani, N., Tse, J. R., & Langlotz, C. P. (2021). Regulatory frameworks for development and evaluation of artificial intelligence–based diagnostic imaging algorithms: Summary and recommendations. *Journal of the American College of Radiology*, *18*(3), 413–424. DOI: 10.1016/j.jacr.2020.09.060 PMID: 33096088

Leontidis, G. (2024). Science in the age of ai: How artificial intelligence is changing the nature and method of scientific research.

Luan, H., Perron, B. E., Victor, B. G., Wan, G., Niu, Y., & Xiao, X. (2024). Using artificial intelligence to support scientometric analysis of scholarly literature: A case example of research on mainland China's left-behind children. *Journal of the Society for Social Work and Research*, *15*(3), 435–457. DOI: 10.1086/731613

Maennig, W. (2014). Inefficiency of the anti-doping system: Cost reduction proposals. *Substance Use & Misuse*, *49*(9), 1201–1205. DOI: 10.3109/10826084.2014.912065 PMID: 24832718

Maguluri, L. P., Arularasan, A. N., & Boopathi, S. (2023). Assessing security concerns for ai-based drones in smart cities. In *Effective AI, Blockchain, and E-Governance Applications for Knowledge Discovery and Management* (pp. 27-47). IGI Global Scientific Publishing. DOI: 10.4018/978-1-6684-9151-5.ch002

Mennella, C., Maniscalco, U., De Pietro, G., & Esposito, M. (2024). Ethical and regulatory challenges of AI technologies in healthcare: A narrative review. *Heliyon*, *10*(4), e26297. DOI: 10.1016/j.heliyon.2024.e26297 PMID: 38384518

Naili, Y. T., Mangkunegara, I. S., Purwono, P., & Baballe, M. A. (2025). Regulatory challenges in ai-based diagnostics: Legal implications of ai use in medical diagnostics. In *BIO Web of Conferences* (Vol. 152, p. 01034). EDP Sciences.

Pesapane, F., Bracchi, D. A., Mulligan, J. F., Linnikov, A., Maslennikov, O., Lanzavecchia, M. B., Tantrige, P., Stasolla, A., Biondetti, P., Giuggioli, P. F., Cassano, E., & Carrafiello, G. (2021). Legal and regulatory framework for AI solutions in healthcare in EU, US, China, and Russia: New scenarios after a pandemic. *Radiation*, *1*(4), 261–276. DOI: 10.3390/radiation1040022

Pesapane, F., Volonté, C., Codari, M., & Sardanelli, F. (2018). Artificial intelligence as a medical device in radiology: Ethical and regulatory issues in Europe and the United States. *Insights Into Imaging*, *9*(5), 745–753. DOI: 10.1007/s13244-018-0645-y PMID: 30112675

Pimpalkar, A. P., Wankhade, N. R., Chole, V., & Golhar, Y. (2024). Women's Empowerment Through AI: Discovering Data Analytics for Predictive Safety Solutions and Future Trends. In *AI Tools and Applications for Women's Safety* (pp. 304-326). IGI Global Scientific Publishing.

Rashid, A. B., & Kausik, A. K. (2024). AI revolutionizing industries worldwide: A comprehensive overview of its diverse applications. *Hybrid Advances*, 100277.

Rodriguez, M. Y., & Storer, H. (2020). A computational social science perspective on qualitative data exploration: Using topic models for the descriptive analysis of social media data. *Journal of Technology in Human Services*, *38*(1), 54–86. DOI: 10.1080/15228835.2019.1616350

San Biagio, M., Cipolla, M., La Mattina, E., & Morreale, V. (2023, December). A Topic Clustering Method to Identify Online Threats against Soft Targets. In *2023 International Conference on Computational Science and Computational Intelligence (CSCI)* (pp. 727-733). IEEE. DOI: 10.1109/CSCI62032.2023.00124

Schünemann, C., Johanning, S., Reger, E., Herold, H., & Bruckner, T. (2024). Complex system policy modelling approaches for policy advice–comparing systems thinking, system dynamics and agent-based modelling. *Political Research Exchange : an ECPR Journal*, *6*(1), 2387438. DOI: 10.1080/2474736X.2024.2387438

Shafik, W. (2024). Data privacy and security safeguarding customer information in ChatGPT systems. In *Revolutionizing the Service Industry Wth OpenAI Models* (pp. 52–86). IGI Global. DOI: 10.4018/979-8-3693-1239-1.ch003

Sheliemina, N. (2024). The use of artificial intelligence in medical diagnostics: Opportunities, prospects and risks. *Health Economics and Management Review*, *5*(2), 104–124. DOI: 10.61093/hem.2024.2-07

Shuja, J., Alanazi, E., Alasmary, W., & Alashaikh, A. (2021). COVID-19 open source data sets: A comprehensive survey. *Applied Intelligence*, *51*(3), 1296–1325. DOI: 10.1007/s10489-020-01862-6 PMID: 34764552

Shukla, R. P., & Taneja, S. (2024). Ethical considerations and data privacy in artificial intelligence. In *Integrating generative AI in education to achieve sustainable development goals* (pp. 86–97). IGI Global. DOI: 10.4018/979-8-3693-2440-0.ch005

Terry, N. (2019). Of regulating healthcare AI and robots. *Yale JL & Tech.*, *21*, 133.

Trotsyuk, A. A., Waeiss, Q., Bhatia, R. T., Aponte, B. J., Heffernan, I. M., Madgavkar, D., Felder, R. M., Lehmann, L. S., Palmer, M. J., Greely, H., Wald, R., Goetz, L., Trengove, M., Vandersluis, R., Lin, H., Cho, M. K., Altman, R. B., Endy, D., Relman, D. A., & Magnus, D. (2024). Toward a framework for risk mitigation of potential misuse of artificial intelligence in biomedical research. *Nature Machine Intelligence*, *6*(12), 1–8. DOI: 10.1038/s42256-024-00926-3

Veluru, C. S. (2024). Responsible Artificial Intelligence on Large Scale Data to Prevent Misuse, Unethical Challenges and Security Breaches. *Journal of Artificial Intelligence & Cloud Computing. SRC/JAICC-349. DOI: doi. org/(3), 331*, 2-6.DOI: 10.47363/JAICC/2024

Verma, A., Rao, K., Eluri, V., & Sharma, Y. (2020). Regulating AI in public health: systems challenges and perspectives. *ORF Occasional Paper, 261.*

Verma, M., & Rohit, K. (2024). Ethical AI Shaping Scholarly Communication: Challenges and Opportunities.

Vyawahare, H., Khandelwal, S., & Rathod, S. (2024). Artificial Intelligence in Detecting and Preventing Online Harassment. In *AI Tools and Applications for Women's Safety* (pp. 14–35). IGI Global Scientific Publishing. DOI: 10.4018/979-8-3693-1435-7.ch002

World Health Organization. (2023). *Regulatory considerations on artificial intelligence for health.* World Health Organization.

Zangana, H. M. (2015). A New Skin Color Based Face Detection Algorithm by Combining Three Color Model Algorithms. *IOSR J. Comput. Eng, 17*, 06-125.

Zangana, H. M. (2017). A new algorithm for shape detection. *IOSR Journal of Computer Engineering (IOSR-JCE), 19*(3), 71-76.

Zangana, H. M. (2017). Library Data Quality Maturity (IIUM as a Case Study). *IOSR Journal of Computer Engineering, 19*(March), 29. DOI: 10.9790/0661-1902033844

Zangana, H. M. (2017). Watermarking System Using LSB. *IOSR Journal of Computer Engineering, 19*(3), 75–79. DOI: 10.9790/0661-1903027579

Zangana, H. M. (2018). Design an information management system for a pharmacy. *International Journal of Advanced Research in Computer and Communication Engineering, 7*(10), 52–55. DOI: 10.17148/IJARCCE.2018.71012

Zangana, H. M. (2018). Developing Data Warehouse for Student Information System (IIUM as a Case Study). *International Organization of Scientific Research, 20*(1), 09-14.

Zangana, H. M. (2018). Implementing a System for Recognizing Optical Characters.

Zangana, H. M. (2019). Issues of Data Management in the Library: A Case Study.

Zangana, H. M. (2019). ITD Data Quality Maturity (A Case Study). *International Journal Of Engineering And Computer Science, 8*(10).

Zangana, H. M. (2020). Mobile Device Integration in IIUM Service. *International Journal (Toronto, Ont.), 8*(5).

Zangana, H. M. (2021). The Global Finical Crisis from an Islamic Point Of View. *Qubahan Academic Journal, 1*(2), 55–59. DOI: 10.48161/qaj.v1n2a39

Zangana, H. M. (2022). Creating a Community-Based Disaster Management System. *Academic Journal of Nawroz University, 11*(4), 234–244. DOI: 10.25007/ajnu.v11n4a1485

Zangana, H. M. (2022). Implementing New Interactive Video Learning System for IIUM. *Academic Journal of Nawroz University, 11*(2), 23–29. DOI: 10.25007/ajnu.v11n2a1281

Zangana, H. M. (2022). Improving The Web Services for Remittance Company: Express Remit as a Case Study. *Academic Journal of Nawroz University (AJNU), 11*(3).

Zangana, H. M., & Abdulazeez, A. M. (2023). Developed Clustering Algorithms for Engineering Applications: A Review. *International Journal of Informatics* [IN-JIISCOM]. *Information System and Computer Engineering*, *4*(2), 147–169.

Zangana, H. M., & Al-Shaikhli, I. F. (2013). A new algorithm for human face detection using skin color tone. *IOSR Journal of Computer Engineering*, *11*(6), 31–38. DOI: 10.9790/0661-1163138

Zangana, H. M., Bazeed, S. M. S., Ali, N. Y., & Abdullah, D. T. (2024). Navigating Project Change: A Comprehensive Review of Change Management Strategies and Practices. *Indonesian Journal of Education and Social Sciences*, *3*(2), 166–179. DOI: 10.56916/ijess.v3i2.735

Zangana, H. M., & Mustafa, F. M. (2024). From Classical to Deep Learning: A Systematic Review of Image Denoising Techniques. *Jurnal Ilmiah Computer Science*, *3*(1), 50–65. DOI: 10.58602/jics.v3i1.36

Zangana, H. M., & Mustafa, F. M. (2024). Review of Hybrid Denoising Approaches in Face Recognition: Bridging Wavelet Transform and Deep Learning. *The Indonesian Journal of Computer Science*, *13*(4). Advance online publication. DOI: 10.33022/ijcs.v13i4.4209

Zangana, H. M., & Mustafa, F. M. (2024). Surveying the Landscape: A Comprehensive Review of Object Detection Algorithms and Advancements. *Jurnal Ilmiah Computer Science*, *3*(1), 1–15. DOI: 10.58602/jics.v3i1.29

Zreik, M. (2024). Harnessing AI for entrepreneurial idea generation: Navigating the new frontier. In *Generating Entrepreneurial Ideas With AI* (pp. 1–18). IGI Global Scientific Publishing. DOI: 10.4018/979-8-3693-3498-0.ch001

Chapter 4

Effect of Research Integrity Challenges on Ethical Compliance Mediating Role of Bureaucratic Barriers in Research Management in the Horn of Africa

Wako Jio
https://orcid.org/0009-0003-6192-459X
Bule Hora University, Ethiopia

shashi kant
https://orcid.org/0000-0003-4722-5736
Bule Hora University, Ethiopia

Hirut Assegid
https://orcid.org/0009-0003-6192-459X
Bule Hora University, Ethiopia

ABSTRACT

This chapter investigates the influence of the problems of the integrity of research on ethical correspondence in the context of research management in Africa, emphasizing the intermediary role of bureaucratic barriers. Using the sample size of 385 researchers in various institutions, we used the Kaiser-Meyer-Lkin (KMO) test to

DOI: 10.4018/979-8-3373-4862-9.ch004

Copyright © 2025, IGI Global Scientific Publishing. Copying or distributing in print or electronic forms without written permission of IGI Global Scientific Publishing is prohibited.

evaluate the adequacy of our sample for factor analysis, reaching the KMO value indicating the adequacy of a good sample. Confirmatory Factor Analysis (CFA) was conducted using AMOS software to validate the measurement model, demonstrating solid construct validity and reliability of the variables involved. Subsequently, Structural Equation Modeling (SEM) was applied to explore the relationships among research integrity challenges, ethical compliance, and bureaucratic barriers. The results show that bureaucratic barriers considerably line up the relationship between the problems of research integrity and ethical correspondence, revealing that increased problems of integrity exacerbate bureaucratic obstacles, thus reducing ethical engagement.

INTRODUCTION

The emphasized global academic environment requires research integrity to achieve reliable scientific results (Zhaksylyk et al., 2023). Research-based solutions to social problems like climate change and public health and social justice place increased importance on ethical research practices in global society (Bain et al., 2022). The need to establish trust in academic outcomes developed research integrity through three primary aspects of the research process that include integrity as well as transparency and accountability. Multiple hurdles to research researches emerge from empirical investigations although these barriers primarily affect developing regions. Ethical research failures happen mainly because researchers lack sufficient training and face resource constraints and institutional demands according to research findings (Eitrem et al., 2024). Bureaucratic barriers involving various regulations and administrative inefficiencies and ethical guideline confusion have proven to intensify integrity challenges which degrade researcher ethical compliance (Asiri et al., 2024). The extensive body of research does not adequately explain how bureaucratic barriers create a connection between research integrity and ethical response problems particularly in Horn of Africa regions (Scott, 2021). The objective of this chapter is to solve previous research deficits by studying intricate game elements and furnish intelligence for forthcoming assessments and political interventions (Zhaksylyk et al., 2023).

The central question leading this research: *how does the question of research integrity affect ethical compliance and what role does a bureaucratic barrier play in these relationships in Africa?* The research assesses practical researcher challenges to provide policy recommendations along with guidance for institutional leaders which create a stronger research environment. The investigation adds to academic literature and provides direction for researcher and stakeholder groups who aim to strengthen ethical research practice standards.

BACKGROUND OF THE STUDY

The study bases its foundation on scrutinizing research integrity combined with ethical compliance practices which exist specifically in the Horn of Africa region (Bain et al., 2022). Several obstacles impede the successful application of research integrity principles in this area because the region is marked by socio-political turmoil and resource scarcity and systemic bureaucratic obstacles (Zhaksylyk et al., 2023). Research integrity includes various ethical procedures which work together to validate research outcomes. Many Horn of African countries experience issues that lead to subverting research integrity standards. Researchers in Ethiopia face practical challenges due to the unstable development of ethical oversight supervision systems throughout their country (Bain et al., 2022). Research delays in obtaining ethical approvals make investigators rush their studies or perform incomplete investigations thus negatively affecting research data quality. The problem gets worse because researchers lack sufficient training about ethical issues although many studies show that they do not understand totally what their work means regarding ethical principles and what standard levels of ethics should be maintained. The development of bureaucratic hurdles in Kenya has been studied through current examinations of public health research activities (Rodríguez et al., 2023). Research organizations face numerous regulatory hurdles that increase project timelines while discouraging pioneering research activities. Excessive documentation requirements coupled with unclear guidelines emerge from bureaucracy which causes researchers to face ethical dilemmas when trying to meet institutional requirements (Eitrem et al., 2024).

Somalia faces ongoing conflict which interrupts research activities by making ethical compliance become subordinate to urgent data collection needs (Bain et al., 2022). Somalia lacks reliable institutions that would maintain ethical compliance resulting in widespread research practices that would be prohibited in controlled environments (Asiri et al., 2024). Research activities occurring in volatile environments make researchers confront ethical challenges when obtaining consent while these obstacles create more hurdles for following research integrity protocols (Zhaksylyk et al., 2023). The series of actual case examples provides a complete view of the obstacles researchers must handle while establishing research integrity practices in the Horn of Africa. Multiple challenges combined with bureaucratic obstacles show why it is essential to study the relationship between these factors that affect ethical compliance standards (Asiri et al., 2024). This analysis looks to establish detailed insights about these dynamics so research integrity capacity for the region can be strengthened. The research aims to develop better policies and frameworks which promote ethical research conduct in order to increase academic quality and credibility across the Horn of Africa (Bain et al., 2022).

STATEMENT OF THE PROBLEM

Research integrity throughout the Horn of Africa faces numerous challenging obstacles which block both ethical practice and solid research administration (Bain et al., 2022). High-quality research should demonstrate transparent actions together with legal responsibility alongside strict ethical guidelines which produces meaningful research outcomes. The true situation in numerous nations in this area differs greatly from the ideal standards. Researchers undergo confusion about the effectiveness of existing ethical frameworks and institutional policies because persistent systemic barriers continue to cause substantial ethical failures (Eitrem et al., 2024). Empirical research about research integrity challenges produces ambiguous outcomes when examining their effects on ethical compliance (Bain et al., 2022). Theoretical gaps in analyzing the relationship between research integrity challenges and ethical compliance create this ambiguity because of the role bureaucratic barriers play in this process (Scott, 2021). Current research about the Horn of Africa neglects the particular social and political factors and inadequate infrastructure that define regional research activities. Knowledge gaps remain unaddressed mainly about how researchers experience ethical compliance and integrity within unique regional environments (Asiri et al., 2024).

Practical obstacles create additional hurdles to the entire system. Researchers encounter monumental bureaucratic obstacles that trigger pragmatic delays which prevent innovation and create conditions where ethical standards face serious risk of degradation. Organization barriers prevent successful research output and drives skepticism among the public about research authenticity (Eitrem et al., 2024). The research establishes its main goal to uncover a full picture of how research integrity obstacles and ethical requirements and bureaucratic processes connect within the Horn of Africa region. This research implements a detailed methodological approach using both extensive participant numbers and advanced analytical methods to uncover intricate research relationships which provides important knowledge for researchers alongside policy developers. The research findings will identify particular intervention points to drive strategic developments in ethical oversight systems which aim to improve research integrity standards. This research initiative aims to enhance academic research ethics in developing areas through its outcomes which will create better strategies for maintaining research integrity and enhancing policy implementation.

THEORIETICAL FOUNDATION

Social Responsibility Theory: Research institutions along with their investigators must conduct research which serves public good to fulfill their ethical requirement according to Social Responsibility Theory (Awa et al., 2024). The field of journalism needs researchers to demonstrate responsibility and maintain transparency when carrying out research activities according to this theoretical framework. Researchers in the Horn of Africa context must consider social results in addition to ethical standards according to the social responsibility theory. The theory insists on ethical communication as an essential tool for achieving knowledge advancement which builds trust needed to tackle community challenges (Awa et al., 2024).

Institutional Theory: According to Institutional Theory different institutions exert influence on the conduct of both organizations and individuals operating in specific settings (Eitrem et al., 2024). The framework identifies different rules which combine with formal and informal elements and structural patterns that shape research standards. The institutional theory examines the impact of bureaucratic challenges and normative rules on ethical standards for researchers in the Horn of Africa region. The theory uses concepts of institutional forces to understand how they interplay with personal actions that help researchers understand regulatory complexity (Eitrem et al., 2024).

Ethical Decision-Making Theory: The ethical decision-making theory examines the systematic approaches through which people choose between ethical options. Several mental processes alongside emotional dynamics act as determinants for people who resolve moral challenges (Ishwara & Mekonnen, 2024). The theory of ethical decision-making demonstrates special significance in situations where research investigators experience stressful situations that endanger ethical morality. The Horn of Africa researchers must handle tough decisions which require them to harmonize fast data acquisition with moral accountability. The theory serves to explain the mental factors which lead researchers toward moral or non-moral conduct (Ishwara & Mekonnen, 2024).

Cognitive Dissonance Theory: Cognitive Dissonance Theory states that human beings develop psychological distress as a result of holding simultaneous contradictory beliefs or performing actions which oppose their core values. Researchers encounter cognitive discomfort when institutions force them to choose results over following ethical guidelines (Chatterjee et al., 2023). The theory sheds light on researcher procedures for maintaining their values even when facing bureaucratic challenges and institutional requirements. Study of dissonance experiences enables researchers to create ethical adherence strategies in research practices (Chatterjee et al., 2023).

The study adopts ***Institutional Theory as its main theoretical framework***. The study bases its decision on evaluating how institutional frameworks and bureaucratic hindrances affect research ethics practices of scholars in the Horn of Africa region. This investigation uses a focus on institutional systems to discover which regulatory limitations create barriers to research integrity so that it can provide recommendations to strengthen ethical standards in these research systems (Eitrem et al., 2024).

DEFINITION AND ORIGIN OF TERMS

Research integrity: defines the practice of following performance standards together with ethical principles during scientific research. Honesty, transparency, accountability and respect for intellectual property together form the whole of research integrity (Zhaksylyk et al., 2023). The concept arose during the late 20th century as scientists started to face mounting concerns about unethical research practices leading to the demand for stronger guidelines (Zhaksylyk et al., 2023).

Ethical Compliance: The extent researchers follow established ethical framework standards and guidelines serve as ethical compliance during the entire research procedure (Asiri et al., 2024). The concept appeared at the same time institutions established both institutional review boards (IRBs) and ethical codes for protecting participant rights and welfare. Research requires ethical compliance as it enables public trust to remain strong throughout the research activity (Asiri et al., 2024).

Bureaucratic Barriers: The impediments to efficient decision-making and research activity execution are known as bureaucratic barriers (Scott, 2021). Nights of approval and muddled documentation and too many governing rules create the problems that stand in the way of research activities. The term bureaucracy, which became a popular organizational idea that characterized organizational structures in the 19th century, was derived from the French word bureau (Scott, 2021).

Horn of Africa: Ethiopia, Somalia, Djibouti, Eritrea, as well as Kenya are all part of the Horn of Africa, a geopolitical area in East Africa (Cavalerie et al., 2021). The Horn name derives from the horn-shaped physical form of this geographical area. Local heritage combined with multiple ethnic cultural variants and ongoing political complications which include security issues alongside economic deprivation together with minimal research capabilities characterize this territory (Cavalerie et al., 2021).

EMPIRICAL LITERATURE REVIEW

Research Integrity Challenges and Ethical Compliance

The empirical literature related to the issue of research integrity and ethical requirements has expanded significantly in recent years, identifying the complex interactions of factors that influence researcher adherence (Zhaksylyk et al., 2023). The central topic of this work is the identification of systemic problems that put research integrity at stake, particularly in developing regions such as the Horn of Africa. Studies have indicated that inadequate institutional support, the lack of clear ethical directives and insufficient training contribute to the ethical towers among researchers. For example, a study conducted in Ethiopia stressed that many researchers did not have access to complete training on ethical practices, leading to involuntary violations of ethical standards. This underscores the need to build possibilities to contribute to the culture of integrity of research institutions. Furthermore, the literature shows that bureaucratic barriers play an important role in shaping ethical communications (Scott, 2021). Kenya's research shows how strict regulatory processes can discourage researchers from respecting ethical standards. This study revealed that long approval times for ethical journals often result in contributions of the procedures required to comply with fundraising and publication. This phenomenon raises important questions about the integrity of the research findings and the possibility that ethical practices will become normal in high pressure environments (Rodríguez et al., 2023).

Furthermore, the research documented the effects of sociocultural factors on ethical compliance (Asiri et al., 2024). In Somalia, for example, researchers declare that traditional values and community expectations are often inconsistent with formal ethical instructions, leading to a decision-making dilemma (Cavalerie et al., 2021). This highlights the need for a contextual and sensitive approach to ethical responses, taking into account local habits and practices with the help of integrity. The literature also highlights the importance of institutional responsibility in promoting ethical research practice. This review states that institutions should take proactive steps to create an environment that contributes to integrity, such as creating reliable mechanisms for ethical supervision and support systems for researchers facing ethical dilemma (Rodríguez et al., 2023). Nevertheless, many institutions in Africa still face limited resources and infrastructure, exacerbating the problems associated with maintaining ethical communications. Despite these ideas, important drawbacks remain in empirical literature. Most existing research focuses on individual factors and pays little attention to the way broader institutional and systematic issues interact to shape the integrity of the research. Furthermore, there is a rare occurrence in research that explores the mediating role of bureaucratic barriers in the relationship between research integrity and ethical compliance challenges (Scott, 2021). This gap highlights the need for more complete research, taking into account the multifaceted nature of ethical compliance in research (Zhaksylyk et al., 2023).

H1: Research Integrity Challenges and Ethical Compliance having empirical association.

Research Integrity Challenges and Bureaucratic Barriers in Research Management

The empirical literature on the intersection of research and bureaucratic barrier integrity in research management presents a multifaceted landscape characterized by systemic disorders that hinder ethical research. Research integrity covers ethical standards, transparency, compliance with accountability, transparency and accountability in research, while bureaucratic barriers are administrative obstacles that complex or hinder the research process (Zhaksylyk et al., 2023). Together, these factors create complex environments that can significantly impair the quality and reliability of research findings. One outstanding topic in the literature is the impact of bureaucratic inefficiency on researchers' ability to maintain integrity (Rodríguez et al., 2023). For example, a study conducted in Uganda has shown that excessive administrative requirements for ethical declarations are often postponed by research projects leading researchers to worry about the ethical protocols of dosage or necessity. Pressure on compliance with financing conditions and publication conditions can create a scenario in which researchers feel obliged to bypass the ethical examination processes, undermining the principles of research integrity. This study underlines how bureaucratic barriers can inadvertently contribute to the environment where ethical differences become commonplace (Scott, 2021).

In addition, the literature indicates that the lack of clear ethical directives and the inconsistent application of the rules are always aggravated by integrity problems. A complete review of research in South Sudan noted that vague ethical standards led to researchers' different interpretations, which led to contradictory compliance with ethical practices (Pendle, 2021). This gap not only influences the quality of research, but also contributes to a culture of distrust. This study highlights the need for well-defined ethical instructions and reliable training programs to improve researchers' understanding of researcher integrity in a particular context. Cultural factors play an important role in training the interaction of research integrity and bureaucratic barriers (Zhaksylyk et al., 2023). In Kenya, this study shows that the cultural norms surrounding authority and hierarchy often discourage researchers from carrying out difficult bureaucratic processes, even when they perceive them as unfair or overreach (Rodríguez et al., 2023). This cultural dynamic can undoubtedly lead to a lack of responsibility for research institutions where ethical obstacles are not properly considered. The results suggest that cultural sensitivity is essential to developing effective strategies to improve research integrity (Zhaksylyk et al., 2023).

Furthermore, the literature highlights the importance of institutional support in the attenuation of bureaucratic barriers (Scott, 2021). This study argues that priority environments should be developed in the field of ethical research by optimizing bureaucratic processes and providing appropriate resources for ethical supervision. Institutions investing in researcher training and support systems are likely to contribute to a culture of integrity, thereby enhancing both ethical adherence and the quality of research. However, many institutions in the African Horn continue to fight limited resources and infrastructure challenges, complicating efforts to improve research management practices. Despite the growing number of literature, a key gap remains by understanding how bureaucratic barriers specifically die the relationship between research integrity and ethical compliance challenges (Asiri et al., 2024). Existing studies have documented the existence of bureaucratic inefficiencies, but only a few have systematically studied the mechanisms by which these barriers influence the researcher's ethical decision process. This gap highlights the need for more purposeful research, where institutional structures, cultural factors, and subtle interactions between individual behaviors in the formation of research integrity, are considered (Zhaksylyk et al., 2023).

> H2: Research Integrity Challenges and Bureaucratic Barriers in Research Management having empirical association.

Bureaucratic Barriers in Research Management and Ethical Compliance

The empirical literature on bureaucratic barriers and the outcomes of ethical responses in the field of research revealed important evidence of how compliance with ethical standards in research could hinder administrative issues (Scott, 2021). Bureaucratic barriers include a range of obstacles, including over-documentation, long-term approval processes, and obscuring government directives. All this can create an environment in which ethical observations are compromised (Asad, 2021). This issue is particularly pronounced in regional development where limited resources and infrastructure flaws exacerbate the problems facing researchers. One important study in Kenya highlights how bureaucratic inefficiency can lead to disappointment among researchers by encouraging them to bypass the ethical testing process (Rodríguez et al., 2023). The authors found that the long term needed to obtain ethical approval leads to the fact that researchers are pressure to accelerate their work, leading to potential ethical disorders. This conclusion is repeated in studies that document similar experiences in Uganda. Researchers reported that the cumbersome nature of administrative requirements not only delayed project timelines but also contributed to a culture where ethical lapses were normalized due to the pressures of meeting external deadlines (Rodríguez et al., 2023).

In addition to delays, the literature indicates that unclear and inconsistent regulatory frameworks further exacerbate bureaucratic barriers (Scott, 2021). It was found that ambiguous ethical recommendations led to various interpretations among researchers in South Sudan (Pendle, 2021). This gap with this field led to the fact that ethical responses are individual discretion and undermines confidence in research findings rather than standardized practices. This study highlights the need for clear, well-defined ethical instructions that can provide researchers with a constant basis for ethical decisions. Cultural dynamics also play an important role in shaping the interaction between bureaucratic barriers and ethical compliance (Asiri et al., 2024). In Somalia, cultural respect for authority has often discouraged researchers from questioning bureaucratic processes, even as they perceived inefficiency and ethical concerns (Cavalerie et al., 2021). This cultural context can create a dynamic force of forces that block open dialogue about ethical practices, further eradicating bureaucratic barriers that hinder compliance. This study suggests that it is important to promote a culture of responsibility and openness to resolve the negative effects of bureaucratic obstacles on ethical research (Scott, 2021).

Furthermore, the literature highlights the importance of institutional support in the attenuation of bureaucratic barrier outcomes. Support that institutions must prioritize the creation of rationalized administrative processes which facilitate ethical compliance. By investing in training programs and resources for ethical surveillance, institutions can allow researchers to meet bureaucratic challenges more effectively. However, many research institutions in the Horn of Africa continue to combat the limited capacity and resources, which complicates efforts to improve ethical compliance (Asiri et al., 2024). Despite these ideas, significant gaps remain in the understanding of specific mechanisms, through which bureaucratic barriers affect ethical observance in research management (Scott, 2021). While existing studies documented the presence of these barriers, only a few systematically studied the nuanced relations between bureaucratic inefficiency, institutional culture and processes of ethical decisions of researchers. This gap highlights the need for further research that examines how these factors interact, particularly within the unique contexts of developing regions.

> H3: Bureaucratic Barriers in Research Management and Ethical Compliance having empirical association.

Research Integrity Challenges, Ethical Compliance and Bureaucratic Barriers in Research Management Mediation

The empirical literature explores mediation of bureaucratic barriers associated with research integrity and ethical response issues, and shows the complex interaction of factors that have a significant impact on researchers' compliance with ethical standards (Scott, 2021). Research integrity issues cover many issues, including misconduct, lack of transparency and inadequate training (Zhaksylyk et al., 2023). All of them can hinder ethical responses. Bureaucratic barriers, including long-term approval processes, excessive documentation requirements, and ambiguous regulatory frameworks, further complicate this landscape, creating an environment where ethical obstacles can often occur. The main study highlighted the intermediate role of Kenya's bureaucratic barriers (Rodríguez et al., 2023). There, researchers reported that the long process of ethics journals led to disappointment and in some cases ethical compromise. The authors found that the pressure to meet external deadlines - combined with long bureaucratic procedures - has often led researchers to completely bypass ethical journals, thus undergoing the integrity of research. This observation is sustained which documented similar experiences in Uganda, indicating that bureaucratic infections were directly correlated to a reduction in compliance with ethical standards, because researchers felt obliged to prioritize the opportunity on integrity (Asad, 2021). Furthermore, the literature shows that obscure and inconsistent regulatory guidelines exacerbate the problems researchers face in maintaining ethical responses. He conducted research in South Sudan, revealing that vague ethical guidelines led to researchers' various interpretations, creating scripts that made ethical communication subjective and rely on individual discretion (Pendle, 2021). This difference highlights the mediation effect of bureaucratic barriers, especially when summarizing the pressures of navigation in ineffective bureaucratic landscapes, as there is no clear standard, which could lead researchers to practice unethical (Asad, 2021).

Cultural factors also play an important role in shaping mediation between bureaucratic barriers and ethical communications (Scott, 2021). Research in Somalia indicated that cultural norms surrounding authority and respect often discouraged researchers from questioning bureaucratic processes, even when they recognized inefficiencies that hampered ethical adherence. This cultural dynamic can strengthen bureaucratic barriers, making it even more difficult for researchers to maintain the integrity of their work (Scott, 2021). This study highlights the importance of promoting a culture of responsibility and openness to counter the negative effects of bureaucratic disability. Institutional support becomes a critical factor when softening the negative impact of bureaucratic obstacles on ethical compliance (Asiri et al., 2024). Indicate that institutions should invest in the creation of optimized processes that facilitate the ethical review and compliance. By providing training and resources, institutions can expand the capabilities of researchers more effectively in bureaucratic problems and support the principles of the integrity of research (Pendle, 2021). However, the literature suggests that many institutions in the Horn of Africa continue to fight limited resources, complicating efforts to improve ethical compliance in a bureaucratic disability setting (Asiri et al., 2024). Despite the substantial ideas provided by existing research, there remains an important gap in understanding the nuanced mechanisms in which bureaucratic barriers mediate the relationship between research integrity and ethical compliance challenges (Zhaksylyk et al., 2023). While many studies documented the presence and influence of these barriers, there is a need for more complete studies that examine the specific interactions between these variables. This includes the study of how institutional culture, training and support systems can buffer the influence of bureaucratic inefficiency on ethical decision –making (Scott, 2021).

H4: Research Integrity Challenges, Ethical Compliance and Bureaucratic Barriers in Research Management Mediation having empirical association.

CONCEPTUAL FRAMEWORK

Figure 1. Conceptual framework

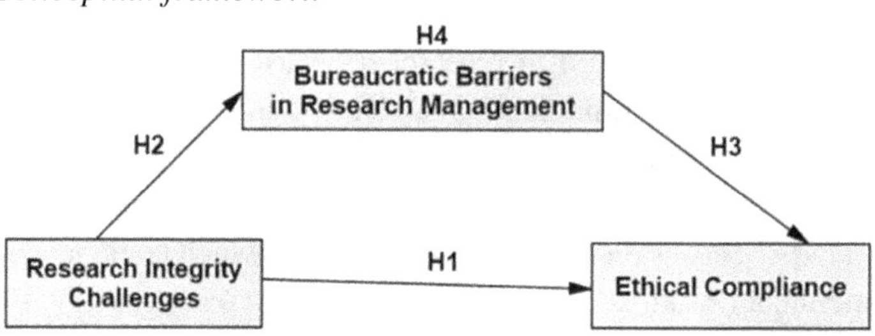

RESEARCH METHODOLOGY

This study used quantitative methodology to study the relationship between research integrity, ethical responses, and bureaucratic barrier issues in research management. A general selection of 385 participants was used (Ghanad, 2023). This included researchers from various African institutions. The choice of participants was carried out using a stratified sampling methodology to ensure the presentation in different fields of research and institutional types. The data were collected using a structured questionnaire, which included elements developed on the basis of the relevant literature, measurement of structures associated with the integrity of research, ethical correspondence and bureaucratic barriers (Ghanad, 2023). In order to assess the adequacy of the sample for the factorial analysis, the Kaiser-Meyer-Lkin (KMO) measure was calculated, which gave the value higher than the recommended threshold 0.6, which indicates that the sample was adapted to this analysis (Tanwar & Agarwal, 2024). Then a research factor analysis (EFA) was carried out to determine the main factor structure of structures. This analysis used analysis of the main component (PCA) with Varimax rotation, allowing it to extract factors that best represent the relationships between variables. After determining the structure of the factors, more concentration analyses were performed using Structural Modeling Equations (SEM) using AMOS software. This approach enabled the researchers to test the hypothesized relationships and assess the overall model fit (Tanwar & Agarwal, 2024).

Scale Development

The scale for this study was developed based on a comprehensive review of related literature, ensuring that it accurately captured the constructs of research integrity challenges, ethical compliance, and bureaucratic barriers (Scott, 2021). Items for the scale were derived from established measures in previous studies, which provided a solid theoretical foundation (Bain et al., 2022). For example, the constructions associated with the integrity of research have been informed, which underline the importance of transparency, responsibility and respect for ethical standards in the practice of research. The elements related to ethical compliance have been adapted to the framework proposed on the principles of respect for people, well-being and justice. Bureaucratic barriers were assessed using items derived from the literature on administrative challenges in research management, particularly the studies. These studies highlighted the impact of excessive documentation, long approval processes, and unclear guidelines on researcher's ability to maintain ethical compliance (Hejazi et al., 2022). Pilot studies were conducted on a subset of participants to further clarify the objects and ensure clarity and relevance. Comments from the pilot study informed formulation adjustments and elemental structure. After finalizing the scale, the questionnaire was administered to the full sample of 385 researchers. The data collected were subjected to EFA, which validated the factor structure of the constructs, confirming the appropriateness of the scale items (Hejazi et al., 2022). After the EFA, the SEM analysis was carried out to study the relationship between constructions and evaluate the adjustment of the model, providing valuable information about the interaction between the problems of the integrity of research, ethical compliance and bureaucratic barriers in the context of research management (Kyriazos & Poga-Kyriazou, 2023).

DATA ANALYSIS

Table 1. KMO and Bartlett's Test

Kaiser-Meyer-Olkin Measure of Sampling Adequacy.		**.850**
Bartlett's Test of Sphericity	Approx. Chi-Square	1419.738
	Df	91
	Sig.	.000

Source: Authors

Table 1 shows the validity of the sampling and results of the Kaiser-Meier Olkin measurement (KMO) of the Bartlett spherical test. A KMO value of 0.850 indicates a good level of sampling validity, as values above 0.8 are considered very well. This suggests that sample size and collected data are sufficient to identify the main structure of the structural factors of the study.

The Bartlett Spheres test also confirms the ability of the data for factor analysis. This provides an approximate value of Chi-Quadrate 1419,738 with a 91 degree of freedom and level of meaning (value P) 0000.

Table 2. Total variance explained

Component	**Initial Eigenvalues**			**Extraction Sums of Squared Loadings**			**Rotation Sums of Squared Loadings**		
	Total	**% of Variance**	**Cumulative %**	**Total**	**% of Variance**	**Cumulative %**	**Total**	**% of Variance**	**Cumulative %**
1	4.51	32.235	32.235	4.51	32.235	32.235	3.00	21.451	21.451
2	1.37	9.787	42.022	1.37	9.787	42.022	2.16	15.491	36.942
3	1.27	9.087	51.110	1.27	9.087	51.110	1.98	14.168	51.110
4	.949	6.782	57.892						
5	.871	6.223	64.115						
6	.773	5.519	69.634						

Extraction Method: Principal Component Analysis.
Source: Authors

Table 2 shows the general variance results explained in the study factor analysis using principal components (ACP) analysis. This table shows the unique initial values, the amount of square load extracted, and the amount of square load rotation for each component identified in the analysis. The first appropriate value for the first component is 4.51, which represents 32.235% of the total variance. This indicates that it reflects an important part of data variation. The total variance explained in this component is 32.235%. The second component with an eigenvalue of 1.37 explains 9.787% of the variance at an additional 9.787%, increasing the cumulative rate by 42.022%. The third component also has its own value above 1.27, which contributes to the total variance of 9.087% and gives the cumulative percentage of 51.110%. Components 4-6 have their own values below 1.0, but show a reduction in yield in terms of the variance explained. More specifically, the eigenvalue for component 4 is 0.949, which contributes to 6.782% to the variance, and the cumulative variance reaches 57.892%. The subsequent components continue to add less than 7% each, with the sixth component explaining a cumulative total of 5.519% and a cumulative total of 69.634%.

Confirmatory Principle Component Examination

Table 3. Covariances

Covariance			Approximation	S.E.	C.R.	P	Hy.
Bureaucratic Barriers in Research Management	<-->	Research Integrity Challenges	.242	.021	8.231	***	H2
Bureaucratic Barriers in Research Management	<-->	Ethical Compliance	.303	.032	7.692	***	**H3**
Research Integrity Challenges	<-->	Ethical Compliance	.254	.24	7.831	***	**H1**

Source: Authors

Table 3 shows the conversation between the concept of bureaucratic impairments in research management, research integrity and ethical observation issues, and appropriate statistical indicators. Each value of covariance indicates the strength and orientation of the relationship between pairs of structures. The incorporation between bureaucratic barriers in research management and research consistency issues is 0.242, with standard error (S.E.) 0.021. The Critical Report (C.R.) is 8.231, and the level of meaning is marked by a star (***), indicating a statistically significant relationship. This conclusion confirms the hypothesis 2 (H2), which suggests that higher bureaucratic barriers are associated with increased problems for studying integrity. Similarly, the conation between bureaucratic barriers in research management and ethical correspondence is reported at 0.303, with S.E. From 0.032 and C.R. 7.692 also significant on p

Table 4. Validity concern

	CR	AVE	MSV	MaxR(H)	RIC	BBRM	EC
RIC	0.732	0.643	0.219	0.852	**0.654**		
BBRM	0.758	0.657	0.132	0.763	0.171	**0.665**	
EC	0.793	0.603	0.274	0.797	0.383	0.193	**0.684**

Note: RIC= Research Integrity Challenges; BBRM= Bureaucratic Barriers in Research Management; EC= Ethical Compliance

Source: Authors

Table 4 presents key validity measures for constructions of research integrity challenges (RIC), bureaucratic barriers in research management (BBRM) and ethical compliance (CE). The table includes composite reliability (CR), the average variance extracted (AVE), maximum shared variance (MSV) and maximum reliability (MAXR (H)) for each construction, providing an overview of their psychometric properties. The composite reliability values indicate satisfactory internal consistency for all structures and RIC - 0.732, BBRM at 0.758 and EC at 0.793. As a rule, CR values greater than 0.7 are considered acceptable, which suggests that the elements of each structure reliably measure alleged concepts. The AVE values also confirm the reliability of the structure, with RICs of 0.643, 0.657, BBRM, and 0.603, EC. AVE values above 0.5 indicate that a significant proportion of the variance within the element is fixed by design, confirming constructive reliability. The maximum shared variance value (MSV) indicates the highest shared variance between structures, with RICs of 0.219, BBRM at 0.132 and EC at 0.274. These values are lower than the corresponding AVE values for each structure. This is a positive indicator, as it suggests that the structures differ from one another and do not overlap. Finally, the maximum reliability value (MAXR(H)) is also higher than the acceptable threshold, with RIC at 0.852, BBRM at 0.763, and EC at 0.797, and EC at 0.797.

Mediating Role Examination

Figure 2. Structural equation model

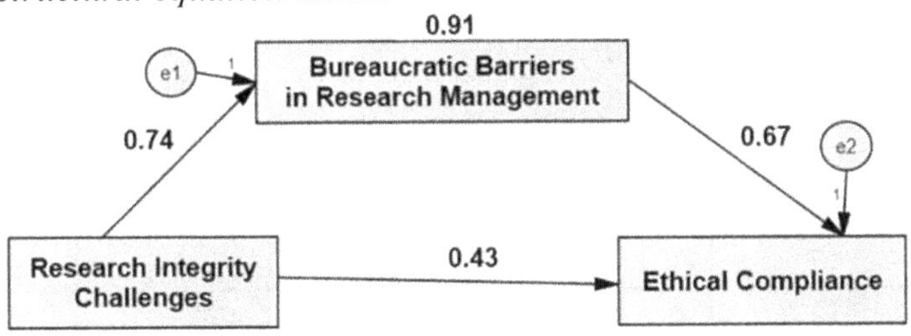

Model Fit Indices

Table 5. Indices for model fit

Sig.	Chi-Sq	RMR	Fitness Goodness	Fitness Confirmatory	TLI	RMSEA
0.004	1.954	.036	0.930	0.912	0.911	.028

Source: Authors

Table 5 provides important tips for assessing model adjustments proposed in the study and provides information on how the model presents the data. The value level (SIG.) was reported at 0.004, indicating that the model is statistically significant, suggesting that there is a significant connection in the data. The Chi-quadrate value is 1.954, which is relatively low, and, combined with the level of meaning, indicates a good correspondence of the model of observed data. It is desirable to reduce cadratis compared to degrees of freedom, as the model suggests that it properly reflects the structure of the data. The mean square root (RMR) is 0.036, which is well below the tolerance threshold of 0.08, indicating good fit. RMR evaluates the mean difference between observed and predicted values, and low values imply the best characteristics of the model. Fitness indices such as the Goodness of Fit Index (GFI) and Confirmatory Fit Index (CFI) are represented by values of 0.930 and 0.912, respectively. Both indices exceed the commonly accepted threshold of 0.90, indicating that the model exhibits a good fit. These signals suggest that the model explains an important part of the data variance. The Tucker-Lewis (TLI) index reported 0.911, exceeding the recommended reduction of 0.90. This shows an even more well -prepared model. Finally, the average square error of approximation (mesa) is very low at 0.028, which is much lower than the threshold of 0.05, which indicates close compliance. RMSEA values less than 0.05 suggest that the model does not significantly deform the data.

Table 6. Regression examination

Relative			**Approx.**	**S.E.**	**C.R.**	**P**	**Ass.**
Bureaucratic Barriers in Research Management	<---	Research Integrity Challenges	.864	.143	7.583	***	H2
Ethical Compliance	<---	Bureaucratic Barriers in Research Management	.328	.131	2.853	***	H3
Ethical Compliance	<---	Research Integrity Challenges	.957	.192	7.958	***	H1

Source: Authors

Table 6 shows the results of regression analysis studying the relationship between research integrity (RIC) problems construction (BBRM) bureaucratic barriers and ethical correspondence (EC). This table includes regression coefficients, standard error (S.E.), critical ratio (C.R.), significance level (P), and related hypotheses. The regression coefficient for the relationship of the problems of research integrity to bureaucratic barriers in research management is 0.864, with S.E. from 0.143 and C.R. 7.583. The level of meaning is marked by stars (***), which indicates that this connection is statistically significant. This strong coefficient suggests that an increase in the integrity of the study is associated with a significant increase in bureaucratic barriers confirming Hypothesis 2 (H2). From bureaucratic barriers to research management of ethical responses, the second regression route shows coefficients of C.R. of 0.131 and 2,853. This observation supports Hypothesis 3 (H3) and shows that high bureaucratic barriers have a negative impact on ethical compliance, but to a lower degree compared to the initial relationship.

Finally, the regression of the research consistency challenge to ethical compliance gives a coefficient of 0.957 using C.R. of 0.192 and 7.958, indicating a very important relationship. This result strongly supports Hypothesis 1 (H1), indicating that challenges related to research integrity are closely associated with ethical compliance, suggesting that as integrity challenges increase, ethical compliance is likely to decline.

Table 7. Mediating role effect

	Worth	Path Influence
Research Integrity Challenges → Ethical Compliance	.43	Direct influence stated
Research Integrity Challenges → Bureaucratic Barriers in Research Management → Ethical Compliance	.74*.67=.48	Indirect Influence Ensued
	.91	Partial mediation

Source: Authors

A mediation analysis through Table 7 establishes how bureaucratic barriers in research management (BBRM) affect the relationship between research integrity challenges (RIC) and ethical compliance (EC). The table determines three levels of influence so researchers can see how components connect. It organizes the effects into direct, indirect, and overall categories to demonstrate the entire coherence structure. The research confirms that changes in Research Integrity Challenges lead directly to 0.43 points decrease in Ethical Compliance. Research integrity directly affects ethical standards so it requires immediate attention. This table also elaborates on the indirect impact of research integrity challenges on ethical compliance through bureaucratic barriers. This indirect route is calculated by multiplying the effect of RIC on BBRM (0.74) by the effect of EC (0.67), resulting in an indirect effect of 0.48. This value means that bureaucratic barriers ensure mediation of the relationship between integrity and suitability issues. The complete or complete effect of the question of research integrity on ethical responses is 0.91, which combines direct and indirect pathways. This high general value indicates a strong general relationship between RIC and EC with the presence of mediation. Finally, the results indicate a partial intermediary effect, which means that although bureaucratic barriers significantly affect the relationship between the problems of the integrity of research and ethical correspondence, the direct effect still exists. This partial mediation emphasizes the complexity of relations between these constructions and emphasizes the need for strategies that solve both the problems of integrity and bureaucratic barriers to improve ethical correspondence in research management.

DISCUSSION

This research produces essential results that reveal how Research Integrity Challenges (RIC) influences relationships between Bureaucratic Barriers in Research Management (BBRM) and Ethical Compliance (EC). RIC holds significant influence over BBRM and EC which proves the essential role of integrity challenges in structuring the research environment. The height of integrity challenges brings forth increased bureaucratic barriers that create obstacles to ethical compliance. The data demonstrates why institutions must take preventive action against integrity issues because active intervention creates less bureaucratic research obstacles leading to an ethical research culture development. BBRM plays a partial mediating role when RIC has an impact on EC according to the research findings. Despite bureaucratic barriers acting as a mediator the direct relationship between integrity challenges and ethical compliance remains strong according to the findings. Research administration should not rely exclusively on bureaucratic obstacle reduction for achieving better ethical compliance because it is essential to address original research integrity problems directly. Organizations should develop extensive strategies which aim to eliminate both these obstacles and integrity vulnerabilities in order to develop an environment friendly to ethical research practices. Strong model fit indices validate the reliability of both proposed relationships thus strengthening the validity of these results. The important covariance between the examined constructs demonstrates that these elements work together which implies modifications in any one area will create effects in other parts of the system. Research management requires comprehensive methods which examine both bureaucratic process implications and integrity together with compliance matters because these domains show interconnectedness.

CONCLUSION

The study demonstrates complex connections that exist between Research Integrity Challenges (RIC) and Bureaucratic Barriers in Research Management (BBRM and Ethical Compliance (EC). Research Integrity challenges result in direct ethical compliance problems as well as creating bureaucratic obstacles which increase complexity in compliance effectiveness. The research finds conclusive evidence that strengthens the argument for simultaneous solutions to integrity problems and bureaucratic obstacles in establishing ethical research practices. The findings demonstrate that BBRM partially explains the connection between RIC and EC yet integrity problems independently create impacts on ethical compliance. So researchers need to create diverse tactics that combat both existing research structure barriers and essential ethical issues in research conduct.

MANAGERIAL IMPLICATIONS

This study provides valuable managerial implications which direct research institutions and their organizations. Research Integrity Challenges play the critical role of determining the development of both bureaucratic barriers and ethical compliance standards. Managers who make identification and mitigation of integrity challenges their priority will develop a better environment for ethical research practices. Managers should create training programs to teach ethical standards along with transparency and discussion methods about integrity issues within the researcher community. The study demonstrates the decision-making obstacles created by bureaucratic procedures which affect the ability to adhere to ethical standards. Managers need to evaluate their present administrative systems to determine which sections slow researchers down while making it harder for them to meet their ethical obligations. Enhanced streamlining of administrative rules and superior support systems decreases researcher workload which enables them to dedicate more effort to their work instead of dealing with time-consuming administrative tasks. The establishment of a workplace atmosphere that promotes shameless communication and teamwork stands essential. The creation of inter professional dialogue between researchers and both administrators and compliance officers enables quick and proactive handling of ethical concerns in workplaces. Organizations benefit from this partnership model because it enables the exchange of both innovative solutions and most effective research ethics best practices. Managers who focus on the combination of organizational structures and workplace culture can enhance ethical compliance throughout their research institutions. Protecting research integrity alongside maintaining public trust in institutional findings serves to enhance responsible and ethical progress of knowledge across institutions.

PRACTICAL IMPLICATIONS

This research study brings forward crucial implications which affect practical operations of institutions that conduct research as well as research management stakeholders. Institutions need to establish complete training systems which focus on educational content about research integrity together with ethical compliance principles. Research training programs must provide understanding and practical skills about integrity challenges and ethical standards as well as the possible consequences of non-compliance to researchers. Institutions should create specific direction manuals and helpful resources which handle bureaucratic barriers. The institution offers simplified administrative procedures and easy-to-use programs to help researchers manage their compliance obligations better. Online platforms that handle research proposal submissions and approve them together with compliance document tracking enable researchers to cut down bureaucracy while lowering effort and time requirements. The practical achievement involves creating opportunities for employees to actively discuss important ethical matters within their workplace environment. The institution should establish periodic workshops and forums that allow researchers to discuss research integrity matters together with compliance issues. The knowledge exchange creates solutions that improve the moral environment across the whole organization. An organization can assist researchers by creating an independent group which both helps them solve integrity issues and provides continuous ethical advice. The purpose of such a committee is to provide both methodology expertise through best practices sharing and to assist with individual ethical cases while guaranteeing researchers have access to needed resources for proper compliance standards.

THEORETICAL IMPLICATIONS

The findings of this study offer significant theoretical implications for the understanding of research integrity, bureaucratic barriers, and ethical compliance. This study describes how constructs link to one another which strengthen current research on behavioral science as well as ethical standards in study environments. Research Integrity Challenges directly affect Ethical Compliance based on existing research that stresses ethical standards in research practices. Future research needs to develop a stronger theoretical foundation which directly explains how integrity challenges affect compliance outcomes because the current findings emphasize this requirement. The study presents Bureaucratic Barriers in Research Management (BBRM) as a key mediator that helps explain how organizational structures affect research ethical conduct. Research theories focused on organizational behavior should adopt an analysis of the dual effects of ethical priorities interacting with bureaucratic procedures to fully understand how organizational factors determine research compliance expectations. The study findings about partial mediation reinforce the need for researchers to identify more potential factors affecting the RIC-EC relationship. Research theories should advance through new pathways which enable scientists to establish more complete models incorporating organizational culture together with leadership styles and institutional policies that affect ethical compliance in research.

RECOMMENDATIONS

Multiple strategic suggestions emerge from this research that organizations need to implement for better research integrity accompanied by improved ethical standards. Research institutions must establish thorough training curriculum focusing on research ethics and integrity for their members. The training programs must teach researchers about their unique research difficulties while educating them about ethical rules and showing them the dangers of non-compliance. Seminar sessions combined with workshops enable researchers to maintain awareness about existing ethical practices as well as mandatory regulatory standards. Organizations need to perform an in-depth evaluation of their bureaucratic systems to find and eliminate redundant obstacles which prevent ethical compliance. The administrative process becomes more efficient as simplification efforts focus on approval management alongside providing easy-to-follow compliance directions leading to reduced laboratory burdens. The implementations of intuitive digital systems which handle research proposals together with compliance documentation both enhance efficiency and makes documentation easier to access. Organizations need to develop an environment where workers maintain open dialogue with each other. The institutions need to enable staff researchers to report their concerns and report about their encounters with research integrity hurdles. A combination of periodic discussion forums and mentorship and discussion programs between researchers enables dual communication for ethical dilemma solutions and information transfer between scientists. Organizations should initiate specific ethics boards that deliver ongoing ethical support and advisory services. The research process benefits from these committees because they assist researchers through ethical challenges while providing best practice information and integrating ethical values into research work since the beginning. To model ethical behavior and demonstrate research integrity leadership needs to play its part wholeheartedly. Leaders who actively back initiatives promoting research integrity together with ethical compliance modeling help develop networks where ethical practices achieve high importance and maintenance.

FUTURE DIRECTIONS

This research reveals important findings that suggest multiple directions to pursue future research focused on research integrity, bureaucratic obstacles and ethical compliance enhancement. The evaluation of organizational policies together with training programs requires extended time-based research to investigate their influence over time on researcher attitudes toward integrity concerns and their adherence to ethical norms. Through this method researchers would obtain greater understanding regarding cause-and-effect relationships while evaluating different programs designed to improve research ethics. Research should investigate how organizational cultures influence the attitudes researchers demonstrate toward research integrity. Culture analysis of different dimensions including openness and accountability and ethical support will guide the discovery of effective practices to develop ethical workplace cultures. Studies comparing various institutions and sectors should analyze how environmental circumstances impact the relationship between integrity threats and bureaucratic problems during ethical compliance procedures. The investigation of precise bureaucratic barriers that affect researchers and their differences between academic fields and research categories would prove useful in creating effective solutions. It becomes important to analyze these particular patterns because they provide guidance for creating specific solutions to simplify processes and decrease research administrative tasks. Future research needs to investigate technology applications for improving research integrity along with compliance practices. The research investigation of how digital tools including artificial intelligence and block chain systems can enhance transparency together with streamlining compliance processes and helping with ethical decision-making could result in innovative solutions to address current challenges.

REFERENCES

Asad, A. (2021). From bureaucratic-centralism management to school based management: managing human resources in the management of education program. *Indonesian Research Journal in Education| IRJE|, 5*(1), 201–225.

Asiri, E. A. S., Bin-Hady, W., & Sahari, Y. (2024). Assessing the Degree of Compliance with the Ethical Principles of the'Translator's Professional Guide'amongst Translators in Saudi Arabia. *Jurnal Arbitrer, 11*(2), 109–122. DOI: 10.25077/ar.11.2.109-122.2024

Awa, H. O., Etim, W., & Ogbonda, E. (2024). Stakeholders, stakeholder theory and corporate social responsibility (CSR). *International Journal of Corporate Social Responsibility, 9*(1), 11. DOI: 10.1186/s40991-024-00094-y

Bain, L. E., Tchuisseu-Kwangoua, L. A., Adeagbo, O., Nkfusai, N. C., Amu, H., Saah, F. I., & Kombe, F. (2022). Fostering research integrity in sub-Saharan Africa: Challenges, opportunities, and recommendations. *The Pan African Medical Journal, 43*(1). Advance online publication. DOI: 10.11604/pamj.2022.43.182.37804 PMID: 36923394

Cavalerie, L., Wardeh, M., Lebrasseur, O., Nanyingi, M., McIntyre, K. M., Kaba, M., Asrat, D., Christley, R., Pinchbeck, G., Baylis, M., & Mor, S. M. (2021). One hundred years of zoonoses research in the Horn of Africa: A scoping review. *PLoS Neglected Tropical Diseases, 15*(7), e0009607. DOI: 10.1371/journal.pntd.0009607 PMID: 34270551

Chatterjee, S., Chaudhuri, R., Kumar, A., Wang, C. L., & Gupta, S. (2023). Impacts of consumer cognitive process to ascertain online fake review: A cognitive dissonance theory approach. *Journal of Business Research, 154*, 113370. DOI: 10.1016/j.jbusres.2022.113370

Eitrem, A., Meidell, A., & Modell, S. (2024). The use of institutional theory in social and environmental accounting research: A critical review. *Accounting and Business Research, 54*(7), 775–810. DOI: 10.1080/00014788.2024.2328934

Ghanad, A. (2023). An overview of quantitative research methods. *International Journal of Multidisciplinary Research and Analysis, 6*(08), 3794–3803. DOI: 10.47191/ijmra/v6-i8-52

Hejazi, S. S., Hosseini, M., Ebadi, A., & Alavi Majd, H. (2022). Development and psychometric properties evaluation of caregiver burden questionnaire in family caregivers of hemodialysis patients. *BMC Nursing, 21*(1), 246. DOI: 10.1186/s12912-022-01025-7 PMID: 36064396

Ishwara, P., & Mekonnen, N. (2024). Ethical decision-making dynamics: Insights from professional accountants. *Cogent Business & Management, 11*(1).

Kyriazos, T., & Poga-Kyriazou, M. (2023). Applied psychometrics: Estimator considerations in commonly encountered conditions in CFA, SEM, and EFA practice. *Psychology (Irvine, Calif.), 14*(5), 799–828. DOI: 10.4236/psych.2023.145043

Pendle, N. (2021). Competing authorities and norms of restraint: Governing community-embedded armed groups in South Sudan. *International Interactions, 47*(5), 873–897. DOI: 10.1080/03050629.2021.1918126

Rodríguez, D. C., Balaji, L. N., Chamdimba, E., Kafumba, J., Koon, A. D., Mazalale, J., Mkombe, D., Munywoki, J., Mwase-Vuma, T., & Namakula, J. (2023). Political economy analysis of subnational health management in Kenya, Malawi and Uganda. *Health Policy andPlanning, 38*(5), 631–647.

Scott, I. (2021). Context and innovation in traditional bureaucracies: A Hong Kong study. *Public Administration and Development, 41*(1), 12–22. DOI: 10.1002/pad.1899

Tanwar, R., & Agarwal, P. K. (2024). Analysis of the determinants of service quality in the multimodal public transport system of Bhopal city using structural equation modelling (SEM) and factor analysis. *Expert Systems with Applications, 256*, 124931. DOI: 10.1016/j.eswa.2024.124931

Zhaksylyk, A., Zimba, O., Yessirkepov, M., & Kocyigit, B. F. (2023). Research integrity: Where we are and where we are heading. *Journal of Korean Medical Science, 38*(47), e405. DOI: 10.3346/jkms.2023.38.e405 PMID: 38050915

KEY TERMS AND DEFINITIONS

Bureaucratic Barriers in Research Management (BBRM): Obstructions to researchers' ethical compliance occur through specific administrative hurdles present in research activity management such as unclear approval systems and complex reporting processes.

Bureaucratic Barriers: Research efficiency can be hindered due to bureaucratic restrictions which primarily stem from elaborate process requirements and tight regulatory compliance requirements and insufficient operational efficiency that stands in the way of ethical practices fulfillment.

Ethical Compliance: Research compliance describes the ways scientists follow existing ethical norms which guide research operations especially regarding human and animal subject treatments alongside data control protocols and publication protocols.

Organizational Culture: Organizational culture encompasses the collective values and beliefs and procedures that control employee behavior to determine how members of the group handle research integrity and ethical compliance practice.

Research Integrity Challenges (RIC): Research integrity remains at risk when factors threatening its process occur such as data fabrication and insufficient oversight and plagiarism because these actions violate ethical guidelines.

Research Integrity: The practice of research follows ethical guidelines along with professional standards for creating research that exists as honest transparent and responsible work.

Training Programs for Research Ethics: Training programs educate researchers about ethical standards alongside providing information about integrity challenges and mandatory compliance requirements which develop their capabilities to execute ethical research.

Chapter 5

Are Textual Prompts in Large Language Models Sufficient for Vulnerability Detection?

Puya Pakshad
https://orcid.org/0000-0003-2834-2769
Illinois Institute of Technology, USA

Sajad Aqanasiri
https://orcid.org/0009-0007-8169-3476
Shahid Beheshti University, Iran

ABSTRACT

Large Language Models (LLMs) have gained traction in domains from software development to cybersecurity, particularly for detecting vulnerabilities in program source code. Their ability to analyze large codebases and identify security weaknesses makes them valuable in software security analysis. However, their effectiveness declines in the absence of intermediate representations such as Abstract Syntax Trees (AST), Control Flow Graphs (CFG), and Data Flow Graphs (DFG), or even tokenized forms of code. In this research study, we assess the performance of LLMs in detecting vulnerabilities directly from raw source code, without structural representations. By designing context-specific prompts, we aim to enhance the model's understanding of code semantics. Our findings show that LLMs can partially identify vulnerabilities from raw code alone, reaching up to 43% accuracy. This indicate both the potential and current limitations of prompt-based LLMs for static vulnerability detection.

DOI: 10.4018/979-8-3373-4862-9.ch005

Copyright © 2025, IGI Global Scientific Publishing. Copying or distributing in print or electronic forms without written permission of IGI Global Scientific Publishing is prohibited.

INTRODUCTION

Vulnerability detection serves as a foundational step in securing modern software, which aims to identify flaws in program source code and software behavior to prevent potential exploitation by malicious adversaries (Ghaffarian & Shahriari, 2017). Recent industry evidence indicates that over 60% of data breaches are caused by unpatched software vulnerabilities, leading to significant business consequences such as data loss, reputational harm, and supply chain disruptions (Ponemon Institute, 2025; Palo Alto Networks Unit 42, 2025). For example, a 2024 analysis by CrowdStrike shows a high-impact software supply chain attack, where an exploited vulnerability in a vendor's source code led to widespread breaches across multiple partner organizations, resulting in multi-million-dollar financial losses and operational disruptions (CrowdStrike, 2024). From a technical perspective, the FBI has reported that over 30% of security incidents in recent years were linked to storage-related security vulnerabilities that allowed unauthorized access to sensitive organizational data (Karie, Sahri, & Yang, 2022). Moreover, global cybercrime damages are projected to reach $10.5 trillion annually by 2025, which represent severe risks to large-size businesses (Gavou, Iliya, & Ihuoma, 2024). These security vulnerabilities often originate in the software development phase, where insecure coding practices by developers introduce exploitable flaws (Hughes & Turner, 2023). These pieces of evidence demonstrate how software vulnerabilities, particularly those left unpatched, serve as primary attack vector with direct and measurable impacts on organizational security and business continuity, which emphasize the critical importance of early vulnerability detection in program source code (IBM Security, 2024).

Numerous techniques have been proposed for software vulnerability detection, typically classified into static, dynamic, and hybrid analysis techniques (Shereen et al., 2024). Traditional methods, such as static code analyzers and runtime behavioral monitors, have laid the groundwork for modern vulnerability detection tools. Over time, these traditional approaches have increasingly been integrated with artificial intelligence, particularly machine learning and deep learning models, which results in higher precision and lower false positive rates (Sheng et al., 2025).

Recently, large language models (LLMs) have emerged as powerful tools in the smart detection of software vulnerabilities, which leverage vast contextual understanding to identify security flaws with high semantic awareness (Shao & Ding, 2024; Khare et al., 2023; Mao et al., 2024). Modern software vulnerability detection technqiues frequently are based on intermediate representations of source code to better convey its structural and semantic properties to LLMs. These include representations such as the Abstract Syntax Tree (AST), Control Flow Graph (CFG), Data Flow Graph (DFG), and Code Property Graph (CPG), which are often fused into Composite Joint Graphs (CJGs) to provide rich input embeddings (Shao & Ding,

2024). Without such structured representations, LLMs which designed primarily for natural language, struggle to fully capture the context-sensitive and flow-sensitive aspects of source code behavior. LLMs fundamentally operate by learning distributional patterns in text, which leverage mechanisms such as cosine similarity and attention-based pattern matching to find analogies between vulnerable and non-vulnerable code sequences (Sheng et al., 2025). However, since the nature of the source code is not merely sequential text but includes semantic relations such as control and data dependencies, IR-guided prompt construction becomes essential for effective vulnerability pattern detection (Shereen et al., 2024).

Despite being inherently text-based, large language models (LLMs) have recently demonstrated exceptional capabilities in cybersecurity knowledge reasoning tasks, as evidenced by their performance on the *CyberMetric* benchmark (Tihanyi, Ferrag, Jain, Bisztray, & Debbah, 2024). This research paper demonstrates that the LLM models outperforming human security experts in both small-scale, 80-item multiple-choice tests and large-scale (up to 10,000-option, benchmark evaluations. This suggests a significant leap in the reasoning capabilities of LLMs, even in specialized domains such as cybersecurity. This growing evidence raises the hypothesis that, although LLMs lack architectural design for vulnerability detection and are not trained specifically on structured code analysis, their extensive knowledge priors could allow them to recognize security flaws using carefully crafted prompts, even in the absence of intermediate representations such as AST or CFG. Such emergent behavior may provide partial effectiveness in detecting vulnerabilities directly from raw source code. In fact, the rapid advancement of knowledge in large language models (LLMs) has raised the question of whether these models may have achieved capabilities beyond what was previously expected, specifically, the potential to identify software vulnerabilities without requiring technical details of the source code structure. Therefore, in this research study, we aim to investigate the extent to which LLMs can effectively detect vulnerabilities in source code without prior knowledge of the technical architecture of the program source code.

Accordingly, this research study aims to address the following two key questions:

- RQ1: To what extent can structure-agnostic large language models (i.e., models without access to intermediate representations) accurately detect software vulnerabilities from source code alone?
- RQ2: Among existing LLMs, which model demonstrates the highest detection performance in this context?

BACKGROUND

Large Language Models (LLMs) are classified into three primary categorizations: decoder-only, encoder-only, and encoder-decoder architectures (Brown et al., 2020). Decoder-only models, such as GPT (Generative Pre-trained Transformer), operate in an autoregressive manner by predicting the next token in a sequence based on previous context (Radford et al., 2019). LLaMA, an optimized autoregressive transformer model by Meta AI, significantly improved computational efficiency for large-scale language modeling (Touvron et al., 2023). Mistral, another decoder-only model, introduces grouped-query attention and sliding window mechanisms for faster context processing (Mistral AI, 2023). These decoder-only models are widely leveraged in natural language generation tasks, but have shown surprising emergent capabilities in domains such as code reasoning (Brown et al., 2020).

Encoder-only models, which utilize the models such as LSTM and GRU, have also been effectively employed for sequence classification tasks by analyzing linguistic patterns and temporal features in user-generated content (Sheikhi et al., 2024). Encoder-only models, such as BERT (Bidirectional Encoder Representations from Transformers), focus on understanding the full input sequence bidirectionally (Devlin et al., 2018). RoBERTa builds upon BERT by using dynamic masking and larger batch sizes to improve language understanding performance (Liu et al., 2019). These encoder-only models excel in tasks involving classification, named entity recognition, and semantic similarity (Devlin et al., 2018). Encoder-decoder models such as T5 (Text-to-Text Transfer Transformer) convert all tasks into a text-to-text format, making them highly versatile (Raffel et al., 2020). BART, which combines BERT's encoder with GPT-based decoding, is effective in sequence-to-sequence tasks such as summarization and translation (Lewis et al., 2020). BLOOM is a multilingual encoder-decoder designed for broad-scale text generation and understanding in multiple languages (BigScience Workshop, 2022).

Recently, LLMs have gained significant traction in vulnerability detection research, where they are applied to identify flaws in raw source code. For example, Guo et al. (2024) evaluated six open-source LLMs for vulnerability detection and highlighted their varying capabilities in code samples (Guo et al., 2024). Lu et al. (2024) proposed GRACE, a framework that integrates graph structures and in-context learning to improve LLM-based vulnerability detection (Lu et al., 2024). Akuthota et al. (2023) demonstrated that LLMs are capable of detecting vulnerabilities in real-world projects with significant accuracy (Akuthota et al., 2023). Yin et al. (2024) conducted a multitask evaluation comparing LLMs with state-of-the-art models in software security contexts (Yin et al., 2024). Tóth et al. (2024) assessed LLM-generated PHP code and uncovered its vulnerabilities and limitations in a web development scenario (Tóth et al., 2024).

Du et al. (2024) introduced Vul-RAG, a retrieval-augmented generation technique that improves detection via knowledge-level inference (Du et al., 2024). Liu et al. (2024) analyzed how code-specific prompts influence LLM vulnerability detection performance, which demonstrate the impact of context placement (Liu et al., 2024). Wang et al. (2023) presented DefectHunter, a hybrid model combining LLMs with conformer-based mechanisms to boost vulnerability detection precision (Wang et al., 2023). Li et al. (2024) explored LLM-assisted static analysis and found that these models significantly improve vulnerability coverage over traditional approaches (Li et al., 2024). Another work by Li et al. (2024) demonstrated that attention-based prompting enables LLMs to precisely locate vulnerable lines of code (Li et al., 2024). These research studies demonstrate the emerging capability of LLMs to serve as the practical tools in vulnerability detection area. Despite not being originally designed for software security, LLMs show promise in generalizing security-relevant patterns when guided with structured or contextual prompts. Thus, the role of LLMs in vulnerability detection continues to expand, especially as hybrid approaches integrate them with code graphs and retrieval systems for enhanced performance.

Recent research by Li et al. (2024) introduced a vulnerability localization strategy that directly leverages LLMs and context-aware prompt construction to guide the model's attention toward vulnerable lines in source code, without relying on structured representations such as AST or CFG (Li et al., 2024). Their approach involves crafting prompts that encourage the LLM to semantically analyze all code lines, based on the assumption that non-vulnerable code minimally affects the model's ability to detect vulnerabilities (Li et al., 2024). Despite leveraging advanced techniques such as chain-of-thought prompting, the authors observed that LLMs still struggle with reasoning over long code sequences, indicating a performance ceiling for prompt-only approaches in lengthy contexts (Li et al., 2024). Unlike their study, which focuses on localizing vulnerabilities, our research investigates whether LLMs can detect the presence of vulnerabilities end-to-end through prompt engineering, even when deprived of all structural inputs such as AST, CFG, or other intermediate representations of program source code.

METHODOLOGY

The proposed architecture in this research study introduces a two-phase architecture designed for structure-independent software vulnerability detection using Large Language Models (LLMs). The full pipeline, as shown in Figure 1, encompasses six main components: raw data input, data preprocessing, dataset unification, prompt engineering (prompt set), LLM-based evaluation, and report generation. The architecture avoids any intermediate representations of code such as Abstract

Syntax Trees (AST), Control Flow Graphs (CFG), or Data Flow Graphs (DFG), and instead focuses solely on textual and contextual reasoning to assess the emergent capabilities of LLMs in detecting software vulnerabilities.

Figure 1. Proposed architecture for prompt-based vulnerability detection using LLMs

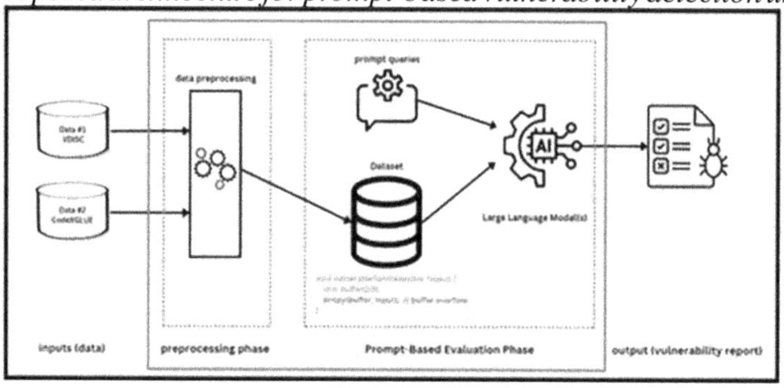

The input to the architecture consists of two widely adopted and well-known datasets in the software vulnerability research community: VDISC and CodeXGLUE. These datasets include thousands of C and C++ source code functions extracted from real-world software repositories. VDISC is curated from the National Vulnerability Database and classifies functions based on Common Weakness Enumeration (CWE) categories, such as CWE-119 (Buffer Errors), CWE-120 (Classic Buffer Overflow), CWE-469 (Incorrect Pointer Scaling), and CWE-476 (NULL Pointer Dereference) (Zhou et al., 2019). On the other hand, the CodeXGLUE Vulnerability Detection dataset includes labeled function samples, each explicitly tagged as either "vulnerable" or "non-vulnerable" (Lu et al., 2021).

The data preprocessing phase is responsible for resolving the structural and semantic inconsistencies between the two datasets. Since CodeXGLUE already provides binary labels, it is directly ingestible. However, VDISC lacks direct binary classification and instead uses vulnerability categories. To resolve this, we re-map all functions labeled with any CWE class in VDISC to a general "vulnerable" tag, while all remaining functions are treated as "non-vulnerable." During this phase, we also clean, tokenize, and normalize the source code, removing unnecessary whitespaces and standardizing code structure to ensure syntactic compatibility. Each instance is then structured into a uniform schema including: function ID, function signature, function body (C/C++ code), and a final label (vulnerable / non-vulnerable). All records are consolidated into a single unified dataset, enabling consistent downstream evaluation.

Once the dataset has been structured, the next critical phase is Prompt-Based Evaluation, which centers around leveraging prompt engineering to guide LLMs in the task of vulnerability detection. To facilitate this, a Prompt set is constructed, which is an organized set of engineered queries tailored to instruct LLMs as if they are expert software security auditors. Each prompt is manually or semi-automatically designed to encode a contextual understanding of vulnerability patterns, alerting the model to behave similar to a cybersecurity analyst who must decide whether the given function is flawed.

In each query, the input provided to the LLM comprises two distinct components: a vulnerability detection prompt and a singular code function. For instance, a representative prompt might be structured as follows:

"Evaluate the subsequent C++ function to determine the presence of a buffer overflow vulnerability. The buffer overflow pattern is demonstrated in **Figure 2**."

Figure 2. Demonstration of the buffer overflow pattern.

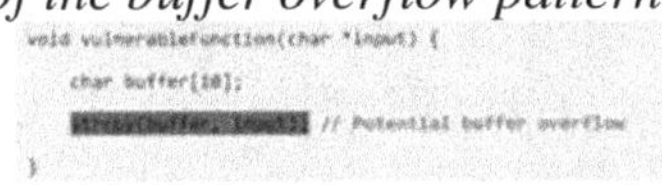

The accompanying function is presented as raw source code. This pairing mimic the real-world activity of a developer or auditor submitting a piece of code to an intelligent system for static analysis.

We evaluate multiple LLM models using this setup, including state-of-the-art decoder-based models capable of few-shot learning and contextual understanding. These models do not receive any additional training or fine-tuning on the dataset; instead, they perform inference-only vulnerability prediction based on the prompt and function input. This is crucial to our research goal of understanding whether LLMs possess inherent reasoning abilities sufficient to detect security flaws without requiring access to structural code graphs or architectural analysis.

The LLM processes each prompt-function pair and outputs a prediction: "vulnerable" or "not vulnerable". These outputs are compared with the ground-truth labels stored in the dataset to compute detection metrics. The final output of the system is a structured vulnerability report, summarizing the model's classification results per all functions. These reports contain key elements such as function ID, predicted label, ground truth label, and binary correctness (match/mismatch). They allow for further statistical evaluation, such as precision, recall, F1-score, and accuracy, to assess the LLM's overall performance. This architectural pipeline simulates a real-world, low-resource vulnerability detection environment, where no structured code representation is available, and models must operate solely based on prompt guidance and code semantics. Such a setup is valuable in assessing the emergent reasoning capacity of LLMs and aligns with recent works investigating few-shot security reasoning via prompting. The system is also modular and extensible as new datasets can be integrated into the preprocessing phase, and different LLMs can be swapped in the evaluation phase. This methodology provides a practical framework for evaluating the potential of LLMs to act as intelligent code auditors in resource-constrained settings.

EVALUATION RESULTS

Setup

To evaluate the feasibility of prompt-based vulnerability detection in the absence of structural code representations, we implemented a two-phase experimental framework and deployed it on a standalone computing environment without GPU acceleration. The experiments were conducted on a Dell Latitude 7400 laptop equipped with a 64-bit Intel Core i7 processor (1.91 GHz, 4 cores), 32 GB of physical RAM (with approximately 20.8 GB available during execution), and Microsoft Windows 11 Pro (Build 26100). Additionally, the system's virtual memory was extended up to 34.6 GB to ensure stable performance during large-scale preprocessing and concurrent API-based interactions with large language models (LLMs). These specifications provided a sufficiently robust environment to process over one million source code functions and perform real-time model querying without encountering significant latency or memory limitations.

The first phase of the framework involved data preprocessing, which was carried out using a custom Python script (dataGenerator.py). This phase unified two widely used vulnerability datasets: VDISC and CodeXGLUE. The VDISC dataset includes functions labeled according to specific Common Weakness Enumeration (CWE) categories (e.g., CWE-119, CWE-476), while CodeXGLUE provides binary vulnerability labels. To achieve format consistency across both datasets, we re-labeled all VDISC samples containing any CWE identifier as "vulnerable," while all other samples were marked "non-vulnerable." After cleaning, tokenizing, and standardizing the function signatures and bodies, we generated 11 structured JSON files containing a total of 1,041,325 unique functions, of which 75,922 were labeled as vulnerable and 965,403 as non-vulnerable.

In the second phase, we evaluated the performance of six state-of-the-art LLMs using prompt-based binary classification. The selected models were: GPT-4o (OpenAI, 2024), Falcon-180B-Chat (Technology Innovation Institute, 2024), GEMINI-pro 1.0 (Google Research, 2024), Mistral-7B-Instruct-v0.2 (Mistral AI, 2024), GPT-3.5 (OpenAI, 2023), and Llama-3-8B (Nvidia, 2024). These models were chosen based on their architectural diversity, public accessibility via API, and prominence in code understanding tasks. Each model was queried through its respective API endpoint using a standardized prompt structure, and no additional fine-tuning or training was performed. This approach ensured consistency in evaluation across models and allowed us to isolate the models' native reasoning capabilities in a structure-agnostic context.

The core of the evaluation was driven by a custom Python script (dataEvaluator.py), which automated the process of sending structured prompts to each model along with raw C/C++ function samples. Each prompt included two illustrative examples one secure and one vulnerable—to simulate expert reasoning and provide context for the model, followed by a new function to be classified. The models were instructed to return a binary label indicating the presence (1) or absence (0) of a vulnerability. To improve reliability, the script incorporated a retry mechanism (up to five attempts per sample) to manage malformed or incomplete API responses, as well as real-time progress monitoring and result logging via the tqdm library. Final outputs included per-function predictions, accuracy scores, and error logs for further analysis.

All prompt templates and evaluation scripts used in this study are publicly available in our GitHub repository (Pakshad, 2025): https://github.com/ppakshad/TextualPromptsLLM-s-. This open-source implementation enables reproducibility and supports future research in prompt-based software vulnerability detection using large language models.

Analysis and Findings

The initial evaluation provided valuable insights into the reasoning potential of LLMs in analyzing raw source code. From the preprocessed dataset, approximately 520,000 functions, representing 50% of the total 1,041,325 functions across 11 JSON files, were selected for evaluation. Due to time and computational constraints associated with querying each LLM model's API separately, combined with the average per-query latency, evaluating the entire dataset was infeasible within a reasonable timeframe. Therefore, we focused on evaluating a representative 50% subset, which still constitutes a substantial volume for performance benchmarking. From the selected subset, a specific batch of 10 functions was sampled and analyzed to illustrate the zero-shot prediction behavior of each model in detail.

The OpenAI GPT-4 model successfully generated predictions for all functions, with 4 out of 10 predictions accurately matching the ground truth labels, resulting in an accuracy rate of 43%. Similarly, Falcon-180B-Chat achieved an accuracy of 42% under the same conditions, while GEMINI-pro 1.0 and Mistral-7B-Instruct-v0.2 recorded accuracy rates of 40% and 38%, respectively. In contrast, GPT-3.5 exhibited a slightly lower accuracy of 37%, and Llama-3-8B demonstrated the lowest accuracy at 27%, which indicate the varying effectiveness of each model in analyzing raw code without the use of structural representations such as AST, CFG, or DFG.

Table 1. Performance comparison of LLMs in vulnerability detection using raw source code, emphasizing the accuracy of proprietary and open-source models under similar conditions.

Model	**Company**	**License**	**Accuracy (%)**
GPT-4o	OPENAI	Proprietary	**~43**
Falcon-180B-Chat	TII	Apache 2.0	~42
GEMINI-pro 1.0	Google	Proprietary	~40
Mistral-7B-Instruct-v0.2	Mistral AI	Apache 2.0	~38
GPT-3.5	OPENAI	Proprietary	~37
Llama-3-8B	Nvidia	Open	~27

Table 1 presents an overview of the performance of each LLM in vulnerability detection using raw source code without intermediate representations. The analysis below provides a structured, model-wise breakdown of the findings, which emphasize accuracy, strengths, and limitations under similar testing conditions.

GPT-4o, developed by OpenAI, achieved the highest accuracy among the evaluated models, recording a correct prediction rate of 43%. This performance was observed under zero-shot inference settings, where the model analyzed 10 sampled functions from a subset of 520,000 functions in the dataset. The model demonstrated strong reasoning capabilities in identifying vulnerable code segments, successfully processing all prompt queries with stable API interaction. However, despite its relatively high accuracy, the model occasionally misclassified complex system functions and domain-specific operations, underscoring its limitations in handling intricate logic flows without structural aids. Moreover, the model exhibited prompt sensitivity, as it performed notably well on buffer overflow patterns but struggled with memory management and pointer dereferencing vulnerabilities, suggesting potential overfitting to certain vulnerability types.

Falcon-180B-Chat, an open-source model by TII with 180 billion parameters, closely matched GPT-4o's accuracy at 42%. Despite its advanced architecture and extensive training dataset, the model's performance remained slightly lower, indicating that parameter size alone may not suffice to compensate for the absence of structural code representations. Falcon-180B-Chat performed well in identifying high-level functions but demonstrated weaknesses in processing nested loops, pointer manipulation, and complex conditional statements, limiting its overall accuracy. GEMINI-pro 1.0, a proprietary model by Google, recorded a moderate accuracy of 40%. The model effectively detected known vulnerability patterns in common coding constructs but underperformed in identifying nuanced vulnerabilities associated with memory management and error handling. Its reliance on textual analysis without leveraging structural graphs constrained its effectiveness in scenarios where logical flow and data dependencies were critical for accurate detection. Mistral-7B-Instruct-v0.2, an open-source model with 7 billion parameters by Mistral AI, secured an accuracy rate of 38%. Despite its smaller size, the model effectively recognized basic security patterns and buffer overflow scenarios, particularly in C and C++ functions. However, its performance declined when faced with advanced constructs such as multi-threading and recursive functions. The Apache 2.0 license offers customization potential, enabling further optimization for domain-specific vulnerability classes. GPT-3.5, a precursor to GPT-4o, exhibited a slightly lower accuracy of 37%. The model struggled to detect subtle vulnerabilities, particularly in functions with complex branching and nested logic. While it managed to identify straightforward patterns, its limited contextual understanding and lack of structural analysis restricted its ability to detect deeper code dependencies. This highlights the impact of architectural advancements in newer models like GPT-4o, which offer enhanced reasoning capabilities in raw code analysis. Llama-3-8B, the smallest model in the dataset with 8 billion parameters and developed by Nvidia, recorded the lowest accuracy at 27%. The model's open-source nature and relatively compact size may have contributed to its limited contextual analysis capabilities. It particularly struggled with functions involving low-level memory manipulation, pointer dereferencing, and security-critical logic flows. Despite these limitations, Llama-3-8B presents a lightweight alternative for rapid assessments, albeit with reduced accuracy in complex code scenarios.

Addressing Research Question 1 (RQ1), the results suggest that structure-agnostic LLMs can detect vulnerabilities to some extent using syntactic cues and contextual information derived solely from raw source code. The best accuracy observed was 43% for GPT-4o, indicating that while LLMs exhibit emergent reasoning capacity, their overall performance remains limited due to the absence of intermediate representations such as AST, CFG, and DFG. The findings suggest that while LLMs can leverage prior knowledge and textual patterns to identify common vulnerability signals, their efficacy is constrained by a lack of structural analysis and deeper semantic understanding.

For Research Question 2 (RQ2), GPT-4o demonstrated the highest detection performance in this context, outperforming other models in the evaluation. Its 43% accuracy indicates that while prompt-driven analysis is promising, significant gaps remain in vulnerability detection without structural hints. This reinforces the need for integrating lightweight structural hints or hybrid approaches to bridge the gap between human-level reasoning and LLM-based analysis.

In conclusion, while the current research results are not production-grade, they indicate the potential of prompt-driven LLMs as foundational tools in static code analysis, capable of identifying vulnerability patterns through syntactic and contextual cues. However, the limited accuracy observed across the evaluated models suggests that relying solely on raw text analysis without structural representations is insufficient for comprehensive vulnerability detection. Future work will explore the expansion of prompt sets, multi-turn reasoning, and the incorporation of lightweight structural hints such as AST or CFG to bridge the gap between human-level understanding and LLM-based classification accuracy. Additionally, hybrid approaches integrating retrieval-augmented generation (RAG) and few-shot learning may further enhance detection capabilities in complex code structures.

LIMITATIONS

While the findings of this research study provide valuable perspective into the capabilities of large language models (LLMs) in detecting software vulnerabilities through prompt-based analysis, several limitations should be acknowledged. First, the scope of evaluated vulnerability types was restricted to six classes, primarily derived from CWE categories represented in the VDISC and CodeXGLUE datasets based on the Owasp Top 10 Standards. Moreover, only four prompt patterns were provided to the models, each corresponding to a generic example of a vulnerability or its secure counterpart. These prompts represented vulnerabilities of moderate complexity, such as buffer overflow, and did not include more sophisticated or context-dependent attack patterns such as race conditions, logic bombs, or memory allocation flaws. As a result, the evaluated models were not tested against the full diversity of real-world software vulnerabilities, and the results should be interpreted within this constrained context.

Second, the prompt-based evaluation inherently relies on the representativeness and clarity of the crafted examples. Given that LLMs operate as probabilistic predictors and are sensitive to prompt phrasing, the limited diversity of prompt structures in this study may have constrained the models' ability to generalize beyond the patterns explicitly encoded in the examples. Additionally, while six LLMs were evaluated using identical prompts and datasets, the analysis was conducted in a zero-shot setting without fine-tuning or model adaptation. This limits the extent to which we can infer each model's true potential in vulnerability detection when provided with broader context or training. Finally, the evaluation was limited to C and C++ source code functions, excluding other programming languages such as Python, Java, or Rust, which may exhibit different vulnerability characteristics. Future work should address these limitations by expanding the range of vulnerability classes, incorporating diverse prompt styles, enabling few-shot or fine-tuned learning, and evaluating across multiple programming languages and real-world software projects.

CONCLUSION

This research study aimed to answer two key research questions to assess the effectiveness of large language models (LLMs) in detecting software vulnerabilities using prompt-based approaches without relying on intermediate code representations such as Abstract Syntax Trees (AST), Control Flow Graphs (CFG), or Data Flow Graphs (DFG).

The first research question investigated the extent to which structure-agnostic LLMs can accurately identify software vulnerabilities from raw source code. The findings show that while models like GPT-4o and Falcon-180B-Chat demonstrated some capability in recognizing vulnerability patterns, their accuracy remained limited due to the absence of structural analysis. The highest accuracy achieved was 43 percent, indicating that relying solely on textual cues is not sufficient for comprehensive vulnerability detection, especially in cases involving complex logic structures and memory management operations.

The second research question focused on identifying the LLM with the highest detection performance under the given conditions. GPT-4o achieved the best accuracy at 43 percent, followed by Falcon-180B-Chat at 42 percent. Despite their relatively better performance, both models struggled with detecting nuanced vulnerabilities such as multi-threading issues, pointer dereferencing, and nested loops, revealing the constraints of prompt-only approaches.

The findings illustrate the potential of prompt-driven LLMs in static code analysis, showing that these models can identify some vulnerability patterns through syntactic and contextual analysis. However, the results emphasize the need to incorporate minimal structural cues or hybrid techniques, such as retrieval-augmented generation (RAG) and few-shot learning, to bridge the gap between human-level vulnerability detection and LLM-based analysis. Future research will focus on expanding prompt sets, refining multi-turn reasoning, and integrating lightweight structural hints to enhance detection capabilities in complex code structures.

REFERENCES

CrowdStrike. (2024). *CrowdStrike 2024 Global Threat Report | CrowdStrike*. Crowdstrike.com. https://www.crowdstrike.com/en-us/global-threat-report/

Gavou, T. P., Iliya, J., Ihuoma, E. C., & Gusen, J. N. (2024). *Cyber security enhancement in Nigeria: A case study of six states in the North Central (Middle Belt) of Nigeria. American Journal of Humanities and Social*

Ghaffarian, S. M., & Shahriari, H. R. (2017). Software Vulnerability Analysis and Discovery Using Machine-Learning and Data-Mining Techniques. *ACM Computing Surveys, 50*(4), 1–36. DOI: 10.1145/3092566

Hughes, C., & Turner, T. (2023). *Software transparency: Supply chain security in an era of a software-driven society*. Wiley.

IBM. (2024). *Cost of a Data Breach 2024*. IBM; IBM. https://www.ibm.com/reports/data-breach

Yalli, J. (n.d.). *A comprehensive review of security challenges and countermeasures in IoT architectural systems. SSRN*. https://doi.org/DOI: 10.2139/ssrn.4752445

2025. *Global Incident Response Report*. (2025). Palo Alto Networks. https://www.paloaltonetworks.com/resources/research/2025-incident-response-report

Akuthota, V., Kasula, R., & Sumona, S. T. (2023). *Vulnerability detection and monitoring using LLM*. IEEE. https://ieeexplore.ieee.org/abstract/document/10456393/

BigScience Workshop. (2022). *BLOOM: A 176B-Parameter Open-Access Multilingual Language Model*. https://huggingface.co/bigscience/bloom

Brown, T., et al. (2020). *Language models are few-shot learners*. NeurIPS.

Devlin, J., Chang, M. W., Lee, K., & Toutanova, K. (2018). *BERT: Pre-training of deep bidirectional transformers for language understanding*. arXiv:1810.04805.

Du, X., Zheng, G., Wang, K., Feng, J., Deng, W., & Liu, M. (2024). *Vul-RAG: Enhancing LLM-based vulnerability detection via knowledge-level RAG*. https://arxiv.org/abs/2406.11147

Sheikhi, F., Fakher, L., & Chekani, D. (2024, February). Depression Detection on e-Risk 2017 using Long Short-term Memory Models. In 2024 20th CSI International Symposium on Artificial Intelligence and Signal Processing (AISP) (pp. 1-6). IEEE.

Google Research. (2024). GEMINI-pro 1.0: Leveraging Large Language Models for Code Analysis. Google. https://gemini.google.com/

Guo, Y., Patsakis, C., Hu, Q., Tang, Q., & Casino, F. (2024). *Outside the comfort zone: Analysing LLM capabilities in software vulnerability detection*. https://link.springer.com/chapter/10.1007/978-3-031-70879-4_14

Khare, A., Dutta, S., Li, Z., Solko-Breslin, A., & Alur, R. (2023). *Understanding the effectiveness of large language models in detecting security vulnerabilities*. arXiv. https://arxiv.org/abs/2311.16169

Lewis, M.. (2020). *BART: Denoising sequence-to-sequence pre-training for natural language generation*. ACL.

Li, Y.. (2024). *Attention is all you need for LLM-based code vulnerability localization*. https://arxiv.org/abs/2410.15288

Li, Y., Li, X., Wu, H., Zhang, Y., Cheng, X., & Zhong, S. (2024). *Attention is all you need for LLM-based code vulnerability localization*. arXiv. https://arxiv.org/abs/2410.15288

Li, Z., Dutta, S., & Naik, M. (2024). *LLM-assisted static analysis for detecting security vulnerabilities*. https://arxiv.org/abs/2405.17238

Liu, Y.. (2019). *RoBERTa: A robustly optimized BERT pretraining approach*. arXiv:1907.11692

Liu, Z., Yang, Z., & Liao, Q. (2024). *Exploration on prompting LLM with code-specific information for vulnerability detection*. https://ieeexplore.ieee.org/abstract/document/10664399/

Lu, G., Ju, X., Chen, X., Pei, W., & Cai, Z. (2024). *GRACE: Empowering LLM-based software vulnerability detection with graph structure and in-context learning*. https://www.sciencedirect.com/science/article/pii/S0164121224000748

Lu, S., Liu, D., Wang, D., & Xu, L. (2021). CodeXGLUE: A Machine Learning Benchmark Dataset for Code Understanding and Generation. *arXiv preprint arXiv:2102.04664*. https://arxiv.org/abs/2102.04664

Mao, Q., Li, Z., Hu, X., Liu, K., Xia, X., & Sun, J. (2024). *Towards effectively detecting and explaining vulnerabilities using large language models*. arXiv. https://arxiv.org/html/2406.09701v2

Mistral, A. I. (2023). *Mistral 7B Model Card*. https://mistral.ai

Nvidia. (2024). Llama-3: Enhanced Code Analysis Capabilities in Compact Models. Nvidia. https://build.nvidia.com/nvidia/llama-3_1-nemotron-70b-instruct

Open, A. I. (2023). GPT-3.5: Bridging the Gap Between GPT-3 and GPT-4. OpenAI. https://platform.openai.com/docs/models/gpt-3-5

Open, A. I. (2024). GPT-4 Technical Report. OpenAI. https://www.openai.com/research/gpt-4

Pakshad, P. (2025). *TextualPromptsLLM-s-* [Source code]. GitHub. https://github.com/ppakshad/TextualPromptsLLM-s-

Ponemon Institute. (2025). Costs and Consequences of Gaps in Vulnerability Response: A global report. ServiceNow. https://www.servicenow.com/lpayr/ponemon-vulnerability-survey.html

Raffel, C.. (2020). *Exploring the limits of transfer learning with a unified text-to-text transformer*. JMLR.

Shao, M., & Ding, Y. (2024). *FVD-DPM: Fine-grained Vulnerability Detection via Conditional Diffusion Probabilistic Models*. USENIX Security Symposium. https://www.usenix.org/conference/usenixsecurity24/presentation/shao

Sheng, Z., Chen, Z., Gu, S., Huang, H., & Gu, G. (2025). *Large Language Models in Software Security: A Survey of Vulnerability Detection Techniques and Insights*. arXiv. https://arxiv.org/abs/2502.07049

Shereen, E., Ristea, D., Vyas, S., & McFadden, S. (2024). *SoK: On Closing the Applicability Gap in Automated Vulnerability Detection*. arXiv. https://arxiv.org/abs/2412.11194

Technology Innovation Institute. (2024). Falcon-180B: Advanced Large Language Models for Open-Source Applications. TII. https://falconllm.tii.ae/falcon-models.html

Tihanyi, N., Ferrag, M. A., Jain, R., Bisztray, T., & Debbah, M. (2024, September). *CyberMetric: A benchmark dataset based on retrieval-augmented generation for evaluating LLMs in cybersecurity knowledge*. In *2024 IEEE International Conference on Cyber Security and Resilience (CSR)* (pp. 296–302). IEEE. DOI: 10.1109/CSR61664.2024.10679494

Tóth, R., Bisztray, T., & Erdődi, L. (2024). *LLMs in web development: Evaluating LLM-generated PHP code*. https://link.springer.com/chapter/10.1007/978-3-031-68738-9_34

Touvron, H.. (2023). *LLaMA: Open and efficient foundation language models*. Meta AI.

Wang, J., Huang, Z., Liu, H., Yang, N., & Xiao, Y. (2023). *DefectHunter: A novel LLM-driven boosted-conformer-based code vulnerability detection mechanism.* https://arxiv.org/abs/2309.15324

Yin, X., Ni, C., & Wang, S. (2024). *Multitask-based evaluation of open-source LLM on software vulnerability*. https://ieeexplore.ieee.org/abstract/document/10706805/

Zhou, Y., Liu, S., Siow, J., Du, X., & Liu, Y. (2019). Devign: Effective vulnerability identification by learning comprehensive program semantics via graph neural networks. *Proceedings of the 2019 ACM SIGSAC Conference on Computer and Communications Security*, 877–892. DOI: 10.1145/3319535.3354211

Chapter 6
Legal Implications of Contract Expiry in Modern Commercial Law:
Towards a Framework for Post-Expiry Obligations and Risk Management

Dilshad Ahmad Mhia-alddin
https://orcid.org/0009-0005-4046-1607
University of Mosul, Iraq

ABSTRACT

In an increasingly complex commercial landscape, the legal implications arising from the expiry of contracts demand critical attention. While contract formation and enforcement have been thoroughly examined in commercial law, post-expiry obligations and the associated risk exposures remain underexplored. This paper investigates the residual responsibilities and liabilities that may persist or emerge following contract termination due to expiry. Drawing on comparative legal analysis, case law, and regulatory frameworks across multiple jurisdictions, this study identifies legal ambiguities and practical challenges that can lead to disputes or financial loss. The research further develops a structured framework aimed at clarifying post-expiry duties and enhancing risk management strategies for both parties. By bridging the gap between legal theory and commercial practice, the proposed framework provides actionable guidance for legal practitioners, businesses, and policymakers to mitigate risks and ensure compliance beyond contract expiration.

DOI: 10.4018/979-8-3373-4862-9.ch006

Copyright © 2025, IGI Global Scientific Publishing. Copying or distributing in print or electronic forms without written permission of IGI Global Scientific Publishing is prohibited.

1. INTRODUCTION

Contracts serve as the foundation of modern commercial transactions, governing relationships, responsibilities, and the allocation of risk between parties. Traditionally, the emphasis of legal analysis has been placed on contract formation, performance, and breach. However, the expiration of a contract—though often perceived as a straightforward conclusion—can generate significant legal and commercial consequences. As markets evolve and complex supply chains, digital agreements, and long-term service arrangements become more common, the precise moment of contract expiry no longer represents a clear-cut end to legal obligations (Mhia-Alddin & Hussein, 2025a; Sullivan, 2015).

Contract expiry has critical implications for both parties involved, particularly when agreements contain post-expiry clauses such as confidentiality, non-compete provisions, intellectual property restrictions, or transition obligations. In many industries, including pharmaceuticals and housing, expiry clauses can significantly affect downstream business decisions and regulatory compliance (Colangelo, 2017; Pomeroy, 2017; Holmen-Jensen & Åsmoen, 2024). Furthermore, digital transformation and AI-powered contract management systems are increasingly involved in enforcing or triggering obligations automatically post-expiry (Mhia-Alddin & Hussein, 2025b), emphasizing the growing complexity of managing these events.

Despite its importance, the legal scholarship and jurisprudence on contract expiry have often overlooked the enduring or residual legal consequences that may persist or arise after termination. Post-expiry disputes can emerge over intellectual property rights, data protection, environmental liabilities, and regulatory obligations—especially in sectors governed by overlapping legal regimes (Goyal, 2017; Drexl, Conde, & Kim, 2025). Additionally, the intersection of public interest and private agreements in sectors like public housing and healthcare further complicates the post-expiry landscape (Cooper, 2018; Read, Botha, & Jamaloodien, 2023).

The commercial sector's evolving risk profile requires a more nuanced approach to expiry-related liabilities. Risk factors such as contractual ambiguity, conflicting jurisdictional regulations, and inconsistent enforcement mechanisms can lead to reputational damage, financial loss, or prolonged litigation (Bharwani & Mathews, 2012; Munton et al., 2021). In cross-border transactions, the uncertainty is further exacerbated by international trade treaties and domestic statutory interpretations (Amani, 2007; Shoraka, 2006).

This study aims to fill the theoretical and practical gaps in current commercial contract law by examining the legal implications and residual obligations arising from contract expiry. Specifically, it seeks to:

1. Analyze the legal doctrines and case law surrounding post-expiry obligations.

2. Evaluate industry practices and regulatory approaches in managing expiry-related risks.
3. Develop a structured legal and operational framework that stakeholders can use to anticipate, manage, and mitigate post-expiry obligations.

By doing so, this research contributes to the modernization of commercial legal practices and aligns with emerging technologies in contract management, such as AI-powered compliance systems (Mhia-Alddin & Hussein, 2025a). It is particularly relevant for corporate legal advisors, regulators, and businesses operating in complex, high-risk environments like pharmaceuticals, intellectual property, and public-private partnerships (Espenlaub et al., 2013; Narayana, Pati, & Padhi, 2019; Samsuri et al., 2017).

2. LITERATURE REVIEW

Contract termination and expiry are critical phases in the contract lifecycle, yet they remain under-theorized in legal and commercial scholarship. This section reviews existing literature on the subject, presents comparative insights between common law and civil law traditions, and identifies persistent gaps in legal and academic discourse.

2.1 Existing Scholarship on Contract Termination and Expiry

A growing body of literature explores contract expiration and termination, particularly in domains such as social housing, intellectual property, and pharmaceutical regulation. For example, Cooper (2018) and Pomeroy (2017) address how contract expiry has significant implications for long-term social housing agreements in the absence of ongoing government subsidies. Similarly, Cooper and Zell (2023) highlight governance challenges in non-profit housing following the expiration of funding contracts.

In the context of technology and pharmaceuticals, Mhia-Alddin and Hussein (2025a, 2025b) emphasize the role of artificial intelligence and machine learning in monitoring contract expiry and compliance, particularly within Science, Technology, and Medicine (STM) research and cybersecurity. They propose the application of deep learning tools to preemptively manage risks and obligations linked to contract lifecycles.

Contract expiry is also pivotal in the pharmaceutical sector, particularly in the transition from exclusivity to generic competition. Works such as Holmen-Jensen and Åsmoen (2024), Schnichels and Sule (2010), Manganelli (2019), and Colangelo

(2017) examine how patent expiration influences pricing, market access, and legal disputes, often triggering complex litigation or regulatory interventions. Narayana et al. (2019) additionally explore reverse logistics post-expiry in the Indian pharmaceutical industry.

On a broader level, Bharwani and Mathews (2012) illustrate how contractual risk—including that related to termination—is managed in the hospitality sector. Similarly, Read et al. (2023) explore the challenges of contract management in public health procurement during the COVID-19 pandemic.

2.2 Comparative Insights: Common Law vs. Civil Law Traditions

The distinction between common law and civil law systems plays a fundamental role in how contract termination and expiry are interpreted and enforced. Hodge (2017) examines the common law development of contract doctrines in the UK, highlighting the judiciary's incremental role in defining contract finality. In contrast, Bousri (2019) presents a comparative analysis of arbitration frameworks in Comoros and Uganda, reflecting differing legal traditions and institutional mechanisms in civil law systems.

Scholars such as McBratney (2004) and Shoraka (2006) note that international economic law—particularly WTO jurisprudence—struggles to harmonize these traditions, especially when addressing disputes rooted in contract expiry and market regulation. The World Trade Organization's dispute resolution framework often requires reconciling these jurisprudential divides (Osei-Tutu, 2001).

In the area of patent law, Lim (2013), Siew-Kuan (2012), and Pai (2018) explore how differing legal traditions shape remedies after patent expiry. While common law jurisdictions focus on equitable relief and economic balancing, civil law systems tend toward codified norms that provide predictable but sometimes rigid outcomes.

Table 1 presents a comparison of how common law and civil law systems address key post-expiry issues in contract law.

Table 1. Comparative approaches to post-expiry contract law

Legal Issue	Common Law Approach	Civil Law Approach
Implied Duties	Based on precedent/custom	Codified or limited
Surviving Clauses	Explicit clauses + judicial interpretation	Mostly codified, limited scope
Enforcement Mechanism	Contractual + equitable relief	Statutory enforcement
Dispute Resolution	Courts and arbitration	Administrative and judicial

2.3 Gaps in Current Academic and Legal Discourse

Despite growing interest, significant gaps persist in understanding the systemic implications of contract expiry across jurisdictions and sectors. First, much of the existing literature tends to be siloed within sectoral studies—such as housing (Sullivan, 2015; Munton et al., 2021), health (Swirnoff & Becker, 2010), or intellectual property (Goyal, 2017; Drexl et al., 2025)—without offering a cohesive, cross-disciplinary framework for analyzing expiry risks and legal responses.

Second, the impact of reverse payments, settlements, and exclusivity extensions post-expiry is underexplored, particularly in light of antitrust concerns (Woodcock, 2019; Espenlaub et al., 2013). There is also insufficient research on the socio-legal consequences of contract termination in development contexts, as noted by Borta et al. (2024) in their survey on drug control agreements in Ethiopia.

Moreover, the integration of artificial intelligence and large language models into contract lifecycle management introduces novel legal questions. As Mhia-Alddin and Hussein (2025a, 2025b) assert, the lack of regulatory clarity surrounding automated expiry alerts, predictive compliance, and algorithmic interpretation poses risks for legal liability and ethical compliance.

Finally, while works such as Amani (2007) and Goyal (2017) deal with overlapping rights and obligations in patent and intellectual property expiry, they highlight the difficulty of reconciling public interest with contractual enforcement mechanisms in a globalized economy.

3. THEORETICAL AND LEGAL FRAMEWORK

A robust understanding of contract termination and expiry necessitates an exploration of the foundational legal theories and principles that underpin contractual obligations and the legal consequences following the cessation of contractual relationships. This section elaborates on central contract law principles, post-expiry obligations, and pertinent legal doctrines that guide judicial reasoning in disputes related to contract expiry.

3.1 Contract Law Principles

The cornerstone of contractual theory lies in two fundamental principles: freedom of contract and pacta sunt servanda. The principle of freedom of contract embodies the autonomy of parties to create legally binding agreements on terms of their choosing, reflecting the liberal notion that individuals are best placed to determine their interests. This principle is particularly pronounced in common law jurisdictions, which traditionally resist judicial interference in private bargains unless public policy or unconscionability is at stake (Hodge, 2017).

On the other hand, pacta sunt servanda, the Latin maxim meaning "agreements must be kept", reflects the binding nature of contracts. Rooted in both civil and common law traditions, it asserts the legal and moral imperative for parties to honor their contractual commitments. This doctrine provides certainty and predictability in commercial relationships, anchoring the enforceability of agreements unless voided by factors such as duress or illegality (Schnichels & Sule, 2010; Pai, 2018).

3.2 Post-Expiry Obligations

While contracts may reach their natural end or be terminated prematurely, certain obligations can persist beyond expiry. Confidentiality clauses, for instance, are routinely drafted to survive termination, preserving the integrity of proprietary information even after contractual relations have ceased (Mhia-Alddin & Hussein, 2025a). Similarly, non-compete clauses—often embedded in employment or licensing agreements—continue to bind parties post-expiry, subject to reasonableness tests under competition and employment laws (Colangelo, 2017; Siew-Kuan, 2012). These post-expiry obligations aim to balance business protection with the individual's right to trade and work freely.

Recent developments in AI-powered contract management systems have highlighted the importance of automatic tracking and enforcement of post-expiry duties, especially in complex multi-jurisdictional settings (Mhia-Alddin & Hussein, 2025b). In sectors such as pharmaceuticals and intellectual property, such obligations are especially critical to safeguarding trade secrets and regulatory compliance (Narayana et al., 2019; Holmen-Jensen & Åsmoen, 2024).

To illustrate the complexity and interconnectivity of obligations that persist beyond contract expiry, Figure 1 presents a conceptual map showing various types of post-expiry responsibilities and their legal foundations.

Figure 1. Conceptual map of post-expiry obligations

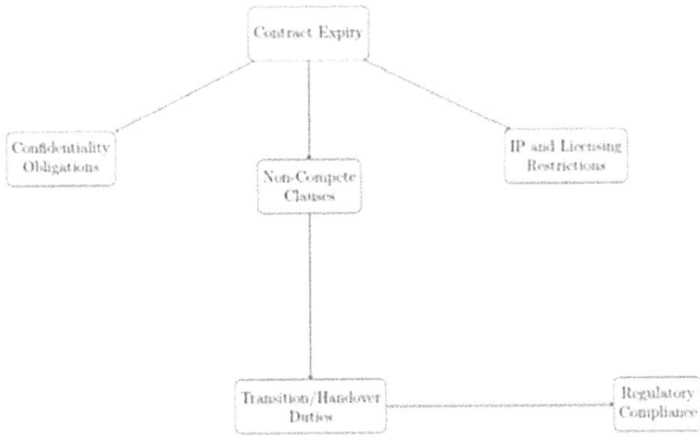

3.3 Legal Doctrines

Three central legal doctrines—implied terms, unjust enrichment, and restitution—further inform the judicial response to disputes arising from contract termination or expiry.

- Implied terms allow courts to read obligations into a contract where necessary to give effect to the parties' intentions or to ensure commercial efficacy. For instance, a duty of good faith or continued support post-termination may be implied in long-term relational contracts (Samsuri et al., 2017).
- Unjust enrichment operates where one party retains a benefit unfairly following the end of a contractual relationship. Courts may order restitution if enrichment occurred without legal justification, even in the absence of a formal contract (Sullivan, 2015; Lim, 2013).
- Restitution ensures a party is restored to their pre-contractual position where performance has occurred but no valid contract exists, or a contract has failed. This doctrine is especially relevant in cases where expiry or invalid termination disrupts the expected allocation of rights and obligations (Swirnoff & Becker, 2010; Munton et al., 2021).

These doctrines reflect an ongoing evolution in legal systems to adapt to modern contractual complexities, including those introduced by global trade, digital contracting, and artificial intelligence (Drexl et al., 2025; Read et al., 2023).

4. METHODOLOGY

This research adopts a qualitative legal research approach, employing doctrinal and comparative legal methodologies to analyze the legal principles, frameworks, and judicial reasoning related to contract termination and expiry. The study focuses on synthesizing authoritative legal texts, judicial decisions, statutory instruments, and academic commentary to understand the doctrinal foundations and practical implications of contract expiry across various jurisdictions.

4.1 Qualitative Legal Research

The primary methodology involves doctrinal legal research, which entails a systematic analysis of legal rules, principles, and case law. This method emphasizes legal reasoning, statutory interpretation, and the evaluation of normative frameworks that govern contractual relationships. Doctrinal research is particularly suitable for exploring how contract expiry is conceptualized and operationalized within different legal systems, especially in light of evolving commercial and technological dynamics. Academic literature, legal commentaries, and policy documents are critically reviewed to identify key theoretical debates, legal doctrines, and interpretive trends that inform judicial and legislative developments.

4.2 Comparative Analysis

A comparative legal analysis is conducted to examine how different jurisdictions approach contract expiry and termination. The study compares legal traditions and practices in common law jurisdictions (such as the United Kingdom, United States, and Australia) with those in civil law jurisdictions, particularly within the European Union and selected non-Western systems. This comparison highlights both convergence and divergence in legal standards, the enforcement of post-expiry obligations, and the interpretation of key principles such as pacta sunt servanda, good faith, and unjust enrichment.

The comparative dimension also allows for an evaluation of how legal systems adapt to new contractual realities, including digital contracting, cross-border obligations, and post-contractual liabilities. The inclusion of emerging jurisdictions—such as Ethiopia (Borta et al., 2024), Comoros, and Uganda (Bousri, 2019)—provides insights into legal pluralism and institutional capacity in managing contract law in transitional economies.

4.3 Case Law Analysis and Statutory Interpretation

The research engages in case law analysis by critically examining landmark judicial decisions that interpret and apply rules concerning contract termination, expiry, and associated legal consequences. Decisions from apex courts and tribunals are assessed to understand evolving judicial attitudes, the role of precedent, and the interpretive techniques employed in different legal cultures (Hodge, 2017; Munton et al., 2021).

In parallel, statutory interpretation is utilized to dissect the language, structure, and legislative intent behind key contractual statutes and regulations. This includes the analysis of national contract law codes, competition regulations, and sector-specific legislation, particularly in areas such as intellectual property, pharmaceuticals, and housing (Colangelo, 2017; Cooper & Zell, 2023). Special attention is given to interpreting clauses that survive contract expiry—such as confidentiality, non-compete, and indemnity provisions—under different legal frameworks.

By triangulating doctrinal research, comparative analysis, and case-based inquiry, this methodology offers a nuanced understanding of the theoretical, normative, and practical dimensions of contract expiry. It enables the identification of legal trends, gaps in existing frameworks, and possible reform pathways, grounded in a global and interdisciplinary legal context.

5. ANALYSIS AND DISCUSSION

This section examines the complex legal terrain surrounding contract expiry, focusing on key doctrinal tensions, interpretive challenges, and practical risks. It draws from statutory frameworks, judicial reasoning, and real-world case studies to uncover how courts and legal systems navigate the legal vacuum that often follows the conclusion of contractual obligations.

5.1 Key Legal Issues: Automatic Renewal, Implied Duties, and Dispute Risks

One of the central legal issues is the automatic renewal of contracts, which can arise either explicitly through renewal clauses or implicitly through conduct. While some contracts include clear terms for extension, others depend on ambiguous or tacit understandings. Jurisdictions such as the UK and Australia generally uphold automatic renewal provisions if they are expressly stated, but disputes often emerge when such clauses are loosely worded or poorly understood by parties (Hodge, 2017; Munton et al., 2021).

Implied duties—such as those relating to confidentiality, good faith, or continued cooperation—pose additional complications. Although contracts may formally expire, obligations like non-disclosure or non-compete may persist based on the intent of the parties or prevailing commercial standards (Schnichels & Sule, 2010; Mhia-Alddin & Hussein, 2025). Courts in common law jurisdictions have sometimes recognized implied terms based on necessity or customary business practice, but these inferences can lead to unpredictable outcomes and increased litigation.

The expiry of a contract can also trigger significant dispute risks, particularly where the delineation of post-contractual responsibilities is vague. Parties may disagree on whether obligations have truly ended, whether informal communications constitute renewal, or whether restitution or compensation is due under doctrines like unjust enrichment or restitution (Swirnoff & Becker, 2010; Lim, 2013). These uncertainties are exacerbated in high-value sectors such as technology licensing, pharmaceuticals, and housing.

Figure 2 outlines a typical flow of legal risks and uncertainties that emerge once a contract expires, particularly when expiry clauses are vague or absent.

Figure 2. Legal risks following contract expiry

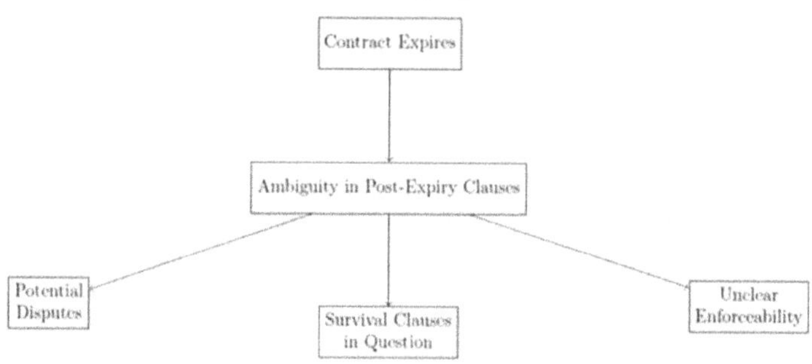

5.2 Case Studies Showing Post-Expiry Litigation or Ambiguity

Real-world examples reveal how ambiguity following contract expiry often leads to litigation or regulatory scrutiny. For instance, in the pharmaceutical industry, cases concerning reverse payment settlements and exclusivity post-patent expiry have sparked judicial intervention in both EU and US jurisdictions (Colangelo, 2017;

Manganelli, 2019). These disputes frequently arise from contracts lacking clear post-expiry clauses, resulting in protracted litigation over market access and pricing.

In the realm of social and affordable housing, contracts between governments and non-profit providers often include layered obligations that outlive the primary funding term. Cooper (2018) and Cooper & Zell (2023) document tensions arising from uncertain expiry procedures and the lack of clear terms about asset control and continued tenant services, highlighting risks not only to institutions but also to vulnerable populations.

Similarly, the COVID-19 vaccine procurement contracts in South Africa, as analyzed by Read, Botha, and Jamaloodien (2023), illustrate how lack of transparency and weak contract management practices after expiry led to administrative inefficiencies and public distrust.

In the energy and natural resources sector, Samsuri et al. (2017) demonstrate how poor handling of operatorship transfer clauses in production sharing contracts created legal friction when expiry conditions were triggered without adequate preparation or mutual understanding.

These examples affirm that litigation frequently follows the expiry of complex contracts, especially where the parties fail to address post-expiry issues during the drafting phase.

5.3 Risks for Businesses and Individuals

The legal and commercial risks of contract expiry are substantial. For businesses, a failure to anticipate post-expiry obligations may lead to financial losses, reputational harm, and regulatory penalties. Ambiguities around renewal or continued service obligations can disrupt supply chains, licensing agreements, or employment relationships, especially in industries such as hospitality (Bharwani & Mathews, 2012), pharmaceuticals (Narayana et al., 2019), and intellectual property (Goyal, 2017; Pai, 2018).

For individuals, especially in employment and tenancy contexts, the expiry of contracts can lead to vulnerability. Cases such as those analyzed by Pomeroy (2017) and Munton et al. (2021) illustrate how the absence of legislative safeguards following contract expiration can result in eviction, job loss, or denial of severance and benefits.

These risks are further amplified in jurisdictions lacking consistent enforcement mechanisms or where legal literacy is low, as noted by Bousri (2019) and Borta et al. (2024). In such settings, both private and public parties may be unaware of their rights or obligations, increasing the likelihood of conflict and legal exposure.

6. PROPOSED LEGAL AND POLICY FRAMEWORK

Given the legal uncertainty and operational risks surrounding contract expiry, it is imperative to develop a clearer and more consistent legal and policy framework. This section offers practical drafting guidelines, policy reform suggestions, and a risk management checklist designed to aid legislators, legal practitioners, and contracting parties in mitigating post-expiry disputes and promoting contractual certainty.

6.1 Guidelines for Drafting Clearer Expiry Clauses

One of the most effective ways to minimize post-expiry ambiguity is through precise and anticipatory drafting. The following best practices should be considered when formulating contract expiry clauses:

1. **Explicit Expiry Date**: Clearly state the contract's expiration date and the conditions under which it will lapse or terminate.
2. **Renewal Procedures**: Outline whether renewal is automatic, conditional, or manual. Specify the required notice period and form of consent for any renewal.
3. **Post-Expiry Obligations**: Detail which obligations (e.g., confidentiality, non-compete, data protection, IP usage) will survive the contract's expiry and for how long.
4. **Dispute Resolution Mechanism**: Incorporate a clause identifying the preferred method of dispute resolution (mediation, arbitration, litigation) to apply post-expiry.
5. **Transition or Exit Plan**: Include provisions for handover, data return, and knowledge transfer where continuity is critical—especially in public-private partnerships or IT services.
6. **Force Majeure and Termination Clauses**: Ensure such clauses include references to the contract's natural expiry and address potential impacts.

Clarity in these areas reduces interpretive burdens on courts and gives parties more confidence in planning the full life cycle of contractual relationships.

6.2 Legislative or Policy Suggestions for Reform

In addition to improved drafting, broader legal reform is needed to harmonize how post-expiry obligations are recognized and enforced. Suggested reforms include:

- **Model Contract Clauses**: Governments and legal bodies should promote standardized expiry templates and model clauses for sectors such as housing, health, and infrastructure.
- **Statutory Implied Terms**: Legislatures may consider codifying key post-expiry obligations (e.g., confidentiality, data protection) to reduce reliance on judicial discretion.
- **Disclosure and Review Mandates**: Regulatory frameworks could mandate periodic review and public disclosure of key contract terms—especially in publicly funded agreements—to ensure expiry risks are identified early.
- **Default Restitution Principles**: Introduce default legal rules for restitution in cases where one party continues performance after contract expiry without formal renewal.
- **Public Procurement Reform**: Update procurement laws to require government contracts to include explicit post-expiry risk assessments and enforcement mechanisms.

Examples from jurisdictions such as Australia and the UK have shown the benefits of such reforms, particularly in the public-private partnership (PPP) domain (Cooper, 2018; Munton et al., 2021).

To clarify proposed legal and policy reforms addressing post-expiry ambiguity, Figure 3 provides a thematic breakdown of recommendations by stakeholder type.

Figure 3. Policy reform recommendations by stakeholder

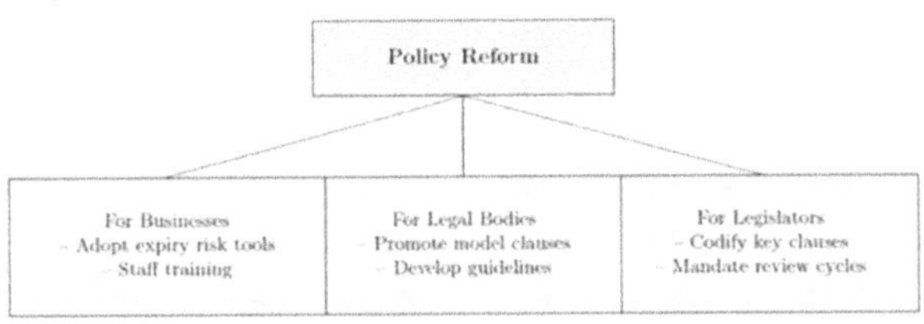

6.3 Checklist for Managing Post-Expiry Risks

To operationalize the legal and policy suggestions above, the following checklist is recommended for both legal drafters and contract managers:

6.3.1 Pre-Contract Stage

- Identify post-expiry obligations based on industry norms and statutory duties.

- Evaluate the legal enforceability of key survival clauses across relevant jurisdictions.
- Consult with stakeholders to define end-of-contract expectations.

6.3.2 Contract Drafting Stage

- Include clear expiry, renewal, and termination provisions.
- Define all continuing obligations and their duration post-expiry.
- Set up monitoring and review processes for the contract's lifespan.

6.3.3 Contract Execution and Management

- Maintain documentation of key communications about contract renewal or expiry.
- Trigger review protocols at least 6 months before expiry.
- Develop and test exit strategies or service continuity plans.

6.3.4 Post-Expiry Stage

- Conduct a formal expiry debrief and document residual obligations.
- Audit for compliance with post-expiry terms (e.g., data deletion, return of property).
- Resolve any outstanding issues through predetermined dispute mechanisms.

This checklist should be tailored to the sector, jurisdiction, and complexity of the contractual arrangement, but it serves as a critical tool for minimizing risk and maintaining legal integrity after expiry.

Figure 4 provides a visual checklist outlining the key actions parties should undertake across the four stages of a contract to minimize post-expiry risk.

Figure 4. Four-stage checklist for post-expiry risk management

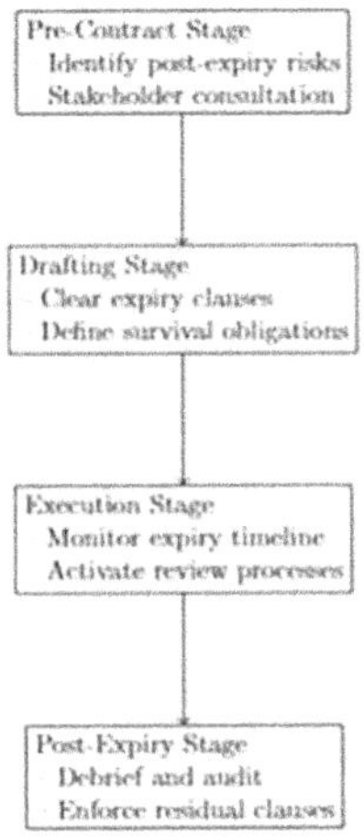

7. CONCLUSION

Contract expiry represents a pivotal yet often underappreciated phase in the lifecycle of legal agreements. As demonstrated throughout this study, the legal complexities that arise at and beyond the point of expiry can result in significant uncertainty, especially when contractual terms are vague, outdated, or silent on post-expiry conduct. This paper has highlighted how both common law and civil law jurisdictions struggle with inconsistencies in handling post-expiry obligations, particularly when issues such as implied duties, automatic renewals, and restitution claims arise.

The analysis revealed that parties frequently overlook or inadequately address the legal consequences that may persist beyond the formal termination of a contract. Obligations such as confidentiality, non-compete clauses, and ongoing liability can survive expiry either by express agreement or legal implication. Furthermore, the risks posed by unjust enrichment, unauthorized continuance of services, or the absence of clear renewal mechanisms present tangible challenges for both individuals and businesses. These challenges are compounded by a lack of harmonized legal standards and varying judicial interpretations across jurisdictions like the UK, US, EU, and Australia.

To address these concerns, this paper proposed a structured legal and policy framework aimed at promoting greater clarity and contractual integrity. Key recommendations included best practices for drafting clearer expiry and survival clauses, legislative reforms to codify essential post-expiry terms, and practical checklists to aid in contract management. If implemented, these measures could significantly reduce litigation risk and improve predictability in commercial and governmental contracting.

Ultimately, managing contract expiry is not just a legal technicality—it is a vital part of strategic planning and risk management. A well-governed expiry process not only safeguards parties' rights but also preserves commercial relationships, protects sensitive information, and fosters trust in legal systems. Therefore, legal practitioners, policymakers, and contracting entities must treat contract expiry with the same rigor and foresight as the formation and performance stages of the agreement.

REFERENCES

Amani, B. (2007). *Merchants missionaries: Patenting life, competing international obligations and the proselytization of a Realistic Utopia.*

Bharwani, S., & Mathews, D. (2012). Risk identification and analysis in the hospitality industry: Practitioners' perspectives from India. *Worldwide Hospitality and Tourism Themes*, *4*(5), 410–427. DOI: 10.1108/17554211211277851

Borta, H. G., Alemu, A., Shute, T., Zewdie, B., Fantaw, D., Shimelis, B., ... & Tamiru, M. T. (2024). Narcotic Drugs and Psychotropic Substances Control System in Ethiopia: A National Survey.

Bousri, M. M. S. (2019). *A comparative analysis of legal and institutional framework for arbitration: Comoros and Uganda* (Doctoral dissertation, School of law).

Colangelo, M. (2017). Reverse payment patent settlements in the pharmaceutical sector under EU and US competition laws: a comparative analysis. *World competition, 40*(3).

Cooper, S., & Zell, S. (2023). *Staying on Board: Non-profit housing provider board capacity in a changing context.* Institute of Urban Studies, The University of Winnipeg.

Cooper, S. E. (2018). *The End of an Era? Social Housing and Social Property in a Post-subsidy World* (Doctoral dissertation, University of Illinois Chicago).

Drexl, J., Conde, B., & Kim, D. (2025). Position Statement of the Max Planck Institute for Innovation and Competition of 25 April 2025 in the framework of the revision of the Technology Transfer Block Exemption Regulation and the accompanying Guidelines. *Max Planck Institute for Innovation & Competition Research Paper*, (25-10).

Espenlaub, S., Goergen, M., Khurshed, A., & Remenar, M. (2013). Do directors trade after IPO lockup expiry? In *Handbook of Research on IPOs* (pp. 275–294). Edward Elgar Publishing. DOI: 10.4337/9781781955376.00024

Goyal, K. (2017). *Overlapping of Intellectual Property Rights: An analysis with reference to conflict vis-à-vis Design, Trademark, Copyright and Patent.* College of Legal Studies, UPES Dehradun.

Hodge, P. S. (2017). Judicial development of the law of contract in the United Kingdom. *Geo. Wash. L. Rev., 85*, 1587.

Holmen-Jensen, P. R., & Åsmoen, O. (2024). Navigating the Patent Cliff.

Lim, D. (2013). Patent misuse and antitrust: Rebirth or false dawn. *Michigan Telecommunications and Technology Law Review*, *20*, 299.

Manganelli, A. G. (2019). Reverse payments and risk of bankruptcy under private information. *International Journal of the Economics of Business*, *26*(3), 411–429. DOI: 10.1080/13571516.2019.1613146

McBratney, A. (2004). Post-WTO China: Competition and Technology Transfer Laws in the 'New' Socialist Market Economy. *Asia Pacific Law Review*, *12*(1), 1–30. DOI: 10.1080/18758444.2004.11788126

Mhia-Alddin, D. A., & Hussein, A. M. (2025). AI-Powered Contract Security: Managing Expiry, Compliance, and Risk Mitigation Through Deep Learning and LLMs. In *Revolutionizing Cybersecurity With Deep Learning and Large Language Models* (pp. 37-64). IGI Global Scientific Publishing.

Mhia-Alddin, D. A., & Hussein, A. M. (2025). Contract Expiry in AI-Driven STM Research: Legal Challenges, Risks, and Regulatory Considerations. In *Ensuring Secure and Ethical STM Research in the AI Era* (pp. 77-110). IGI Global Scientific Publishing.

Munton, J., Stewart, A., McCrystal, S., Hardy, T., & Orifici, A. (2021). Submission to the Senate Education and Employment Legislation Committee Inquiry in the Fair Work Amendment (Supporting Australia's Jobs and Economic Recovery) Bill 2020.

Munton, J., Stewart, A., McCrystal, S., Hardy, T., & Orifici, A. (2021). The (Omni) bus that Broke Down: Changes to Casual Employment and the Remnants of the Coalition's Industrial Relations Agenda. *Australian Journal of Labour Law*.

Narayana, S. A., Pati, R. K., & Padhi, S. S. (2019). Market dynamics and reverse logistics for sustainability in the Indian Pharmaceuticals industry. *Journal of Cleaner Production*, *208*, 968–987. DOI: 10.1016/j.jclepro.2018.10.171

Osei-Tutu, J. J. (2001). Trips and domestic control: implications for developing countries.

Pai, Y. (2018). Patent Injunction Heuristics in India. *Pai, Yogesh, Patent Injunction Heuristics in India in Rafal Sikorski (Ed.) Patent Law Injunctions, Kluwer Law International BV (2019).*

Pomeroy, S. (2017). *Discussion paper: Envisioning a modernized social and affordable housing sector in Canada*. Carleton University Centre for Urban Research and Education.

Read, A., Botha, R., & Jamaloodien, K. (2023). COVID-19 vaccination procurement and contract management in a South African context. *Journal of Strategic Contracting and Negotiation*, *7*(1-2), 33–43. DOI: 10.1177/20555636231198053

Samsuri, A., Zakaria, Z., Manaf, K. H., & Ismail, I. (2017). Key enablers in a production sharing contract operatorship transfer exercise. *Journal of Advanced Review on Scientific Research, 36*(1), 1–13.

Schnichels, D., & Sule, S. (2010). The pharmaceutical sector inquiry and its impact on competition law enforcement. *Journal of European competition law & practice, 1*(2), 93-111.

Shoraka, S. (2006). *World trade dispute resolution and developing countries: Taking a development approach to fair adjudication in the context of WTO law*. London School of Economics and Political Science.

Siew-Kuan, E. (2012). Evolving landscape of patent remedies in a changing marketplace. *Singapore Academy of Law Journal, 24*, 634-668.

Sullivan, C. (2015). Interim dilapidations. *Journal of Building Survey. Appraisal & Valuation, 3*(4), 323–334. DOI: 10.69554/UTKA7017

Swirnoff, A. H., & Becker, D. M. (2010). Judicial developments in the US Hatch-Waxman infringement safe harbor. *Expert Opinion on Therapeutic Patents, 20*(4), 451–458. DOI: 10.1517/13543771003604737 PMID: 20302449

Woodcock, R. (2019). Using Price Regulation Instead of Competition to Reduce Prices after Patents Expire. *Available atSSRN* 3466473. DOI: 10.2139/ssrn.3466473

Chapter 7
Case Studies of Misuse and Mitigation in AI-Driven STM Research

Angel Justo Jones
https://orcid.org/0009-0007-9740-6611
University of Virginia, USA

Bianca Montes Jones
https://orcid.org/0009-0007-5175-5867
Capitol Technology University, USA

ABSTRACT

Integrating Artificial Intelligence (AI) in Science, Technology, and Medicine (STM) research has led to groundbreaking advancements. However, it has also introduced significant security, ethics, and potential misuse challenges. This chapter explores several case studies in which AI-driven approaches in STM research have been misapplied, resulting in ethical violations, security breaches, or unintended consequences. Additionally, it examines strategies for addressing these issues, focusing on regulatory frameworks, ethical guidelines, and technological safeguards. This chapter analyzes real-world examples and highlights the importance of maintaining secure and ethical practices in AI-enhanced STM research. It offers insights into the evolving landscape of AI within this field.

DOI: 10.4018/979-8-3373-4862-9.ch007

Copyright © 2025, IGI Global Scientific Publishing. Copying or distributing in print or electronic forms without written permission of IGI Global Scientific Publishing is prohibited.

1. INTRODUCTION

Artificial Intelligence (AI) is revolutionizing industries and academic domains worldwide, significantly transforming various sectors, including finance, healthcare, cybersecurity, education, and many more. As AI advances, its applications grow more diverse and sophisticated, driving innovation, enhancing productivity, and reshaping how businesses and societies operate. In particular, the ethical considerations surrounding AI technologies have become a critical area of focus, especially considering their rapid integration into everyday operations. These considerations extend across multiple dimensions, including fairness, transparency, privacy, and accountability, necessitating ongoing discussions about the responsible use of AI.

The introduction of generative AI models has further amplified the need for ethical frameworks, as these systems can create realistic data, such as text, images, or even videos, often making it difficult to distinguish between genuine and fabricated content. The proliferation of generative AI in finance, cybersecurity, and education is causing a paradigm shift in how organizations approach technology, governance, and compliance. The evolving landscape of generative AI presents immense opportunities and significant challenges, making understanding the complex interplay between technological advancement and ethical considerations essential.

This chapter will explore the ethical implications of AI, focusing particularly on generative AI, and how these technologies can be effectively integrated while addressing societal concerns. We will draw on a diverse body of literature to examine AI's ethical challenges and opportunities, specifically focusing on its application in finance, cybersecurity, and other critical sectors. As part of this exploration, we will engage with recent studies and perspectives to assess how AI can be harnessed for the greater good while minimizing potential harms.

Recent works have highlighted the importance of ethical AI governance, particularly in sectors like finance, where AI-driven decision-making is increasingly shaping policy and business strategies. For instance, Ali and Aysan (2024) provide a comprehensive exploration of the future of generative AI in finance, using machine learning to analyze academic and grey literature to predict trends in the sector. Their work underscores the potential for AI to revolutionize financial services, pointing to the pressing ethical issues that need to be addressed to ensure fairness and equity in these systems. Similarly, in their follow-up study, Ali, Zafar, and Aysan (2024) delve deeper into the multi-level machine learning analysis of AI's impact on the financial sector, shedding light on both the benefits and challenges associated with the integration of these advanced systems into financial decision-making processes.

Beyond finance, the ethical dimensions of AI are also critically relevant in cybersecurity, where AI systems are being used to enhance security measures but also raise concerns about privacy and potential misuse. Al-Sinani and Mitchell (2024) explore the role of AI-enhanced ethical hacking, focusing on using AI in the context of Linux-based systems, a critical area in cybersecurity. Their work highlights the potential of AI to improve security protocols while raising questions about the ethical implications of AI-driven hacking techniques. Al-Sinani et al. (2025) continue this exploration, proposing experimental studies that advance the use of AI in ethical hacking, focusing on enhancing the security of Linux-based environments.

AI's impact is also felt in other sectors, such as agriculture, defense, and border protection, where AI-driven systems are being leveraged for monitoring and decision-making. Arya and Rastogi (2024) explore the use of AI in aerial monitoring systems across various domains, emphasizing AI's critical role in enhancing operational efficiency and ensuring security. Similarly, the ethical considerations surrounding AI in warfare, as discussed by Batabyal (2024), bring attention to the legal and moral questions surrounding AI-driven military technologies.

As AI becomes increasingly integrated into societal frameworks, the need for comprehensive policies and regulations to govern its use has never been more urgent. The introduction of the European Union's AI Act, discussed by Butt (2024), marks a significant step toward regulating AI systems and ensuring their ethical deployment. This legal framework seeks to balance innovation with safety, transparency, and accountability, offering insights into how other regions might approach AI governance.

In the context of scientific research, AI is transforming the way data is analyzed and interpreted. Luan et al. (2024) demonstrate how AI can support scientometric analysis, improving how scholarly literature is explored and understood. Similarly, Filetti et al. (2024) discuss how AI tools can assist researchers in designing and writing scholarly articles, providing new opportunities for efficient academic publishing.

Ethical considerations in AI are not limited to technical concerns but also societal and human factors, particularly regarding privacy, security, and fairness. Shukla and Taneja (2024) examine the ethical issues surrounding AI in education, highlighting the challenges of integrating generative AI into educational systems while safeguarding data privacy and ensuring equitable access to learning opportunities.

Finally, as AI continues to evolve, there is an increasing need for frameworks to mitigate the potential misuse of AI technologies. Trotsyuk et al. (2024) propose a risk mitigation framework for the misuse of AI in biomedical research, emphasizing the need for robust safeguards to prevent harmful applications of AI technologies.

In summary, the ethical dimensions of AI are complex and multifaceted, requiring a nuanced understanding of these advanced systems' technological and societal implications. This chapter will further explore these themes, drawing on a wide range of studies to present a comprehensive overview of the ethical challenges and opportunities in the evolving landscape of AI.

2. FRAMEWORK FOR EVALUATING MISUSE IN AI RESEARCH

The rapid evolution of artificial intelligence (AI) across various domains has brought about immense opportunities and significant challenges. A critical concern that has surfaced is the potential for misuse of AI technologies, particularly in cybersecurity, ethics, privacy, and governance. The need for a robust framework to evaluate and mitigate the misuse of AI has never been more pressing. This section outlines a comprehensive framework for assessing the misuse of AI in research, focusing on identifying, preventing, and mitigating unethical practices and harmful applications. The framework incorporates theoretical perspectives and practical strategies, drawing on insights from various disciplines, including machine learning, ethics, and system design.

2.1. Understanding AI Misuse: Conceptual Overview

AI misuse can be broadly categorized into several types, including malicious use, unethical applications, and unintended harmful consequences. Misuse in AI research can manifest through practices such as exploiting AI for surveillance, discrimination, biased decision-making, and violation of privacy. AI-driven systems, such as deep learning models and generative AI, while powerful tools, can be repurposed for harmful uses. The misuse of AI in research not only jeopardizes the integrity of academic work but also threatens public trust in AI systems (Ali & Aysan, 2024). To address this challenge, a clear understanding of misuse types is essential.

2.2. Defining Ethical Boundaries in AI Research

One of the key pillars of an AI misuse framework is the definition and enforcement of ethical boundaries. Ethical considerations should guide AI research and deployment to ensure that technologies align with societal values and legal frameworks. For instance, AI applications in sensitive areas like healthcare, defense, and finance require robust ethical oversight to prevent harm. Researchers must engage with AI's ethical implications, considering accountability, transparency, fairness, and privacy (Ali, Zafar, & Aysan, 2024). The inclusion of ethical AI guidelines, as demonstrated by organizations like the EU AI Act (Butt, 2024), serves as a vital starting point for curbing misuse in AI research.

2.3. AI in Security and Privacy: Risk Assessment and Control

Assessing its impact on security and privacy is a critical aspect of evaluating AI misuse. AI technologies, particularly generative models, pose risks to personal data, intellectual property, and national security. The framework should include a risk assessment protocol to identify vulnerabilities associated with AI technologies. For instance, in the case of AI-enhanced ethical hacking, security researchers may unintentionally create new vulnerabilities or misuse AI tools for illegal activities (Al-Sinani & Mitchell, 2024). A comprehensive risk control strategy would involve preventative measures like encryption and anonymization, and responsive measures like breach detection and mitigation (Trotsyuk et al., 2024).

2.4. Framework for Evaluating Ethical AI in Multidisciplinary Contexts

AI research spans multiple domains, each with unique ethical challenges. Therefore, a multidisciplinary approach to evaluating AI misuse is essential. For example, using AI for high-frequency trading or market manipulation in finance presents significant ethical dilemmas (Ali & Aysan, 2025). Similarly, in the defense sector, the integration of AI in warfare raises concerns about accountability and the potential for autonomous weapons systems to act outside of human control (Batabyal, 2024). The framework should adopt a cross-domain analysis, considering the ethical implications of AI in various contexts and ensuring the development of domain-specific guidelines for ethical AI use.

2.5. Data Governance: Preventing Misuse through Responsible Data Management

Data misuse is a significant risk in AI research, as improper data collection, processing, or sharing can lead to harmful consequences. A robust framework for evaluating AI misuse must include strategies for responsible data governance. This includes ensuring data privacy, integrity, and adherence to data protection regulations, such as GDPR. Additionally, it is important to examine the impact of AI on vulnerable populations, ensuring that AI systems are not biased or discriminatory (Shukla & Taneja, 2024). Researchers must adopt best practices in data management to prevent misuse, including the responsible use of data sets, rigorous data validation, and transparency in data sourcing.

2.6. AI for Social Good: Harnessing Positive Potential While Mitigating Misuse

While AI misuse poses significant challenges, AI has great potential for societal benefit. Frameworks must focus on mitigating negative impacts and promoting AI's use for social good. For instance, AI applications in agriculture, healthcare, and disaster management can potentially improve lives on a large scale (Arya & Rastogi, 2024). A balanced framework would highlight how AI can be directed toward addressing pressing global challenges, such as climate change, poverty, and public health, while implementing safeguards to minimize the risk of misuse (Pimpalkar et al., 2024).

2.7. Regulatory and Legal Frameworks for AI Misuse

Regulation plays a crucial role in preventing the misuse of AI in research. Legal frameworks such as the EU AI Act (Butt, 2024) and national AI policies aim to ensure AI systems are developed and deployed responsibly. These regulatory mechanisms should be integrated into the misuse evaluation framework, providing clear guidelines for compliance. Additionally, the framework must include mechanisms for continuous monitoring and enforcement of regulations, with penalties for violations and incentives for ethical AI research practices (Eisenberg, 2024).

2.8. Ethical AI Training and Awareness

A practical framework for evaluating AI misuse also requires education and training programs aimed at raising awareness about AI ethics among researchers, developers, and policymakers. Ensuring that AI professionals understand the ethical implications of their work and are equipped with the skills to identify and address misuse is key to reducing risks. AI education should include technical skills and ethical training, focusing on how AI can be applied responsibly in various domains (Luan et al., 2024). Training programs should also encourage collaboration between AI researchers and ethicists to foster a deeper understanding of AI's societal impact.

2.9. Case Studies: Learning from Real-World Examples

Evaluating AI misuse can be further enhanced by learning from real-world case studies. The framework should incorporate lessons from AI research projects and deployments that have encountered misuse or ethical challenges. For instance, AI-based drones in smart cities may pose security risks if misused for surveillance or attacks (Maguluri et al., 2023). By studying such cases, researchers can identify common patterns of misuse and develop more effective strategies to prevent these occurrences in future AI research.

2.10. Continuous Improvement and Feedback Loops

The final element of the AI misuse evaluation framework is the integration of continuous feedback mechanisms. As AI technologies evolve, so must the frameworks used to assess and prevent misuse. Regular audits, updates to ethical guidelines, and engagement with stakeholders, including the public and regulatory bodies, are necessary to keep the framework relevant and practical. Continuous improvement ensures that AI research meets societal needs and ethical standards (Shafik, 2024).

2.11 Summary

Developing a comprehensive framework for evaluating the misuse of AI in research is essential for ensuring the responsible development and deployment of AI technologies. This framework should encompass various dimensions, including ethical boundaries, risk assessment, data governance, regulation, education, and real-world case studies. By applying these principles, AI researchers can mitigate the risks associated with misuse while harnessing the transformative potential of AI for societal good. The continued evolution of AI technologies necessitates ongoing dialogue and cooperation among researchers, policymakers, and ethical bodies to ensure that AI remains a positive force in shaping the future.

The following flowchart illustrates the comprehensive framework outlined in this section to provide a clear overview of the steps involved in evaluating AI misuse in research.

Figure 1. Flowchart of framework for evaluating AI misuse

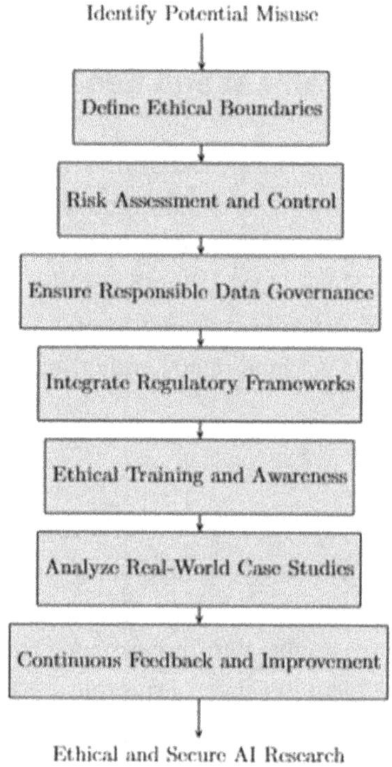

3. CASE STUDY 1: BIASED ALGORITHMS IN MEDICAL DIAGNOSTICS

The application of Artificial Intelligence (AI) in medical diagnostics has revolutionized healthcare, promising enhanced accuracy, speed, and efficiency in diagnosing various diseases. However, despite its potential, integrating AI systems in healthcare raises ethical concerns, particularly regarding bias in algorithmic decision-making. This case study examines the issue of biased algorithms in medical diagnostics, exploring its impact on patient care, the causes of bias, and potential solutions.

3.1 The Role of AI in Medical Diagnostics

AI systems have been employed in healthcare for tasks such as image analysis, diagnosis of diseases, and predictive analytics. AI-powered tools, such as deep learning algorithms, are now widely used to analyze medical images (e.g., X-rays,

MRIs, and CT scans), assist in diagnostic procedures, and predict patient outcomes. The benefits of AI in these areas are evident in efficiency, as AI can process and analyze large datasets much faster than human clinicians. In terms of accuracy, AI can identify subtle patterns in medical data that human doctors may miss.

However, despite these advantages, AI systems in healthcare are not free from flaws. One of the most critical issues is the presence of bias in these algorithms, which can have significant implications for healthcare outcomes.

3.2 Causes of Bias in AI Algorithms

AI algorithms, including those used in medical diagnostics, are only as unbiased as the data they are trained on. Bias in medical AI systems typically arises from several sources:

1. **Skewed Training Data**: Many AI systems in healthcare are trained on historical data, which may reflect biases present in past medical practices or patient demographics. If the training data underrepresents specific populations (e.g., racial minorities, women, or the elderly), the algorithm may fail to provide accurate predictions for these groups (Zangana & Al-Shaikhli, 2013; Ali & Aysan, 2024). This issue of unrepresentative data is especially problematic in medical diagnostics, where the stakes are high, and the cost of misdiagnosis can be life-threatening (Al-Sinani & Mitchell, 2024).
2. **Data Labeling Bias**: Medical datasets often require human labeling for supervised learning. This process is subjective, and the individuals involved in labeling may knowingly or unknowingly introduce their biases into the dataset. For instance, if medical professionals label images of skin conditions in a way that reflects racial bias, AI systems may be less accurate at diagnosing conditions in darker-skinned individuals (Butt, 2024).
3. **Algorithmic Bias**: Even when the data is unbiased, the design of AI algorithms can introduce bias. Algorithms may prioritize certain variables over others, leading to skewed outcomes. For example, an AI model trained to predict heart disease might focus disproportionately on risk factors like cholesterol levels and age, which may not be as relevant for certain ethnic groups (Shukla & Taneja, 2024).

To better understand the primary contributors to bias in AI medical diagnostics, the following pie chart provides a visual breakdown of the leading causes discussed.

Figure 2. Primary causes of bias in medical AI diagnostics

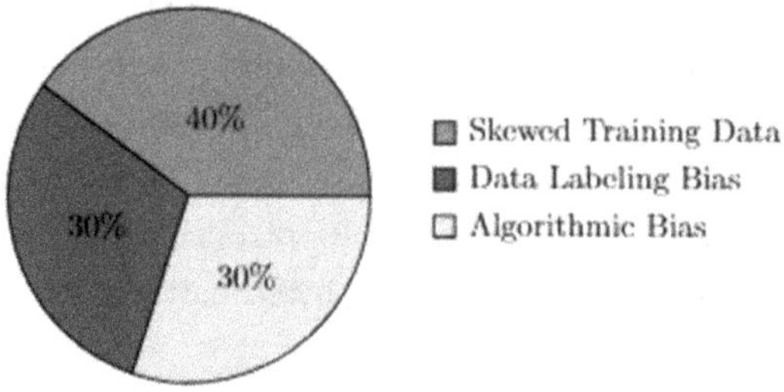

3.3 Consequences of Biased Medical AI

The consequences of biased AI algorithms in medical diagnostics can be severe:

1. **Disparities in Healthcare Outcomes**: Biased algorithms can result in misdiagnosis or delayed diagnosis, particularly for underrepresented groups. For example, if an AI system is trained on data predominantly from one ethnic group, it may perform poorly when diagnosing diseases in other ethnicities. This can exacerbate health disparities and worsen outcomes for marginalized populations (Veluru, 2024).
2. **Patient Trust and Confidence**: The perceived or real presence of bias in medical AI systems can undermine patient trust in healthcare technologies. When patients feel that AI systems are not accurate or equitable, they may be less likely to rely on AI-driven diagnoses or participate in clinical trials involving AI (Rashid & Kausik, 2024).
3. **Legal and Ethical Implications**: Using biased algorithms can lead to legal challenges, especially if patients experience harm due to incorrect diagnoses or delayed treatments. Moreover, healthcare organizations may face ethical dilemmas if they are found to be using AI systems that disproportionately affect specific patient populations (Trotsyuk et al., 2024; Zangana & Al-Shaikhli, 2017).

3.4 Mitigating Bias in Medical AI

To address the issue of bias in medical AI, several strategies can be employed:

1. **Diverse and Representative Data**: Ensuring that training data is diverse, and representative of different demographics is crucial. This includes collecting data from various ethnic, gender, and age groups to ensure the AI system performs well across all populations (Fenwick, Molnar, & Frangos, 2024; Ali & Aysan, 2024).
2. **Bias Audits and Testing**: Regular audits of AI algorithms are essential to detect and mitigate bias. These audits should focus on evaluating how well the algorithm performs across different population groups and identifying any disparities in accuracy (Maguluri et al., 2023; Leontidis, 2024).
3. **Transparency and Explainability**: AI systems in healthcare should be transparent, with clear explanations of how decisions are made. This can help clinicians understand how the algorithm arrived at a particular diagnosis and identify potential biases influencing the outcome (Shafik, 2024).
4. **Ethical AI Design**: Researchers and practitioners in AI should adopt ethical frameworks when designing medical AI systems. This includes prioritizing fairness, accountability, and transparency and ensuring that AI systems are subject to rigorous testing before being deployed in real-world medical settings (Ali, Zafar, & Aysan, 2024; Batabyal, 2024).

3.5 Summary

While AI holds immense promise for improving medical diagnostics, we must address the issue of biased algorithms. We can mitigate the risks associated with bias in healthcare AI by ensuring that AI systems are trained on diverse, representative data, subjecting them to regular audits, and adopting ethical design principles. As AI plays an increasingly important role in medical diagnostics, we must remain vigilant to ensure fairness and equity in healthcare outcomes.

4. CASE STUDY 2: UNAUTHORIZED DATA USE IN ENVIRONMENTAL AI RESEARCH

Integrating Artificial Intelligence (AI) in environmental research has brought transformative benefits, including enhanced data analysis, improved prediction models, and more efficient resource management. However, the rapid adoption of AI technologies in this domain has raised significant ethical concerns, particularly regarding unauthorized data use. Environmental AI research often relies on large datasets, including sensitive or proprietary data from various sources such as governmental databases, satellite imagery, or environmental monitoring systems. This data's improper or unauthorized use can lead to privacy breaches, misrepresentation of research outcomes, and damage to trust in AI systems.

In this case study, we examine a real-world scenario in which a prominent AI research institute working on environmental sustainability projects used unauthorized data to train its models. The project, aimed at predicting air quality trends in urban areas, relied on publicly available data and some proprietary datasets from partner organizations. However, an internal investigation revealed that the team had incorporated data from private sources without obtaining explicit consent from the data owners, leading to a significant breach of ethical standards.

4.1 The Ethical Implications

The unauthorized use of data in environmental AI research underscores several ethical concerns often overlooked in pursuing scientific advancement. The primary issue is the violation of data privacy and intellectual property rights. According to Shukla and Taneja (2024), data privacy is crucial in maintaining research integrity, particularly when the data is sensitive or personally identifiable. Unauthorized access to and use of data, whether intentional or inadvertent, can negatively affect individuals' trust in research institutions and the overall credibility of AI-driven studies.

Furthermore, this case highlights the challenge of maintaining transparency in AI research. While AI models are often viewed as powerful tools for decision-making, their effectiveness is directly tied to the quality and legitimacy of the data used to train them. As Eisenberg (2024) noted, the responsible use of AI in research requires a commitment to transparency regarding data sources and the methods used to collect and analyze them.

4.2 Legal and Regulatory Considerations

The unauthorized use of data also brings up legal and regulatory concerns. In this case, the data used without permission fell under the protection of intellectual property laws, and its unauthorized use could result in legal consequences. Butt (2024) discusses the emergence of regulatory frameworks such as the European Union's Artificial Intelligence Act, which seeks to establish legal guidelines for AI development and use, including the protection of data privacy and intellectual property rights. However, the implementation of such regulations remains inconsistent across different regions, making it challenging to hold institutions accountable for unethical data practices.

Moreover, using unauthorized data can also violate environmental laws and regulations governing data sharing and usage. As environmental data often falls under government or public ownership, the misuse of such data can lead to violations of national or international agreements. In the case of environmental AI research, the unauthorized use of data may not only breach ethical standards. However, it could also result in non-compliance with environmental protection and sustainability regulations.

4.3 Impacts on Research and Public Trust

The ramifications of unauthorized data use in AI-driven environmental research are not limited to legal and ethical violations; they extend to the broader impact on scientific integrity. As discussed by Luan et al. (2024), research that relies on data obtained without proper authorization can lead to inaccurate or misleading results. In the context of environmental AI, this could have serious consequences for public policy and decision-making, as stakeholders may rely on faulty predictions to address critical issues such as climate change, pollution, and resource management.

Additionally, the unauthorized use of data erodes public trust in AI systems, especially in sensitive domains like environmental research. Public trust is essential for the widespread acceptance and integration of AI technologies into society. Rashid and Kausik (2024) observed that AI-driven technologies can only be successful if they are trusted by the public, which in turn requires the responsible and ethical use of data. When AI researchers and organizations fail to adhere to ethical standards, they risk damaging the entire field's reputation, ultimately hindering AI's potential to contribute to sustainable development goals.

The following diagram illustrates the cascading impacts resulting from the unauthorized use of data in AI-driven environmental research.

Figure 3. Impacts of unauthorized data use in environmental AI research

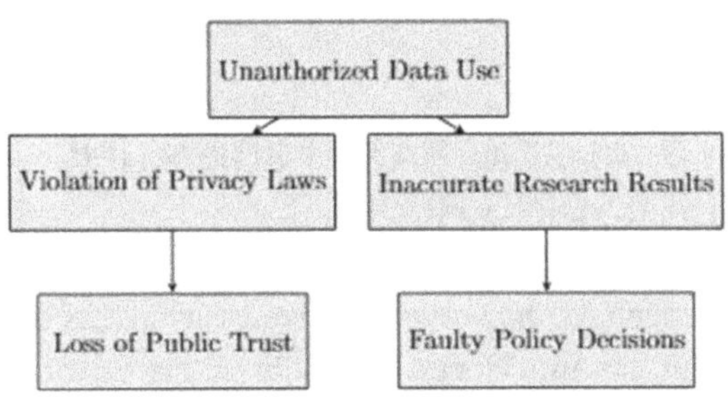

4.4 The Role of AI Ethics in Preventing Data Misuse

To prevent unauthorized data use, it is crucial to establish clear ethical guidelines and standards for data collection, storage, and usage in AI research. These guidelines should prioritize transparency, informed consent, and respect for intellectual property rights. Verma and Rohit (2024) highlight that ethical AI frameworks are pivotal in guiding researchers and institutions to make responsible decisions about data use. Institutions must ensure that data is used for its intended purpose and that proper permissions are obtained before incorporating it into research models.

Moreover, AI ethics should encourage researchers to consider the long-term consequences of data misuse. As Trotsyuk et al. (2024) argue, AI should be seen as a tool for technological advancement and a mechanism for promoting fairness, justice, and social responsibility. Researchers must be trained to recognize their work's ethical implications and adopt best practices for data handling that align with these principles.

4.5 Summary

The case study of unauthorized data use in environmental AI research serves as a reminder of the ethical challenges that arise when AI technologies are applied to sensitive areas such as environmental sustainability. Unauthorized data use not only compromises the integrity of the research but also undermines public trust in AI systems and violates legal and regulatory frameworks. To prevent such issues, AI researchers must adopt ethical guidelines prioritizing transparency, data privacy, and respect for intellectual property. By doing so, they can ensure that AI-driven environmental research contributes positively to society while maintaining the highest standards of ethical practice.

5. CASE STUDY 3: AI-GENERATED SCIENTIFIC FRAUD AND MISLEADING RESULTS

Artificial Intelligence (AI) has revolutionized various sectors, including scientific research. While it has introduced groundbreaking advancements, the rise of AI has also exposed vulnerabilities in research practices, particularly concerning generating fraudulent or misleading results. AI's potential for producing seemingly legitimate findings, manipulating data, and fabricating research outcomes raises critical concerns regarding the integrity of scientific inquiry. This case study explores the risks and challenges associated with AI-generated scientific fraud, focusing on its implications for research validity, ethical standards, and regulatory frameworks.

5.1. Introduction

The increasing adoption of AI technologies in scientific research reshapes how studies are conducted, analyzed, and disseminated. AI systems, including machine learning algorithms and natural language models, can now generate research papers, analyze vast datasets, and even make predictions based on incomplete information. While these advancements bring efficiency and innovation, they also create opportunities for misconduct, primarily when AI tools are used to fabricate results or misrepresent scientific findings.

A critical concern in this domain is the potential for AI to generate pseudo-scientific results that appear valid but lack empirical grounding. These AI-generated outcomes could mislead researchers, decision-makers, and the public, disseminating false information that could influence policy, funding decisions, and public health initiatives.

5.2. The Role of AI in Scientific Research

AI plays a significant role in streamlining various aspects of scientific research, from data collection and processing to hypothesis generation and result analysis. For example, generative AI models have been employed to write research papers by synthesizing existing data and literature (Ali & Aysan, 2024). While these tools have helped researchers accelerate the writing process, they have also raised concerns about the accuracy and authenticity of the generated content (Ali & Aysan, 2025). As AI becomes increasingly integrated into research workflows, the line between genuine human-driven discovery and AI-generated content blurs, presenting new challenges for research integrity.

5.3. AI-Generated Scientific Fraud: A Growing Threat

AI-generated scientific fraud can take various forms, including data fabrication, image manipulation, and the generation of false results or citations. One notable example is the use of AI models to simulate research data, which may appear credible but are entirely fabricated. This has significant consequences for the reliability of published scientific knowledge and undermines the trust in academic institutions.

Researchers have highlighted how AI tools can automate the creation of fraudulent research outcomes by manipulating existing datasets or generating false conclusions based on biased or incomplete inputs (Ali, Zafar, & Aysan, 2024). In some cases, AI models can even generate entire papers with fabricated data, citations, and references, severely threatening academic publishing and peer review processes (Leontidis, 2024).

The bar chart below categorizes the different forms of AI-generated scientific fraud highlighted in this section.

Figure 4. Prevalence of different types of AI-generated scientific fraud

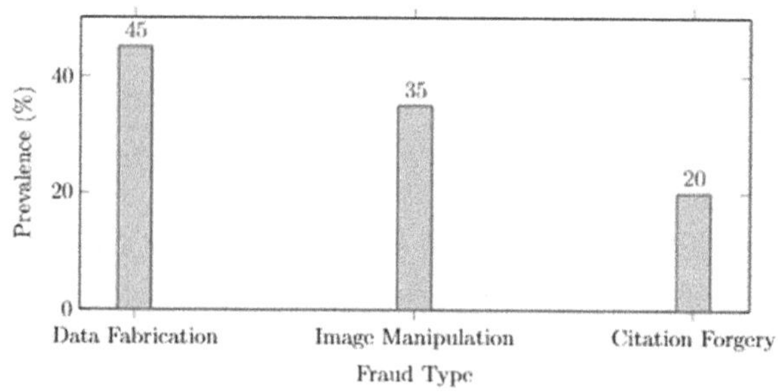

5.3.1 Data Fabrication and Manipulation

One of the most concerning aspects of AI-generated scientific fraud is its ability to fabricate data. AI models trained on large datasets can identify patterns and trends in the data. However, if the model is fed with biased or incomplete data, it can produce misleading or false results. The widespread use of AI in data analysis also means that errors or intentional manipulations can be amplified, leading to widespread misinformation across scientific fields.

For instance, researchers using AI-based tools to analyze financial data may unknowingly rely on fabricated datasets generated by the AI, leading to erroneous conclusions about market trends or financial predictions (Ali & Aysan, 2024). These fabricated results can then be published, cited, and incorporated into further research, perpetuating a cycle of misinformation.

5.3.2 Image Manipulation

AI's ability to manipulate images is another area of concern, particularly in biomedical research. AI tools can alter images to make experimental results appear more promising or consistent with hypotheses. This manipulation of research images can be difficult to detect, especially when high-quality AI algorithms are employed to edit images seamlessly.

For example, studies that rely on imaging techniques such as microscopy or MRI scans may be altered using AI tools to enhance visual features, creating the illusion of more significant findings. This practice compromises the scientific rigor of studies and undermines trust in medical research (Ali, Zafar, & Aysan, 2024).

5.4. Implications of AI-Generated Scientific Fraud

The rise of AI-generated scientific fraud has profound implications for research integrity, ethical standards, and public trust in scientific institutions. Manipulating research data and outcomes can undermine the credibility of entire scientific fields, especially when false findings are published and widely disseminated. Moreover, fraudulent research can lead to misguided policies, ineffective treatments, and wasteful investments in scientific endeavors.

For example, AI-generated fraud in healthcare could lead to the approval of ineffective or harmful medical treatments, jeopardizing patient safety (Ali & Aysan, 2025). Similarly, fraudulent research in environmental sciences could result in misguided policies that fail to address pressing ecological challenges. These consequences highlight the critical need for stringent ethical guidelines and regulatory frameworks to prevent AI misuse in research.

5.4.1 Ethical Concerns

The ethical implications of AI-generated scientific fraud are multifaceted. On one hand, the misuse of AI for fraudulent purposes violates the ethical standards of academic research, which prioritize honesty, transparency, and integrity. On the other hand, AI's role in research complicates traditional notions of authorship and accountability. Who is responsible when an AI system generates false data or conclusions? Is it the researcher who used the AI tool, the developer, or the institution that published the research?

Ethical dilemmas also arise when AI tools manipulate results to align with specific agendas, such as promoting biased research or supporting preconceived notions. As AI evolves, researchers must carefully consider the ethical implications of relying on AI for critical scientific endeavors (Shafik, 2024).

5.5. Preventing AI-Generated Scientific Fraud

Preventing AI-generated scientific fraud requires a multifaceted approach that combines technological, ethical, and regulatory measures. One of the most effective ways to combat AI-driven misconduct is by developing robust detection tools to identify fraudulent data, images, or research conclusions. Advances in AI itself, such as deep learning algorithms designed to detect inconsistencies in datasets or images, can be employed to verify the authenticity of research findings (Veluru, 2024).

Additionally, implementing stricter ethical guidelines and regulatory frameworks is essential to ensure that AI tools are used responsibly in scientific research. Scholars and policymakers are increasingly calling for comprehensive legislation to regulate AI's role in research and academic publishing (Butt, 2024). International efforts to establish AI ethics standards, such as the European Union's AI Act, are essential in curbing AI misuse and ensuring that AI-generated research adheres to established scientific norms (Trotsyuk et al., 2024).

Furthermore, academic institutions and journals must adopt rigorous peer review processes that account for using AI tools in research. This includes verifying the authenticity of datasets and results, conducting in-depth checks for image manipulation, and ensuring that AI-generated papers are reviewed thoroughly for quality and credibility (Fenwick et al., 2024).

5.6. Summary

AI-generated scientific fraud poses a significant threat to the integrity of scientific research, with the potential to undermine public trust and hinder the progress of knowledge. As AI technologies continue to evolve, researchers, institutions, and policymakers must address the risks of AI misuse through robust ethical frameworks, regulatory oversight, and the development of advanced detection tools. By doing so, the scientific community can ensure that AI serves as a force for good, advancing knowledge and innovation while maintaining the integrity of research practices.

6. CASE STUDY 4: CYBERSECURITY BREACH IN AI-ENABLED RESEARCH INFRASTRUCTURE

In this case study, we explore the cybersecurity breach that occurred in an AI-enabled research infrastructure, specifically in the context of academic and industrial collaborations that leverage artificial intelligence (AI) for research purposes. This breach compromised the integrity of the research data and highlighted the significant risks associated with AI technologies in sensitive sectors, including academic, industrial, and governmental research.

6.1. Background of the Incident

The breach occurred in a research institution that integrated AI technologies to support advanced scientific studies, including quantum computing, cybersecurity, and machine learning. The institution had implemented AI-driven tools to streamline research data processing, enhance computational power, and foster collaboration with industrial partners. However, the reliance on these technologies created vulnerabilities that were exploited by cybercriminals.

The attackers, believed to have exploited weaknesses in the AI-enabled systems, gained unauthorized access to a critical AI research platform for developing machine learning algorithms. This platform was connected to the institution's internal systems and collaborated with external research labs, government bodies, and private sector stakeholders. The breach allowed the cybercriminals to access sensitive intellectual property, research methodologies, and, potentially, classified data.

6.2. Impact of the Breach

The breach had widespread consequences:

- **Data Theft and Intellectual Property Loss**: Sensitive research data were stolen, including unpublished findings and proprietary machine learning algorithms. This compromised years of research efforts, leading to potential financial losses and reputational damage for the institution and its partners.
- **Disruption of Research**: The breach temporarily halted ongoing research projects as the institution scrambled to contain the damage and restore its systems. This disrupted collaborative efforts, delaying critical milestones in various AI-based initiatives.
- **Security Repercussions**: The breach revealed significant security gaps in the AI-enabled infrastructure, specifically in how AI systems interacted with external entities. The institution's reliance on cloud-based AI tools exposed it to risks that were previously underestimated.

6.3. Root Cause Analysis

Upon conducting a thorough investigation, several key factors contributing to the breach were identified:

- **Insufficient Security Protocols**: The AI-enabled infrastructure had not implemented adequate security protocols to protect against external threats. Although the system incorporated advanced AI-driven anomaly detection, the breach was carried out by attackers who were sophisticated enough to bypass these defenses.
- **Lack of AI-Specific Security Measures**: AI systems, particularly those designed for research purposes, are often more complex and challenging to secure. As highlighted by Al-Sinani and Mitchell (2024), traditional cybersecurity frameworks do not adequately address the unique security needs of AI systems, leaving vulnerabilities that malicious actors can exploit.
- **Inadequate Authentication Mechanisms**: The breach occurred due to weak authentication mechanisms for remote access to the research systems. The AI infrastructure relied on basic password-based access, which was insufficient for securing sensitive academic and research data (Veluru, 2024).

6.4. AI and Cybersecurity Intersection

AI technologies offer promising solutions to enhance cybersecurity, as seen in various implementations in fields like ethical hacking and phishing detection (Ali & Aysan, 2024). However, the breach also underscored the paradox of relying on the same technology to protect against threats while exposing new vulnerabilities. The attackers likely exploited the AI systems designed to safeguard the infrastructure, making it clear that there is a pressing need to integrate advanced cybersecurity measures into AI-driven research tools.

According to Rashid and Kausik (2024), integrating AI into cybersecurity must be approached cautiously, ensuring that vulnerabilities are not introduced as part of the technology stack. They suggest that AI-based cybersecurity systems must incorporate robust self-learning capabilities to adapt to evolving threats and stronger encryption methods to protect sensitive research data.

The following flowchart maps the events and key vulnerabilities that led to the cybersecurity breach in AI-enabled research infrastructure.

Figure 5. Flowchart of cybersecurity breach in AI-enabled research infrastructure

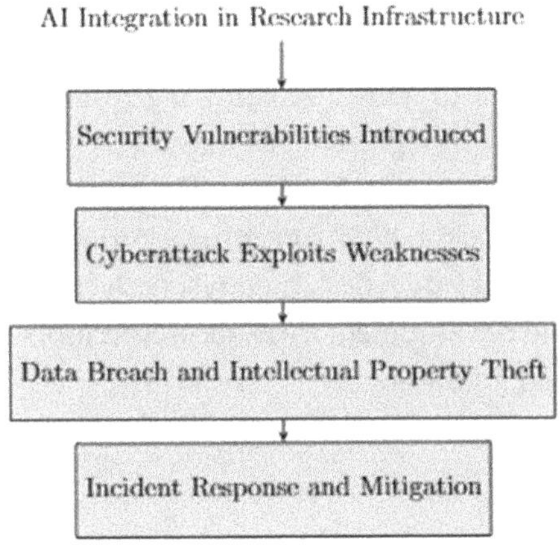

6.5. The Role of Ethical AI in Cybersecurity

Ethical AI considerations are also crucial in preventing cybersecurity breaches in AI-enabled research infrastructures. AI systems used in research must be designed to uphold ethical principles, ensuring that data privacy and security are safeguarded from potential misuse. As Shafik (2024) emphasizes, a failure to implement ethical AI can expose organizations to significant risks, including data breaches and unauthorized access to critical information. Furthermore, as Ali et al. (2024) discuss in their studies, AI-driven systems should be designed to enhance transparency and accountability, particularly when sensitive data is involved.

In response to the breach, the institution began exploring adopting ethical hacking practices, as suggested by Al-Sinani et al. (2025). By leveraging AI in penetration testing and vulnerability scanning, the institution aimed to identify and mitigate vulnerabilities before they could be exploited.

6.6. Mitigation Strategies

In the aftermath of the breach, the institution took several key steps to improve its cybersecurity posture:

- **Strengthening AI-Specific Security**: The institution worked closely with cybersecurity experts to develop tailored security measures for its AI systems. This included implementing advanced threat detection systems, multi-factor authentication, and more stringent access controls (Ali & Aysan, 2025).

- **AI-Driven Monitoring Tools**: To prevent future breaches, the institution incorporated AI-driven monitoring tools that continuously analyze system behavior and identify anomalies that could signal potential threats. These tools were designed to work in real-time, allowing researchers and administrators to respond quickly to emerging security issues.
- **Collaboration with Industry Experts**: The institution also forged partnerships with industry leaders in AI and cybersecurity to co-develop solutions to address the unique risks of AI-enabled research infrastructures. This collaboration allowed the development of AI-powered tools to detect sophisticated attacks and respond autonomously.

6.7. Summary

The cybersecurity breach in this AI-enabled research infrastructure is a stark reminder of the vulnerabilities inherent in relying on AI technologies for sensitive research purposes. While AI offers immense potential to transform research capabilities, it also introduces significant risks if not adequately secured. Ethical AI, robust cybersecurity frameworks, and ongoing collaboration between academia, industry, and cybersecurity experts are essential to mitigate these risks and protect the integrity of research data.

By learning from this breach, the institution has taken critical steps to strengthen its AI-enabled systems and ensure that future research is conducted in a secure and ethical environment. This case study highlights the urgent need for comprehensive cybersecurity strategies specifically tailored to the challenges posed by AI-driven research infrastructures.

7. CROSS-CASE ANALYSIS AND COMMON THEMES

In analyzing the diverse applications and ethical dimensions of artificial intelligence (AI), several common themes have emerged across the various cases explored in the literature. These themes underscore the complex interplay of technological, ethical, and practical considerations in integrating AI across sectors such as finance, cybersecurity, and agriculture. By examining these cases, it becomes evident that while AI offers transformative potential, it also presents significant challenges that must be addressed holistically.

7.1. Ethical Concerns in AI Deployment

One of the most prevalent themes from the cross-case analysis is the ethical implications surrounding AI deployment. AI, particularly in generative models, is becoming increasingly central in industries like finance (Ali & Aysan, 2024), healthcare (Zangana & Mustafa, 2024), and cybersecurity (Al-Sinani et al., 2025). While the technology provides remarkable capabilities for innovation, it also raises concerns regarding fairness, accountability, and transparency.

For instance, Ali, H., & Aysan, A. F. (2025) delve into the ethical dimensions of generative AI by using machine learning structural topic modeling to understand the various ethical concerns related to AI's proliferation across industries. These concerns include data privacy, algorithmic bias, and potential misuse. As discussed by Al-Sinani et al. (2024), ethical hacking highlights the importance of employing AI responsibly, especially within cybersecurity contexts where the stakes for ethical breaches are high.

7.2. The Role of AI in Decision-Making and Governance

AI's impact on decision-making processes and governance structures across various industries also forms a significant theme. The need for clear governance frameworks becomes paramount as AI systems increasingly take over complex decision-making tasks. For example, Butt (2024) examines the European Union's AI Act, which represents a pivotal step toward creating a regulatory environment that ensures the responsible use of AI technologies in the context of both corporate governance and governmental policy.

In the realm of warfare, Batabyal (2024) explores how AI-driven technologies are reshaping military decision-making, raising questions about the ethical use of AI in warfare and its implications for international law. This theme emphasizes the need for policies that address the ethical deployment of AI while ensuring compliance with global standards and regulations.

7.3. AI and Human-Centric Adoption

Another recurring theme in the case studies is the need for a human-centric approach to AI adoption. While AI holds vast potential, its integration into organizational structures and societal frameworks must be done with careful consideration of human impact. Fenwick, Molnar, & Frangos (2024) argue that AI-driven digital transformations should focus on human workers, emphasizing developing human-

AI collaborations rather than replacing human roles. This perspective is essential to achieving long-term sustainability and acceptability for AI technologies.

The importance of a human-centric approach is also highlighted in the context of women's safety, where Pimpalkar et al. (2024) discuss how AI tools can empower women through predictive safety solutions. Similarly, Vyawahare, Khandelwal, & Rathod (2024) focus on the role of AI in preventing online harassment, further emphasizing the need for AI systems that prioritize ethical considerations and societal welfare.

7.4. Interdisciplinary Integration of AI

AI increasingly intersects with other technological fields, and this interdisciplinary integration brings challenges and opportunities. Campus (2024) illustrates how AI is being leveraged alongside quantum computing to enhance technological advancements in various fields, including semiconductor technology. Such interdisciplinary approaches promise to open new frontiers in AI capabilities, but they also necessitate rethinking traditional approaches to research and development.

In agriculture, Arya & Rastogi (2024) examine the application of AI in aerial monitoring systems for agricultural practices. The integration of AI with sensors and satellite technology in this context underscores the broad potential of AI to optimize industries by improving efficiency, sustainability, and resilience. However, this convergence of technologies also raises issues related to data privacy and environmental impacts, which must be carefully managed.

7.5. Security Challenges and Risk Mitigation

Security concerns are a significant theme when considering AI applications, especially in the context of smart cities, e-commerce, and the biomedical sector. Maguluri, Arularasan, & Boopathi (2023) analyze the security vulnerabilities of AI-based drones in smart cities, highlighting the need for robust risk mitigation strategies. Similarly, Trotsyuk et al. (2024) propose a framework for managing the potential misuse of AI in biomedical research, underscoring the importance of proactive measures to safeguard against malicious applications of AI technologies.

The growing importance of AI in cybersecurity is also evidenced by the work of Shafik (2024), who discusses the need for AI-based systems to safeguard customer data in service industries. The pervasive nature of AI in security applications calls for constant vigilance and the development of adaptive security protocols to mitigate emerging risks.

7.6. Regulation and Policy Development

Finally, the regulatory landscape for AI technologies is evolving rapidly. As AI systems become more integrated into everyday life, there is an urgent need for comprehensive legal frameworks to govern their use. The European Union's AI Act, discussed by Butt (2024), is a key example of an attempt to regulate AI on a broad scale. Additionally, Luan et al. (2024) point to the role of AI in supporting scientometric analysis, an area where ethical and regulatory considerations must guide how AI tools influence scholarly communication.

Shukla & Taneja (2024) examine the ethical considerations and data privacy concerns surrounding the use of AI in education, illustrating the complexities of implementing AI within sensitive sectors where personal data is involved. These regulatory discussions ensure that AI technologies are deployed responsibly and aligned with societal values.

7.7 Summary

Through the cross-case analysis, it is clear that the integration of AI into various domains must be approached carefully, considering ethical, security, and governance issues. While AI offers unprecedented opportunities for innovation, its potential for misuse, ethical dilemmas, and security challenges must not be overlooked. The cases analyzed in this chapter highlight the need for interdisciplinary approaches, human-centric design, and robust regulatory frameworks to ensure the responsible deployment of AI technologies. Moving forward, continued research and policy development will be essential to mitigate risks and maximize the benefits of AI across diverse sectors.

8. LESSONS LEARNED AND RECOMMENDATIONS

In recent years, artificial intelligence (AI) has made significant strides across multiple domains, offering transformative solutions and presenting new challenges that must be addressed with foresight and responsibility. Integrating AI into finance, defense, healthcare, and agriculture industries demonstrates the vast potential for efficiency gains and innovation. However, as AI systems continue to evolve, lessons learned from these applications can provide valuable insights into the ethical, operational, and regulatory hurdles encountered and guidance for future development.

8.1 Ethical and Regulatory Challenges

One of the primary lessons learned from the rapid adoption of AI is the critical importance of ethical considerations. The work by Ali and Aysan (2024) highlights the growing role of AI in finance, yet stresses the need for robust ethical frameworks to ensure that these technologies are used responsibly. As AI systems increasingly influence financial decision-making, data bias, privacy concerns, and transparency must be addressed to maintain trust in these systems (Ali & Aysan, 2025). The lack of ethical oversight in AI development can lead to negative consequences, including algorithmic discrimination and unintended social impacts.

Similarly, the advancement of AI-enhanced ethical hacking, as demonstrated by Al-Sinani et al. (2024, 2025), underscores the duality of AI technologies. While they can be leveraged for security and ethical use cases, they can also be misused. Researchers have called for a stronger regulatory framework, as seen in the analytical study by Butt (2024) on the EU AI Act. The study points out that despite being a pioneering regulatory effort, the EU's approach is still evolving and faces challenges in keeping pace with the fast-moving AI landscape.

8.2 Advancements in AI Applications

AI's potential to revolutionize traditional industries is evident. In agriculture, for instance, Arya and Rastogi (2024) demonstrate how AI-driven aerial monitoring systems are being employed to enhance decision-making and sustainability. These systems monitor crops, forests, and borders, providing real-time data that aids in resource management. However, despite these advancements, a key lesson from this area is that widespread adoption requires careful attention to environmental impacts, regulatory compliance, and balancing efficiency with sustainability.

In the defense sector, Batabyal (2024) discusses the role of AI in warfare and the ethical dilemmas it poses. The increasing autonomy of AI-driven military systems raises questions about accountability, decision-making in life-and-death scenarios, and the potential for misuse. A clear recommendation here is the development of international norms and standards for using AI in warfare to ensure that ethical considerations are prioritized when deploying these technologies.

8.3 Human-Centric AI Integration

AI's integration into business processes, as explored by Fenwick et al. (2024), emphasizes the shift towards human-centric adoption. Human resource management (HRM) is experiencing a paradigm shift, where AI systems are not just tools for automation but are integral to the strategic development of human capital. However, the key lesson here is ensuring that AI adoption complements human workers rather than replacing them. Recommendations suggest that companies focus on reskilling employees to work alongside AI, fostering collaboration between humans and machines.

Similarly, the advancement of AI tools for women's safety, such as those outlined by Pimpalkar et al. (2024) and Vyawahare et al. (2024), shows AI's capacity to empower vulnerable groups. These tools leverage data analytics to predict and prevent safety threats, offering a new dimension of protection. Nevertheless, the lesson learned from these applications is the importance of developing AI systems that are inclusive, equitable, and designed with a diverse set of user needs in mind.

8.4 Future Directions

Looking ahead, several critical areas need attention. First, addressing data privacy concerns will be paramount, as Shafik (2024) outlined. With the proliferation of AI systems that process vast amounts of personal data, securing this information from breaches and misuse is a primary concern. Developing AI systems that are both secure and transparent, adhering to privacy regulations, will be crucial for maintaining public trust.

Furthermore, the use of AI in scientific research is expanding, as seen in the work of Luan et al. (2024), who applied AI for scientometric analysis in social work literature. AI's potential to analyze large volumes of scholarly data is helping to accelerate research across disciplines. However, as AI becomes increasingly involved in scientific inquiry, it is essential to ensure that AI methodologies are interpretable, and that human oversight is maintained. Recommendations include the development of clear guidelines for integrating AI into research, emphasizing transparency and reproducibility.

In addition, as AI continues to evolve, the intersection of AI and quantum computing holds immense potential. As explored by Campus (2024) and Eswaran and Eswaran (2025), quantum computing could significantly enhance AI's capabilities, particularly in processing power. However, this technological leap comes with challenges, including the need for specialized knowledge, secure systems, and ethical considerations regarding its impact on society.

8.5 Summary

The future of AI is undeniably bright, with countless opportunities for innovation. However, the lessons learned from current applications reveal the importance of approaching AI with caution, responsibility, and ethical foresight. As AI systems continue to evolve, it will be essential to prioritize human-centric approaches, establish robust regulatory frameworks, and ensure that AI is deployed in ways that benefit society. Moving forward, researchers, policymakers, and industry leaders must collaborate to address the challenges and unlock the full potential of AI.

9. CONCLUSION

Integrating artificial intelligence (AI) across multiple domains has proven to be a transformative force, influencing industries, technologies, and societal frameworks. As explored throughout this chapter, the convergence of AI with fields such as finance, healthcare, defense, and ethical hacking underscores the profound potential and challenges associated with AI implementation. Notably, the application of generative AI and its ethical implications, especially in domains like finance and security, highlights the dual-edged nature of AI advancements.

Several key lessons have emerged from the analysis. First, AI's capabilities extend beyond traditional automation, offering insights into complex decision-making, pattern recognition, and risk assessment. However, the use of AI also raises critical ethical and privacy concerns, emphasizing the need for robust regulatory frameworks and responsible AI governance (Ali & Aysan, 2024; Ali et al., 2025). Additionally, sectors like agriculture, defense, and healthcare have demonstrated that AI's role can be preventative and predictive, enhancing operational efficiency, security, and societal wellbeing (Arya & Rastogi, 2024; Maguluri et al., 2023).

Considering these developments, the implementation of AI must be approached with caution, considering both the potential benefits and the risks of misuse. Responsible AI development requires technological advancements and a commitment to transparency, fairness, and inclusivity. As the growing body of literature indicates, interdisciplinary collaboration between AI researchers, policymakers, and industry practitioners is critical to achieving sustainable and ethical AI integration (Fenwick et al., 2024; Shafik, 2024).

Moreover, the future of AI holds promising avenues for enhancement, particularly through the synergy of AI with quantum computing (Campus, 2024; Eswaran & Eswaran, 2025). This convergence may drive innovations in biomedical research, smart city infrastructure, and personalized medicine, enabling new efficiency and problem-solving capabilities. However, this future is fraught with complexities, particularly in safeguarding data privacy, ensuring compliance with ethical standards, and mitigating the risk of AI misuse (Trotsyuk et al., 2024; Shukla & Taneja, 2024).

While AI continues reshaping industries and academic research, a balanced approach that prioritizes ethics, security, and societal impact is essential. The role of AI in shaping the future is undeniable. However, its success will depend on our ability to guide its evolution through responsible governance and innovation, ensuring its benefits are maximized while minimizing risks.

In conclusion, the future of AI is one of both promise and responsibility. It is essential that researchers, practitioners, and policymakers continue to engage in thoughtful dialogue, informed by AI's technological potential and the societal responsibilities it entails. With these considerations, AI can become a tool for transformative change, driving innovation across sectors while safeguarding the rights and interests of individuals and communities.

REFERENCES

Al-Sinani, H. S., & Mitchell, C. J. (2024). AI-enhanced ethical hacking: A Linux-focused experiment. *arXiv preprint arXiv:2410.05105.*

Al-Sinani, H. S., Sahli, N., Mitchell, C. J., & Al-Siyabi, M. (2025). Advancing ethical hacking with AI: A Linux-based experimental study. *Proceedings of ITASEC and SERICS, Bologna, Italy (Feb 2025),* https://www. chrismitchell. net/Papers/aehwaa. pdf

Ali, H., & Aysan, A. F. (2024). Decoding the Future of Generative AI in Finance: A Machine Learning Exploration of Academic and Grey Corpus. *Available atSSRN* 4787211. DOI: 10.2139/ssrn.4787211

Ali, H., & Aysan, A. F. (2025). Ethical dimensions of generative AI: A cross-domain analysis using machine learning structural topic modeling. *International Journal of Ethics and Systems, 41*(1), 3–34. DOI: 10.1108/IJOES-04-2024-0112

Ali, H., Zafar, M. B., & Aysan, A. F. (2024). Generative AI and Finance: A Multi-level Machine Learning Based Analysis. *Available atSSRN* 5129013.

Arya, L., & Rastogi, R. (2024). Study on Aerial Monitoring System in Agriculture, Forestry, Defense, and Border Protection Using Artificial Intelligence (AI). In *Agriculture and Aquaculture Applications of Biosensors and Bioelectronics* (pp. 392-407). IGI Global Scientific Publishing.

Batabyal, G. S. (2024). Ethics, laws on war and artificial intelligence-driven warfare. In *Artificial intelligence, ethics and the future of warfare* (pp. 187–215). Routledge India. DOI: 10.4324/9781003421849-9

Butt, J. (2024). Analytical study of the world's first EU Artificial Intelligence (AI) Act. *International Journal of Research Publication and Reviews, 5*(3), 7343–7364. DOI: 10.55248/gengpi.5.0324.0914

Campus, M. T. (2024). Quantum Machine Learning, Leveraging Al, and. *Integration of AI, Quantum Computing, and Semiconductor Technology*, 57.

Eisenberg, D. (2024). *Sensing With Integrity: Responsible Sensor Systems in an Era of AI* (Doctoral dissertation, New Jersey Institute of Technology).

Eswaran, U., & Eswaran, V. (2025). Quantum Machine Learning, Leveraging AI, and Semiconductor Technology. In *Integration of AI, Quantum Computing, and Semiconductor Technology* (pp. 57-78). IGI Global.

Fenwick, A., Molnar, G., & Frangos, P. (2024). The critical role of HRM in AI-driven digital transformation: A paradigm shift to enable firms to move from AI implementation to human-centric adoption. *Discover Artificial Intelligence*, *4*(1), 34. DOI: 10.1007/s44163-024-00125-4

Filetti, S., Fenza, G., & Gallo, A. (2024). Research design and writing of scholarly articles: New artificial intelligence tools available for researchers. *Endocrine*, *85*(3), 1104–1116. DOI: 10.1007/s12020-024-03977-z PMID: 39085566

Flannery, J., Ajayi, S. O., & Oyegoke, A. S. (2021). Alcohol and substance misuse in the construction industry. *International Journal of Occupational Safety and Ergonomics*, *27*(2), 472–487. DOI: 10.1080/10803548.2019.1601376 PMID: 30935301

Gaurav, A., Chui, K. T., Arya, V., Attar, R. W., Bansal, S., Alhomoud, A., & Psannis, K. (2024). Optimized AI-Driven Semantic Web Approach for Enhancing Phishing Detection in E-Commerce Platforms. [IJSWIS]. *International Journal on Semantic Web and Information Systems*, *20*(1), 1–13. DOI: 10.4018/IJSWIS.359767

Jamro, M. Y., & Jamro, F. A. (2023). AI Matters: Chatbot Integration in Holistic STEM Education.

Karim, R., Galar, D., & Kumar, U. (2023). *AI factory: theories, applications and case studies*. CRC Press. DOI: 10.1201/9781003208686

Leontidis, G. (2024). Science in the age of ai: How artificial intelligence is changing the nature and method of scientific research.

Luan, H., Perron, B. E., Victor, B. G., Wan, G., Niu, Y., & Xiao, X. (2024). Using artificial intelligence to support scientometric analysis of scholarly literature: A case example of research on mainland China's left-behind children. *Journal of the Society for Social Work and Research*, *15*(3), 435–457. DOI: 10.1086/731613

Maennig, W. (2014). Inefficiency of the anti-doping system: Cost reduction proposals. *Substance Use & Misuse*, *49*(9), 1201–1205. DOI: 10.3109/10826084.2014.912065 PMID: 24832718

Maguluri, L. P., Arularasan, A. N., & Boopathi, S. (2023). Assessing security concerns for ai-based drones in smart cities. In *Effective AI, Blockchain, and E-Governance Applications for Knowledge Discovery and Management* (pp. 27-47). IGI Global Scientific Publishing. DOI: 10.4018/978-1-6684-9151-5.ch002

Pimpalkar, A. P., Wankhade, N. R., Chole, V., & Golhar, Y. (2024). Women's Empowerment Through AI: Discovering Data Analytics for Predictive Safety Solutions and Future Trends. In *AI Tools and Applications for Women's Safety* (pp. 304-326). IGI Global Scientific Publishing.

Rashid, A. B., & Kausik, A. K. (2024). AI revolutionizing industries worldwide: A comprehensive overview of its diverse applications. *Hybrid Advances*, 100277.

Rodriguez, M. Y., & Storer, H. (2020). A computational social science perspective on qualitative data exploration: Using topic models for the descriptive analysis of social media data. *Journal of Technology in Human Services*, *38*(1), 54–86. DOI: 10.1080/15228835.2019.1616350

San Biagio, M., Cipolla, M., La Mattina, E., & Morreale, V. (2023, December). A Topic Clustering Method to Identify Online Threats against Soft Targets. In *2023 International Conference on Computational Science and Computational Intelligence (CSCI)* (pp. 727-733). IEEE. DOI: 10.1109/CSCI62032.2023.00124

Schünemann, C., Johanning, S., Reger, E., Herold, H., & Bruckner, T. (2024). Complex system policy modelling approaches for policy advice–comparing systems thinking, system dynamics and agent-based modelling. *Political Research Exchange : an ECPR Journal*, *6*(1), 2387438. DOI: 10.1080/2474736X.2024.2387438

Shafik, W. (2024). Data privacy and security safeguarding customer information in ChatGPT systems. In *Revolutionizing the Service Industry Wth OpenAI Models* (pp. 52–86). IGI Global. DOI: 10.4018/979-8-3693-1239-1.ch003

Shuja, J., Alanazi, E., Alasmary, W., & Alashaikh, A. (2021). COVID-19 open source data sets: A comprehensive survey. *Applied Intelligence*, *51*(3), 1296–1325. DOI: 10.1007/s10489-020-01862-6 PMID: 34764552

Shukla, R. P., & Taneja, S. (2024). Ethical considerations and data privacy in artificial intelligence. In *Integrating generative AI in education to achieve sustainable development goals* (pp. 86–97). IGI Global. DOI: 10.4018/979-8-3693-2440-0.ch005

Trotsyuk, A. A., Waeiss, Q., Bhatia, R. T., Aponte, B. J., Heffernan, I. M., Madgavkar, D., Felder, R. M., Lehmann, L. S., Palmer, M. J., Greely, H., Wald, R., Goetz, L., Trengove, M., Vandersluis, R., Lin, H., Cho, M. K., Altman, R. B., Endy, D., Relman, D. A., & Magnus, D. (2024). Toward a framework for risk mitigation of potential misuse of artificial intelligence in biomedical research. *Nature Machine Intelligence*, *6*(12), 1–8. DOI: 10.1038/s42256-024-00926-3

Veluru, C. S. (2024). Responsible Artificial Intelligence on Large Scale Data to Prevent Misuse, Unethical Challenges and Security Breaches. *Journal of Artificial Intelligence & Cloud Computing. SRC/JAICC-349. DOI: doi. org/(3), 331*, 2-6.DOI: 10.47363/JAICC/2024

Verma, M., & Rohit, K. (2024). Ethical AI Shaping Scholarly Communication: Challenges and Opportunities.

Vyawahare, H., Khandelwal, S., & Rathod, S. (2024). Artificial Intelligence in Detecting and Preventing Online Harassment. In *AI Tools and Applications for Women's Safety* (pp. 14–35). IGI Global Scientific Publishing. DOI: 10.4018/979-8-3693-1435-7.ch002

Zangana, H. M. (2015). A New Skin Color Based Face Detection Algorithm by Combining Three Color Model Algorithms. *IOSR J. Comput. Eng, 17*, 06-125.

Zangana, H. M. (2017). A new algorithm for shape detection. *IOSR Journal of Computer Engineering (IOSR-JCE), 19*(3), 71-76.

Zangana, H. M. (2017). Library Data Quality Maturity (IIUM as a Case Study). *IOSR Journal of Computer Engineering, 19*(March), 29. DOI: 10.9790/0661-1902033844

Zangana, H. M. (2017). Watermarking System Using LSB. *IOSR Journal of Computer Engineering, 19*(3), 75–79. DOI: 10.9790/0661-1903027579

Zangana, H. M. (2018). Design an information management system for a pharmacy. *International Journal of Advanced Research in Computer and Communication Engineering, 7*(10), 52–55. DOI: 10.17148/IJARCCE.2018.71012

Zangana, H. M. (2018). Developing Data Warehouse for Student Information System (IIUM as a Case Study). *International Organization of Scientific Research, 20*(1), 09-14.

Zangana, H. M. (2018). Implementing a System for Recognizing Optical Characters.

Zangana, H. M. (2019). Issues of Data Management in the Library: A Case Study.

Zangana, H. M. (2019). ITD Data Quality Maturity (A Case Study). *International Journal Of Engineering And Computer Science, 8*(10).

Zangana, H. M. (2020). Mobile Device Integration in IIUM Service. *International Journal (Toronto, Ont.), 8*(5).

Zangana, H. M. (2021). The Global Finical Crisis from an Islamic Point Of View. *Qubahan Academic Journal, 1*(2), 55–59. DOI: 10.48161/qaj.v1n2a39

Zangana, H. M. (2022). Creating a Community-Based Disaster Management System. *Academic Journal of Nawroz University, 11*(4), 234–244. DOI: 10.25007/ajnu.v11n4a1485

Zangana, H. M. (2022). Implementing New Interactive Video Learning System for IIUM. *Academic Journal of Nawroz University, 11*(2), 23–29. DOI: 10.25007/ajnu.v11n2a1281

Zangana, H. M. (2022). Improving The Web Services for Remittance Company: Express Remit as a Case Study. *Academic Journal of Nawroz University (AJNU), 11*(3).

Zangana, H. M., & Abdulazeez, A. M. (2023). Developed Clustering Algorithms for Engineering Applications: A Review. *International Journal of Informatics* [INJIISCOM]. *Information System and Computer Engineering*, *4*(2), 147–169.

Zangana, H. M., & Al-Shaikhli, I. F. (2013). A new algorithm for human face detection using skin color tone. *IOSR Journal of Computer Engineering*, *11*(6), 31–38. DOI: 10.9790/0661-1163138

Zangana, H. M., Bazeed, S. M. S., Ali, N. Y., & Abdullah, D. T. (2024). Navigating Project Change: A Comprehensive Review of Change Management Strategies and Practices. *Indonesian Journal of Education and Social Sciences*, *3*(2), 166–179. DOI: 10.56916/ijess.v3i2.735

Zangana, H. M., & Mustafa, F. M. (2024). From Classical to Deep Learning: A Systematic Review of Image Denoising Techniques. *Jurnal Ilmiah Computer Science*, *3*(1), 50–65. DOI: 10.58602/jics.v3i1.36

Zangana, H. M., & Mustafa, F. M. (2024). Review of Hybrid Denoising Approaches in Face Recognition: Bridging Wavelet Transform and Deep Learning. *The Indonesian Journal of Computer Science*, *13*(4). Advance online publication. DOI: 10.33022/ijcs.v13i4.4209

Zangana, H. M., & Mustafa, F. M. (2024). Surveying the Landscape: A Comprehensive Review of Object Detection Algorithms and Advancements. *Jurnal Ilmiah Computer Science*, *3*(1), 1–15. DOI: 10.58602/jics.v3i1.29

Zreik, M. (2024). Harnessing AI for entrepreneurial idea generation: Navigating the new frontier. In *Generating Entrepreneurial Ideas With AI* (pp. 1–18). IGI Global Scientific Publishing. DOI: 10.4018/979-8-3693-3498-0.ch001

Chapter 8 The Role of Language in Regulating AI and Agricultural Technologies: Legal Perspectives from a Globalized World

Hewa Majeed Zangana
https://orcid.org/0000-0001-7909-254X
Duhok Polytechnic University, Iraq

Pratiwi Amelia
https://orcid.org/0000-0001-9778-6772
Universitas Muhammadiyah Bangka Belitung, Indonesia

Senny Luckyardi
https://orcid.org/0000-0001-9954-7433
Universitas Komputer Indonesia, Indonesia

Firas Mahmood Mustafa
https://orcid.org/0000-0002-8757-5303
Duhok Polytechnic University, Iraq

Shuai Li
University of Oulu, Finland

ABSTRACT

Language plays a pivotal role in shaping the legal and regulatory frameworks that

DOI: 10.4018/979-8-3373-4862-9.ch008

Copyright © 2025, IGI Global Scientific Publishing. Copying or distributing in print or electronic forms without written permission of IGI Global Scientific Publishing is prohibited.

govern the development and deployment of artificial intelligence (AI) and agricultural technologies. In a globalized context, regulatory language not only influences legal interpretation and policy implementation but also impacts international cooperation, compliance standards, and ethical discourse. This chapter explores how linguistic nuances, translation challenges, and semantic ambiguities can affect the formulation and harmonization of legal norms across jurisdictions. By examining case studies and regulatory instruments from diverse legal systems, the chapter highlights the complexities of crafting clear, inclusive, and enforceable legal language in the face of rapidly evolving scientific and technological landscapes. The chapter argues that a multilingual and interdisciplinary approach is essential for creating robust regulatory ecosystems that promote innovation while safeguarding societal and environmental interests.

1. INTRODUCTION

The rapid advancement of artificial intelligence (AI) has profoundly reshaped contemporary scientific landscapes, revolutionizing domains as diverse as agriculture, education, environmental science, and academic writing. What was once an emerging concept is now a transformative force driving productivity, innovation, and decision-making across sectors (Groumpos, 2023; Girasa, 2020). The integration of AI technologies into academic and scientific domains is increasingly accompanied by critical questions surrounding ethics, governance, regulation, and trustworthiness (Cath, 2018; Farah & Varela, 2023).

In the field of academic writing, AI-powered tools such as ChatGPT and other large language models (LLMs) have dramatically enhanced researchers' capabilities to draft, edit, and translate content with unprecedented efficiency and fluency. However, these tools have raised significant ethical concerns, particularly around authorship, plagiarism, data fabrication, and the erosion of scholarly rigor (Casal & Kessler, 2023; Guleria et al., 2023; Chetwynd, 2024). The ongoing discourse surrounding responsible use underscores the need for well-defined ethical standards and institutional guidelines (Dinçer, 2024; Alahdab, 2024; Harati, 2024; AlSamhori & Alnaimat, 2024).

Simultaneously, AI has emerged as a key enabler in agriculture and environmental sustainability, promising to address global challenges such as food security, climate adaptation, and land degradation. The Fourth Agricultural Revolution—often referred to as Agriculture 4.0—leverages AI for precision farming, crop monitoring, yield prediction, and efficient resource allocation (Araújo et al., 2021; Chen et al., 2024; Bhat & Huang, 2021). Studies have shown how machine learning models and robotics can optimize agronomic practices, reduce environmental footprints, and empower developing economies to bridge longstanding technological divides (Ahmad et al., 2024; Aderibigbe et al., 2023; Aggarwal et al., 2024).

Yet, this promise is tempered by a parallel increase in cybersecurity risks, data governance concerns, and the need for ethical AI deployment in rural and low-resource contexts (Ali et al., 2024; Ali et al., 2024; Gardezi et al., 2024; Alexander et al., 2024). Privacy preservation, data ownership, and federated learning models are now critical areas of research, particularly as AI systems ingest sensitive agricultural data (Dembani et al., 2025; Gavai et al., 2025). Calls for robust frameworks to govern AI applications in agriculture are echoed by scholars advocating for "responsible AI" that centers transparency, fairness, and stakeholder engagement (Dara et al., 2022; Devare et al., 2023; Benabed & Tudoran, 2023).

In higher education, AI's role is similarly transformative. Beyond writing assistance, AI is reshaping pedagogical approaches, enabling personalized learning, and automating administrative processes. However, its deployment in academic institutions has prompted rigorous debate around academic integrity, student authorship, and the potential deskilling of critical thinking and scholarly engagement (Alghamdy, 2023; Aithal & Aithal, 2023; Aljuaid, 2024; Espino et al., 2024). Scholars and educators are calling for AI literacy, regulatory oversight, and interdisciplinary dialogue to responsibly navigate this evolving landscape (Fedoriv et al., 2024; Eberlin, 2024; Ajiye & Omokhabi, 2025).

This chapter explores the ethical, legal, and practical dimensions of AI in agriculture and academic writing, drawing upon interdisciplinary research and global perspectives. It offers a comparative analysis of current applications, highlights emerging regulatory models, and outlines best practices to guide the responsible integration of AI technologies. By anchoring the discussion in empirical studies and expert insights, the chapter aims to provide a comprehensive framework for scholars, educators, policymakers, and technologists seeking to align innovation with integrity.

2. UNDERSTANDING THE LANGUAGE-LAW-TECHNOLOGY NEXUS

The interplay between language, law, and technology forms a complex and evolving nexus, particularly in the context of scientific writing, agricultural innovation, and artificial intelligence (AI). This intersection has significant implications for knowledge production, dissemination, and regulatory governance.

Language functions as both a conduit and a constraint within scientific and technological development. As Posner (2009) argues, the interpretation of language in legal and scientific discourse profoundly shapes outcomes in both disciplines. Legal language, in particular, has the power to delimit or expand technological practices, while the language of scientific writing frames how research is understood and evaluated (Swales, 1990).

Technological developments in AI are reshaping the contours of this nexus. For instance, the integration of AI in scientific writing and publishing, as explored by Bagheri and Kardan (2021), demonstrates how machine learning algorithms can aid in plagiarism detection, text generation, and even peer review. While such advancements promise efficiency, they also raise ethical and epistemological concerns (Hagendorff, 2020). Questions arise about authorship, originality, and the capacity of algorithms to make value-based judgments (Mittelstadt et al., 2016).

In the agricultural sector, AI and robotics are being increasingly utilized to improve productivity and sustainability. Cai et al. (2022) provide a comprehensive review of AI applications in smart agriculture, including crop monitoring and automated harvesting. Similarly, techniques like image denoising and pattern recognition are vital for precision agriculture (Mohammadi et al., 2018). Yet, these developments necessitate robust regulatory frameworks to address concerns related to data privacy, labor displacement, and environmental impact (Stilgoe et al., 2013).

The convergence of AI and legal systems also requires an understanding of how language influences both technological design and legal interpretation. Binns (2018) emphasizes the role of transparency in algorithmic decision-making, advocating for regulatory measures that ensure accountability. These concerns are echoed in the development of explainable AI, where the goal is to make algorithmic processes intelligible to human users (Samek et al., 2017).

Scientific language itself is evolving in response to technological mediation. Hyland (2004) discusses how academic discourse communities shape norms and expectations in scholarly communication, which are now being challenged by AI-generated texts. The tension between traditional peer review and algorithmic assessment methods further complicates the relationship between scientific integrity and technological mediation (Roosendaal & Geurts, 1997).

Moreover, ethical considerations are at the forefront of this nexus. AI systems, particularly those used in healthcare, agriculture, and publishing, must align with principles of fairness, accountability, and transparency (Jobin et al., 2019). Legal frameworks must evolve to accommodate the rapidly changing landscape of AI applications, ensuring that innovations do not outpace regulation (Floridi et al., 2018).

In summary, the language-law-technology nexus is a dynamic and multifaceted domain that demands interdisciplinary attention. As AI continues to permeate various fields, including scientific writing and agriculture, it is crucial to develop legal and ethical frameworks that are responsive to the linguistic and technological complexities inherent in this convergence.

To better conceptualize the interconnected relationship between language, legal interpretation, and technological innovation, the following flowchart illustrates how language acts as both a medium and a constraint in regulating AI and agricultural technologies.

Figure 1. Flowchart of the language-law-technology nexus

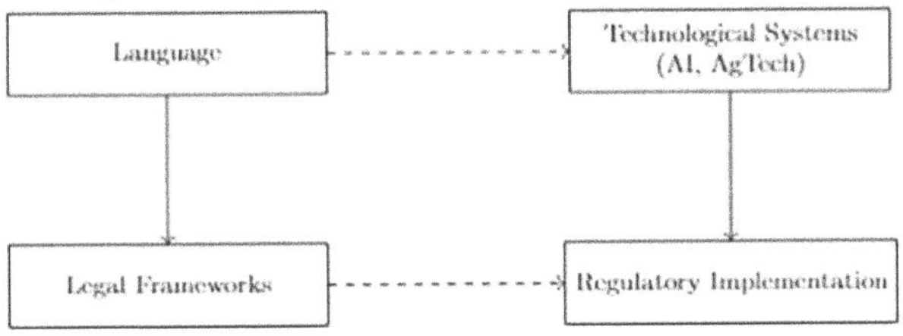

3. AI AND AGRICULTURAL TECHNOLOGIES: A REGULATORY OVERVIEW

The rapid integration of Artificial Intelligence (AI) into agricultural technologies marks a significant transformation in global food systems, with profound implications for productivity, environmental sustainability, and regulatory governance. As AI redefines precision farming, crop monitoring, supply chain management, and pest control, it also introduces ethical, legal, and technical challenges that demand comprehensive regulatory responses (Chen et al., 2024; Alexander et al., 2024).

3.1 AI-Driven Agricultural Innovation and Governance

AI applications in agriculture have revolutionized traditional farming practices, enabling data-driven decisions, predictive analytics, and automation. From soil monitoring and yield prediction to autonomous tractors and smart irrigation systems, AI is reshaping the agri-food value chain (Aggarwal et al., 2024; Bhat & Huang, 2021). These advancements are especially pivotal in developing countries, where AI presents both opportunities to bridge food security gaps and challenges linked to infrastructural and educational deficits (Ahmad et al., 2024; Ali et al., 2024; Aderibigbe et al., 2023).

However, the pace of innovation has outstripped regulatory readiness. Governments often lack coherent frameworks to manage AI deployment in agriculture, particularly concerning ethical standards, data protection, liability, and accountability (Benabed & Tudoran, 2023; Goh & Vinuesa, 2021). This regulatory lag can lead to uneven AI adoption, favoring large agribusinesses while marginalizing smallholder farmers and exacerbating digital divides (Dara et al., 2022).

3.2 Ethical, Legal, and Policy Challenges

AI in agriculture introduces complex ethical dilemmas, such as algorithmic transparency, autonomy, data privacy, and consent. Regulatory frameworks must ensure responsible innovation while protecting human rights and environmental sustainability (Cath, 2018; Alahdab, 2024; Ersöz & Engin, 2024). For instance, the collection and use of agricultural data—often generated from remote sensing or farm-based IoT devices—raises serious concerns about ownership, usage rights, and the exploitation of farmers' data by private corporations (Devare et al., 2023; Gavai et al., 2025).

Moreover, AI systems trained on biased datasets may yield inaccurate predictions, disproportionately affecting vulnerable communities and ecosystems (Adanma & Ogunbiyi, 2024). Ethical AI implementation requires inclusive policy dialogues and multidisciplinary frameworks that align technological capabilities with social values (Araújo et al., 2021; Alghamdy, 2023).

3.3 Cybersecurity and AI Regulation in Smart Agriculture

The proliferation of AI and IoT in agriculture—termed Agriculture 4.0—has also intensified cybersecurity risks, such as data breaches, cyber-physical attacks, and malicious algorithm manipulation (Ali et al., 2024; Bhangar & Shahriyar, 2023). Regulatory agencies must evolve beyond traditional models to incorporate cybersecurity protocols, ethical AI standards, and real-time compliance mechanisms (Denhere & Shao, 2024; Groumpos, 2023).

Legal scholars have emphasized the necessity of adaptive governance mechanisms that respond dynamically to the pace of AI evolution. These include sandbox regulatory environments, AI certification programs, and cross-sectoral coordination between agricultural, environmental, and data protection bodies (Farah & Varela, 2023; Gardezi et al., 2024; Bahrini et al., 2023).

3.4 Trust, Accountability, and Responsible Innovation

Building trust in AI-driven agricultural systems is critical for widespread adoption. Farmers and stakeholders must be confident in the reliability, fairness, and transparency of AI tools (Alexander et al., 2024; Gardezi et al., 2024). Accountability mechanisms—such as transparent algorithmic auditing and stakeholder feedback loops—can enhance legitimacy and ensure that AI deployment aligns with public interest (Ali et al., 2024; Chetwynd, 2024).

AI's role in agriculture must also be seen through the lens of international regulatory harmonization. Inconsistent standards across borders can hinder technology transfer, limit cooperation, and create regulatory arbitrage (Benabed & Tudoran, 2023). Collaborative frameworks such as those advocated by the OECD or FAO could facilitate ethical alignment and sustainability goals (Chen et al., 2024; Goh & Vinuesa, 2021).

3.5 Educational and Institutional Readiness

Ensuring effective regulatory oversight requires capacity-building in both educational and institutional settings. Universities and research institutions must prepare future agricultural professionals to understand the ethical and legal implications of AI use, beyond its technical capabilities (BaHammam, 2023; Ajiye & Omokhabi, 2025; Aljuaid, 2024). Training curricula should integrate interdisciplinary perspectives encompassing law, computer science, environmental science, and agronomy (Aslam & Nisar, 2024; Espino et al., 2024).

Moreover, scientific communication and academic publishing have seen increased use of AI, raising concerns about authenticity and ethical authorship (Abd-Elsalam & Abdel-Momen, 2023; Casal & Kessler, 2023; Eberlin, 2024). This further underscores the need for regulatory clarity and best practices in AI-assisted research and writing (Dinçer, 2024; Fedoriv et al., 2024).

3.6 Summary: Towards Holistic Regulatory Models

To realize AI's full potential in agriculture while mitigating associated risks, a holistic regulatory approach is essential—one that integrates ethical principles, legal safeguards, technical standards, and institutional support. This includes proactive policies on data privacy, cybersecurity, algorithmic fairness, and inclusive innovation (Groumpos, 2023; Gardezi et al., 2024; Dembani et al., 2025).

Regulatory models must also be dynamic, forward-looking, and participatory, involving stakeholders from farm to policy table. AI is not merely a technological tool but a transformative force that reshapes the socio-economic fabric of agriculture. Addressing its challenges requires legal ingenuity, ethical vigilance, and global collaboration (Girasa, 2020; Granjeiro et al., 2025).

4. LANGUAGE AS A BARRIER AND ENABLER IN GLOBAL REGULATION

Language plays a dual role in the global regulation of artificial intelligence (AI)—it can either act as a bridge to foster collaboration or as a barrier that impedes consensus and equitable implementation. As AI technologies permeate diverse sectors such as agriculture, scientific writing, education, and environmental management, the language-law-technology nexus becomes central to understanding how regulatory efforts are developed and enforced globally.

4.1 Linguistic Inequities and Global AI Governance

Language discrepancies impact the framing, dissemination, and enforcement of AI regulations. In global contexts, English often dominates regulatory documents, technical standards, and scholarly discourse, sidelining non-English speaking communities from active participation in AI governance (Benabed & Tudoran, 2023; Farah & Varela, 2023). This creates an asymmetry in knowledge exchange and legal interpretation, particularly disadvantaging developing nations (Aderibigbe et al., 2023; Ahmad et al., 2024).

For example, AI research in agriculture, especially in regions where local dialects or indigenous languages prevail, faces challenges in aligning with internationally recognized standards (Ali et al., 2024; Gavai et al., 2025). Furthermore, language barriers can obstruct ethical reviews, data-sharing protocols, and collaborative policy-making across borders (Devare et al., 2023; Dara et al., 2022).

4.2 AI Language Models as Regulatory Enablers

Ironically, AI itself offers potential solutions. Language models like ChatGPT can serve as linguistic equalizers by translating complex regulatory texts and scientific publications into multiple languages, thus democratizing access to AI-related knowledge (Aithal & Aithal, 2023; Aljuaid, 2024). This potential has been recognized in the realm of academic writing and scientific communication, where AI tools help non-native English speakers enhance the clarity and structure of their work (Abd-Elsalam & Abdel-Momen, 2023; Alahdab, 2024; Ajiye & Omokhabi, 2025).

However, the uncritical use of such tools also presents ethical dilemmas. Concerns regarding the authenticity of AI-generated text, potential plagiarism, and the masking of linguistic identity have been raised (Casal & Kessler, 2023; Chetwynd, 2024; Espino et al., 2024). These concerns necessitate clear ethical guidelines and regulatory frameworks that address the linguistic dimensions of AI usage in research and policy (Ersöz & Engin, 2024; AlSamhori & Alnaimat, 2024).

4.3 Cross-Cultural Interpretations of Ethics and Law

Language also influences the cultural interpretation of AI ethics and regulation. Terms like "responsibility," "privacy," or "bias" may carry varied connotations in different cultural and linguistic contexts, affecting how AI policies are received and implemented (Cath, 2018; Alexander et al., 2024). For instance, in agriculture, divergent understandings of data ownership and environmental stewardship complicate the harmonization of global AI ethics (Gardezi et al., 2024; Goh & Vinuesa, 2021).

Similarly, ethical standards for AI use in academic writing vary across cultures, with some viewing AI assistance as enhancement and others as academic misconduct (Dinçer, 2024; Eberlin, 2024; Granjeiro et al., 2025). Without multilingual and culturally sensitive policy frameworks, these differences can hinder the adoption of consistent international regulations.

4.4 The Role of Translation and Local Contextualization

To overcome linguistic barriers, stakeholders must invest in localized translations of regulatory documents and engage local experts in policymaking. AI tools should be leveraged not only for real-time translation but also for contextualizing content to reflect regional legal norms and cultural practices (Bhangar & Shahriyar, 2023; Ali et al., 2024; Gardezi et al., 2024). Research has shown that when local languages are integrated into digital agriculture platforms, both user trust and regulatory compliance improve (Chen et al., 2024; Araújo et al., 2021).

Moreover, incorporating local languages into data labeling, voice command systems, and interface designs can make AI applications more inclusive and effective, especially in agriculture and education (Ahmed et al., 2024; Aggarwal et al., 2024; Adanma & Ogunbiyi, 2024).

4.5 Ethical and Legal Implications

Linguistic representation must be a key consideration in ethical AI governance. Legal scholars have highlighted that multilingual accessibility in regulatory texts enhances transparency, fosters accountability, and reduces the risk of misinterpretation (Girasa, 2020; Goh & Vinuesa, 2021). The European Union's AI Act, for example, mandates documentation in multiple languages to accommodate all member states—an approach worth emulating globally (Benabed & Tudoran, 2023).

In sum, while language can pose a barrier to equitable AI regulation, it also holds the key to inclusive governance. The future of global AI regulation lies in balancing the standardization of legal frameworks with the linguistic and cultural diversity of the global community. Encouraging multilingualism in AI development, policy drafting, and educational outreach is no longer optional but imperative for ethical and effective regulation.

To ensure inclusive governance, multilingualism should be embedded at all levels of AI regulation. The following layered model proposes an architecture that integrates global, national, and local language standards.

Figure 2. Layered multilingual integration in AI Policy frameworks

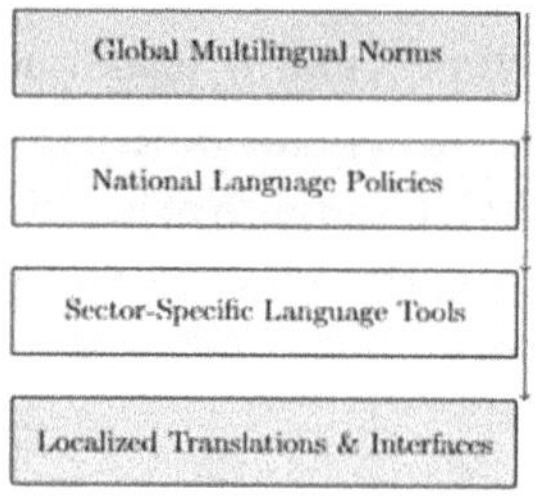

5. ETHICAL AND EQUITY IMPLICATIONS

The integration of artificial intelligence (AI) into scientific writing and agricultural innovation presents significant ethical and equity concerns, particularly within the domains of data ownership, algorithmic transparency, research integrity, and global disparities in technological access and implementation.

5.1 Algorithmic Bias and Epistemic Inequity

AI systems often reflect and reproduce the biases embedded in their training data, which can exacerbate epistemic injustices, particularly for researchers and farmers from the Global South. Aderibigbe et al. (2023) emphasize that many AI tools are developed in and for technologically advanced nations, which may marginalize local agricultural knowledge systems in developing countries. This bias is compounded by the lack of localized datasets, which makes AI less effective and potentially misleading when applied in underrepresented regions (Ahmad et al., 2024; Alexander et al., 2024).

In the realm of scientific writing, this issue manifests through the over-standardization of language and style by AI-based tools like ChatGPT, potentially diminishing linguistic diversity and creativity (Casal & Kessler, 2023; Abd-Elsalam & Abdel-Momen, 2023). Alghamdy (2023) and Aljuaid (2024) caution that AI may inadvertently reinforce Eurocentric norms in academic communication, privileging certain dialects and epistemologies over others.

AI adoption in both scientific writing and agriculture brings unique and shared ethical challenges. The Venn diagram below visualizes overlapping concerns between these two domains.

Figure 3. Overlapping ethical concerns of AI in science and agriculture

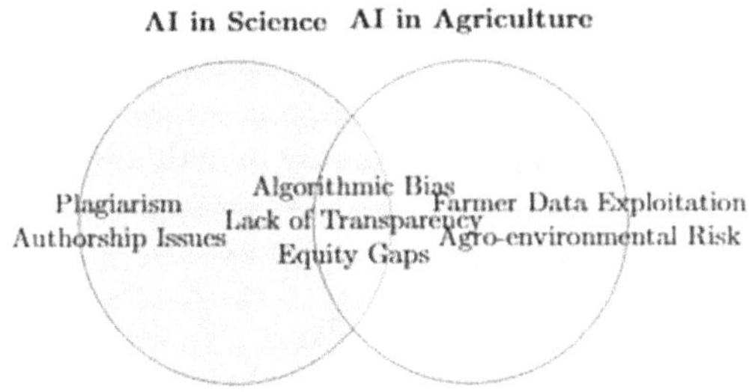

5.2 Intellectual Integrity and Plagiarism Concerns

AI-assisted writing tools raise questions of academic authorship, originality, and intellectual responsibility. Ajiye and Omokhabi (2025) argue that the ease of generating text through AI challenges conventional notions of authorship and accountability. Similarly, Alahdab (2024) and AlSamhori and Alnaimat (2024) discuss the ethical gray areas surrounding the use of AI for manuscript preparation, noting concerns about ghostwriting and the erosion of critical thinking skills among students and researchers.

Ethical use guidelines are thus paramount. Dinçer (2024) and Ersöz and Engin (2024) recommend establishing transparent authorship disclosures and delineating AI-assisted contributions from human-generated content. The misuse of these tools without proper attribution may constitute a new form of academic dishonesty (Eberlin, 2024; Chetwynd, 2024).

5.3 Equity in Access and Technological Disparities

The implementation of AI in agriculture and scientific research is not evenly distributed. Goh and Vinuesa (2021) highlight that low-income countries often lack the infrastructure to adopt AI technologies effectively, leading to a growing digital divide. This concern is echoed by Ali et al. (2024), who underline that without targeted interventions, AI may deepen global inequalities rather than alleviate them.

Bhangar and Shahriyar (2023) and Aggarwal et al. (2024) note that access to AI tools and the digital literacy to use them remain major barriers in many rural communities. Gender disparities and social inequities further complicate these issues, limiting equitable participation in AI-driven agricultural initiatives (Ahmed et al., 2024; Gardezi et al., 2024).

5.4 Data Privacy and Consent

AI applications in precision agriculture rely heavily on personal and ecological data, raising urgent ethical questions about data privacy, ownership, and informed consent. Gavai et al. (2025) and Dembani et al. (2025) review the emerging strategies for securing agricultural data, including federated learning, but caution that current frameworks remain inadequate in addressing stakeholder consent and rights.

Devare et al. (2023) stress the need for governance models that balance data utility with privacy protections, particularly for smallholder farmers. The commodification of agricultural data without equitable benefit-sharing mechanisms may result in exploitative practices (Benabed & Tudoran, 2023; Farah & Varela, 2023).

5.5 Cybersecurity and Ethical Use of AI

The intersection of AI with cybersecurity introduces additional ethical challenges, especially when AI systems are deployed in agricultural monitoring, irrigation management, or crop surveillance. Ali et al. (2024) and Adanma and Ogunbiyi (2024) point out that these systems are vulnerable to cyber threats that can compromise sensitive data and disrupt essential services.

Moreover, as Bahrini et al. (2023) outline, malicious use of AI—such as deepfakes, data poisoning, or misinformation—can undermine trust in scientific outputs and jeopardize food security systems. Ethical safeguards must thus extend beyond individual use to systemic resilience.

5.6 Frameworks for Responsible AI Use

Scholars have proposed multiple frameworks and guidelines for the responsible deployment of AI in scientific writing and agriculture. Cath (2018) and Dara et al. (2022) suggest that ethical AI use should be guided by principles of transparency, accountability, and inclusivity. This includes designing AI systems that are explainable, culturally adaptive, and co-created with stakeholders (Chen et al., 2024; Araújo et al., 2021).

BaHammam (2023) and Granjeiro et al. (2025) advocate for institutional policies that embed ethics into AI tool development and usage from the outset. Educational reforms that promote AI literacy, ethical reasoning, and participatory design can further empower users to engage critically with AI technologies (Aithal & Aithal, 2023; Aslam & Nisar, 2024).

5.7 Cultivating Trust and Social Acceptance

Trust is central to the adoption and ethical deployment of AI systems. Gardezi et al. (2024) note that farmers are more likely to adopt AI when they understand how it works and perceive it as fair and beneficial. This requires transparent communication, user-centric design, and participatory governance (Espino et al., 2024; Denhere & Shao, 2024).

Importantly, AI development must not be isolated from the communities it intends to serve. Alexander et al. (2024) emphasize the importance of building "responsible AI" through collaborative models that reflect local needs, values, and ecological knowledge.

6. BEST PRACTICES AND EMERGING SOLUTIONS

As artificial intelligence (AI) continues to revolutionize scientific writing and agriculture, adopting best practices and identifying emerging solutions is essential to ensure ethical deployment, promote innovation, and foster public trust. These solutions must account for technological, ethical, pedagogical, and regulatory perspectives that govern AI systems.

6.1 Ethical Governance and Responsible Use

AI implementation in agriculture and academia must prioritize transparency, data privacy, and human oversight. Best practices include adopting **ethical frameworks** for data management, particularly in agriculture, where federated learning and platform governance have been proposed to address privacy concerns (Dembani et al., 2025; Gavai et al., 2025; Devare et al., 2023). In the academic domain, responsible AI usage must include citation transparency, disclosure of AI use in manuscripts, and prevention of plagiarism or data fabrication (Chetwynd, 2024; Eberlin, 2024; Dinçer, 2024).

AI tools like ChatGPT, while offering unprecedented efficiency in drafting and editing, should be accompanied by **ethical literacy training** for students and researchers to mitigate misuse (AlSamhori & Alnaimat, 2024; Casal & Kessler, 2023). As BaHammam (2023) argues, maintaining integrity in research means balancing innovation with ethical conduct.

6.2 AI for Sustainable and Precision Agriculture

Best practices in AI for agriculture emphasize precision farming, resource optimization, and sustainability. AI-powered solutions—such as crop monitoring, disease detection, and yield forecasting—are enhancing food security and minimizing environmental impact (Ahmad et al., 2024; Ahmed et al., 2024; Gardezi et al., 2024). These approaches support the sustainable development goals (Goh & Vinuesa, 2021) and address the socio-technical challenges identified in smart agriculture systems (Ali et al., 2024; Chen et al., 2024).

Emerging solutions include the integration of AI with IoT devices and drones for real-time data collection (Bhat & Huang, 2021; Bhangar & Shahriyar, 2023), as well as data linkage and ontology-based systems for plant data interoperability (Devare et al., 2023; Araújo et al., 2021).

Effective AI integration in agriculture depends on a lifecycle that incorporates ethics, policy, and stakeholder input. The following diagram maps this process from design to field deployment.

Figure 4. Responsible AI lifecycle in agricultural technologies

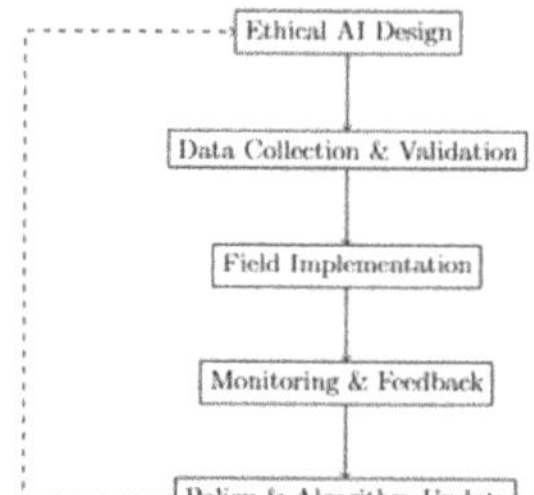

6.3 Academic Writing Enhancement Through AI

In higher education, AI can support multilingual learners, streamline research workflows, and improve academic writing through grammar correction, coherence analysis, and style optimization (Aljuaid, 2024; Abd-Elsalam & Abdel-Momen, 2023; Granjeiro et al., 2025). However, educators must guide learners in understanding the role of AI as a **supportive tool** rather than a replacement for human critical thinking and originality (Alghamdy, 2023; Aithal & Aithal, 2023).

To promote ethical use, institutions are encouraged to develop **AI policies** and incorporate AI literacy into curricula (Espino et al., 2024; Ersöz & Engin, 2024). As Fedoriv et al. (2024) and Aslam and Nisar (2024) highlight, contextual and cultural awareness must underpin the adoption of AI tools in academic writing, especially in English as a Foreign Language (EFL) settings.

6.4 Cybersecurity and Data Protection in AI Systems

AI systems in agriculture and academic platforms are vulnerable to cyber threats, including data breaches and algorithm manipulation. Establishing **robust cybersecurity protocols** is a key best practice (Ali et al., 2024; Adanma & Ogunbiyi, 2024). Encryption, access control, and ethical hacking are among the tools suggested to enhance system resilience in smart agricultural ecosystems.

6.5 Global Collaboration and Regulatory Development

Harmonizing AI regulations across borders is crucial for fostering innovation while ensuring ethical compliance. Global best practices involve multi-stakeholder governance frameworks, transparency standards, and accountability protocols (Benabed & Tudoran, 2023; Farah & Varela, 2023). According to Cath (2018), inclusive policymaking that integrates legal, ethical, and technical considerations is central to the future of AI.

Legal scholars emphasize the importance of **adaptive regulatory models** that evolve with technology while upholding human rights and academic freedom (Girasa, 2020; Dara et al., 2022; Alexander et al., 2024). These frameworks must be sensitive to geopolitical, environmental, and socio-economic differences, particularly when implementing AI in developing nations (Aderibigbe et al., 2023; Ahmad et al., 2024).

6.6 Building Trust in AI Technologies

Trust is a cornerstone of AI adoption in both science and agriculture. Gardezi et al. (2024) recommend participatory approaches involving farmers, researchers, and policymakers to co-design AI systems. Similarly, in academia, building trust in AI-enhanced writing requires transparency, ethical oversight, and academic rigor (Ajiye & Omokhabi, 2025; Alahdab, 2024).

6.7 Summary

Adopting best practices and developing emerging solutions in AI for scientific writing and agriculture requires a holistic and interdisciplinary approach. By prioritizing ethical governance, data privacy, regulatory alignment, and inclusive education, AI can be leveraged as a transformative force that enhances productivity, fosters innovation, and maintains the integrity of research and agrifood systems.

7. POLICY RECOMMENDATIONS

The rapid integration of Artificial Intelligence (AI) in scientific writing, academic research, and agriculture presents transformative opportunities as well as complex challenges. To harness AI's potential responsibly and sustainably, policymakers must craft comprehensive frameworks addressing ethical, legal, technological, and socio-economic dimensions. The following policy recommendations draw on current scholarship to guide governments, academic institutions, and industry stakeholders in enabling AI's benefits while mitigating risks.

7.1. Establish Clear Ethical Guidelines and Accountability Mechanisms

AI's use in scientific writing and agriculture must be underpinned by transparent ethical standards to uphold integrity, trust, and fairness (Eberlin, 2024; Dinçer, 2024; Espino et al., 2024). Policies should mandate disclosures of AI assistance in academic outputs to prevent plagiarism and maintain scholarly rigor (Alahdab, 2024; Casal & Kessler, 2023). Furthermore, responsibility for AI-driven decisions, especially in agriculture, must be clearly defined to avoid accountability gaps (Alexander, Yarborough, & Smith, 2024; Kaushik et al., 2024). Institutions should create ethics committees to oversee AI deployments and ensure compliance with best practices (Aslam & Nisar, 2024).

7.2. Promote Inclusive Access and Capacity Building in Developing Countries

AI technologies risk exacerbating global inequalities if their adoption remains uneven. Policies must prioritize investment in digital infrastructure, training, and support systems to enable developing nations to benefit from AI innovations in agriculture and research (Aderibigbe et al., 2023; Ahmad et al., 2024; Ali et al., 2024). Capacity-building initiatives, including partnerships with international organizations, will foster localized AI solutions attuned to socio-cultural and environmental contexts (Abd-Elsalam & Abdel-Momen, 2023; Bhangar & Shahriyar, 2023).

7.3. Develop Robust Regulatory Frameworks for AI in Agriculture and Research

Effective governance requires harmonized legal frameworks balancing innovation with safety and privacy. Governments should enact laws regulating data collection, usage, and sharing in agricultural AI platforms to safeguard farmers' privacy and prevent data misuse (Dembani et al., 2025; Gavai et al., 2025; Devare et al., 2023). Simultaneously, research institutions must adopt policies ensuring ethical use of AI tools in manuscript preparation, such as limiting AI to assistive rather than authorship roles (AlSamhori & Alnaimat, 2024; Aljuaid, 2024).

A review of current AI policies in agriculture and science reveals significant governance gaps. The bar chart below ranks key areas lacking adequate policy attention.

Figure 5. Ranking of key policy gaps in AI governance

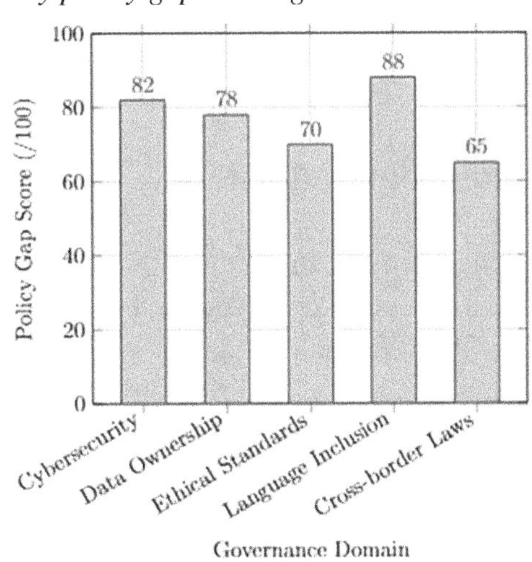

7.4. Encourage Transparency and Explainability in AI Systems

Transparency is essential for building trust among users and stakeholders, particularly where AI influences critical decisions in farming or academic publishing (Cath, 2018; He et al., 2021). Regulatory bodies should require AI developers to provide explainable models and audit trails that clarify how conclusions or recommendations are generated (Holzinger et al., 2021; Kapoor, 2025). This approach will also facilitate better identification of biases and errors (Gardezi et al., 2024).

7.5. Address Cybersecurity Risks in AI-Driven Agricultural Systems

As agriculture increasingly incorporates smart technologies, vulnerabilities to cyberattacks multiply, threatening food security and data integrity (Ali et al., 2024; Kaushik et al., 2024; Jerhamre, Carlberg, & van Zoest, 2022). Policies must enforce rigorous cybersecurity standards, continuous threat monitoring, and incident response mechanisms specific to AI-powered agricultural networks (Bhat & Huang, 2021; Ali et al., 2024). Cross-sector collaboration is crucial to share intelligence and best practices (Kaushik et al., 2024).

7.6. Foster Interdisciplinary Research and Collaboration

Bridging gaps between AI technology developers, agronomists, ethicists, legal experts, and end-users is vital to anticipate challenges and craft holistic solutions (Farah & Varela, 2023; Girasa, 2020; Goh & Vinuesa, 2021). Funding agencies and institutions should incentivize collaborative projects addressing AI's societal impact, including frameworks for responsible AI adoption in agriculture and academic writing (Granjeiro et al., 2025; Groumpos, 2023).

7.7. Support Development of AI Literacy and Digital Skills

Widespread AI adoption depends on equipping researchers, students, farmers, and policymakers with the necessary knowledge and skills to utilize AI responsibly (Aithal & Aithal, 2023; Khup & Bantugan, 2025; Alghamdy, 2023). Educational curricula should integrate AI literacy, covering ethical use, risk mitigation, and critical evaluation of AI-generated content (Espino et al., 2024; Dinçer, 2024).

7.8. Encourage the Adoption of Federated Learning and Data Privacy Technologies

Emerging techniques like federated learning enable AI training on distributed datasets without compromising privacy—a critical consideration for sensitive agricultural and research data (Dembani et al., 2025; Gavai et al., 2025). Policymakers should support development and deployment of such privacy-preserving methods through grants and regulatory incentives (Bahrini et al., 2023).

7.9. Monitor and Update Policies in Response to AI Evolution

AI technologies and their implications evolve rapidly; thus, regulatory frameworks must be adaptable and continuously reviewed (Benabed & Tudoran, 2023; Kirov, 2023). Governments and institutions should establish dedicated task forces to monitor AI developments and update policies accordingly, engaging stakeholders in an iterative, transparent process (Bhangar & Shahriyar, 2023; Khalifa & Albadawy, 2024).

7.10. Promote Responsible AI Research and Development Funding

Funding agencies should incorporate ethical and societal impact criteria into AI research grants to ensure innovations align with public interest and sustainable development goals (Chen et al., 2024; Kapoor, 2025; Goh & Vinuesa, 2021). Grants can prioritize projects that explicitly address AI's risks and develop mitigation strategies, including in agricultural supply chains and academic publishing (Kanyepe et al., 2025; Aggarwal, Bansal, & Goel, 2024).

7.11 Summary

The integration of AI in scientific writing and agriculture is poised to revolutionize knowledge creation and food production. However, without proactive and comprehensive policy frameworks, these advancements risk undermining ethical standards, equity, security, and public trust. By adopting the above policy recommendations grounded in interdisciplinary scholarship and global best practices, stakeholders can foster an AI ecosystem that is innovative, responsible, and inclusive.

8. CONCLUSION

The integration of artificial intelligence (AI) in scientific writing, academic research, and agricultural technologies represents a transformative shift with profound potential to enhance productivity, innovation, and sustainability. This chapter has highlighted both the opportunities and challenges associated with AI adoption in these critical domains, emphasizing the need for balanced, ethical, and policy-driven approaches.

AI-driven tools have significantly streamlined scientific writing and research processes, enabling faster data analysis, improved manuscript quality, and broader access to knowledge (Abd-Elsalam & Abdel-Momen, 2023; Khalifa & Albadawy, 2024). However, these benefits come with concerns regarding ethical use, authorship integrity, and potential misuse, underscoring the importance of clear guidelines and responsible practices (Aslam & Nisar, 2024; Dinçer, 2024; AlSamhori & Alnaimat, 2024).

In agriculture, AI technologies offer unprecedented capabilities for precision farming, crop monitoring, and supply chain optimization, which are vital for global food security and sustainable environmental management (Aggarwal, Bansal, & Goel, 2024; Ahmad et al., 2024; Chen et al., 2024). Nonetheless, challenges such as data privacy, cybersecurity threats, and equitable access must be addressed to ensure inclusive and safe deployment (Ali et al., 2024; Dembani et al., 2025; Gavai et al., 2025).

Policy frameworks play a critical role in shaping AI development and usage, especially by fostering trust, transparency, and ethical accountability in both academia and agriculture (Benabed & Tudoran, 2023; Cath, 2018; Farah & Varela, 2023). As AI continues to evolve rapidly, it is imperative that policymakers, researchers, and practitioners collaborate to develop adaptive regulations that protect human rights, promote innovation, and prevent unintended consequences (Girasa, 2020; Goh & Vinuesa, 2021; Kapoor, 2025).

In conclusion, while AI presents transformative opportunities for scientific writing and agricultural innovation, realizing its full potential requires an integrated approach. This approach must combine technological advancement with ethical considerations, robust policy measures, and continuous stakeholder engagement to build a future where AI empowers human creativity, enhances food security, and upholds scientific integrity.

REFERENCES

Abd-Elsalam, K. A., & Abdel-Momen, S. M. (2023). Artificial intelligence's development and challenges in scientific writing. *Egyptian Journal of Agricultural Research, 101*(3), 714–717. DOI: 10.21608/ejar.2023.220363.1414

Adanma, U. M., & Ogunbiyi, E. O. (2024). Artificial intelligence in environmental conservation: Evaluating cyber risks and opportunities for sustainable practices. *Computer Science & IT Research Journal*, *5*(5), 1178–1209. DOI: 10.51594/csitrj.v5i5.1156

Aderibigbe, A. O., Ohenhen, P. E., Nwaobia, N. K., Gidiagba, J. O., & Ani, E. C. (2023). Artificial intelligence in developing countries: Bridging the gap between potential and implementation. *Computer Science & IT Research Journal*, *4*(3), 185–199. DOI: 10.51594/csitrj.v4i3.629

Aggarwal, S., Bansal, S., & Goel, R. (2024). Ai In Agriculture: A Looming Challenge, A Gleaming Opportunity. *International Journal of Engineering Science and Humanities, 14*(Special Issue 1), 43-52.

Ahmad, A., Liew, A. X., Venturini, F., Kalogeras, A., Candiani, A., Di Benedetto, G., Ajibola, S., Cartujo, P., Romero, P., Lykoudi, A., De Grandis, M. M., Xouris, C., Lo Bianco, R., Doddy, I., Elegbede, I., D'Urso Labate, G. F., García del Moral, L. F., & Martos, V. (2024). AI can empower agriculture for global food security: Challenges and prospects in developing nations. *Frontiers in Artificial Intelligence*, *7*, 1328530. DOI: 10.3389/frai.2024.1328530 PMID: 38726306

Ahmed, M. N., Singh, A. P., Hussain, M. R., Rasool, M. A., Khan, I. M., & Dildar, M. S. (2024, July). Enhancing Crop Production using Artificial Intelligence in Agricultural Revolution. In *2024 IEEE 7th International Conference on Advanced Technologies* [ATSIP]. *Signal and Image Processing : an International Journal*, *1*, 432–437.

Aithal, P. S., & Aithal, S. (2023). Application of ChatGPT in higher education and research–A futuristic analysis. [IJAEML]. *International Journal of Applied Engineering and Management Letters*, *7*(3), 168–194. DOI: 10.47992/IJAEML.2581.7000.0193

Ajiye, O. T., & Omokhabi, A. A. (2025). THE POTENTIAL AND ETHICAL ISSUES OF ARTIFICIAL INTELLIGENCE IN IMPROVING ACADEMIC WRITING. *ShodhAI: Journal of Artificial Intelligence*, *2*(1), 1–9. DOI: 10.29121/shodhai.v2.i1.2025.24

Alahdab, F. (2024). Potential impact of large language models on academic writing. *BMJ Evidence-Based Medicine*, *29*(3), 201–202. DOI: 10.1136/bmjebm-2023-112429 PMID: 37620013

Alexander, C. S., Yarborough, M., & Smith, A. (2024). Who is responsible for 'responsible AI'?: Navigating challenges to build trust in AI agriculture and food system technology. *Precision Agriculture*, *25*(1), 146–185. DOI: 10.1007/s11119-023-10063-3

Alghamdy, R. Z. (2023). Pedagogical and ethical implications of artificial intelligence in EFL context: A review study. *English Language Teaching*, *16*(10), 87–98. DOI: 10.5539/elt.v16n10p87

Ali, A., Anderson, L., Venturini, F., Athanasios, K., Candiani, A., Di Benedetto, G., ... & Martos, V. (2024). AI can empower agriculture for global food security: challenges and prospects in developing nations.

Ali, G., Mijwil, M. M., Buruga, B. A., Abotaleb, M., & Adamopoulos, I. (2024). A survey on artificial intelligence in cybersecurity for smart agriculture: State-of-the-art, cyber threats, artificial intelligence applications, and ethical concerns. *Mesopotamian Journal of Computer Science*, *2024*, 53–103. DOI: 10.58496/MJCSC/2024/007

Aljuaid, H. (2024). The impact of artificial intelligence tools on academic writing instruction in higher education: A systematic review. *Arab World English Journal (AWEJ) Special Issue on ChatGPT*.

AlSamhori, A. F., & Alnaimat, F. (2024). Artificial intelligence in writing and research: Ethical implications and best practices. *Central Asian Journal of Medical Hypotheses and Ethics = Central'noaziatskij Zurnal Medicinskich Gipotez i Etiki = Medicinalyk Gipoteza Men Ètikanyn Orta Aziâlyk Zurnaly*, *5*(4), 259–268. DOI: 10.47316/cajmhe.2024.5.4.02

Araújo, S. O., Peres, R. S., Barata, J., Lidon, F., & Ramalho, J. C. (2021). Characterising the agriculture 4.0 landscape—Emerging trends, challenges and opportunities. *Agronomy (Basel)*, *11*(4), 667. DOI: 10.3390/agronomy11040667

Aslam, M. S., & Nisar, S. (2024). Ethical Considerations for Artificial Intelligence Tools in Academic Research and Manuscript Preparation: A Web Content Analysis. In *Digital Transformation in Higher Education, Part B: Cases, Examples and Good Practices* (pp. 155-196). Emerald Publishing Limited. DOI: 10.1108/978-1-83608-424-220241007

BaHammam, A. S. (2023). Balancing innovation and integrity: The role of AI in research and scientific writing. *Nature and Science of Sleep*, •••, 1153–1156. PMID: 38170140

Bahrini, A., Khamoshifar, M., Abbasimehr, H., Riggs, R. J., Esmaeili, M., Majdabadkohne, R. M., & Pasehvar, M. (2023, April). ChatGPT: Applications, opportunities, and threats. In *2023 Systems and Information Engineering Design Symposium (SIEDS)* (pp. 274-279). IEEE. DOI: 10.1109/SIEDS58326.2023.10137850

Benabed, A., & Tudoran, L. (2023). Artificial intelligence towards international regulations, frameworks and laws in the world of globalization: Implications and challenges. *Persp. L. Pub. Admin.*, *12*, 268.

Bhangar, N. A., & Shahriyar, A. K. (2023). Iot and ai for next-generation farming: Opportunities, challenges, and outlook. *International Journal of Sustainable Infrastructure for Cities and Societies*, *8*(2), 14–26.

Bhat, S. A., & Huang, N. F. (2021). Big data and ai revolution in precision agriculture: Survey and challenges. *IEEE Access : Practical Innovations, Open Solutions*, *9*, 110209–110222. DOI: 10.1109/ACCESS.2021.3102227

Casal, J. E., & Kessler, M. (2023). Can linguists distinguish between ChatGPT/AI and human writing?: A study of research ethics and academic publishing. *Research Methods in Applied Linguistics*, *2*(3), 100068. DOI: 10.1016/j.rmal.2023.100068

Cath, C. (2018). Governing artificial intelligence: Ethical, legal and technical opportunities and challenges. *Philosophical Transactions. Series A, Mathematical, Physical, and Engineering Sciences*, *376*(2133), 20180080. DOI: 10.1098/rsta.2018.0080 PMID: 30322996

Chen, T., Lv, L., Wang, D., Zhang, J., Yang, Y., Zhao, Z., & Tao, D. (2024). Empowering agrifood system with artificial intelligence: A survey of the progress, challenges and opportunities. *ACM Computing Surveys*, *57*(2), 1–37.

Chetwynd, E. (2024). Ethical use of artificial intelligence for scientific writing: Current trends. *Journal of Human Lactation*, *40*(2), 211–215. DOI: 10.1177/08903344241235160 PMID: 38482810

Dara, R., Hazrati Fard, S. M., & Kaur, J. (2022). Recommendations for ethical and responsible use of artificial intelligence in digital agriculture. *Frontiers in Artificial Intelligence*, *5*, 884192. DOI: 10.3389/frai.2022.884192 PMID: 35968036

Dembani, R., Karvelas, I., Akbar, N. A., Rizou, S., Tegolo, D., & Fountas, S. (2025). Agricultural data privacy and federated learning: A review of challenges and opportunities. *Computers and Electronics in Agriculture, 232*, 110048. DOI: 10.1016/j.compag.2025.110048

Denhere, V., & Shao, D. (2024). Artificial Intelligence in Agritourism: Utilitarian Analysis of Opportunities, Challenges, and Ethical Considerations in the African Context. *Agritourism in Africa*, 17-36.

Devare, M., Arnaud, E., Antezana, E., & King, B. (2023). Governing agricultural data: Challenges and recommendations. *Towards Responsible Plant Data Linkage: Data Challenges for Agricultural Research and Development, 201.*

Dinçer, S. (2024). The use and ethical implications of artificial intelligence in scientific research and academic writing. *Educational Research & Implementation, 1*(2), 139–144. DOI: 10.14527/edure.2024.10

Eberlin, M. N. (2024). The Art of Scientific Writing and Ethical Use of Artificial Intelligence. *Journal of the Brazilian Chemical Society, 35*(1), e-20230121.

Ersöz, A. R., & Engin, M. (2024). Exploring Ethical Dilemmas in the Use of Artificial Intelligence in Academic Writing: Perspectives of Researchers. *Journal of Uludag University Faculty of Education, 37*(3), 1190–1208. DOI: 10.19171/uefad.1514323

Espino, A. R. C., Esto, M. R. A., Manalo, C. G. S., Santiago, C. S., & Pragacha, R. N. (2024, June). Ethical Implications of Using Assistive Writing Tools in the Academe: A Literature Review. In *International Conference on Frontiers of Intelligent Computing: Theory and Applications* (pp. 133-145). Singapore: Springer Nature Singapore.

Farah, P. D., & Varela, J. C. (2023). Science, Technology, Society, and Law. In *Science, Technology, Policy and International Law* (pp. 1-19). Routledge.

Fedoriv, Y., Shuhai, A., & Pirozhenko, I. (2024). Foundations of Ethical Use of AI in EFL Academic Writing.

Gardezi, M., Joshi, B., Rizzo, D. M., Ryan, M., Prutzer, E., Brugler, S., & Dadkhah, A. (2024). Artificial intelligence in farming: Challenges and opportunities for building trust. *Agronomy Journal, 116*(3), 1217–1228. DOI: 10.1002/agj2.21353

Gavai, A. K., Bouzembrak, Y., Xhani, D., Sedrakyan, G., Meuwissen, M. P., Souza, R. G. S., ... & van Hillegersberg, J. (2025). Agricultural data Privacy: Emerging platforms & strategies. *Food and Humanity*, 100542.

Girasa, R. (2020). *Artificial intelligence as a disruptive technology: Economic transformation and government regulation*. Springer Nature. DOI: 10.1007/978-3-030-35975-1

Goh, H. H., & Vinuesa, R. (2021). Regulating artificial-intelligence applications to achieve the sustainable development goals. *Discover Sustainability*, *2*(1), 1–6. DOI: 10.1007/s43621-021-00064-5 PMID: 35425914

Granjeiro, J. M., Cury, A. A. D. B., Cury, J. A., Bueno, M., Sousa-Neto, M. D., & Estrela, C. (2025). The Future of Scientific Writing: AI Tools, Benefits, and Ethical Implications. *Brazilian Dental Journal*, *36*, e25–e6471. DOI: 10.1590/0103-644020256471 PMID: 40197923

Groumpos, P. P. (2023, July). A critical historic overview of artificial intelligence: Issues, challenges, opportunities, and threats. *Artificial Intelligence and Applications (Commerce, Calif.)*, *1*(4), 181–197. DOI: 10.47852/bonviewAIA3202689

Guleria, A., Krishan, K., Sharma, V., & Kanchan, T. (2023). ChatGPT: Ethical concerns and challenges in academics and research. *Journal of Infection in Developing Countries*, *17*(09), 1292–1299. DOI: 10.3855/jidc.18738 PMID: 37824352

Gupta, D. K., Pagani, A., Zamboni, P., & Singh, A. K. (2024). AI-powered revolution in plant sciences: Advancements, applications, and challenges for sustainable agriculture and food security. *Exploration of Foods and Foodomics*, *2*(5), 443–459. DOI: 10.37349/eff.2024.00045

Harati, K. (2024). ChatGPT and AI-Powered Writing Tools: Unveiling Risks and Ethical Challenges in Scientific Writing. *Journal of Research in Medical Sciences : the Official Journal of Isfahan University of Medical Sciences*, *4*(1), 1–6.

He, H., Gray, J., Cangelosi, A., Meng, Q., McGinnity, T. M., & Mehnen, J. (2021). The challenges and opportunities of human-centered AI for trustworthy robots and autonomous systems. *IEEE Transactions on Cognitive and Developmental Systems*, *14*(4), 1398–1412. DOI: 10.1109/TCDS.2021.3132282

Holzinger, A., Weippl, E., Tjoa, A. M., & Kieseberg, P. (2021, August). Digital transformation for sustainable development goals (sdgs)-a security, safety and privacy perspective on ai. In *International cross-domain conference for machine learning and knowledge extraction* (pp. 1-20). Cham: Springer International Publishing.

Jerhamre, E., Carlberg, C. J. C., & van Zoest, V. (2022). Exploring the susceptibility of smart farming: Identified opportunities and challenges. *Smart Agricultural Technology*, 2, 2. DOI: 10.1016/j.atech.2021.100026

Kanyepe, J., Chibaro, M., Morima, M., & Moeti-Lysson, J. (2025). AI-Powered Agricultural Supply Chains: Applications, Challenges, and Opportunities. *Integrating Agriculture, Green Marketing Strategies, and Artificial Intelligence*, 33-64.

Kapoor, P. (2025). Harvesting Ethics: Forging Responsible Paths in AI and ML for the Agri-Food Industry. In *Food and Industry 5.0: Transforming the Food System for a Sustainable Future* (pp. 305–315). Springer Nature Switzerland. DOI: 10.1007/978-3-031-76758-6_19

Kaushik, K., Khan, A., Kumari, A., Sharma, I., & Dubey, R. (2024). Ethical considerations in AI-based cybersecurity. In *Next-generation cybersecurity: AI, ML, and Blockchain* (pp. 437–470). Springer Nature Singapore. DOI: 10.1007/978-981-97-1249-6_19

Khalifa, M., & Albadawy, M. (2024). Using artificial intelligence in academic writing and research: An essential productivity tool. *Computer Methods and Programs in Biomedicine Update*, *5*, 100145. DOI: 10.1016/j.cmpbup.2024.100145

Khup, V. K., & Bantugan, B. (2025). Exploring the Impact and Ethical Implications of Integrating AI-Powered Writing Tools in Junior High School English Instruction: Enhancing Creativity, Proficiency, and Academic Outcomes. *International Journal of Research and Innovation in Social Science*, *9*(IIIS, 3s), 361–378. DOI: 10.47772/IJRISS.2025.903SEDU0022

Kirov, B. (2023, September). Artificial Intelligence in Creation of Scientific Written Works: Weighing the Benefits and Ethical Dilemmas-Should We Use It? In *2023 International Scientific Conference on Computer Science (COMSCI)* (pp. 1-5). IEEE. DOI: 10.1109/COMSCI59259.2023.10315821

Kochupillai, M., Kahl, M., Schmitt, M., Taubenböck, H., & Zhu, X. X. (2022). Earth observation and artificial intelligence: Understanding emerging ethical issues and opportunities. *IEEE Geoscience and Remote Sensing Magazine*, *10*(4), 90–124. DOI: 10.1109/MGRS.2022.3208357

Kochupillai, M., & Köninger, J. (2023). Creating a digital marketplace for agrobiodiversity and plant genetic sequence data: Legal and ethical considerations of an ai and blockchain based solution. *Towards Responsible Plant Data Linkage: Data Challenges for Agricultural Research and Development*, 223.

Leong, Y. M., Lim, E. H., Subri, N. F. B., & Jalil, N. B. A. (2023, September). Transforming agriculture: Navigating the challenges and embracing the opportunities of artificial intelligence of things. In *2023 IEEE International Conference on Agrosystem Engineering, Technology & Applications (AGRETA)* (pp. 142-147). IEEE. DOI: 10.1109/AGRETA57740.2023.10262747

Li, J., Zong, H., Wu, E., Wu, R., Peng, Z., Zhao, J., Yang, L., Xie, H., & Shen, B. (2024). Exploring the potential of artificial intelligence to enhance the writing of english academic papers by non-native english-speaking medical students-the educational application of ChatGPT. *BMC Medical Education*, *24*(1), 736. DOI: 10.1186/s12909-024-05738-y PMID: 38982429

Liu, Y., Kong, W., & Merve, K. (2025). ChatGPT applications in academic writing: A review of potential, limitations, and ethical challenges. *Arquivos Brasileiros de Oftalmologia*, *88*(3), e2024–e0269. DOI: 10.5935/0004-2749.2024-0269 PMID: 39879415

Lund, B. D., Wang, T., Mannuru, N. R., Nie, B., Shimray, S., & Wang, Z. (2023). ChatGPT and a new academic reality: Artificial Intelligence-written research papers and the ethics of the large language models in scholarly publishing. *Journal of the Association for Information Science and Technology*, *74*(5), 570–581. DOI: 10.1002/asi.24750

Malhotra, K., & Firdaus, M. (2022). Application of artificial intelligence in IoT security for crop yield prediction. *ResearchBerg Review of Science and Technology*, *2*(1), 136–157.

Manning, L., Brewer, S., Craigon, P. J., Frey, J., Gutierrez, A., Jacobs, N., Kanza, S., Munday, S., Sacks, J., & Pearson, S. (2022). Artificial intelligence and ethics within the food sector: Developing a common language for technology adoption across the supply chain. *Trends in Food Science & Technology*, *125*, 33–42. DOI: 10.1016/j.tifs.2022.04.025

Mark, R. (2019). Ethics of using AI and big data in agriculture: The case of a large agriculture multinational. *The ORBIT Journal*, *2*(2), 1–27. DOI: 10.29297/orbit.v2i2.109

Miao, J., Thongprayoon, C., Suppadungsuk, S., Garcia Valencia, O. A., Qureshi, F., & Cheungpasitporn, W. (2023). Ethical dilemmas in using AI for academic writing and an example framework for peer review in nephrology academia: A narrative review. *Clinics and Practice*, *14*(1), 89–105. DOI: 10.3390/clinpract14010008 PMID: 38248432

Molligan, J., & Pérez-López, E. (2024). Artificial intelligence in academia: Opportunities, challenges, and ethical considerations. *Biochemistry and Cell Biology*, *103*, 1–3. DOI: 10.1139/bcb-2024-0216 PMID: 39611424

Nam, B. H., & Bai, Q. (2023). ChatGPT and its ethical implications for STEM research and higher education: A media discourse analysis. *International Journal of STEM Education*, *10*(1), 66. DOI: 10.1186/s40594-023-00452-5

Neupane, S., Mitra, S., Fernandez, I. A., Saha, S., Mittal, S., Chen, J., Pillai, N., & Rahimi, S. (2024). Security considerations in ai-robotics: A survey of current methods, challenges, and opportunities. *IEEE Access : Practical Innovations, Open Solutions*, *12*, 22072–22097. DOI: 10.1109/ACCESS.2024.3363657

Nurchurifiani, E., Maximilian, A., Ajeng, G. D., Wiratno, P., Hastomo, T., & Wicaksono, A. (2025). Leveraging AI-Powered Tools in Academic Writing and Research: Insights from English Faculty Members in Indonesia. *International Journal of Information and Education Technology (IJIET)*, *15*(2), 312–322. DOI: 10.18178/ijiet.2025.15.2.2244

Ocampo, T. S. C., Silva, T. P., Alencar-Palha, C., Haiter-Neto, F., & Oliveira, M. L. (2023). ChatGPT and scientific writing: A reflection on the ethical boundaries. *Imaging Science in Dentistry*, *53*(2), 175. DOI: 10.5624/isd.20230085 PMID: 37405199

Omodan, B. I., & Marongwe, N. (2024). The role of artificial intelligence in decolonising academic writing for inclusive knowledge production. *Interdisciplinary Journal of Education Research*, *6*(s1), 1–14. DOI: 10.38140/ijer-2024.vol6.s1.06

Otieno, M. (2023). An extensive survey of smart agriculture technologies: Current security posture. *World J. Adv. Res. Rev*, *18*(3), 1207–1231. DOI: 10.30574/wjarr.2023.18.3.1241

Pandey, D. K., & Mishra, R. (2024). *Towards sustainable agriculture: Harnessing AI for global food security*. Artificial Intelligence in Agriculture.

Pedro, F., Subosa, M., Rivas, A., & Valverde, P. (2019). Artificial intelligence in education: Challenges and opportunities for sustainable development.

Peng, S. Y., Lin, C. F., & Streinz, T. (Eds.). (2021). *Artificial intelligence and international Economic law*. Cambridge University Press. DOI: 10.1017/9781108954006

Perkins, M. (2023). Academic Integrity considerations of AI Large Language Models in the post-pandemic era: ChatGPT and beyond. *Journal of University Teaching & Learning Practice*, *20*(2), 1–24. DOI: 10.53761/1.20.02.07

Salvagno, M., Taccone, F. S., & Gerli, A. G. (2023). Can artificial intelligence help for scientific writing? *Critical Care*, *27*(1), 75. DOI: 10.1186/s13054-023-04380-2 PMID: 36841840

Senoo, E. E. K., Anggraini, L., Kumi, J. A., Luna, B. K., Akansah, E., Sulyman, H. A., & Aritsugi, M. (2024). IoT solutions with artificial intelligence technologies for precision agriculture: Definitions, applications, challenges, and opportunities. *Electronics (Basel)*, *13*(10), 1894. DOI: 10.3390/electronics13101894

Shafik, W., Tufail, A., De Silva, C. L., Haji, R. A. A., & Apong, M. (2025). The Role, Application, and Impact of Artificial Intelligence in the Agriculture Industry. In *Future Tech Startups and Innovation in the Age of AI* (pp. 36–60). CRC Press.

Shofiah, N., Putera, Z. F., & Solichah, N. (2023, December). Challenges and opportunities in the use of artificial intelligence in education for academic writing: A scoping review. In *Conference Psychology and Flourishing Humanity (PFH 2023)* (pp. 174-193). Atlantis Press. DOI: 10.2991/978-2-38476-188-3_20

Sood, A., Sharma, R. K., & Bhardwaj, A. K. (2022). Artificial intelligence research in agriculture: A review. *Online Information Review*, *46*(6), 1054–1075. DOI: 10.1108/OIR-10-2020-0448

Sparrow, R., & Howard, M. (2021). Robots in agriculture: prospects, impacts, ethics, and policy. *precision agriculture, 22*, 818-833.

Sparrow, R., Howard, M., & Degeling, C. (2021). Managing the risks of artificial intelligence in agriculture. *NJAS: Impact in Agricultural and Life Sciences*, *93*(1), 172–196. DOI: 10.1080/27685241.2021.2008777

Subaveerapandiyan, A., Kalbande, D., & Ahmad, N. (2025). Perceptions of effectiveness and ethical use of AI tools in academic writing: A study Among PhD scholars in India. *Information Development*, •••, 02666669251314840. DOI: 10.1177/02666669251314840

Tai, A. M. Y., Meyer, M., Varidel, M., Prodan, A., Vogel, M., Iorfino, F., & Krausz, R. M. (2023). Exploring the potential and limitations of ChatGPT for academic peer-reviewed writing: Addressing linguistic injustice and ethical concerns. *Journal of Academic Language and Learning*, *17*(1), T16–T30.

Tasa-Fuster, V. (2024). The Legal Rationales of the Leading Technological Models: The Challenges of Regulating Linguistic and Gender Biases. In *Gendered Technology in Translation and Interpreting* (pp. 27-65). Routledge.

Turner, J. (2018). *Robot rules: Regulating artificial intelligence*. Springer.

Tzachor, A., Devare, M., King, B., Avin, S., & Ó hÉigeartaigh, S. (2022). Responsible artificial intelligence in agriculture requires systemic understanding of risks and externalities. *Nature Machine Intelligence*, *4*(2), 104–109. DOI: 10.1038/s42256-022-00440-4

Uddin, M., Chowdhury, A., & Kabir, M. A. (2024). Legal and ethical aspects of deploying artificial intelligence in climate-smart agriculture. *AI & Society*, *39*(1), 221–234. DOI: 10.1007/s00146-022-01421-2

Ugwu, N. F., Igbinlade, A. S., Ochiaka, R. E., Ezeani, U. D., Okorie, N. C., Opele, J. K., Onayinka, T. S., Iroegbu, O., Onyekwere, O. K., Adams, A. B., Aigbona, P., & Ojobola, F. B. (2024). Clarifying Ethical Dilemmas in Using Artificial Intelligence in Research Writing: A Rapid Review. *Higher Learning Research Communications, 14*(2), 29–47. DOI: 10.18870/hlrc.v142.1549

Uplaonkar, S. S., Veershetty, R., Bahar, Z., & Sangeeta, G. (2024). The role of productive AI: A supporter or challenger in the future of agricultural librarianship. *IJAR, 10*(4), 46–53.

Wei, H., Xu, W., Kang, B., Eisner, R., Muleke, A., Rodriguez, D., deVoil, P., Sadras, V., Monjardino, M., & Harrison, M. T. (2024). Irrigation with artificial intelligence: Problems, premises, promises. *Human-Centric Intelligent Systems, 4*(2), 187–205. DOI: 10.1007/s44230-024-00072-4

Williamson, H. F., Brettschneider, J., Caccamo, M., Davey, R. P., Goble, C., Kersey, P. J., May, S., Morris, R. J., Ostler, R., Pridmore, T., Rawlings, C., Studholme, D., Tsaftaris, S. A., & Leonelli, S. (2023). Data management challenges for artificial intelligence in plant and agricultural research. *F1000 Research, 10*, 324. DOI: 10.12688/f1000research.52204.2 PMID: 36873457

Wiwanitmkit, S., & Wiwanitkit, V. (2024). Artificial Intelligence, Academic Publishing, Scientific Writing, Peer Review, and Ethics. *Brazilian Journal of Cardiovascular Surgery, 39*(4), e20230377. DOI: 10.21470/1678-9741-2023-0377 PMID: 39038191

Ya'u, M. S., & Mohammed, M. S. (2025). AI-Assisted Writing and Academic Literacy: Investigating the Dual Impact of Language Models on Writing Proficiency and Ethical Concerns in Nigerian Higher Education. *International Journal of Education and Literacy Studies, 13*(2), 593–604. DOI: 10.7575/aiac.ijels.v.13n.2p.593

Zangana, H. M., Amelia, P., Mustafa, F. M., & Li, S. (2025). The Role of English Language and AI in Scientific Writing: Ethical and Academic Implications. In Zangana, H., & Omar, M. (Eds.), *Ensuring Secure and Ethical STM Research in the AI Era* (pp. 191–218). IGI Global Scientific Publishing., DOI: 10.4018/979-8-3373-4252-8.ch005

Zangana, H. M., Luckyardi, S., Mustafa, F. M., & Li, S. (2025). Enhancing Agricultural Cybersecurity: Leveraging Deep Learning and Large Language Models for Smart Farming Protection. In Zangana, H., Al-Karaki, J., & Omar, M. (Eds.), *Revolutionizing Cybersecurity With Deep Learning and Large Language Models* (pp. 307–338). IGI Global Scientific Publishing., DOI: 10.4018/979-8-3373-3296-3.ch010

Zangana, H. M., Luckyardi, S., Mustafa, F. M., & Li, S. (2025). Ethical and Secure AI Applications in Agricultural Research: Challenges and Opportunities. In Zangana, H., & Omar, M. (Eds.), *Ensuring Secure and Ethical STM Research in the AI Era* (pp. 43–76). IGI Global Scientific Publishing., DOI: 10.4018/979-8-3373-4252-8.ch002

Zohouri, M., Sabzali, M., & Golmohammadi, A. (2024). Ethical considerations of ChatGPT-assisted article writing. *Synesis (ISSN 1984-6754), 16*(1), 94-113.

Chapter 9
Navigating Legal Barriers in Climate and Environmental Technologies

Hermano Jorge Da Silva De Queiroz
https://orcid.org/0000-0001-6738-6321
Lindsey Wilson College, USA

ABSTRACT

As global efforts intensify to combat climate change and advance sustainable development, climate and environmental technologies have emerged as critical tools in achieving environmental resilience and innovation. However, deployment and scaling of such technologies often encounter complex legal and regulatory barriers that can hinder progress. This chapter explores the legal challenges surrounding the development, implementation, and diffusion of climate technologies. It examines international treaties, national regulations, intellectual property regimes, liability standards, and market mechanisms such as carbon trading. Particular attention is given to environmental justice, technology transfer, and public-private partnerships in addressing these legal constraints. By analyzing case studies from developed and developing jurisdictions, the chapter identifies key friction points and proposes reform pathways. Ultimately, it provides a strategic lens through which STM stakeholders can navigate legal complexities while promoting ethical and sustainable technological innovation.

DOI: 10.4018/979-8-3373-4862-9.ch009

Copyright © 2025, IGI Global Scientific Publishing. Copying or distributing in print or electronic forms without written permission of IGI Global Scientific Publishing is prohibited.

1. INTRODUCTION

Artificial Intelligence (AI) has ushered in a new era of possibilities across numerous sectors, with healthcare and medical diagnostics at the forefront of its transformative impact. From enhancing radiological interpretations to improving clinical decision-making systems, AI has demonstrated immense potential in increasing diagnostic accuracy, reducing human error, and optimizing healthcare delivery. However, these advancements also pose unprecedented ethical, legal, and regulatory challenges that necessitate robust policy responses (Pesapane et al., 2021; Leontidis, 2024).

The increasing integration of AI into healthcare systems globally has amplified the urgency for comprehensive and adaptive regulatory frameworks. Regulatory gaps, ethical uncertainties, and technical complexities around AI's deployment in sensitive health-related contexts have sparked growing scholarly attention (Mennella et al., 2024; Sheliemina, 2024). Issues such as data privacy, algorithmic bias, patient safety, and explainability are critical concerns that regulators, developers, and healthcare practitioners must address collaboratively (Terry, 2019; Shukla & Taneja, 2024).

The global landscape offers diverse regulatory models, ranging from the European Union's Artificial Intelligence Act—the first of its kind aiming to impose binding obligations on high-risk AI systems (Butt, 2024)—to the more fragmented regulatory approaches observed in the United States, China, and Russia (Pesapane et al., 2021). As highlighted by Naili et al. (2025), existing legal systems are often ill-equipped to address the dynamic and interdisciplinary nature of AI in medical diagnostics, particularly in balancing innovation with accountability.

Furthermore, the rapid pace of AI innovation has outstripped the ability of traditional legal mechanisms to ensure equitable and safe usage. Researchers such as Trotsyuk et al. (2024) and Veluru (2024) have stressed the importance of establishing preventive frameworks to mitigate the misuse of AI technologies, particularly in biomedical contexts where the stakes are high.

Adding to this complexity is the intersection of AI with broader systemic and environmental challenges. Scholars like Daniel (2024), Ali (2024), and Saikia (2024) have emphasized the importance of aligning AI governance in healthcare with global sustainability goals and legal innovations in environmental law. For instance, as AI is increasingly used in energy-efficient diagnostic systems and predictive modeling for climate-related diseases, the integration of environmental legal principles into AI policy becomes relevant (Akindele & Chabinga, 2024; Singh & Kaunert, 2025).

Ethical hacking and cybersecurity also play pivotal roles in maintaining the integrity of AI systems in healthcare. Al-Sinani and Mitchell (2024), as well as Al-Sinani et al. (2025), have demonstrated how AI-enhanced ethical hacking can be leveraged to detect vulnerabilities in medical software environments, an area crucial for regulatory oversight. Similarly, Shafik (2024) and Maguluri et al. (2023) raise alarms about the cybersecurity risks associated with AI-based healthcare tools, emphasizing the need for secure and transparent frameworks.

Moreover, the ethical implications of deploying AI in sensitive domains like healthcare necessitate a reevaluation of human rights, data sovereignty, and informed consent frameworks (Ho, 2023; Batabyal, 2024). AI's capabilities to automate decision-making introduce legal ambiguities around liability, informed autonomy, and fairness—an issue explored by Pesapane et al. (2018) and further dissected through machine learning analysis by Ali and Aysan (2025).

This chapter aims to explore these multidimensional regulatory challenges and responses in a structured and comparative manner. It will critically examine current legal frameworks, emerging models, and best practices for governing AI in healthcare and diagnostics. It will also consider the evolving nature of AI technologies, drawing insights from recent scholarship on generative AI, quantum machine learning, and the ethics of automation (Ali & Aysan, 2024; Campus, 2024; Eswaran & Eswaran, 2025).

By situating these issues within broader socio-political, technological, and environmental contexts, the chapter contributes to the growing discourse on responsible AI governance. Through a comprehensive review of interdisciplinary sources, including empirical studies, policy analyses, and technological assessments, it aims to provide actionable insights for lawmakers, healthcare professionals, and AI developers.

2. OVERVIEW OF CLIMATE AND ENVIRONMENTAL TECHNOLOGIES

Climate and environmental technologies encompass a broad spectrum of innovations aimed at mitigating climate change, enhancing sustainability, and promoting environmental resilience. These technologies integrate advancements in renewable energy, artificial intelligence (AI), legal frameworks, and ethical considerations to address the multifaceted challenges posed by environmental degradation and climate change.

2.1. Renewable Energy and Storage Solutions

The transition to renewable energy sources, such as solar and wind, is pivotal in reducing greenhouse gas emissions. However, the intermittent nature of these energy sources necessitates efficient storage solutions. Battery storage systems, particularly lithium-ion batteries, are widely used but present environmental concerns related to raw material extraction and disposal (NenPower, 2025). Alternative storage methods, like compressed-air energy storage (CAES), offer environmentally friendly options by utilizing natural geological formations, though they require careful site selection to minimize ecological disruption (Wikipedia, 2025).

Innovative concepts like quantum batteries are emerging, leveraging quantum mechanics to potentially enhance energy storage efficiency. While still in experimental stages, these technologies could revolutionize energy storage by offering faster charging times and higher energy densities (Quach et al., 2023).

2.2. Artificial Intelligence in Climate Monitoring and Management

AI has become an indispensable tool in climate science, offering enhanced capabilities in data analysis, prediction, and decision-making. AI-driven models improve weather forecasting accuracy, enabling better preparation for extreme weather events (Financial Times, 2025). In agriculture, AI assists in optimizing resource use, predicting crop yields, and managing pests, thereby promoting sustainable farming practices (Appen, 2024).

Moreover, AI facilitates the monitoring of deforestation and biodiversity loss through satellite imagery analysis, aiding in conservation efforts (World Economic Forum, 2024). In waste management, AI systems like those developed by Greyparrot enhance recycling efficiency by accurately sorting materials, reducing landfill contributions (Freethink, 2024).

2.3. Legal and Ethical Frameworks

The integration of advanced technologies in environmental management raises significant legal and ethical considerations. International environmental law plays a crucial role in guiding sustainable practices and ensuring compliance with climate agreements (Akindele & Chabinga, 2024). Legal strategies are essential in overcoming regulatory barriers to renewable energy expansion and promoting innovation (Oduro et al., 2024).

Ethical considerations are paramount in the deployment of AI technologies. Ensuring transparency, accountability, and fairness in AI applications is critical to prevent biases and protect individual rights (Ali & Aysan, 2025). The development of ethical guidelines and regulatory frameworks is necessary to govern the use of AI in environmental contexts (Mennella et al., 2024).

2.4. Socioeconomic Implications and Global Equity

The adoption of climate and environmental technologies has profound socio-economic impacts. AI and renewable energy technologies can drive economic growth and job creation, but they also risk exacerbating inequalities if access is uneven (Grantham Research Institute, 2024). Ensuring equitable distribution of technological benefits is essential to avoid widening the gap between developed and developing regions.

Efforts to promote inclusivity involve capacity-building initiatives, technology transfer, and the development of infrastructure in underserved areas. Programs like the United Nations' IKI Project utilize AI to support communities in Africa vulnerable to climate change, enhancing resilience through improved planning and resource management (Freethink, 2024).

2.5. Future Directions and Challenges

The ongoing evolution of climate and environmental technologies presents both opportunities and challenges. Advancements in AI, renewable energy, and storage solutions hold promise for more effective climate change mitigation. However, addressing the environmental impacts of technology production, ensuring ethical AI deployment, and fostering global cooperation remain critical challenges.

Continued interdisciplinary collaboration among scientists, policymakers, industry leaders, and communities is essential to navigate these complexities. Developing robust legal frameworks, ethical guidelines, and inclusive policies will support the responsible advancement of climate and environmental technologies, contributing to a sustainable and equitable future.

To navigate the multidimensional nature of climate and environmental technologies, an interdisciplinary integration of legal, technological, ethical, and environmental components is essential. The following flowchart visualizes how these domains intersect to form a cohesive innovation and governance framework.

Figure 1. Interdisciplinary integration of climate technologies and law

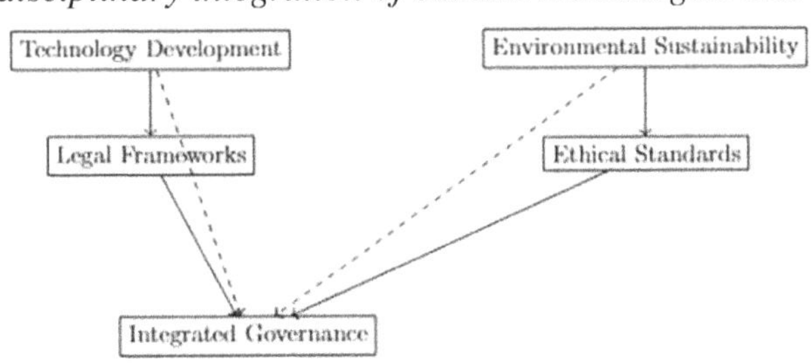

3. LEGAL BARRIERS TO DEVELOPMENT AND DEPLOYMENT

The deployment of artificial intelligence (AI) technologies in healthcare and medical diagnostics holds transformative potential but is heavily constrained by a range of legal barriers. These barriers stem from fragmented regulatory frameworks, jurisdictional inconsistencies, the complexity of liability allocation, data protection mandates, ethical ambiguities, and insufficient international harmonization. As innovation outpaces regulation, these legal challenges risk impeding not only technological advancement but also equitable access to its benefits (Mennella et al., 2024; Naili et al., 2025).

3.1 Fragmented Regulatory Landscapes

One of the core legal barriers is the lack of harmonized regulatory frameworks across jurisdictions. While the European Union (EU) has initiated formalized approaches such as the Artificial Intelligence Act (Butt, 2024), other regions remain governed by a patchwork of laws that inadequately address the specifics of AI-driven diagnostics. In the healthcare context, this fragmentation leads to divergent approval processes, compliance burdens, and data governance standards (Pesapane et al., 2018; Pesapane et al., 2021). This disjointedness is further complicated by the overlap of data protection laws (e.g., GDPR), medical device regulations, and AI governance norms.

In emerging economies, regulatory efforts often lag behind due to limited institutional capacity and the dominance of foreign technologies (Akindele & Chabinga, 2024; Aloamaka, 2024). For instance, while Nigeria has made strides in environmental and international law, its governance of AI in healthcare is still evolving within broader digital health policies.

3.2 Jurisdictional and Liability Challenges

A recurring legal question is: who is liable when an AI system causes harm? The traditional principles of tort law are often ill-suited to address the distributed agency of AI systems (Batabyal, 2024). This challenge is especially acute in diagnostic AI, where black-box models may produce erroneous predictions without transparent reasoning. Regulatory scholarship has thus called for an updated liability framework that accounts for shared responsibilities between developers, deployers, and healthcare providers (Darvishi et al., 2022; Mennella et al., 2024).

In regions like the U.S., the FDA's Digital Health Software Precertification Program provides a precedent for risk-based AI governance. However, this model still falls short of resolving complex accountability issues (Larson et al., 2021). In countries like Pakistan, legal compliance mechanisms often suffer from enforcement gaps and limited awareness among practitioners (Soomro et al., 2025).

3.3 Data Governance and Privacy Concerns

AI-based diagnostics rely on vast volumes of personal and often sensitive health data, making compliance with privacy regulations an inherent barrier. Laws such as HIPAA in the U.S. and GDPR in the EU impose strict obligations on data collection, storage, and processing. These legal constraints, while necessary for safeguarding patient rights, often inhibit innovation due to ambiguity around anonymization standards and cross-border data transfer (Shafik, 2024; Shukla & Taneja, 2024).

Moreover, generative AI applications in healthcare further complicate the data privacy landscape by introducing models trained on heterogeneous and, at times, publicly sourced datasets (Ali & Aysan, 2024; Ali et al., 2024). The use of such datasets in diagnostic systems raises questions about consent, bias, and dataset provenance.

3.4 Ethical-Legal Intersections and Unclear Standards

Another significant legal barrier lies in the insufficient integration of ethical standards into binding legal frameworks. While numerous guidelines propose ethical AI principles—transparency, fairness, accountability—they are often non-binding or inconsistently applied (Ho, 2023; Trotsyuk et al., 2024). Consequently, legal systems struggle to operationalize abstract ethical ideals into enforceable norms.

For example, there is an ongoing debate on whether the "right to explanation" under GDPR can be meaningfully applied to deep learning models used in diagnostics. Researchers argue that current standards do not mandate explainability or interpretability, leaving patients and providers vulnerable to decisions made by opaque systems (Filetti et al., 2024; Eisenberg, 2024).

3.5 International Legal Imbalances and Inequities

There is also a growing recognition that current regulatory paradigms are skewed towards high-income countries, thereby marginalizing lower-resource settings. Legal structures in many developing nations are not equipped to assess or regulate AI technologies, let alone ensure fair access (Daniel, 2024; Singh & Kaunert, 2025).

Regulatory asymmetries may widen the digital divide and create new forms of health injustice.

This is echoed in global discourses around climate and environmental technologies, where legal strategies play a crucial role in enabling sustainable innovation but often exclude the Global South from shaping regulatory agendas (Ali, 2024; Saikia, 2024; Sakapaji et al., 2024). Similar dynamics are evident in the deployment of AI in healthcare.

3.6 Innovation-Stifling Compliance Structures

The necessity of rigorous safety and efficacy evaluations often results in cumbersome regulatory pipelines that stifle innovation. For startups and academic institutions lacking legal resources, the cost and complexity of compliance can be prohibitive (Fenwick et al., 2024; Maguluri et al., 2023). This is particularly problematic for rapidly evolving technologies such as AI-enhanced ethical hacking in digital health environments, where legal ambiguity discourages experimental development (Al-Sinani & Mitchell, 2024; Al-Sinani et al., 2025).

Furthermore, legal rigidity in medical device classification fails to adapt to novel AI functionalities, leading to either underregulation or overregulation (Patra, 2025; Mennella et al., 2024). These structural barriers must be addressed through regulatory sandboxes, adaptive compliance models, and international cooperation.

To assess the most prevalent legal challenges in the deployment of AI and climate technologies, the following bar chart summarizes the frequency with which key legal barriers are mentioned in recent literature.

Figure 2. Prevalence of legal barriers in literature on AI and climate technologies

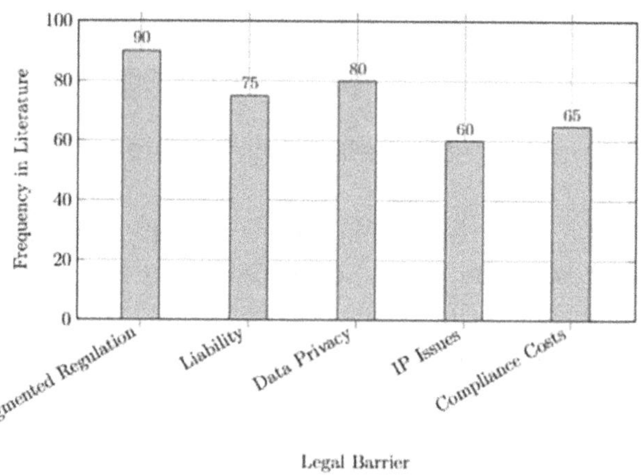

3.7 Legal Barriers in AI-Driven Green Health Technologies

In the broader context of AI-enabled sustainability, including applications like environmental monitoring, drone diagnostics, and quantum health systems, regulatory inertia can severely limit deployment (Arya & Rastogi, 2024; Campus, 2024; Eswaran & Eswaran, 2025; Jafarizadeh et al., 2024). Legal misalignment between environmental, medical, and technological domains creates overlapping or contradictory requirements (Oduro et al., 2024; Emon et al., 2025).

Additionally, regulatory uncertainty surrounding AI-generated scientific research impedes the adoption of these tools in public health and climate diagnostics (Leontidis, 2024; Luan et al., 2024; Chowdhury, 2024).

4. REGULATORY FRAMEWORKS AFFECTING CLIMATE TECHNOLOGIES

The global expansion of climate technologies—ranging from renewable energy systems and carbon capture solutions to AI-enabled environmental monitoring—necessitates sophisticated regulatory frameworks that balance innovation, environmental goals, and social equity. As the urgency of climate action intensifies, regulatory environments must adapt rapidly to ensure that technological advancements contribute meaningfully to sustainability and justice.

4.1. International Environmental Law and Climate Technology Governance

International frameworks, including the Paris Agreement and the United Nations Framework Convention on Climate Change (UNFCCC), have laid foundational principles for climate technology adoption. Countries are increasingly using these instruments to mandate technology transfer, funding, and cooperative innovation efforts. Akindele and Chabinga (2024) emphasize Nigeria's strategic legal navigation in international climate governance, showcasing how nations in the Global South align national policies with global sustainability goals.

Further, Aloamaka (2024) explores the evolution of international environmental law in accommodating emerging climate tech, underscoring the tension between sovereign interests and the collective need for climate resilience. These dynamics are echoed by Singh and Kaunert (2025), who examine the biodiversity and sustainability legal landscapes under the SDGs, emphasizing the vital role of enforceable international agreements.

4.2. National Regulatory Models and Legal Adaptation

National governments have developed diverse legal pathways to support climate technologies. Daniel (2024) outlines how environmental statutes, constitutional mandates, and judicial interpretations have created a layered legal environment conducive to sustainable development. In Africa, countries like Nigeria and Kenya have initiated climate technology incentives, while nations like Pakistan still face regulatory inertia (Soomro, Suhrab, & Abbasi, 2025).

Chowdhury (2024) argues that climate justice should be at the heart of regulatory design, suggesting that law must evolve to reflect the disproportionate burdens of climate change on vulnerable populations. Saikia (2024) similarly underscores the need for ecological law frameworks to mitigate the negative impacts of oil and gas industries while fostering clean-tech alternatives.

4.3. GreenTech, Renewable Energy, and Innovation Pathways

The GreenTech sector requires agile, forward-looking legal systems that facilitate innovation while ensuring public accountability. Emon et al. (2025) stress the importance of regulatory strategies that promote AI-integrated green solutions, while Oduro, Uzougbo, and Ugwu (2024) present a comprehensive overview of how legal strategies can dismantle regulatory barriers to renewable energy expansion.

Jafarizadeh et al. (2024) provide a technical and policy analysis of renewable energy storage, identifying gaps in large-scale integration due to outdated or rigid legal frameworks. Their findings illustrate the need for coordinated legal reform, financial instruments, and public-private partnerships to drive sustainable infrastructure development.

4.4. AI, Quantum, and Ethical Legal Oversight

With AI playing a transformative role in climate prediction, environmental modeling, and smart energy grids, legal systems must address the ethical and governance challenges that emerge. Campus (2024) and Eswaran and Eswaran (2025) advocate for regulatory frameworks that integrate AI, quantum computing, and semiconductor technologies with sustainability standards.

Ali and Aysan (2025) argue for a cross-domain ethical oversight model for generative AI, which has implications for climate tech applications involving autonomous decision-making. Darvishi, Liu, and Lim (2022) explore the broader nexus between law and emerging technologies, stressing the importance of adaptive legal instruments to account for the uncertainty and scale of technological change.

The development of sustainable Industry 4.0 technologies, as explored by Patra (2025), also demands comprehensive legal integration of environmental metrics into industrial AI systems.

AI's increasing role in climate and health domains introduces overlapping legal concerns. The following Venn diagram highlights areas of convergence and distinct focus across AI regulation, climate law, and health law.

Figure 3. Overlap between AI, climate, and health legal frameworks

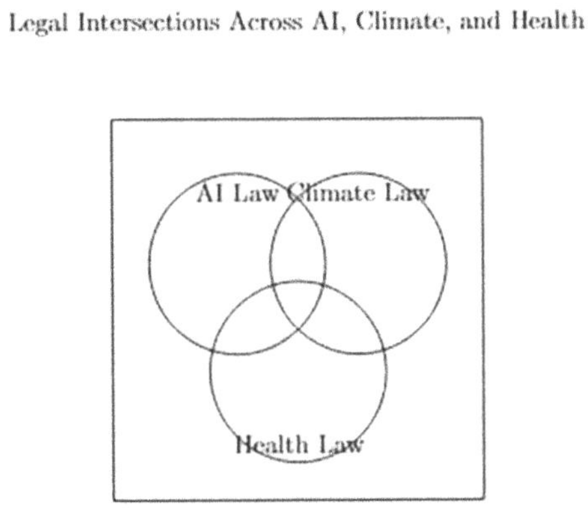

4.5. Regulatory Challenges and Comparative Legal Approaches

Comparative legal scholarship highlights how countries navigate regulatory bottlenecks. Butt (2024) offers insights into the EU's AI Act, revealing parallels in regulating climate-centric AI tools. Mennella et al. (2024) provide a narrative review of regulatory and ethical challenges in healthcare AI, with potential applicability in environmental health surveillance. Similarly, Pesapane et al. (2018, 2021) explore the regulatory intricacies in deploying AI as a device, which can be adapted to AI-driven climate sensors and environmental diagnostics.

Terry (2019) warns of regulatory lag in fast-moving domains, advocating for anticipatory governance models—a stance supported by Trotsyuk et al. (2024), who propose risk mitigation frameworks against AI misuse in biomedical and environmental research contexts.

4.6. Human Rights, Indigenous Systems, and Inclusive Frameworks

Effective climate technology regulation must be inclusive, safeguarding indigenous knowledge systems and community rights. Sakapaji et al. (2024) discuss how indigenous socioecological systems require legal recognition to foster sustainability and resilience. Ho (2023) calls for the implementation of the human right to science within AI regulation, which can empower marginalized groups through accessible, responsible innovation.

Ali (2024) underscores the political dynamics of policy alignment for net-zero goals, emphasizing that governance must reflect not just scientific priorities but also socio-political realities. This aligns with Fenwick, Molnar, and Frangos (2024), who highlight the need for human-centric policy frameworks, even in highly technical fields like AI and climate informatics.

4.7. Systemic Integration and Future Directions

Integrated legal frameworks that consider environmental, technological, economic, and ethical factors are vital. Schünemann et al. (2024) compare modeling approaches—systems thinking, dynamics, and agent-based modeling—to propose policy mechanisms that can simulate and preemptively resolve regulatory conflicts.

As nations and organizations continue to align their legal instruments with emerging technologies, a comprehensive regulatory paradigm must address innovation incentives, ecological justice, cross-border governance, and adaptive policymaking.

5. CROSS-JURISDICTIONAL AND TRANSBOUNDARY LEGAL CHALLENGES

The rapid integration of Artificial Intelligence (AI) into healthcare systems worldwide has brought forth a series of complex cross-jurisdictional and transboundary legal challenges. As AI-driven diagnostics, decision support tools, and robotic systems transcend national boundaries, the fragmentation in legal systems, regulatory approaches, and ethical norms among nations becomes increasingly pronounced (Mennella et al., 2024; Pesapane et al., 2018).

One of the primary challenges arises from the asymmetry of regulatory frameworks across different countries. While regions such as the European Union have developed comprehensive policies like the EU Artificial Intelligence Act to address AI risks in healthcare (Butt, 2024), other jurisdictions still lack robust legislative mechanisms. For example, countries in the Global South face legal ambiguities in AI governance due to limited institutional capacity and evolving digital infrastructures (Akindele & Chabinga, 2024; Soomro et al., 2025).

This inconsistency in legal standards impairs interoperability, trust, and accountability among AI healthcare systems deployed in multinational contexts. When medical devices or diagnostic algorithms developed in one country are deployed in another, there is a risk of non-compliance with local health and data protection laws (Terry, 2019; Pesapane et al., 2021). Such inconsistencies necessitate the development of harmonized regulatory principles and mutual recognition agreements for AI certification and data governance.

Another pressing transboundary issue involves cross-border data flows and sovereignty concerns, especially when personal health information is transferred for training or validating AI models. These challenges are amplified by the lack of unified global standards on data privacy, security, and ethical consent mechanisms (Shafik, 2024; Shukla & Taneja, 2024). AI systems trained on data from one demographic region may also suffer from biases and lack generalizability in others, leading to inequities in healthcare outcomes (Ali & Aysan, 2025; Leontidis, 2024).

Furthermore, geopolitical tensions and uneven AI development raise concerns about digital colonialism and technological dependencies, where lower-income countries become consumers of AI technologies without having a say in their design, ethical configuration, or application (Aloamaka, 2024; Singh & Kaunert, 2025). These dynamics underscore the urgent need for inclusive international legal instruments to ensure fair participation in shaping AI standards globally (Daniel, 2024; Saikia, 2024).

In addition, the increasing use of cloud-based and decentralized AI platforms in healthcare raises jurisdictional ambiguity over legal liability in the case of algorithmic errors or harm. It remains unclear which laws apply when a patient in Country A is diagnosed by an AI model developed in Country B, hosted in the cloud infrastructure of Country C (Naili et al., 2025; Al-Sinani et al., 2025). Such scenarios illustrate the necessity for multi-stakeholder treaties and conventions that can clarify legal obligations in cross-border healthcare AI.

Efforts to create global ethical guidelines, such as those proposed by UNESCO and the World Health Organization, offer a promising direction. However, enforcement mechanisms remain weak, and most countries retain sovereign discretion over the application of such principles (Chowdhury, 2024; Ho, 2023). Some scholars suggest AI-specific bilateral and multilateral agreements, inspired by treaties on biotechnology or pharmaceuticals, could be leveraged to address legal harmonization and ethical convergence (Ali, 2024; Oduro et al., 2024).

At the same time, emerging technologies like quantum computing and AI convergence introduce further complications in regulatory oversight due to their novelty and unpredictability (Eswaran & Eswaran, 2025; Campus, 2024). Such advances may blur jurisdictional boundaries even more as AI systems become capable of autonomous decision-making, challenging existing notions of liability, negligence, and informed consent (Batabyal, 2024; Darvishi et al., 2022).

Moreover, indigenous legal traditions and socioecological systems often fall outside the scope of mainstream AI regulations. There is a critical need to integrate localized governance mechanisms that reflect indigenous values, cultural norms, and environmental sustainability in transboundary regulatory frameworks (Sakapaji et al., 2024; Arya & Rastogi, 2024).

To mitigate these cross-jurisdictional legal risks, experts recommend the establishment of international AI registries, global audit protocols, and intergovernmental oversight boards for high-risk applications in healthcare (Larson et al., 2021; Emon et al., 2025). Additionally, cross-domain ethical assessment tools are being explored to foster a shared understanding of risks across contexts (Ali & Aysan, 2025; Eisenberg, 2024).

As AI continues to redefine the healthcare landscape, navigating its transboundary legal complexities demands sustained cooperation among governments, international organizations, civil society, and the private sector. Legal harmonization, grounded in ethical universality and technological adaptability, is essential to ensure that AI-driven healthcare systems serve global health equity rather than deepen existing divides.

6. FINANCING AND INCENTIVE LEGAL STRUCTURES

The acceleration of AI technologies in healthcare and climate tech sectors demands not only regulatory oversight but also structured financial and incentive mechanisms to foster ethical development, safe implementation, and equitable distribution. These legal structures span public-private partnerships, tax incentives, venture funding provisions, green finance frameworks, and performance-based subsidies. As the interplay between sustainability goals and technological innovation grows stronger, the financial backbone supporting these transitions must evolve to ensure both resilience and accountability.

6.1 Public and Private Financing Dynamics

Effective climate and health-tech innovation, particularly those involving AI and emerging technologies, rely heavily on sustainable financing models. Ali (2024) underscores that aligning environmental policy with sustainable finance instruments is central to supporting net-zero objectives. Public financing remains foundational in the early phases of development, especially for high-risk AI research and medical diagnostics, while private investment surges during commercialization and scaling.

Governments have responded by creating financial frameworks that de-risk investment through co-funding, innovation grants, and legal safeguards.

Akindele and Chabinga (2024) emphasize that in regions like Nigeria, international legal instruments play a key role in directing climate financing, particularly through mechanisms enshrined in treaties and multilateral aid structures. However, local implementation depends on well-articulated legal standards that ensure funds are allocated efficiently and equitably, particularly in underrepresented and vulnerable communities.

6.2 Tax and Incentive Schemes

Targeted tax relief and credits for R&D in AI and health technologies have proven effective in catalyzing innovation. In the U.S. and EU, policies include accelerated depreciation, investment tax credits, and refundable R&D credits aimed at firms investing in healthcare AI (Pesapane et al., 2018; Pesapane et al., 2021). These schemes often come with regulatory conditions that enforce ethical guidelines and promote transparency, ensuring that public money supports socially responsible innovation.

Daniel (2024) explains that embedding sustainability principles within national legal systems enables more robust and enforceable financing structures. These structures include performance-based tax incentives that reward developers for achieving specific sustainability or health impact milestones. This results in better alignment between public policy objectives and private sector innovation strategies.

6.3 Green and Climate Finance Integration

Green finance mechanisms are increasingly being utilized to support AI-driven solutions in environmental and health sectors. Instruments such as green bonds, climate investment funds, and sustainability-linked loans are being extended to projects involving AI-based diagnostics, renewable-powered healthcare infrastructure, and eco-efficient medical technologies (Oduro et al., 2024). These financial tools are buttressed by international agreements that mandate climate accountability, such as the Paris Agreement and SDG frameworks (Saikia, 2024).

As Eswaran and Eswaran (2025) and Campus (2024) argue, the fusion of quantum computing, AI, and sustainability requires not just technical innovation but integrated legal and economic mechanisms that ensure financial flows support resilience, transparency, and long-term ecological benefit. Such multi-layered innovation ecosystems are only possible when financial instruments are embedded within enforceable regulatory structures.

To support the advancement of AI-enabled environmental technologies, multiple financing and incentive mechanisms are legally structured across public and private domains. The following flow diagram illustrates the main pathways.

Figure 4. Legal financing pathways for climate and AI innovation

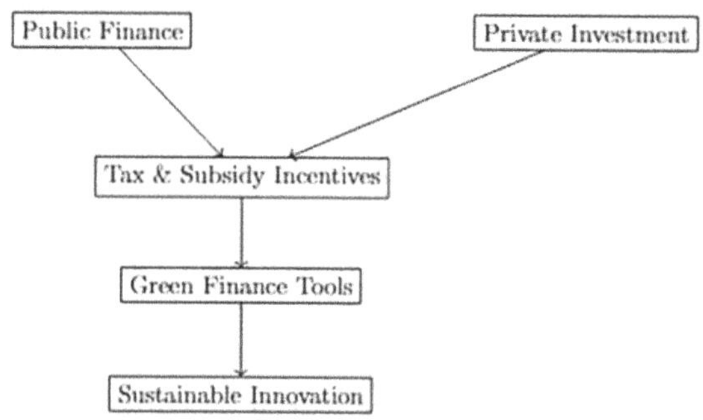

6.4 Legal Frameworks for Risk Mitigation and Investor Protection

Investors in emerging tech, especially those involving high-stakes healthcare applications, require clear legal structures that address risk, intellectual property rights, and data governance. Ali and Aysan (2025) stress the ethical and financial risks posed by generative AI, which demand that financing be conditioned on rigorous due diligence, impact assessments, and transparent audit trails. This is especially true in the medical diagnostics space, where patient data sensitivity and liability concerns are heightened (Mennella et al., 2024).

Moreover, Naili et al. (2025) emphasize the growing importance of legal instruments that protect investors from regulatory volatility in AI diagnostics. These include legal predictability clauses in public-private contracts, data protection regulations harmonized with financial disclosure norms, and legal safe harbors for compliance with international ethical standards.

6.5 Incentivizing Ethical AI Development

Legal incentive structures must prioritize not only financial return but also ethical integrity. Al-Sinani et al. (2025) advocate for incentives that fund ethical hacking and red-team testing for AI systems, especially in critical infrastructure such as healthcare. Similarly, Fenwick et al. (2024) argue for funding frameworks that incorporate human-centric AI adoption, balancing financial metrics with social value and equity.

Government programs and international institutions are increasingly requiring that financing for AI-based health applications includc safeguards for data privacy, transparency in algorithmic decision-making, and inclusion of underserved populations (Butt, 2024; Larson et al., 2021). The inclusion of AI ethics impact assessments as a precondition for funding is one emerging legal strategy that could align technical excellence with social responsibility (Terry, 2019; Ali & Aysan, 2024).

6.6 International Cooperation and Legal Harmonization

Given the transnational nature of AI and healthcare technologies, international financial coordination is essential. Singh and Kaunert (2025) emphasize the importance of biodiversity and environmental legal landscapes in shaping international financing mechanisms. Harmonizing laws across jurisdictions ensures that financial incentives are not misused for regulatory arbitrage. This is supported by Aloamaka (2024), who explores how the evolution of international environmental law can frame sustainable financing practices, especially in the Global South.

Soomro et al. (2025) further argue that green regulatory frameworks in developing countries require government support to overcome compliance and legal interpretation challenges. These can be addressed through legal instruments like soft law guidance, harmonized reporting standards, and cross-border incentive programs tied to international sustainability benchmarks.

6.7 Integrating AI into Legal and Economic Financing Models

The role of AI in structuring, analyzing, and administering financial incentives is also growing. AI-driven analysis enables more precise targeting of subsidies and better fraud detection in grant disbursement. Ali, Zafar, and Aysan (2024) and Leontidis (2024) demonstrate how AI and machine learning are being used to optimize financial systems, enhance transparency, and automate regulatory compliance in healthcare and climate finance sectors.

As Darvishi et al. (2022) note, the convergence of legal reasoning and economic forecasting models via AI tools can yield more adaptive financing structures capable of responding to rapidly evolving innovation landscapes. This is especially relevant in managing the long-term costs and risks associated with AI integration in healthcare systems.

7. INTELLECTUAL PROPERTY AND INNOVATION LAW

The integration of artificial intelligence (AI) into healthcare and medical diagnostics has prompted an urgent need to revisit and redefine intellectual property (IP) and innovation law. As AI continues to redefine scientific research, data analysis, and diagnostic capabilities, existing IP frameworks must evolve to accommodate non-human creators, data-driven inventions, and collaborative innovations that transcend traditional patent paradigms.

7.1 The Evolution of Innovation in the AI Era

AI systems in healthcare are increasingly capable of generating diagnostic models, designing molecular compounds, and even drafting scientific articles (Filetti et al., 2024; Leontidis, 2024). These capabilities challenge the foundational notion that human intellect is central to innovation—a notion on which most IP regimes are based. As Eisenberg (2024) argues, AI-based sensor systems can autonomously refine their algorithms through machine learning, raising questions about inventorship, ownership, and accountability in innovation.

The dual-use nature of AI—where a single algorithm may serve civilian and security functions—further complicates the patentability of such technologies. For example, technologies developed for AI-based diagnostics might also be applied in military or surveillance systems (Batabyal, 2024), which prompts a reassessment of innovation boundaries and their ethical dimensions.

7.2 Ownership, Inventorship, and Data as Intellectual Capital

A critical issue in AI-generated healthcare solutions is determining the rightful owner of the resulting intellectual property. Traditional IP laws assign inventorship to humans, but when an AI model significantly contributes to or independently generates a medical diagnosis or drug discovery, attributing ownership becomes legally murky (Mennella et al., 2024; Pesapane et al., 2018). Ali and Aysan (2025) demonstrate how generative AI's role in content creation spans disciplines, yet innovation laws remain limited in addressing AI as a potential co-inventor or contributor.

Moreover, the data fueling AI systems in healthcare—ranging from patient imaging to genomic information—is itself a form of intellectual capital. This data is often collected from public institutions, private healthcare providers, or even open-source repositories (Shuja et al., 2021), raising questions about data ownership, licensing rights, and consent. Shafik (2024) underscores the importance of safeguarding such data, particularly when used to train models like ChatGPT that may later be commercialized.

7.3 Patentability and Regulatory Fragmentation

Differences in how jurisdictions interpret patent eligibility for AI-assisted inventions exacerbate legal uncertainty. The European Union, United States, and China differ in their approaches to regulating AI as a medical device (Pesapane et al., 2021). While the EU AI Act (Butt, 2024) introduces classification-based regulation for high-risk AI, including in diagnostics, it does not offer concrete direction on patent law adjustments, potentially stifling cross-border innovation.

According to Naili et al. (2025), the absence of cohesive IP frameworks poses challenges for AI startups entering the medical diagnostics domain, particularly in jurisdictions where health-related innovations are heavily regulated but IP protections are underdeveloped. The resulting fragmentation can hinder collaborative research and discourage the open sharing of AI models across borders.

7.4 Incentivizing Innovation in Sustainable and Equitable AI

In light of climate concerns and sustainability goals, innovation law must also incentivize "green" AI and equitable access. As Jafarizadeh et al. (2024) note, innovation in renewable energy storage is increasingly reliant on AI for efficiency, mirroring trends in healthcare. Legal strategies should similarly reward AI developments that promote ethical medical diagnostics and responsible use of resources (Oduro et al., 2024).

Further, innovation law must address structural inequities in global healthcare systems. Singh and Kaunert (2025) argue for legal mechanisms that ensure biodiversity protection and access to essential health technologies, particularly in underserved regions. In this context, IP law should support open innovation models that prioritize global health outcomes over profit maximization.

Ali (2024) and Akindele and Chabinga (2024) both emphasize that net-zero policies and international environmental law can inspire similar frameworks in AI regulation—ones that balance innovation with long-term sustainability. These perspectives suggest that future IP regimes in AI healthcare should not only protect the rights of inventors but also embed social and ecological responsibilities into innovation incentives.

7.5 Challenges and Opportunities in IP Law Modernization

As AI systems advance, IP law must address the challenges of algorithmic opacity, collaborative authorship, and rapid iteration cycles. Rodriguez and Storer (2020) and Luan et al. (2024) highlight how AI-driven topic modeling and scientometric analyses enhance scholarly output but complicate the attribution of intellectual contribution.

Emon et al. (2025) suggest that GreenTech innovations, much like AI in medicine, require legal frameworks that both protect and promote innovation. Similarly, Eswaran and Eswaran (2025) propose that innovation law must now consider the convergence of quantum computing, semiconductors, and AI—a reality that further destabilizes traditional patent models.

Finally, Campus (2024) and Darvishi et al. (2022) assert that future-ready innovation laws must integrate both legal and economic implications of emerging technologies, ensuring that commercialization, compliance, and creativity coexist without sacrificing public trust or ethical standards.

8. ENVIRONMENTAL JUSTICE AND EQUITY CONSIDERATIONS

The intersection of artificial intelligence (AI), healthcare, and environmental justice is a critical domain in the discourse of equitable technological governance. As AI technologies expand their reach into healthcare and environmental management, the imperative to consider distributive and procedural justice becomes increasingly salient. The equity implications of AI deployment are multifaceted, encompassing access to healthcare, exposure to environmental risks, and the rights of marginalized communities.

8.1 Equity in Access to AI-Enhanced Healthcare

AI-based diagnostic tools and medical systems have the potential to improve outcomes and reduce healthcare disparities. However, unequal access to digital infrastructure, data, and healthcare systems exacerbates existing inequalities. Disparities in healthcare delivery often correlate with environmental injustices, particularly in regions facing high pollution levels, lack of clean water, or exposure to toxic substances (Ali & Aysan, 2025; Chowdhury, 2024). Without intentional design and deployment strategies, AI systems risk reinforcing structural inequalities, particularly in underserved communities.

For instance, underrepresented populations may be excluded from the training datasets that inform AI diagnostics, leading to biased outcomes and misdiagnoses. These algorithmic biases may disproportionately affect communities already burdened by environmental degradation and limited access to medical services (Sheliemina, 2024; Mennella et al., 2024). Ensuring justice in AI development requires incorporating diverse datasets, localized ethical considerations, and participatory regulatory mechanisms (Shukla & Taneja, 2024).

8.2 Environmental Burdens and Health Impacts

Environmental injustice is also manifest in the placement of industrial and healthcare-related waste disposal facilities, often located near marginalized communities. The intersection of AI with environmental technologies must not ignore these pre-existing patterns of inequity. AI-driven green technologies, when equitably implemented, can mitigate environmental hazards and promote cleaner, healthier living conditions (Emon et al., 2025; Oduro, Uzougbo, & Ugwu, 2024).

Akindele and Chabinga (2024) emphasize the role of international environmental law in correcting historical injustices and promoting sustainable development. Their study of Nigeria's role illustrates how international cooperation and legal frameworks can enhance equity by aligning global environmental strategies with local needs. Similarly, Singh and Kaunert (2025) underscore the necessity of biodiversity protection and environmental resilience as integral to sustainable development, particularly for vulnerable ecosystems and communities.

8.3 Indigenous and Socioecological Systems

Equity considerations also demand attention to indigenous rights and local knowledge systems. As noted by Sakapaji et al. (2024), indigenous socioecological systems often face the dual burden of environmental degradation and exclusion from policy decisions. Inclusive regulatory frameworks must integrate indigenous perspectives to achieve both environmental justice and technological equity. The development and governance of AI must be culturally sensitive and acknowledge the environmental stewardship historically practiced by indigenous communities.

In parallel, Saikia (2024) explores the role of international mechanisms in ensuring sustainability within the oil and gas sector, highlighting how global legal instruments can offer protection against ecological exploitation in resource-rich, vulnerable regions. These lessons are transferable to the governance of AI in healthcare, especially in the context of environmental exposures impacting public health outcomes.

8.4 Governance, Participation, and Procedural Justice

Procedural justice entails meaningful community participation in regulatory decision-making. Ali (2024) emphasizes the importance of aligning policy, politics, and governance structures to achieve environmental sustainability. Democratic engagement is essential not only for ensuring accountability in AI deployment but also for tailoring interventions to the unique environmental health profiles of different communities (Daniel, 2024; Darvishi, Liu, & Lim, 2022).

Flannery, Ajayi, and Oyegoke (2021) argue that environmental and occupational health must be addressed simultaneously, particularly in high-risk industries like construction. The same logic applies to AI-enhanced healthcare: workers involved in its development and maintenance should be protected from environmental hazards and digital exploitation, ensuring a just transition to AI-augmented systems.

Moreover, equity should extend to educational and professional opportunities in AI development. Pimpalkar et al. (2024) discuss the empowerment of women through AI, highlighting how targeted inclusion strategies can reduce gender-based disparities in emerging technological domains. Equitable participation across gender, racial, and economic lines fosters diverse perspectives essential for ethical AI governance.

8.5 Emerging Legal and Ethical Models

Recent scholarly attention emphasizes the convergence of environmental ethics, legal protections, and digital technology. Aloamaka (2024) traces the evolution of international environmental law and its relevance to AI governance, suggesting that adaptive legal mechanisms can evolve in response to novel environmental-health challenges posed by emerging technologies.

Similarly, Butt (2024) analyzes the EU AI Act and its implications for global AI ethics, suggesting the potential for regulatory harmonization that includes environmental justice as a core component. Campus (2024) and Eswaran and Eswaran (2025) also advocate for the integration of quantum computing and AI to improve energy efficiency and sustainability, underscoring the dual benefits of technological advancement and ecological protection.

Ultimately, environmental justice within AI-enhanced healthcare governance is not merely a moral imperative—it is a prerequisite for sustainable and equitable progress. As AI continues to reshape both environmental and health landscapes, regulatory systems must adopt a justice-centered approach that proactively addresses structural inequities, ensures diverse participation, and safeguards both human health and ecological integrity.

9. EMERGING LEGAL MODELS AND BEST PRACTICES

The rapid evolution of artificial intelligence (AI), climate technology, and environmental science has catalyzed the development of new legal models aimed at ensuring ethical governance, regulatory agility, and interdisciplinary coherence. These emerging models increasingly reflect the need to balance innovation with sustainability, public safety, and data privacy. Drawing on comparative legal systems, international frameworks, and sector-specific innovations, this section outlines key legal developments and best practices shaping the future of responsible AI and climate governance.

9.1. Adaptive and Human-Centered AI Regulation

AI governance is transitioning from static rule-making to adaptive and human-centric models. Butt (2024) provides a thorough analysis of the EU Artificial Intelligence Act, illustrating how the law is shifting toward risk-based classification and continuous monitoring frameworks. Similarly, Ho (2023) emphasizes incorporating the human right to science into AI governance, particularly in healthcare, thus prioritizing ethical use and access to innovation.

To facilitate interdisciplinary cooperation, Mennella et al. (2024) argue for hybrid models that bridge medical ethics, algorithmic accountability, and clinical practices. This approach ensures AI solutions in healthcare are validated not only for technical accuracy but also for their socio-ethical impact (Pesapane et al., 2018; Pesapane et al., 2021). Naili et al. (2025) further advocate for transparent regulatory pathways in medical diagnostics that include liability frameworks and real-time auditability.

9.2. Climate Technology and International Environmental Law

Emerging legal models in environmental governance have become increasingly transnational. Akindele and Chabinga (2024) discuss Nigeria's evolving role in international environmental law, highlighting collaborative frameworks under the Paris Agreement. Aloamaka (2024) further analyzes international legal mechanisms that facilitate state compliance with climate objectives through enforcement-oriented treaties and adaptive policy instruments.

At a regional level, Singh and Kaunert (2025) present biodiversity protection as a legal imperative integrated into broader sustainability trajectories. They propose legal pluralism and ecological constitutionalism as foundational to emerging environmental jurisprudence. These approaches are reflected in Saikia's (2024) study on the oil and gas industry, where ecologically informed legal instruments are used to mitigate exploration risks.

9.3. Sustainability-Oriented Industrial and Technological Models

Best practices are also emerging in industrial contexts where AI and green technologies intersect. Ali (2024) outlines governance strategies to align policy, politics, and net-zero objectives, advocating for agile regulatory mechanisms that adapt to scientific uncertainty. Emon et al. (2025) propose multi-stakeholder models to navigate GreenTech challenges, including innovation subsidies and open data platforms to reduce implementation bottlenecks.

Patra (2025) further explores Industry 4.0 legal landscapes, suggesting digital compliance frameworks and carbon accountability protocols as the future of sustainable manufacturing. Oduro et al. (2024) reinforce this view, recommending legal tools such as energy innovation zones and flexible licensing to accelerate renewable adoption.

9.4. Digital Ethics, Data Privacy, and AI Transparency

Emerging models also foreground digital rights and algorithmic ethics. Ali and Aysan (2025) examine ethical dimensions of generative AI, promoting structural topic modeling as a method for legislative foresight. Their earlier work (Ali & Aysan, 2024; Ali et al., 2024) leverages machine learning to assess ethical risk in financial AI, emphasizing proactive governance and explainability.

Ethical governance also calls for AI transparency. Shukla and Taneja (2024) emphasize data privacy-by-design in educational AI, while Shafik (2024) details regulatory safeguards for customer information in generative AI systems like ChatGPT. These practices align with global trends toward embedding digital ethics into legal compliance.

9.5. Integrating Emerging Technologies with Existing Legal Systems

As AI integrates with quantum computing, sensor systems, and biosensor technologies, emerging legal frameworks are beginning to accommodate these advancements. Eisenberg (2024) advocates for integrity-first models in sensor design that include legal safeguards for autonomous data collection. Campus (2024) and Eswaran and Eswaran (2025) explore the interface of quantum machine learning with AI law, urging the establishment of integrated compliance protocols for dual-use technologies.

Arya and Rastogi (2024) extend this conversation to drone use in defense and agriculture, proposing spatial regulation zones and real-time ethics monitoring. These practices are especially critical in jurisdictions where security and civil liberties intersect, requiring fine-tuned legal oversight (Maguluri et al., 2023).

9.6. Participatory Governance and Legal Innovation

Another trend in emerging legal models is participatory governance, especially within marginalized or indigenous communities. Sakapaji et al. (2024) propose legal frameworks that protect indigenous socioecological systems through resilience-based governance and co-drafted legal codes. Chowdhury (2024) underscores the role of procedural justice in climate law, where public deliberation and community engagement are embedded in regulatory design.

Darvishi et al. (2022) advocate for legal innovation through economic-legal synergy, showing how legal systems can encourage ethical tech entrepreneurship. This is mirrored in Luan et al. (2024), where AI is used for legal research and policy tracking, facilitating more responsive and evidence-based governance.

9.7. Legal Readiness and Institutional Best Practices

Best practices are increasingly institutionalized through legal education, policy modeling, and AI-assisted compliance. Schünemann et al. (2024) compare systems thinking and agent-based models to advise legal readiness, advocating simulation-based regulatory testing. Daniel (2024) emphasizes modular environmental laws with built-in adaptability to changing climate data.

Rodriguez and Storer (2020) and Jamro and Jamro (2023) present how computational tools like topic modeling and chatbots can support legal outreach and policy literacy. Leontidis (2024) and Filetti et al. (2024) reinforce the role of AI in accelerating legal scholarship, making legal best practices more accessible and evidence-driven.

9.8. Sector-Specific Regulatory Innovations

Sectors such as defense, education, finance, and healthcare are developing bespoke legal models. Batabyal (2024) explores ethical and legal norms in AI-driven warfare, recommending an update to international humanitarian law to include autonomous weapon systems. Pimpalkar et al. (2024) advocate for predictive safety protocols in women's safety applications, suggesting a regulatory model based on dynamic data analysis and preemptive risk governance.

Fenwick et al. (2024) highlight HRM's critical role in transitioning to human-centric AI adoption in business, stressing internal ethics codes and employee-focused legal instruments. Rashid and Kausik (2024) propose domain-specific compliance standards to address the diverse impacts of AI across sectors, supported by regulatory sandboxes and innovation hubs.

10. FUTURE DIRECTIONS AND RECOMMENDATIONS

The rapid evolution of artificial intelligence (AI), environmental sustainability frameworks, and regulatory landscapes necessitates a forward-looking approach that aligns technological innovation with ethical governance and legal compliance. This section outlines key future directions and strategic recommendations across AI governance, sustainability, legal frameworks, and interdisciplinary collaboration to ensure responsible advancement in healthcare, finance, climate technology, and security domains.

10.1. Enhancing Regulatory Frameworks for AI in Healthcare and Diagnostics

The increasing integration of AI in healthcare diagnostics demands regulatory models that balance innovation with patient safety and ethical considerations. Current frameworks in the EU, US, China, and Russia demonstrate significant variation, necessitating harmonization efforts to enable global standards (Pesapane et al., 2021; Pesapane, Volonté, Codari, & Sardanelli, 2018). Future regulations must incorporate dynamic mechanisms for continuous evaluation, transparency, and explainability, addressing challenges identified in AI-driven diagnostic tools (Mennella, Maniscalco, De Pietro, & Esposito, 2024; Naili, Mangkunegara, Purwono, & Baballe, 2025).

Moreover, the World Health Organization (2023) advocates for inclusive frameworks that support equitable access while ensuring privacy and security safeguards. Emphasizing the human right to science, governance should focus on patient-centric AI deployment in healthcare settings (Ho, 2023). To this end, regulators must engage multi-stakeholder dialogues to shape adaptive policies responsive to rapid AI advances (Larson et al., 2021; Terry, 2019).

10.2. Addressing Ethical and Security Challenges in AI Applications

Ethical AI development remains a critical concern, particularly in fields such as finance, cybersecurity, and warfare. Emerging research highlights the ethical complexities of generative AI systems and the imperative for cross-domain ethical standards (Ali & Aysan, 2025; Batabyal, 2024). In cybersecurity, AI-enhanced ethical hacking offers promising avenues for threat detection but requires rigorous oversight to mitigate misuse and unintended consequences (Al-Sinani & Mitchell, 2024; Al-Sinani, Sahli, Mitchell, & Al-Siyabi, 2025).

Furthermore, large-scale AI deployments risk data privacy breaches and algorithmic biases that must be proactively managed through robust data governance and transparent audit trails (Shafik, 2024; Veluru, 2024; Shukla & Taneja, 2024). Financial systems leveraging generative AI need multi-level analyses to anticipate risks and reinforce ethical compliance (Ali, Zafar, & Aysan, 2024; Ali & Aysan, 2024).

10.3. Promoting Sustainable Environmental Governance Through Legal Innovation

Addressing climate change requires coordinated international legal strategies that foster sustainability while enabling innovation. Nigeria's role in international environmental law exemplifies the growing importance of national contributions to global climate governance (Akindele & Chabinga, 2024). Legal frameworks must evolve to support net zero policies that harmonize political, social, and economic dimensions for environmental sustainability (Ali, 2024; Aloamaka, 2024).

Future environmental law must integrate mechanisms for indigenous socioecological resilience and biodiversity protection, recognizing local knowledge systems alongside scientific innovation (Sakapaji, García Molinos, Parilova, Gavrilyeva, & Yakovleva, 2024; Singh & Kaunert, 2025). Legal strategies should also address regulatory barriers hindering renewable energy expansion and green technology adoption (Oduro, Uzougbo, & Ugwu, 2024; Jafarizadeh et al., 2024).

10.4. Leveraging AI and Quantum Technologies for Sustainable Industry and Science

The intersection of AI, quantum computing, and semiconductor technology presents transformative potential across sectors, from diagnostics to renewable energy (Campus, 2024; Eswaran & Eswaran, 2025). Future research should prioritize responsible AI integration that safeguards against misuse while enhancing scientific discovery and industrial sustainability (Leontidis, 2024; Trotsyuk et al., 2024).

Industry 4.0 frameworks require legal foresight to navigate challenges of automation, data ownership, and intellectual property rights, ensuring innovation does not compromise ethical or environmental standards (Patra, 2025). The rise of AI in STEM education and entrepreneurial idea generation further underscores the need for inclusive policies fostering equitable technology access and workforce development (Jamro & Jamro, 2023; Zreik, 2024).

10.5. Strengthening Cross-sectoral Collaboration and Human-Centric AI Adoption

The transition from AI implementation to human-centric adoption requires organizational transformations in human resource management and digital culture (Fenwick, Molnar, & Frangos, 2024). Bridging technological innovation with ethical and social responsibility necessitates collaborative governance models involving policymakers, technologists, ethicists, and civil society (Darvishi, Liu, & Lim, 2022).

AI tools must be developed with transparency and designed to enhance women's safety, prevent online harassment, and empower marginalized communities through predictive analytics (Pimpalkar, Wankhade, Chole, & Golhar, 2024; Vyawahare, Khandelwal, & Rathod, 2024). Proactive identification of emerging threats using AI-driven semantic analysis can improve security in e-commerce and soft targets (Gaurav et al., 2024; San Biagio, Cipolla, La Mattina, & Morreale, 2023).

10.6. Recommendations for Policy and Governance

- **Develop Adaptive and Inclusive Regulatory Frameworks:** Policies must be flexible to keep pace with rapid AI evolution, incorporating international harmonization and stakeholder engagement (Butt, 2024; Daniel, 2024).
- **Integrate Ethical AI Principles Across Domains:** Implement cross-sectoral ethical guidelines addressing data privacy, security, and accountability (Shukla & Taneja, 2024; Ali & Aysan, 2025).
- **Enhance Transparency and Explainability:** Foster AI systems with interpretable decision-making processes to build public trust and enable effective oversight (Mennella et al., 2024; Luan et al., 2024).
- **Support Green and Sustainable Technology Innovation:** Align climate and environmental policies with legal frameworks that promote renewable energy, biodiversity, and indigenous rights (Chowdhury, 2024; Saikia, 2024; Soomro, Suhrab, & Abbasi, 2025).

- **Promote Interdisciplinary Research and Education:** Invest in AI literacy, STEM education, and collaborative research that merges legal, technological, and ethical perspectives (Jamro & Jamro, 2023; Filetti, Fenza, & Gallo, 2024).

By following these recommendations, policymakers, industry leaders, and researchers can collaboratively navigate the complex terrain of AI and sustainability to foster innovation that is ethical, equitable, and environmentally responsible.

Future-ready legal systems must be multilayered, integrating global ethics, sector-specific governance, and technological responsiveness. The following diagram presents a conceptual model for a layered regulatory framework governing AI at the climate-health interface.

Figure 5. Layered regulatory model for AI at the climate-health nexus

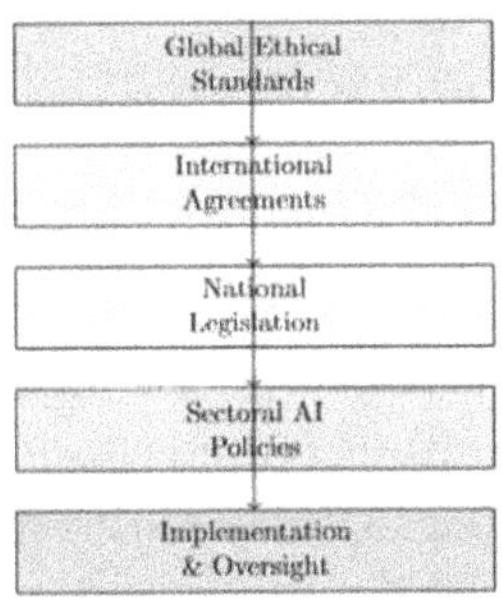

11. CONCLUSION

The dynamic intersection of artificial intelligence, environmental sustainability, and regulatory frameworks presents both unprecedented opportunities and complex challenges for the future. This chapter has explored the evolving landscape of regulatory responses to AI applications in healthcare and medical diagnostics, emphasizing the need for adaptable, transparent, and ethically grounded governance structures. As AI technologies continue to advance rapidly, their integration within sensitive domains such as healthcare demands rigorous oversight to ensure patient safety, data privacy, and equitable access to benefits (Mennella et al., 2024; Pesapane et al., 2021; World Health Organization, 2023).

Moreover, the expanding role of AI in addressing global climate change and sustainability challenges underscores the importance of harmonizing legal frameworks with innovative technologies to promote resilience and responsible stewardship of natural resources (Akindele & Chabinga, 2024; Ali, 2024; Singh & Kaunert, 2025). The intersection of AI with international environmental law and policy offers pathways to accelerate climate action, but it also requires careful navigation of geopolitical and socio-economic complexities (Aloamaka, 2024; Chowdhury, 2024; Saikia, 2024).

Ethical considerations permeate every aspect of AI deployment, from healthcare diagnostics to environmental monitoring and finance. The imperative to embed ethics into AI governance is echoed across multiple domains, urging stakeholders to prioritize transparency, accountability, and human rights (Ali & Aysan, 2025; Batabyal, 2024; Shukla & Taneja, 2024). Regulatory models must evolve to anticipate emerging risks, including misuse, bias, and security vulnerabilities, while fostering innovation and public trust (Al-Sinani et al., 2025; Veluru, 2024; Trotsyuk et al., 2024).

Looking ahead, multi-disciplinary collaboration among technologists, policymakers, legal experts, and civil society will be critical to crafting robust regulatory ecosystems that balance technological progress with societal values. The integration of AI with quantum computing and other frontier technologies will further complicate governance but also expand the potential for transformative solutions (Campus, 2024; Eswaran & Eswaran, 2025). Continuous research, education, and inclusive policy dialogues will be essential in shaping a future where AI acts as a force multiplier for sustainable development, healthcare improvement, and environmental protection (Luan et al., 2024; Fenwick et al., 2024; Zreik, 2024).

In sum, the future of AI regulation in healthcare and sustainability is not merely a technical challenge but a fundamental question of societal choice. The policies and frameworks we develop today will define the ethical, legal, and practical contours of AI's impact for decades to come, making proactive, informed, and inclusive governance indispensable.

REFERENCES

Akindele, A., & Chabinga, R. (2024). Navigating Climate Change and Sustainability Solutions: Nigeria's Role in International Environmental Law. *African Journal of Climate Change and Resource Sustainability*, *3*(1), 331–344. DOI: 10.37284/ajccrs.3.1.2188

Al-Sinani, H. S., & Mitchell, C. J. (2024). AI-enhanced ethical hacking: A Linux-focused experiment. *arXiv preprint arXiv:2410.05105.*

Al-Sinani, H. S., Sahli, N., Mitchell, C. J., & Al-Siyabi, M. (2025). Advancing ethical hacking with AI: A Linux-based experimental study. *Proceedings of ITASEC and SERICS, Bologna, Italy (Feb 2025),* https://www. chrismitchell. net/Papers/aehwaa. pdf

Ali, A. (2024). Navigating Road for Net Zero Policies to Aligning Policy, Politics, and Governance for Environmental Sustainability. In *Transition Towards a Sustainable Future: Net Zero Policies and Environmental Sustainability* (pp. 205–230). Springer Nature Singapore. DOI: 10.1007/978-981-97-5756-5_10

Ali, H., & Aysan, A. F. (2024). Decoding Future of Generative AI in Finance: A Machine Learning Exploration of Academic and Grey Corpus. *Available atSSRN* 4787211. DOI: 10.2139/ssrn.4787211

Ali, H., & Aysan, A. F. (2025). Ethical dimensions of generative AI: A cross-domain analysis using machine learning structural topic modeling. *International Journal of Ethics and Systems*, *41*(1), 3–34. DOI: 10.1108/IJOES-04-2024-0112

Ali, H., Zafar, M. B., & Aysan, A. F. (2024). Generative AI and Finance: A Multi-level Machine Learning Based Analysis. *Available atSSRN* 5129013.

Aloamaka, P. C. (2024). Navigating the Climate Crisis: Exploring International Law's Evolution and Application. *GLS Law Journal*, *6*(1), 48–58. DOI: 10.69974/glslawjournal.v6i1.127

Arya, L., & Rastogi, R. (2024). Study on Aerial Monitoring System in Agriculture, Forestry, Defense, and Border Protection Using Artificial Intelligence (AI). In *Agriculture and Aquaculture Applications of Biosensors and Bioelectronics* (pp. 392-407). IGI Global Scientific Publishing.

Batabyal, G. S. (2024). Ethics, laws on war and artificial intelligence-driven warfare. In *Artificial intelligence, ethics and the future of warfare* (pp. 187–215). Routledge India. DOI: 10.4324/9781003421849-9

Butt, J. (2024). Analytical study of the world's first EU Artificial Intelligence (AI) Act. *International Journal of Research Publication and Reviews*, *5*(3), 7343–7364. DOI: 10.55248/gengpi.5.0324.0914

Campus, M. T. (2024). Quantum Machine Learning, Leveraging Al, and. *Integration of AI, Quantum Computing, and Semiconductor Technology*, 57.

Chowdhury, S. (2024). Towards a Just Climate: Navigating Complexities and Challenges in Climate Change Discourse and Action. *Issue 2 Int'l JL Mgmt. &. Human.*, *7*, 1807.

Daniel, J. (2024). *Environmental Law: Navigating Legal Pathways for a Sustainable Future.* Pencil.

Darvishi, K., Liu, L., & Lim, S. (2022). Navigating the Nexus: Legal and Economic Implications of Emerging Tech-nologies. *Law and Economics*, *16*(3), 172–186. DOI: 10.35335/laweco.v16i3.59

Eisenberg, D. (2024). *Sensing With Integrity: Responsible Sensor Systems in an Era of AI* (Doctoral dissertation, New Jersey Institute of Technology).

Emon, M. M. H., Khan, T., Rahman, M. A., Hamid, A. B. A., & Yaakub, N. I. (2025). GreenTech revolution: Navigating challenges and seizing opportunities. In *AI and green technology applications in society* (pp. 63–90). IGI Global Scientific Publishing.

Eswaran, U., & Eswaran, V. (2025). Quantum Machine Learning, Leveraging AI, and Semiconductor Technology. In *Integration of AI, Quantum Computing, and Semiconductor Technology* (pp. 57-78). IGI Global.

Fenwick, A., Molnar, G., & Frangos, P. (2024). The critical role of HRM in AI-driven digital transformation: A paradigm shift to enable firms to move from AI implementation to human-centric adoption. *Discover Artificial Intelligence*, *4*(1), 34. DOI: 10.1007/s44163-024-00125-4

Filetti, S., Fenza, G., & Gallo, A. (2024). Research design and writing of scholarly articles: New artificial intelligence tools available for researchers. *Endocrine*, *85*(3), 1104–1116. DOI: 10.1007/s12020-024-03977-z PMID: 39085566

Flannery, J., Ajayi, S. O., & Oyegoke, A. S. (2021). Alcohol and substance misuse in the construction industry. *International Journal of Occupational Safety and Ergonomics*, *27*(2), 472–487. DOI: 10.1080/10803548.2019.1601376 PMID: 30935301

Gaurav, A., Chui, K. T., Arya, V., Attar, R. W., Bansal, S., Alhomoud, A., & Psannis, K. (2024). Optimized AI-Driven Semantic Web Approach for Enhancing Phishing Detection in E-Commerce Platforms. [IJSWIS]. *International Journal on Semantic Web and Information Systems, 20*(1), 1–13. DOI: 10.4018/IJSWIS.359767

Ho, C. W. (2023). Implementing the human right to science in the regulatory governance of artificial intelligence in healthcare. *Journal of Law and the Biosciences, 10*(2), lsad026. DOI: 10.1093/jlb/lsad026 PMID: 37854168

Jafarizadeh, H., Yamini, E., Zolfaghari, S. M., Esmaeilion, F., Assad, M. E. H., & Soltani, M. (2024). Navigating challenges in large-scale renewable energy storage: Barriers, solutions, and innovations. *Energy Reports, 12*, 2179–2192. DOI: 10.1016/j.egyr.2024.08.019

Jamro, M. Y., & Jamro, F. A. (2023). AI Matters: Chatbot Integration in Holistic STEM Education.

Karim, R., Galar, D., & Kumar, U. (2023). *AI factory: theories, applications and case studies*. CRC Press. DOI: 10.1201/9781003208686

Larson, D. B., Harvey, H., Rubin, D. L., Irani, N., Tse, J. R., & Langlotz, C. P. (2021). Regulatory frameworks for development and evaluation of artificial intelligence–based diagnostic imaging algorithms: Summary and recommendations. *Journal of the American College of Radiology, 18*(3), 413–424. DOI: 10.1016/j.jacr.2020.09.060 PMID: 33096088

Leontidis, G. (2024). Science in the age of ai: How artificial intelligence is changing the nature and method of scientific research.

Luan, H., Perron, B. E., Victor, B. G., Wan, G., Niu, Y., & Xiao, X. (2024). Using artificial intelligence to support scientometric analysis of scholarly literature: A case example of research on mainland China's left-behind children. *Journal of the Society for Social Work and Research, 15*(3), 435–457. DOI: 10.1086/731613

Maennig, W. (2014). Inefficiency of the anti-doping system: Cost reduction proposals. *Substance Use & Misuse, 49*(9), 1201–1205. DOI: 10.3109/10826084.2014.912065 PMID: 24832718

Maguluri, L. P., Arularasan, A. N., & Boopathi, S. (2023). Assessing security concerns for ai-based drones in smart cities. In *Effective AI, Blockchain, and E-Governance Applications for Knowledge Discovery and Management* (pp. 27-47). IGI Global Scientific Publishing. DOI: 10.4018/978-1-6684-9151-5.ch002

Mennella, C., Maniscalco, U., De Pietro, G., & Esposito, M. (2024). Ethical and regulatory challenges of AI technologies in healthcare: A narrative review. *Heliyon*, *10*(4), e26297. DOI: 10.1016/j.heliyon.2024.e26297 PMID: 38384518

Naili, Y. T., Mangkunegara, I. S., Purwono, P., & Baballe, M. A. (2025). Regulatory challenges in ai-based diagnostics: Legal implications of ai use in medical diagnostics. In *BIO Web of Conferences* (Vol. 152, p. 01034). EDP Sciences.

Oduro, P., Uzougbo, N. S., & Ugwu, M. C. (2024). Renewable energy expansion: Legal strategies for overcoming regulatory barriers and promoting innovation. *International Journal of Applied Research in Social Sciences*, *6*(5), 927–944. DOI: 10.51594/ijarss.v6i5.1145

Patra, S. P. (2025). Navigating the legal landscape of sustainable Industry 4.0. *Industry 4.0 for Manufacturing Systems: Concepts, Technologies, and Applications*, 109.

Pesapane, F., Bracchi, D. A., Mulligan, J. F., Linnikov, A., Maslennikov, O., Lanzavecchia, M. B., Tantrige, P., Stasolla, A., Biondetti, P., Giuggioli, P. F., Cassano, E., & Carrafiello, G. (2021). Legal and regulatory framework for AI solutions in healthcare in EU, US, China, and Russia: New scenarios after a pandemic. *Radiation*, *1*(4), 261–276. DOI: 10.3390/radiation1040022

Pesapane, F., Volonté, C., Codari, M., & Sardanelli, F. (2018). Artificial intelligence as a medical device in radiology: Ethical and regulatory issues in Europe and the United States. *Insights Into Imaging*, *9*(5), 745–753. DOI: 10.1007/s13244-018-0645-y PMID: 30112675

Pimpalkar, A. P., Wankhade, N. R., Chole, V., & Golhar, Y. (2024). Women's Empowerment Through AI: Discovering Data Analytics for Predictive Safety Solutions and Future Trends. In *AI Tools and Applications for Women's Safety* (pp. 304-326). IGI Global Scientific Publishing.

Rashid, A. B., & Kausik, A. K. (2024). AI revolutionizing industries worldwide: A comprehensive overview of its diverse applications. *Hybrid Advances*, 100277.

Rodriguez, M. Y., & Storer, H. (2020). A computational social science perspective on qualitative data exploration: Using topic models for the descriptive analysis of social media data. *Journal of Technology in Human Services*, *38*(1), 54–86. DOI: 10.1080/15228835.2019.1616350

Saikia, B. (2024). Ecologically-Informed approaches: International mechanisms for navigating environmental challenges and ensuring sustainability in the oil and gas exploration and production industry. *Proceedings of the International Academy of Ecology and Environmental Sciences*, *14*(2), 60.

Sakapaji, S. C., García Molinos, J., Parilova, V., Gavrilyeva, T., & Yakovleva, N. (2024). Navigating legal and regulatory frameworks to achieve the resilience and sustainability of indigenous socioecological systems. *Resources*, *13*(4), 56. DOI: 10.3390/resources13040056

San Biagio, M., Cipolla, M., La Mattina, E., & Morreale, V. (2023, December). A Topic Clustering Method to Identify Online Threats against Soft Targets. In *2023 International Conference on Computational Science and Computational Intelligence (CSCI)* (pp. 727-733). IEEE. DOI: 10.1109/CSCI62032.2023.00124

Schünemann, C., Johanning, S., Reger, E., Herold, H., & Bruckner, T. (2024). Complex system policy modelling approaches for policy advice–comparing systems thinking, system dynamics and agent-based modelling. *Political Research Exchange : an ECPR Journal*, *6*(1), 2387438. DOI: 10.1080/2474736X.2024.2387438

Shafik, W. (2024). Data privacy and security safeguarding customer information in ChatGPT systems. In *Revolutionizing the Service Industry Wth OpenAI Models* (pp. 52–86). IGI Global. DOI: 10.4018/979-8-3693-1239-1.ch003

Sheliemina, N. (2024). The use of artificial intelligence in medical diagnostics: Opportunities, prospects and risks. *Health Economics and Management Review*, *5*(2), 104–124. DOI: 10.61093/hem.2024.2-07

Shuja, J., Alanazi, E., Alasmary, W., & Alashaikh, A. (2021). COVID-19 open source data sets: A comprehensive survey. *Applied Intelligence*, *51*(3), 1296–1325. DOI: 10.1007/s10489-020-01862-6 PMID: 34764552

Shukla, R. P., & Taneja, S. (2024). Ethical considerations and data privacy in artificial intelligence. In *Integrating generative AI in education to achieve sustainable development goals* (pp. 86–97). IGI Global. DOI: 10.4018/979-8-3693-2440-0.ch005

Singh, B., & Kaunert, C. (2025). Navigating the Terrain of Sustainability Trajectories of Environment: Biodiversity Protection and Legal Landscapes. In *Community Resilience and Climate Change Challenges: Pursuit of Sustainable Development Goals (SDGs)* (pp. 355-374). IGI Global Scientific Publishing.

Soomro, J. A., Suhrab, M., & Abbasi, B. A. (2025). Navigating Green Regulations in the Business Ecosystem: Government Support, Compliance, and Obstacles in the Context of Pakistan. In *Government Influences on Eco-Friendly Practices in Business* (pp. 55-86). IGI Global.

Terry, N. (2019). Of regulating healthcare AI and robots. *Yale JL & Tech.*, *21*, 133.

Trotsyuk, A. A., Waeiss, Q., Bhatia, R. T., Aponte, B. J., Heffernan, I. M., Madgavkar, D., Felder, R. M., Lehmann, L. S., Palmer, M. J., Greely, H., Wald, R., Goetz, L., Trengove, M., Vandersluis, R., Lin, H., Cho, M. K., Altman, R. B., Endy, D., Relman, D. A., & Magnus, D. (2024). Toward a framework for risk mitigation of potential misuse of artificial intelligence in biomedical research. *Nature Machine Intelligence*, *6*(12), 1–8. DOI: 10.1038/s42256-024-00926-3

Veluru, C. S. (2024). Responsible Artificial Intelligence on Large Scale Data to Prevent Misuse, Unethical Challenges and Security Breaches. *Journal of Artificial Intelligence & Cloud Computing. SRC/JAICC-349. DOI: doi. org/(3), 331*, 2-6.DOI: 10.47363/JAICC/2024

Verma, A., Rao, K., Eluri, V., & Sharma, Y. (2020). Regulating AI in public health: systems challenges and perspectives. *ORF Occasional Paper, 261.*

Verma, M., & Rohit, K. (2024). Ethical AI Shaping Scholarly Communication: Challenges and Opportunities.

Vyawahare, H., Khandelwal, S., & Rathod, S. (2024). Artificial Intelligence in Detecting and Preventing Online Harassment. In *AI Tools and Applications for Women's Safety* (pp. 14–35). IGI Global Scientific Publishing. DOI: 10.4018/979-8-3693-1435-7.ch002

Wang, Q. (2024). Maritime law enforcement concerning offshore energy platforms: Navigating international law constraints and challenges. *Marine Policy*, *170*, 106370. DOI: 10.1016/j.marpol.2024.106370

World Health Organization. (2023). *Regulatory considerations on artificial intelligence for health.* World Health Organization.

Zreik, M. (2024). Harnessing AI for entrepreneurial idea generation: Navigating the new frontier. In *Generating Entrepreneurial Ideas With AI* (pp. 1–18). IGI Global Scientific Publishing. DOI: 10.4018/979-8-3693-3498-0.ch001

Chapter 10
Managing the Adoption and Implementation of Zero Trust Architecture Cybersecurity:
Overcoming Organizational, Cultural, and Compliance Challenges

Noble Antwi
https://orcid.org/0009-0000-5123-5051
Illinois Institute of Technology, USA

ABSTRACT

The growing sophistication of cyber threats and complexity of digital ecosystems demand a shift in cybersecurity strategy. This paper examines the organizational, strategic, and regulatory challenges of adopting Zero Trust Architecture (ZTA). It argues that ZTA is not just a technical solution but a management-driven framework requiring leadership, cultural change, and compliance alignment. Through analysis of leadership roles, regulatory demands (e.g., GDPR, HIPAA), and resource allocation, the study highlights barriers to adoption. It recommends best practices such as phased implementation, identity governance, automation, and continuous monitoring. Emerging technologies like AI and blockchain are explored for their role in enhancing ZTA. The research emphasizes the need for a proactive security culture in cloud-first and remote work environments and offers actionable strategies for sustainable ZTA implementation. Ultimately, Zero Trust is presented as a foundational model for resilient, future-ready cybersecurity governance.

DOI: 10.4018/979-8-3373-4862-9.ch010

Copyright © 2025, IGI Global Scientific Publishing. Copying or distributing in print or electronic forms without written permission of IGI Global Scientific Publishing is prohibited.

INTRODUCTION

Overview of Zero Trust Architecture

Zero Trust Architecture is a significant step in the methods organizations use to implement cybersecurity; however, effective deployment requires more than just technological improvement. Strong leadership and strategic direction are also necessary for successful transformation at all levels within an organization. Zero Trust realization involves a considerable shift in attitude within each department, to become an environment where security is considered a shared responsibility.

The Zero Trust model converges with management, undermining the traditional way of thinking that assumes internal systems are trustworthy by nature. Management will need to drive the redefinition of security policies and resource allocation while ensuring all stakeholders, from the board to IT teams, are aligned to ZTA principles. For example, effective implementation of Zero Trust involves collaboration among IT security teams, HR, and executive leadership to ensure seamless integration with business processes. The leadership also must address the possible operational disruptions that might happen during the transition and assure minimal impact on business continuity (Kindervag & Balaouras, 2010).

The Role of Zero Trust in Modern Cybersecurity Management

As a cybersecurity management approach, the Zero Trust model provides a holistic framework that closely aligns with current organizational strategies highlighting resilience and adaptability. However, effective Zero Trust implementation requires more than just technical deployment; it drives leaders to lead organizational transformations through several major management challenges (Rais, Morillo, Gilman, & Barth, 2024).

- Leadership and Decision-Making: Top management plays a critical role in the implementation of Zero Trust principles. Effective leaders will be needed to articulate the role of Zero Trust in the context of the organization's overall security strategy so that both information technology and non-information technology teams understand the long-term benefits. The effective implementation of this program is contingent upon having visionary leadership that can advocate the necessary investments in security technologies and people training.
- Cultural Change: Adaptation to Zero Trust is always resisted, as it is actually a change in culture. Most of the staff would resent the additional layers of security, which may be perceived as intrusive or inconvenient. Management

needs to lead from the front in bringing on board a security-sensitive culture that ensures the protocols are welcomed and not rebelled against. Besides, the concepts of change management through awareness training and constant communication will help a leader to make the employees understand how Zero Trust can reduce insider threats and protect sensitive information.

- Compliance and Regulatory Management: The other key challenge for management in implementing Zero Trust is getting into compliance with it. From the viewpoint of regulations like GDPR and HIPAA, the control on how data access and usage must be done is very restricted, so management has to ensure that these Zero Trust policies keep up with their demands. It will require not only technical solutions but also writing comprehensive internal policies and having regular audits done in order to confirm compliance.
- Resource allocation and budgeting are among the major roles of the management. The cost of implementing Zero Trust is expensive in adding cybersecurity capabilities and training personnel. It thus calls for hard decisions by leaders in apportioning the scarce budgetary resources to such investments amidst competing organizational needs. Long-term financial planning by the management for sustaining the Zero Trust system involves periodic review and testing.

Research Objectives and Scope

This study will investigate challenges concerning management in the context of adopting and implementing Zero Trust Architecture. Specifically, it will focus on the roles of organizational leadership, changing corporate culture, and issues of compliance that impact the effective adoption of Zero Trust within today's cybersecurity management. The following objectives shall guide the research:

- To examine how leadership influences the adoption and implementation of Zero Trust across various organizational levels.
- To explore the cultural barriers that hinder the acceptance of Zero Trust within organizations and how these challenges can be mitigated through change management strategies.
- To analyze the compliance challenges that organizations face when implementing Zero Trust, focusing on industry-specific regulations like GDPR and HIPAA, and the role management plays in ensuring regulatory alignment.
- To develop best practices and recommendations for management to overcome these challenges, ensuring the sustainable and effective implementation of Zero Trust across the organization.

This research will focus on organizations across multiple industries, particularly those in highly regulated sectors, such as healthcare and finance, where the implementation of Zero Trust is critical to maintaining compliance and security.

BACKGROUND

Historical Evolution of Cybersecurity Management Approaches

The evolution of cybersecurity management has seen a shift from traditional perimeter-based defenses, which focused on securing the network's boundaries through firewalls and antivirus software, to more advanced models like Zero Trust. This approach assumes no one, inside or outside the network, should be trusted by default, and access is granted only after continuous authentication and verification (Howard, 2024). This approach was effective when networks were relatively isolated, and threats primarily originated from external sources. However, as the internet expanded, so did the complexity of cyber threats, leading to the development of more sophisticated security measures. Figure 1 below illustrates a traditional Perimeter Security

Figure 1. Traditional perimeter security model

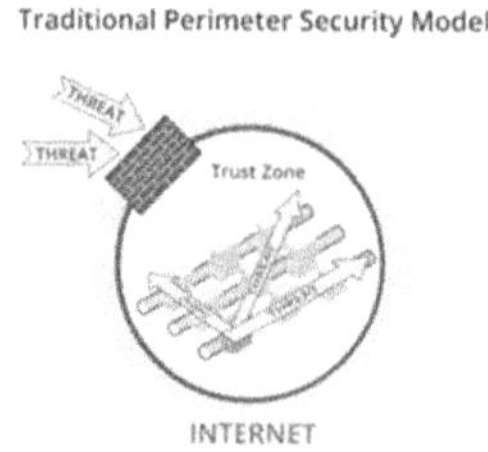

(Howard, 2024).

According to Whitman and Mattord (2019), in the early 2000s, the focus shifted towards network security, emphasizing the protection of data in transit and the establishment of secure communication channels. This period saw the rise of intrusion detection systems (IDS) and intrusion prevention systems (IPS), which aimed to detect and mitigate unauthorized access attempts in real-time

The advent of cloud computing and mobile technologies in the 2010s introduced new challenges, necessitating a more dynamic approach to cybersecurity. This era marked the beginning of the transition towards more holistic security frameworks, such as the Zero Trust Architecture (ZTA), that focus on continuous verification, making use of the principle of least privilege and assume that threats can originate from both inside and outside the network (Bush & Mashatan, 2022). Figure 2 illustrates a holistic approach to Zero Trust architecture, highlighting its integration across identities, endpoints, networks, and more (Microsoft, n.d.)

Figure 2. Zero trust architecture model

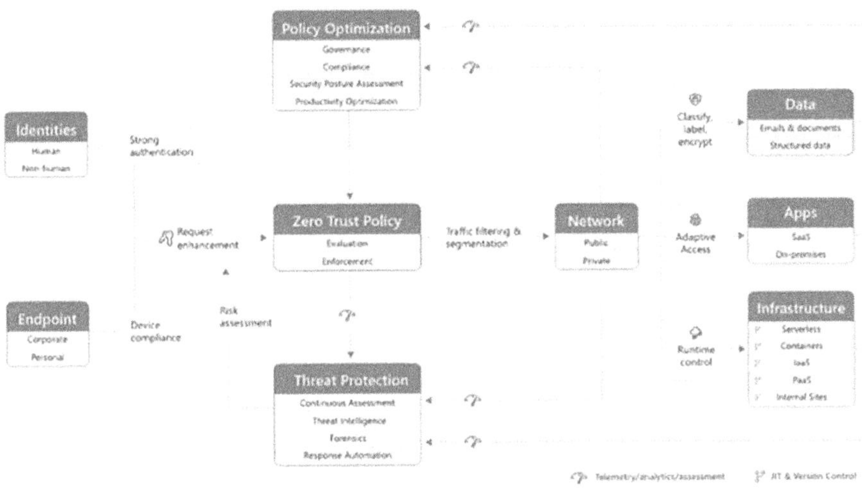

(Microsoft, n.d.).

Limitations of Traditional Perimeter-Based Security and the Management Implications

Traditional perimeter-based security models rely on the fact that threats originate from outside the network, and once inside, it may be trusted. Such an approach has significant limitations, especially for modern, highly interconnected environments.

One major limitation is the inability to handle insider threats effectively. Because perimeter-based models inherently trust insiders, malicious insiders or compromised internal accounts can use this assumption to their advantage in accessing sensitive information (Chen, 2005). Another challenge is that modern information landscapes are typified by complex networks of cloud services, IoT devices, and remote access that make the definition of a clear perimeter rather obtuse (Kang et al., 2023; Ghasemshirazi et al., 2023).

These limitations from a management perspective demand a shift towards adaptive and resilient security architectures like Zero Trust. The need for managers to understand that "constant surveillance and verification of each and every subject regardless of their position in the network" has become paramount. This shift also requires significant level of investment in training and awareness programs to ensure that all staff understand and adhere to the new security methods of operation adopted. Whitman & Mattord, 2019.

The next table gives a bit more detail to distinguish Traditional Perimeter-Based Security from Zero Trust Identity.

Table 1. Comparison of perimeter-based and zero trust security models

Feature	Perimeter-Based Security	Zero Trust Security
Authentication Mechanisms	Single authentication point; typically relies on network location or perimeter entry as proof of trust.	Continuous authentication and verification for every user and device, regardless of location.
Access Controls	Broad access is often granted once inside the network, trusting users implicitly.	Granular, least-privilege access is enforced, allowing only necessary permissions for specific roles or tasks.
Trust Models	Assumes entities inside the network are inherently trustworthy.	Assumes no entity is trustworthy by default, whether inside or outside the network.
Monitoring and Detection	Limited or periodic monitoring focused on detecting external threats.	Continuous, real-time monitoring and analysis of all activities to detect anomalies or breaches.
Threat Response	Reactive response after identifying threats, often delayed by lack of visibility.	Proactive threat detection with automated responses to anomalies or breaches.
Network Architecture	Strong focus on perimeter defense using firewalls and VPNs to secure the boundary	Emphasizes network segmentation, micro-segmentation, and securing individual access points.
User Experience	Simplified but less secure experience, with fewer authentication prompts.	May introduce additional security steps (e.g., multi-factor authentication), balanced with adaptive policies.

Key Principles of Zero Trust and Their Relevance to Information Security Management (Verification, Least Privilege, Continuous Monitoring)

Figure 3. Core principles of zero trust.

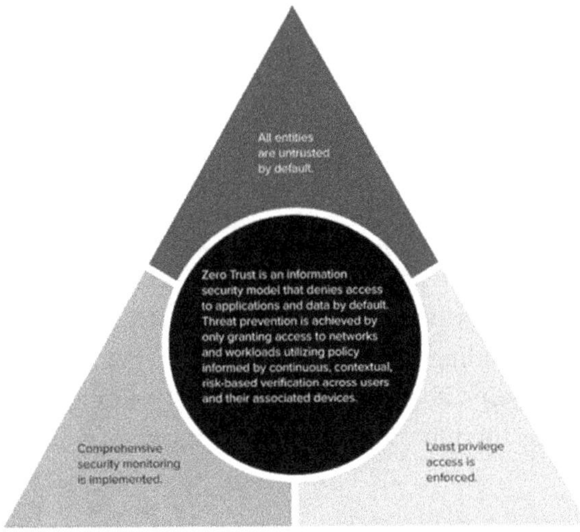

Adapted from Durrett (2022).

Zero Trust Architecture (ZTA) is built on three core principles: verification, least privilege, and continuous monitoring. These principles are crucial for modern information security management.

- **Verification:** ZTA operates on the principle of "never trust, always verify." This means that every access request, whether from inside or outside the network, must be authenticated and authorized. This approach helps mitigate the risk of unauthorized access and ensures that only legitimate users can access sensitive resources (Daah, Qureshi, Awan, & Konur, 2024)
- **Least Privilege:** The principle of least privilege dictates that users should only have the minimum level of access necessary to perform their tasks. This minimizes the potential damage from compromised accounts and reduces the attack surface. Implementing least privilege requires a thorough understanding of user roles and responsibilities, as well as robust access control mechanisms (Ma, Li, Lu, Lu, & Dong, 2011)
- **Continuous Monitoring/ Assume Breach:** Continuous monitoring involves the ongoing assessment of network activity to detect and respond to potential threats in real-time. It is hinged on the fact that; organization must assume

their enterprise has already been compromised by bad actors in the digital space. This principle is essential for maintaining a proactive security posture and ensuring that any anomalies are quickly identified and addressed. Effective continuous monitoring relies on advanced analytics and automated response systems to manage the vast amounts of data generated by modern networks (Dempsey, Chawla, Johnson, Johnston, Jones, Orebaugh, Scholl, & Stine, 2011)

These principles are essential for contemporary information security management because they tackle the weaknesses of older security models. Traditional approaches often assumed that once inside the network, users and devices could be trusted. However, this assumption is no longer valid in today's complex and interconnected environments. By reducing trust assumptions and continuously validating every access request, these modern principles ensure that security measures are always active and vigilant, thereby providing a more robust defense against potential threats. This continuous validation helps in promptly identifying and mitigating risks, making the overall security posture more resilient and adaptive to emerging

STRATEGIC MANAGEMENT OF ZERO TRUST IMPLEMENTATION

Leadership's Role in Driving Zero Trust Adoption

According to Backman, 2023, ZTA requires effective leadership. Its success demands a skilled leader to lead the Zero Trust initiative, clearly explain its importance, and knit it into the greater security structure of the institution. In addition, the leader should help in setting a security-conscious culture and make the different departments aware of the benefits accompanying Zero Trust. But they must also be the advocates for necessary investments in technology and training that will make it possible. Indeed, solving such complex problems with Zero Trust implementation and leading organizational change requires transformational leadership.

Aligning Zero Trust with Organizational Goals and Business Objectives

Federici et al. (2023) make a point that Zero Trust should be integrated with the organization's overall goals and objectives if it is to work. It is not solely an IT-related project; it forms part of the strategic outlook of the organization in terms of how best business processes can be reinforced and other wider objectives met. In that way, it assures that security services enable business-things, such as remote access and collaboration, without losing data integrity. The leadership should engage the business units in embedding Zero Trust principles in the ways of working and make the security enhancements to make workflows secure and productive.

Managing Change: Overcoming Resistance from Key Stakeholders and Departments

Zero Trust is implemented only when the resistance of stakeholders is overcome; these would feel that enhanced security protocols intrude into their privacy. Effective change management strategies need to be implemented to overcome such fears by communicating transparently about the benefits of ZTA and how these align with organizational objectives, states Uwaoma (2023). Early stakeholder involvement, along with training, will help overcome resistance. Demonstrating quick wins with the help of pilot projects can further generate excitement and ownership at different levels.

Resource Allocation and Financial Management for Zero Trust Projects

Resource planning will be required for proper Zero Trust implementation. In this regard, financial investments should be made in core technologies like identity management systems, network segmentation tools, and solutions for continuous monitoring. The security measures to be implemented include MFA, endpoint detection and response systems, and data encryption, among others Wang, Sadjadi, Rishe, & Mahara, 2024.

In addition, the financial management should consider a number of other continuous expenses that would relate to the upkeep and refresh of the security systems. Resources can be scaled effectively and efficiently to invest in technologies and security controls that ensure the organization's Zero Trust initiatives are actionable and sustainable long. Figure 4 is a flowchart showing one possible phased ZTA implementation strategy.

Figure 4. Flowchart of a phased ZTA implementation strategy

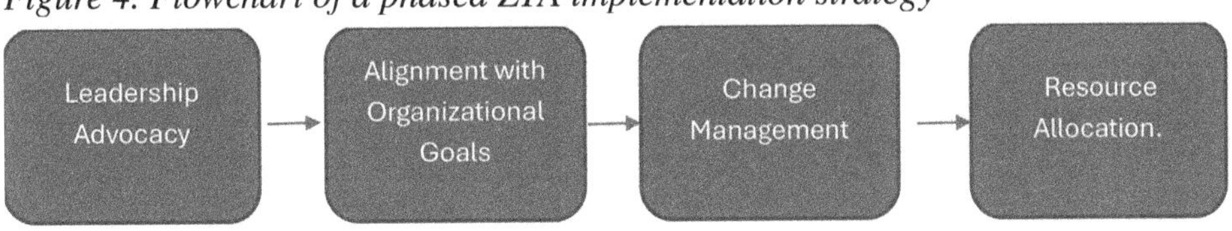

ORGANIZATIONAL AND CULTURAL CHALLENGES

Shifting from a Trust-Based to a Zero-Trust Security Culture

The Zero Trust security model requires a sea change in how an organization thinks about and manages trust inside the network. Traditional models implicitly trust internal users and systems, which is simply no longer practical in light of advanced cyber threats. The Zero Trust framework, articulated by the tenet of "never trust, always verify," mandates that continuous authentication of all users and devices occurs, independent of their position within the network. This transition demands a cultural transformation in which security is emphasized at all organizational tiers, promoting a milieu in which vigilance and verification become routine practices (Gajbhiye, Jain, & Goel, 2023).

Managing the Impact on Employee Productivity and User Experience

Implementing Zero Trust can initially slow down employee productivity and affect user experience because of the extra authentication steps and access controls. Organizations need to find a balance between security and usability to keep disruptions to a minimum (Ismail & Abd El-Gawad, 2023).

Using technologies like single sign-on (SSO) and adaptive authentication can make the process smoother while still keeping security strong. It's also important to clearly explain to employees why these security measures are necessary and how they help protect the organization's assets (Ismail & Abd El-Gawad, 2023).

Training and Awareness Programs to Support Zero Trust Adoption

Training and awareness programs are essential for adopting Zero Trust principles. Employees need to understand the new security protocols, why they are important, and their role in keeping the environment secure (Ali, Gregory, & Li, 2023). Regular training sessions, workshops, and informational resources can help create a knowledgeable workforce ready to adapt to new security measures. Encouraging a proactive approach to security through continuous learning opportunities ensures that employees stay engaged and informed about evolving threats and best practices (Ali, Gregory, & Li, 2023).

Addressing Internal Resistance and Fostering a Proactive Security Culture

Resistance to change is pretty common when rolling out new security frameworks like Zero Trust. To tackle this, it's important to get stakeholders involved early, be transparent about any concerns, and show how Zero Trust supports the organization's goals (Gajbhiye et al., 2023).

Creating a culture that values proactive security measures can help employees feel more responsible for cybersecurity. Leaders should set an example by prioritizing security initiatives and recognizing staff efforts. Award schemes that highlight these efforts can motivate others to take security seriously (Gajbhiye et al., 2023).

COMPLIANCE AND GOVERNANCE IN ZERO TRUST MANAGEMENT

Navigating Regulatory Requirements (GDPR, CCPA, HIPAA, PCI-DSS) in a Zero Trust Environment

Navigating the General Data Protection Regulation, California Consumer Privacy Act, Health Insurance Portability and Accountability Act, and Payment Card Industry Data Security Standard compliance within a Zero Trust framework involves the alignment of security practices to strict data protection and privacy mandates. Zero Trust principles, which emphasize continuous verification and least privilege access, inherently support compliance by ensuring that data access is tightly controlled and monitored (Bhusa & Shrestha, 2024). Organizations must ensure that their Zero Trust implementations are designed to meet specific regulatory requirements, such as data encryption, access logs, and breach notification protocols. This alignment helps to implement compliance and improves security posture by mitigating unauthorized access to data. Organizations must incorporate regulatory requirements into their Zero Trust framework in the initial phases. To do so, it involves:

- Data Encryption: Ensuring that all sensitive data, both at rest and in transit, is encrypted using strong encryption algorithms. This protects data by rendering it useless in the event of it been intercepted as bad actors may not possess the decryption keys to access the sensitive data.
- Access Logs: Implementing extensive logging and monitoring systems, in which every access attempt and activities taking place in the network are logged and making sure these logs are very detailed and securely stored for easy auditing and investigations in case of a security incident.

- Breach Notification Protocols: Formulate clear policies for identifying, responding to, and reporting data breaches. This will include immediate notification to the affected individuals and concerned regulatory bodies as required by law such as under the General Data Protection Regulation (GDPR) and the California Consumer Privacy Act (CCPA).
- Regular Audits and Assessments: Conducting regular security audits and assessments to ensure ongoing compliance with regulatory standards. This helps identify and address any gaps or weaknesses in the security posture.
- Employee Training and Awareness: Providing continuous training and awareness programs for employees to ensure they understand the importance of regulatory compliance and their role in maintaining security.

Implementing these regulatory mandates in the Zero Trust framework, it gives an organization a chance to lay down a security infrastructure that is resilient and accomplishes the requirements legally at the same time looking forward and minimizing probable threats. That is, with this holistic approach, security measures are certainly not reactive; they become part of a deliberate strategy for safeguarding sensitive information and assurance among stakeholders.

Establishing Governance Structures to Support Continuous Zero Trust Monitoring

In the Zero Trust model, effective governance structures make monitoring continuous. Such frameworks should define clear roles and responsibilities for security personnel, formulate access management policies, and ensure that security protocols are reviewed periodically (Miracle, 2024). Governance structures have to support the integration of automated technologies that provide real-time insight into network operations and identified potential vulnerabilities. In doing so, organizations have to integrate SIEM tools, that are very critical in collecting, analyzing, and correlating security event data emanating from multiple sources. By leveraging advanced SIEM tools for governance frameworks, organizations will gain insights into network activity in real-time, an optimum time for detecting possible threats and overall fortification of their security stature. This proactive approach does not just help in maintaining compliance with regulatory standards but ensures that the entire IT environment is more resilient and secure.

Auditing and Reporting for Zero Trust Compliance

Miracle (2024) articulates auditing and reporting, these are very critical components of operating within a Zero Trust framework. Frequent audits will help to ensure that designed security measures are in place and the regulations around access are enforced consistently across the organization. In this respect, strong reporting mechanisms must be put in place to document where and how compliance with regulatory requirements is occurring to give transparency to stakeholders and demonstrate due diligence in protection efforts around sensitive data. This documentation becomes very important during regulatory assessments or any events that require forensic analysis. Tools like Security Information and Event Management (SIEM) systems are helpful in terms of continuously overseeing and documenting compliance (Seaman, 2020).

Risk Management and Zero Trust: Integrating Risk Assessment into Security Strategy

Integration of risk assessment within a Zero Trust framework means identifying possible threats and vulnerabilities, assessing their consequences, and establishing controls aimed at mitigating these risks. This process, therefore, is continuous and ensures security controls are always updated and aligned with the current threat landscape and organizational objectives (Rose, Borchert, Mitchell, & Connelly, 2020).

BEST PRACTICES FOR ZERO TRUST MANAGEMENT

Conducting a Comprehensive Organizational Asset Inventory

Zero Trust Architecture consists of a crucial initial phase where all organizational assets are inventoried in a thorough manner. This process includes the identification and systematic cataloging of hardware, software, data, and other network elements to establish what should be protected and how the various components are related. A detailed asset inventory helps organizations implement appropriate security measures and monitor access appropriately, hence ensuring that all the assets are acknowledged within the Zero Trust concept. (Rose, Borchert, Mitchell, & Connelly, 2020; Fischer et al., 2022).

Developing a Phased and Scalable Zero Trust Implementation Strategy

Formulation of the phased and scalable implementation strategy is critical to effective Zero-Trust adoption. This approach will allow organizations to integrate Zero-Trust principles progressively, starting from the most critical systems and expanding to cover the whole network. Organizations can maximize their management of resources and reduce disruptions to business operations by focusing on high-risk sectors and by the systematic application of security measures. A scalable design ensures that the Zero Trust architecture is able to adapt to the evolution of organizational needs and technological advance. (AWS, 2024; DAU, 2023)

Establishing and Managing Effective Identity Governance Frameworks

Effective identity governance is at the core of Zero Trust; that is, it ensures only authorized users can access specific resources. Strong identity governance frameworks are implemented through the use of technologies like multi-factor authentication and identity access management systems, where these are continuously used to verify the identity of the users (Securing Digital Identity in the Zero Trust Architecture, 2024). The frameworks should contain policies for user onboarding and offboarding, access rights management, and regular auditing of all activities related to identity for the prevention of unauthorized access (Ghasemshirazi et al., 2023).

Implementing Least Privilege and Zero Trust Network Access (ZTNA) in the Workplace

The principle of least privilege is the bedrock of Zero Trust, which demands that a user have only the access required to perform their role. Implementing ZTNA demands network segmentation with strict controls on access; in this way, access is only permitted to the extent of roles and responsibilities of the users. In this manner, the attack surfaces are minimized, and risk from inward threats is reduced since users cannot access sensitive data or systems beyond their scope of work. World Economic Forum. (2024).

Leveraging Automation to Manage and Monitor Zero Trust Systems

The installation of automation ensures that the Zero Trust systems can be effectively managed and supervised. Automating solutions can also be useful in optimizing procedures related to threat detection, incident response, and compliance documentation by enabling immediate insights into network operations (Karanam, 2024). Automation allows for the sustainability of a proactive stance in security by quickly identifying anomalies and any risks that might accompany them without human interference. Instruments like SOAR allow for the automation of routine tasks, thereby ensuring the uniformity of security policies and more rapid responses to threats. This way, much burden is taken off security personnel, while their general posture in security is enhanced (Nicolai, Richmond, & Morrow, 2022).

FUTURE TRENDS AND CONSIDERATIONS IN ZERO TRUST MANAGEMENT

The Role of Emerging Technologies (AI, Blockchain) in Supporting Management of Zero Trust Systems

Similarly, emerging technologies such as AI and Blockchain help in keeping Zero Trust frameworks significantly up to date. For example, AI might be used in threat detection and response in real time by automatically highlighting anomalies and possible violations of security in a network. The latter offers the possibility of adopting proactive security through persistent analysis of large data volumes for any suspicious activity (Kaur et al., 2024).

The decentralized and immutable nature of blockchain provides a strong base for the realization of the ZTA. Application of permissioned blockchain platforms, such as Hyperledger, would thus be able to improve network security in supporting open and secure transactions (Liu, Tan, Wu, et al., 2024). In that case, blockchain will ensure that there will always be a protected ledger for recording access and transactions that echoes the Zero Trust principle of “never trust, always verify,” ensuring that every interaction in the system is properly authenticated and authorized.

The integration of AI and Blockchain technologies with architectures of Zero Trust increases security in consideration of the ever-evolving landscape of cyber threats. The role of AI in cybersecurity,more so within Zero Trust frameworks—holds a lot of promise in its benefits, including:

- **Dynamic Threat Identification**: AI algorithms can analyze network traffic patterns and user behaviors to detect anomalies that could indicate security breaches.
- **Automated Response**: AI-powered systems can initiate immediate countermeasures upon detecting potential threats, reducing response times and minimizing damage.
- **Continuous Learning**: Machine learning models can adapt to new threat patterns, improving the accuracy of threat detection over time.

Similarly, Blockchain technology strengthens Zero Trust systems by providing:

- **Immutable Audit Trails**: Blockchain offers a tamper-resistant record of all network activities and access attempts, enhancing accountability and forensic capabilities (Gai et al., 2022).
- **Decentralized Authentication**: Blockchain's distributed nature enables organizations to implement secure and transparent authentication mechanisms.
- **Smart Contract Enforcement**: Blockchain-based smart contracts can automate policy enforcement, ensuring consistent application of security protocols across the network (Gai et al., 2022).

The integrated interplay between Artificial Intelligence and Blockchain technologies within Zero Trust frameworks gives a holistic view toward the enhancement of cybersecurity and answers the challenges inducted by the increasingly complex digital ecosystems and sophisticated cyber threats. This will help organizations shifting to more efficient, adaptive, and resilient security protocols that can protect against emerging risks (Malik, 2024).

Managing Zero Trust in Cloud-First and Remote Work Environments

The shift to cloud-first and remote work environments has produced a need to incorporate Zero Trust principles into the security of distributed networks. In these environments, traditional perimeter-centric security models prove insufficient because there is no clear network boundary. Zero Trust provides a systematic approach that ensures all users, regardless of location, face continuous verification before access to resources is granted (Microsoft, 2024). ZTA in cloud environments includes micro-segmentation for workload protection and tight identity verification processes for access management. It contributes toward the security of sensitive data from unauthorized access but allows secure collaboration among remote teams (Kappel, 2024).

Long-Term Implications for Cybersecurity Governance and Policy Development

The adoption of Zero Trust brings major implications for cybersecurity governance and policy development. It calls on organizations to rethink their security frameworks, emphasizing continuous monitoring and verification. The shift is now affecting regulatory landscapes with a focus on new policies that center on proactive security measures and accountability in the practice of cybersecurity. Governments are increasingly putting in place regulations to beef up cybersecurity resilience (World Economic Forum, 2024).

Challenges and Opportunities in Managing Zero Trust Across Multi-National Organizations

Zero Trust management in multi-national companies brings some unique challenges and opportunities. Such organizations have to navigate different regulatory environments while keeping consistency in their security policies in global operations. Adoption of ZTA can help build alignment with security policies as corporations expand globally, but careful coordination is needed to ensure that local compliance requirements are met in light of cultural and legal differences (Diaz Rivera et al., 2024). Moreover, the decentralized, blockchain-enabled multi-factor authentication (MFA) system would help improve digital identity security and facilitate privacy and compliance with multiple regulatory frameworks. Such a capacity, which leverages the knowledge base of worldwide perspectives on threat patterns and security methodologies, shows promise of better defensive strategy developments.

Through the use of global data in different regions, organizations can enhance their threat detection capabilities and create adaptive security measures that change with each new risk involved (Diaz Rivera et al., 2024). Yet, the organizations have to face all challenges, including varying levels of technology development as well as differences in regional cybersecurity preparedness. Some regions might have infrastructure in place and policies already developed, while others might have limitations in resources or a gradual rollout of new technologies (Malik, 2024). These kinds of factors call for an advanced approach to Zero Trust in which global security standards are adapted to local technology and regulatory ecosystems.

QUANTITATIVE INSIGHTS ON ZERO TRUST ADOPTION AND EFFECTIVENESS

The adoption of Zero Trust has demonstrated significant benefits in enhancing organizational security and mitigating cyber threats. However, empirical data highlights the necessity for widespread implementation and optimization of this framework.

Adoption Rates

A 2023 Gartner survey revealed that 63% of organizations are presently planning or implementing Zero Trust strategies, a response to growing threats and compliance mandates. This high rate of implementation shows that Zero Trust is now more widely recognized as one of the components necessary to include in modern cybersecurity architectures. Moreover, 43% of respondents reported that their organizations have already implemented Zero Trust solutions, while 46% are in the process of transitioning to a zero-trust framework (Statista, 2023).

Challenges Highlighted by Data

Despite its benefits, 38% of organizations cited resistance to cultural change as a top barrier to Zero Trust adoption (Cisco Security, 2024). Much of this resistance to adopting Zero Trust stems from the large change in mindset and practices that implementation requires. The other big barrier relates to resource constraints: in a Forrester survey, 41% of respondents cited high costs, among other expenses incurred by advanced technologies and training (Forrester Research, 2023). It was also underlined in the Okta 2023 State of Zero Trust Security report that the biggest hindrances to the implementation of Zero Trust security measures are financial constraints, technology gaps, and privacy regulations.

Future Outlook

As Zero Trust continues to be applied more widely, you can expect:

- Further integration of AI and machine learning into enhancing the detection of threats and automating security responses.
- More attention to Zero Trust education and training programs, to close the skill gap.
- Development of industry specific Zero Trust frameworks to meet the unique demands of each sector.

CONCLUSION

The implementation and management of Zero Trust Architecture (ZTA) marks a transformative shift in modern cybersecurity management, driven by the need to counteract increasingly sophisticated cyber threats. This research has underscored the critical role of leadership, cultural adaptation, and strategic governance in ensuring the successful adoption of ZTA. By embedding principles such as continuous verification, least privilege, and proactive monitoring, organizations can effectively overcome the limitations of traditional perimeter-based security models.

Key findings from the study highlight that Zero Trust is not merely a technical solution but a holistic approach requiring alignment with organizational goals, robust resource allocation, and the mitigation of resistance through effective change management. Additionally, the integration of regulatory compliance frameworks, along with leveraging emerging technologies like AI and blockchain, reinforces ZTA's potential as a resilient and scalable cybersecurity framework.

The research also emphasizes the importance of fostering a culture of security awareness, implementing phased strategies, and utilizing automation to maintain operational efficiency while enhancing security measures. As organizations increasingly operate in cloud-first and remote work environments, Zero Trust provides a versatile foundation to secure dynamic, distributed networks.

Looking ahead, the evolution of Zero Trust will likely be shaped by emerging technologies and global regulatory developments, posing both challenges and opportunities. Organizations must remain adaptable, embracing innovation while tailoring ZTA principles to their unique operational and compliance landscapes.

In conclusion, Zero Trust represents a paradigm shift that addresses the complexities of modern cybersecurity. By adopting this approach, organizations can not only fortify their security postures but also drive a culture of continuous vigilance, ultimately ensuring sustainable protection against the evolving threat landscape.

REFERENCES

Ali, B., Gregory, M. A., & Li, S. (2023). Trust-aware task load balancing in multi-access edge computing based on blockchain and a Zero Trust security capability framework. *Transactions on Emerging Telecommunications Technologies*, *34*(12), 34. DOI: 10.1002/ett.4845

AWS. (2024). Phased approach to Zero Trust. *Amazon Web Services*. Retrieved fromhttps://docs.aws.amazon.com/prescriptive-guidance/latest/strategy-zero-trust - a rchitecture/phased-migration.html

Backman, S. (2023). *Making sense of large-scale cyber incidents: International cybersecurity beyond threat-based security perspectives. Department of Economic History and I nternational Relations*. Stockholm University.

Bhusa, G., & Shrestha, B. (2024). *The role of PASTA in addressing future trends in regulatory compliance: Emerging cyber threats. International Journal of Innovative Science and Research Technology*. IJISRT.

Bush, M., & Mashatan, A. (2022). From Zero to One Hundred. *ACM Queue; Tomorrow's Computing Today*, *20*(4), 80–106. DOI: 10.1145/3561799

Chen, S., & Song, Q. (2005). Perimeter-based defense against high bandwidth DDoS attacks. *IEEE Transactions on Parallel and Distributed Systems*, *16*(6), 526–537. DOI: 10.1109/TPDS.2005.74

Cisco. (n.d.). *Zero trust outcomes report*. Cisco. h t t p s : //www.cisco.com/c/en/us/products/security/zero-trust-outcomes-report.html

Daah, C., Qureshi, A., Awan, I., & Konur, S. (2024). Enhancing zero trust models in the f inancial industry through blockchain integration: A proposed framework. *Electronics (Basel)*, *13*(5), 865. DOI: 10.3390/electronics13050865

Dempsey, K., Chawla, N., Johnson, L., Johnston, R., Jones, A., Orebaugh, A., Scholl, M., & Stine, K. (2011). Information security continuous monitoring (ISCM) for federal i nformation systems and organizations (NIST Special Publication 800-137). National Institute of Standards and Technology. https://csrc.nist.gov/publications/detail/sp/800- 137/final

Diaz Rivera, J. J., Muhammad, A., & Song, W. (2024). Securing digital identity in the zero trust architecture: A blockchain approach to privacy-focused multi-factor authentication. *IEEE Open Journal of the Communications Society, 5*, 2792-2814. https://DOI: <ALIGNMENT.qj></ALIGNMENT>10.1109/OJCOMS.2024.3250511

Durrett, D. M. (2022, January 28). *(Zero) Trust but Verify*. Stamus Networks. Retrieved from https://www.stamus-networks.com/blog/zero-trust-but-verify

Federici, F., Martintoni, D., & Senni, V. (2023). A zero-trust architecture for remote access in industrial IoT infrastructures. *Electronics, 12*(3), 566. h t t p s://DOI: 10.3390/electronics12030566

Fischer, A., Fuhry, B., Kußmaul, J., Janneck, J., Kerschbaum, F., & Bodden, E. (2022). C omputation on encrypted data using dataflow authentication. *ACM Transactions on Privacy and Security*, *25*(3), 1–36. DOI: 10.1145/3513005

Forrester. (n.d.). *Building a Zero Trust roadmap: A practical guide*. Forrester. ht t ps://www.forrester.com/blogs/building-a-zero-trust-roadmap-a-practical-guide/

Gai, K., She, Y., Zhu, L., Choo, K. R., & Wan, Z. (2022). A blockchain-based access control scheme for zero trust cross-organizational data sharing. *ACM Transactions on Internet Technology*, *23*(3), 1–25. DOI: 10.1145/3511899

Gajbhiye, B., Jain, S., & Goel, O. (2023). *Defense in depth strategies for Zero Trust security models*. Darpan International Research Analysis.

Gartner. (2024, April 22). Gartner survey reveals 63 percent of organizations worldwide have implemented a Zero Trust strategy. Gartner. ht t p s : / /www.gartner.com/en/newsroom/press-releases/2024-04-22-gartner-survey-reveals-63- percent-of-organizations-worldwide-have-implemented-a-zero-trust-strategy

Ghasemshirazi, S., Shirvani, G., & Alipour, M. A. (2023). Zero trust: Applications, challenges, and opportunities. *arXiv Preprint*. https://arxiv.org/pdf/2309.03582v1

Howard. (2024, May 24). From perimeter to zero trust: The evolution of cyber defense. *FS.com*. https://community.fs.com/article/from-perimeter-to-zero-trust-the -evolution-of-cyber- defense.html

Ismail, M., & Abd El-Gawad, A. F. (2023). *Revisiting Zero-Trust security for Internet of Things*. Sustainable Machine Intelligence Journal. DOI: 10.61185/SMIJ.2023.33106

Kang, H., Liu, G., Wang, Q., & Liu, J. (2023). Theory and application of zero trust security: A brief survey. *Entropy (Basel, Switzerland)*, *25*(12), 1595. DOI: 10.3390/e25121595 PMID: 38136475

Kappel, K. (2024). Navigating Zero Trust security in the remote work era: Guidance for o rganizations. *KPMG*. Retrieved from https://kpmg.com/us/en/media/news/navigating- zero-trust-security-in-the-remote-work-era-2024.html

Karanam, R. (2024). Zero Trust architecture in DevSecOps: Enhancing security in cloud-native environments. *International Journal for Research in Applied Science and Engineering Technology*, *12*(8), 1071–1077. DOI: 10.22214/ijraset.2024.64045

Kaur, J., Hasan, S. N., Orthi, S. M., Miah, M. A., Goffer, M. A., Barikdar, C. R., & Hassan, J. (2024). Advanced cyber threats and cybersecurity innovation: Strategic approaches and emerging solutions. *Journal of Computer Science and Technology Studies.*

Kindervag, J., & Balaouras, S. (2010). No more chewy centers: Introducing the zero trust model of information security. *Forrester Research, 3.*

Liu, C., Tan, R., Wu, Y., Feng, Y., Jin, Z., Zhang, F., Liu, Y., & Liu, Q. (2024). Dissecting zero trust: Research landscape and its i mplementation in IoT. *Cybersecurity*, *7*(1), 20. DOI: 10.1186/s42400-024-00212-0

Ma, X., Li, R., Lu, Z., Lu, J., & Dong, M. (2011). Specifying and enforcing the principle of least privilege in role-based access control. *Concurrency and Computation*, *23*(2), 203–215. DOI: 10.1002/cpe.1731

Malik, V. (2024). Securing AI-native application workloads with zero trust: Preventing LLM attacks and poisoning. *Cloud Security Alliance*. Retrieved from h t t ps://c loudsecurityalliance.org/blog/2024/05/23/securing-ai-native-application-workloads - with-zero-trust-preventing-llm-attacks-and-poisoning

Microsoft. (n.d.). *Illustration of the Zero Trust model* [Illustration]. Retrieved from h ttps://www.microsoft.com/en-us/security/business/zero-trust

Miracle, N. O. (2024). The importance of network security in protecting sensitive data and information. *International Journal of Research and Innovation in Applied Science.*

Nicolai, M., Richmond, N., & Morrow, T. (2022). *Industry best practices for Zero Trust a rchitecture*. Software Engineering Institute. Retrieved from h t t p s://resources .sei.cmu.edu/asset_files/WhitePaper/2022_019_001_890272.pdf

Okta. (2023). *SOZT report*. Okta. https://www.okta.com/sites/default/files/2023- 0 9 /SOZT_Report.pdf

Rais, R., Morillo, C., Gilman, E., & Barth, D. (2024). *Zero Trust Networks: Building Secure Systems in Untrusted Networks*. O'Reilly Media, Incorporated.

Seaman, J. (2020). *PCI DSS: An integrated data security standard guide*. Apress. DOI: 10.1007/978-1-4842-5808-8

Shaw, P. (2023, March 16). Zero trust. *Defense Acquisition University.* https://www.dau.edu/sites/default/files/Migrate/EventAttachments/885/DAU%20Zero%20Trust%20Shaw%20%2020230316.pdf

Statista. (2024). *Zero trust adoption stage among companies worldwide*. Statista. https://www.statista.com/statistics/1422664/zero-trust-adoption-stage-companies/

Uwaoma, C. (2023). *The challenges and processes of achieving optimal implementation of Zero Trust Architecture in the workplace*. SIGMIS-CPR. DOI: 10.1145/3579168.3632735

Wang, W., Sadjadi, S. M., Rishe, N., & Mahara, A. (2024). Applying transparent shaping for Zero Trust Architecture implementation in AWS: A case study. *arXiv preprint a rXiv:2405.01412v2*. https://arxiv.org/pdf/2405.01412v2

Whitman, M. E., & Mattord, H. J. (2019). Management of information security (6th ed.). C engage Learning.

World Economic Forum. (2022). The Zero Trust model in cybersecurity: Towards understanding and deployment. https://www3.weforum.org/docs/WEF_The_Zero_Trust_Model_in_Cybersecurity_2022.pdf

World Economic Forum. (2024). Cybersecurity rules saw big changes in 2024. *World Economic Forum*. Retrieved from https://www.weforum.org/agenda/2024/10/cybersecurity- r egulation-changes-nis2-eu-2024/

Chapter 11

Governing AI-Driven Agriculture: Policy, Ethics, and the Role of Language in Knowledge Transfer

Hewa Majeed Zangana
https://orcid.org/0000-0001-7909-254X
Duhok Polytechnic University, Iraq

Pratiwi Amelia
https://orcid.org/0000-0001-9778-6772
Universitas Muhammadiyah Bangka Belitung, Indonesia

Senny Luckyardi
https://orcid.org/0000-0001-9954-7433
Universitas Komputer Indonesia, Indonesia

Firas Mahmood Mustafa
https://orcid.org/0000-0002-8757-5303
Duhok Polytechnic University, Iraq

Shuai Li
University of Oulu, Finland

ABSTRACT

Artificial intelligence (AI) is transforming agriculture by enabling precision farming, predictive analytics, and automated decision-making, thereby enhancing productivity and sustainability. However, this rapid technological advancement raises complex policy and ethical challenges, particularly regarding data governance, equitable access, environmental impact, and transparency. This chapter explores the regulatory

DOI: 10.4018/979-8-3373-4862-9.ch011

Copyright © 2025, IGI Global Scientific Publishing. Copying or distributing in print or electronic forms without written permission of IGI Global Scientific Publishing is prohibited.

frameworks shaping AI-driven agricultural practices and emphasizes the critical role of language in facilitating effective knowledge transfer among diverse stakeholders, including farmers, policymakers, and researchers. By analyzing interdisciplinary approaches, the chapter highlights how linguistic clarity and ethical considerations underpin responsible AI governance in agriculture, ensuring innovations serve public interest while mitigating risks. Ultimately, it advocates for comprehensive policies that balance innovation with accountability and inclusivity in the evolving landscape of agri-tech.

1. INTRODUCTION

Artificial Intelligence (AI) has become a transformative force across many disciplines, notably in scientific writing and agricultural technologies. Its rapid development is reshaping how researchers generate, analyze, and disseminate knowledge, as well as how agricultural systems operate to meet the pressing challenges of global food security and environmental sustainability. However, the expansion of AI applications brings forth complex challenges related to ethics, governance, cybersecurity, and equitable access, especially in developing countries (Abd-Elsalam & Abdel-Momen, 2023; Aderibigbe et al., 2023; Aggarwal et al., 2024).

In the realm of scientific writing, AI-powered tools such as large language models (LLMs) and automated writing assistants are increasingly adopted to enhance productivity, improve clarity, and assist non-native speakers (Aithal & Aithal, 2023; Alahdab, 2024; Khalifa & Albadawy, 2024). These innovations promise to democratize academic authorship, making scientific knowledge creation more accessible. Nonetheless, they raise profound ethical questions about authorship, originality, transparency, and accountability (Ajiye & Omokhabi, 2025; Dinçer, 2024; Ersöz & Engin, 2024). Scholars have warned of risks including potential misuse, plagiarism, and the dilution of human intellectual contribution (BaHammam, 2023; Casal & Kessler, 2023; Harati, 2024). Furthermore, regulatory frameworks and best practices to govern the ethical use of AI in academia are still nascent, calling for multidisciplinary dialogue and international collaboration (Benabed & Tudoran, 2023; Cath, 2018; AlSamhori & Alnaimat, 2024).

Concurrently, AI's integration into agriculture — often framed as Agriculture 4.0 — is revolutionizing food production, supply chain management, and environmental conservation (Araújo et al., 2021; Bhangar & Shahriyar, 2023; Chen et al., 2024). AI-enabled precision agriculture leverages big data, remote sensing, and machine learning to optimize crop yields, reduce resource waste, and predict pest outbreaks (Ahmed et al., 2024; Bhat & Huang, 2021; Gupta et al., 2024). This potential is critical to addressing the food demands of a growing global population, especially in developing countries facing infrastructural and resource constraints (Ahmad et al., 2024; Ali et al., 2024). Yet, these advancements also expose new cybersecurity vulnerabilities, data privacy issues, and ethical dilemmas related to data ownership, algorithmic bias, and equitable benefit sharing (Ali et al., 2024; Alghamdy, 2023; Dembani et al., 2025; Gavai et al., 2025; Kapoor, 2025). The governance of AI in agriculture demands policies that balance innovation with transparency, accountability, and inclusivity (Alexander et al., 2024; Dara et al., 2022; Devare et al., 2023; Farah & Varela, 2023).

Moreover, the ethical and social implications of AI intersect critically in the context of education and capacity building, especially in regions where digital divides persist. For instance, AI tools in academic writing have pedagogical impacts that must be carefully managed to foster genuine learning and creativity without compromising academic integrity (Aljuaid, 2024; Khup & Bantugan, 2025; Alghamdy, 2023). Similarly, in agritourism and smallholder farming contexts, AI adoption must be sensitive to local socio-economic realities and cultural norms (Denhere & Shao, 2024; Kanyepe et al., 2025). These considerations underscore the need for culturally aware and ethically informed AI deployment strategies.

This chapter aims to provide a comprehensive overview of AI's role in scientific writing and agricultural technologies, addressing the intertwined technological advancements, ethical challenges, and regulatory landscapes. By synthesizing insights from diverse studies and disciplines, it will highlight best practices and emerging models for responsible AI use, aiming to bridge the gap between AI's potential and its practical, equitable implementation (Groumpos, 2023; Granjeiro et al., 2025; Jerhamre et al., 2022; Girasa, 2020).

In sum, understanding and navigating the complex Language-Law-Technology nexus is vital to harness AI's promise while mitigating its risks, ensuring that this powerful technology serves society's broader goals of sustainability, knowledge advancement, and social justice (Farah & Varela, 2023; Goh & Vinuesa, 2021; Holzinger et al., 2021).

2. AI IN AGRICULTURE: TECHNOLOGIES AND USE CASES

Artificial Intelligence (AI) has become a transformative force in modern agriculture, enabling precision, efficiency, and sustainability in food production. With global food demand increasing and climate-related challenges intensifying, AI presents critical tools to support data-driven decision-making, enhance productivity, and ensure food security, particularly in developing regions (Ahmad et al., 2024; Ali et al., 2024).

2.1 Key AI Technologies in Agriculture

Modern agricultural practices are increasingly embracing AI-driven technologies, including:

- **Machine Learning (ML) and Deep Learning (DL):** These are used to predict crop yields, detect diseases, and optimize irrigation (Bhat & Huang, 2021).
- **Computer Vision:** Deployed in drones and automated machinery to monitor crop health and detect weeds or pests in real time (Chen et al., 2024).
- **Natural Language Processing (NLP):** Facilitates communication in smart farming platforms and decision support systems (Araújo et al., 2021).
- **Robotics and Autonomous Systems:** Used for harvesting, planting, and spraying with minimal human intervention (Aggarwal et al., 2024).

The integration of these technologies is shaping what is known as Agriculture 4.0, a term denoting the convergence of digital tools in farming (Araújo et al., 2021; Bhangar & Shahriyar, 2023).

The convergence of various AI technologies within modern agricultural practices can be best understood through a structured flowchart. This diagram illustrates how technologies like machine learning, computer vision, NLP, and robotics collectively shape the ecosystem of Agriculture 4.0.

Figure 1. Core AI technologies driving agriculture 4.0

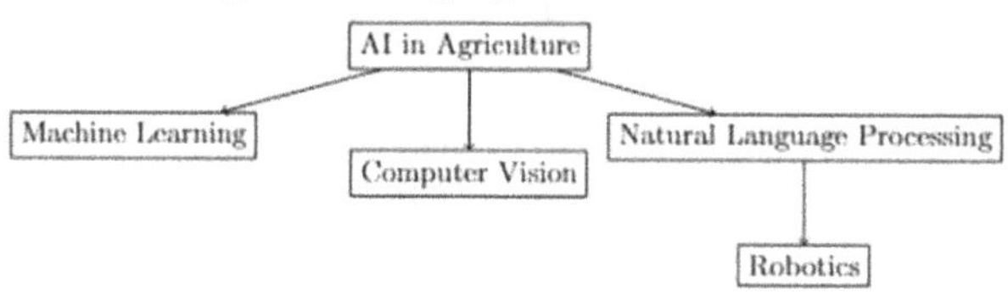

2.2 Use Cases and Applications

AI applications in agriculture are diverse and expanding. Notable examples include:

- **Crop Monitoring and Disease Detection:** AI systems equipped with satellite imagery and IoT sensors provide farmers with early warnings of plant diseases or infestations (Ahmed et al., 2024).

- **Precision Farming:** AI optimizes resource use (water, fertilizer) and enhances yields through data analytics (Aggarwal et al., 2024; Gardezi et al., 2024).
- **Supply Chain Management:** AI algorithms streamline logistics, storage, and distribution, minimizing food loss and waste (Chen et al., 2024).
- **Climate Adaptation:** AI models predict weather patterns and inform planting decisions, enhancing resilience to climate variability (Adanma & Ogunbiyi, 2024).

In developing countries, AI has the potential to bridge gaps in infrastructure and education by enabling access to real-time agronomic advice and market data (Aderibigbe et al., 2023; Ahmad et al., 2024).

2.3 Ethical, Legal, and Governance Considerations

While the benefits are significant, the deployment of AI in agriculture raises ethical and legal challenges. Questions about data privacy, algorithmic bias, and the digital divide must be addressed. The need for responsible AI is especially urgent in food systems where trust and safety are paramount (Alexander et al., 2024; Gardezi et al., 2024; Dara et al., 2022).

Governance mechanisms must align with ethical standards, emphasizing transparency and inclusivity (Cath, 2018; Farah & Varela, 2023; Girasa, 2020). Emerging frameworks and international collaborations are exploring ways to regulate AI while encouraging innovation (Benabed & Tudoran, 2023; Goh & Vinuesa, 2021).

Additionally, agricultural data privacy is a growing concern. As AI relies heavily on data, secure and ethical data-sharing models, such as federated learning, are being explored to protect farmers' rights (Dembani et al., 2025; Gavai et al., 2025; Devare et al., 2023).

2.4 Cybersecurity in Smart Agriculture

The integration of AI and IoT in agriculture has increased exposure to cyber threats. Ensuring the cybersecurity of agricultural data systems is crucial to maintaining operational continuity and trust (Ali et al., 2024). Developing secure AI models and adopting best practices in cybersecurity are essential to safeguard digital farming ecosystems.

2.5 Challenges and Opportunities

Despite its promise, AI adoption in agriculture faces hurdles such as lack of infrastructure, high implementation costs, and limited technical expertise in rural areas (Aggarwal et al., 2024; Ahmad et al., 2024). Additionally, the ethical use of AI must be championed through inclusive policies and educational initiatives (Denhere & Shao, 2024; Alexander et al., 2024).

Opportunities lie in interdisciplinary collaboration and public-private partnerships to develop context-specific AI solutions. Transparent and fair regulatory models are essential to maximize benefits while mitigating risks (Dara et al., 2022; Benabed & Tudoran, 2023).

In developing regions, the implementation of AI in agriculture faces both critical challenges and promising opportunities. This chart juxtaposes the relative frequency of key issues and benefits reported in recent studies.

Figure 2. Challenges and opportunities of AI in agriculture in developing regions

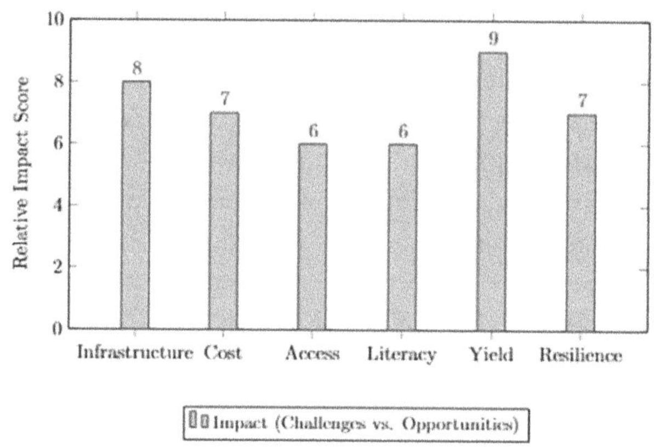

3. POLICY AND REGULATORY LANDSCAPE

The rapid integration of artificial intelligence (AI) into agriculture, environmental science, and scientific writing has created an urgent need for comprehensive policy frameworks and regulatory oversight. The current policy landscape is characterized by a combination of fragmented national initiatives, emerging international standards, and significant regulatory gaps. As AI technologies continue to evolve, policymakers and regulatory bodies face the challenge of balancing innovation with ethical responsibility, data protection, transparency, and accountability.

3.1 Global Policy Trends and Regulatory Gaps

Despite the transformative potential of AI, many developing countries face considerable challenges in implementing effective AI governance frameworks due to infrastructural, economic, and legal limitations (Aderibigbe et al., 2023). In agricultural sectors, these challenges are magnified by the diversity of stakeholders, data sources, and application contexts (Ahmad et al., 2024; Alexander et al., 2024).

Current global efforts to establish harmonized AI regulations, such as the European Union's AI Act and UNESCO's Recommendation on the Ethics of Artificial Intelligence, are beginning to provide a foundation for transnational collaboration. However, as Benabed and Tudoran (2023) point out, these initiatives often struggle to address the nuanced requirements of agriculture-specific AI applications and their ethical implications. Similarly, Cath (2018) emphasizes the need for legal and technical harmonization in AI governance to ensure that AI development aligns with international human rights and safety standards.

3.2 Agricultural Data and Privacy Regulation

Agriculture 4.0 has introduced advanced data-driven systems that require robust data governance frameworks. The complexity of managing agricultural data is highlighted by Devare et al. (2023), who underscore the importance of linking plant data responsibly. Gavai et al. (2025) and Dembani et al. (2025) stress that protecting privacy in agricultural data-sharing environments necessitates innovative approaches like federated learning and the development of secure platforms.

Furthermore, issues of cybersecurity in smart agriculture demand urgent regulatory attention. Ali et al. (2024) and Adanma and Ogunbiyi (2024) provide critical insights into cyber threats facing precision farming systems and emphasize the dual need for both defensive strategies and ethical AI applications.

3.3 Intellectual Property, Scientific Writing, and Ethical AI Use

As AI becomes a tool for academic and scientific writing, questions around authorship, intellectual property rights, and academic integrity have become prominent. Several scholars have called for policy frameworks that govern the ethical use of AI tools in research and writing (Casal & Kessler, 2023; Eberlin, 2024; Espino et al., 2024). Aithal and Aithal (2023), Aljuaid (2024), and Alahdab (2024) advocate for a balance between leveraging AI's potential and maintaining rigorous academic standards.

Ajiye and Omokhabi (2025) and Dinçer (2024) emphasize the need for institutional policies that address ethical dilemmas related to AI-assisted writing, such as transparency in disclosure and the accuracy of AI-generated content. Regulatory efforts must therefore integrate these ethical concerns into broader data and innovation policy frameworks.

3.4 Regulatory Innovation and Governance Models

Emerging governance models propose a combination of soft law approaches, including codes of conduct, voluntary standards, and public-private partnerships (Farah & Varela, 2023; Goh & Vinuesa, 2021). These frameworks aim to foster adaptive regulation that can evolve alongside technological innovation.

The work of Girasa (2020) and Gardezi et al. (2024) highlights the importance of adaptive regulatory instruments that not only govern AI innovation but also build public trust. Trustworthy AI systems, especially in sensitive areas like food systems and education, require multidimensional policies that incorporate ethical, legal, and socio-economic considerations (Aggarwal et al., 2024; Alghamdy, 2023; Aslam & Nisar, 2024).

3.5 Cross-Sectoral Harmonization

Given the interdisciplinary nature of AI applications in agriculture, scientific writing, and environmental management, regulatory harmonization is essential. Chen et al. (2024) and Araújo et al. (2021) advocate for sector-specific guidelines within a broader regulatory ecosystem to address overlapping policy domains.

Stakeholder involvement, particularly from the scientific, agricultural, and legal communities, is crucial in shaping practical and inclusive regulatory policies (Ahmed et al., 2024; Ersöz & Engin, 2024; BaHammam, 2023). Policymakers must therefore engage in continuous dialogue with these communities to ensure policies are context-sensitive and future-proof.

3.6 Summary

The policy and regulatory landscape governing the use of AI in agriculture and scientific writing is at a pivotal stage. While the potential of AI to revolutionize these sectors is evident, the risks associated with ethical misuse, data breaches, and inequitable access necessitate proactive and inclusive regulation. Developing a coherent policy framework requires harmonized international collaboration, sector-specific guidance, and dynamic governance models that are capable of evolving alongside AI technologies.

By incorporating ethical standards, data governance, intellectual property rights, and cybersecurity measures, stakeholders can ensure that AI contributes to sustainable development and scientific advancement while upholding societal trust and legal accountability.

4. ETHICAL CONSIDERATIONS IN AI-DRIVEN AGRICULTURE

The integration of artificial intelligence (AI) into agriculture has significantly transformed the sector, offering powerful tools for enhanced productivity, sustainability, and food security. However, this digital evolution brings forth a multitude of ethical challenges that must be addressed to ensure responsible and equitable application. Issues such as data privacy, algorithmic bias, environmental impacts, transparency, accountability, and the socio-economic divide between regions and communities raise profound ethical considerations in the context of AI-driven agriculture.

One of the most critical concerns is data privacy and ownership. AI applications in agriculture rely heavily on big data collected from farms, sensors, drones, and satellites (Bhat & Huang, 2021). The ethical dilemma arises when ownership of this data becomes ambiguous. Farmers often do not have control over how their data is collected, used, or monetized (Dembani et al., 2025; Devare et al., 2023). This raises questions about informed consent and the equitable sharing of benefits derived from data analytics (Gavai et al., 2025).

The ethical challenges associated with AI in agriculture are multidimensional, encompassing data privacy, algorithmic fairness, and environmental sustainability. The following diagram categorizes and connects these major ethical themes.

Figure 3. Key ethical dimensions of AI in agriculture

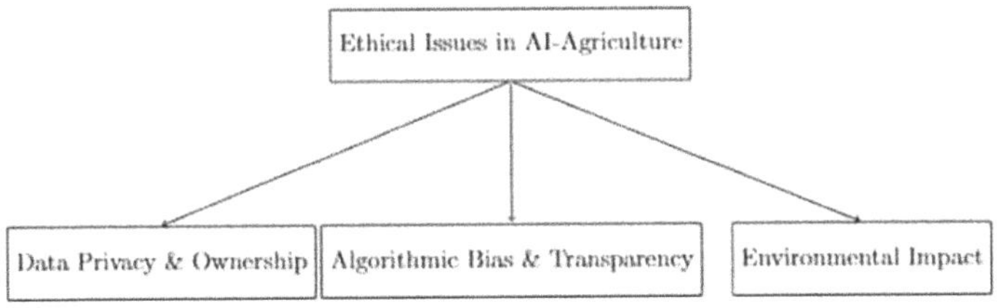

Moreover, algorithmic transparency and accountability are central to ethical AI deployment. Many AI systems operate as "black boxes," making it difficult to interpret or audit decisions (Alexander et al., 2024; Dara et al., 2022). This opacity undermines farmers' trust and may lead to decisions that are not aligned with local agricultural needs or socio-economic contexts (Gardezi et al., 2024). Efforts to promote explainable AI in agriculture must be prioritized to bridge the gap between technological innovation and ethical integrity (Chen et al., 2024; Alahdab, 2024).

Equity and access also present significant ethical concerns. AI technologies, while promising, may exacerbate existing disparities between technologically advanced and underdeveloped regions (Aderibigbe et al., 2023; Ahmad et al., 2024). In many developing countries, access to AI infrastructure, education, and digital literacy remains limited, potentially sidelining smallholder farmers and creating an uneven playing field (Ali et al., 2024; Aggarwal et al., 2024). Ethical deployment of AI should ensure inclusive access and address the digital divide (Denhere & Shao, 2024).

Environmental ethics are particularly pertinent in the context of AI-enhanced precision farming. While AI can optimize resource use and reduce environmental harm, it can also contribute to ecological overexploitation if not carefully monitored (Adanma & Ogunbiyi, 2024; Bhangar & Shahriyar, 2023). Ethical agricultural AI must therefore integrate sustainability frameworks and consider long-term ecological consequences.

Cybersecurity is another underexplored but vital ethical dimension. As smart farms become increasingly connected, they become vulnerable to cyber threats that could compromise food supply chains (Ali et al., 2024). Ethical frameworks must encompass strategies for cybersecurity resilience in agriculture to safeguard both data integrity and food safety.

Ethical AI literacy and governance play crucial roles in shaping the responsible use of AI in agriculture. As emphasized by Benabed and Tudoran (2023), the lack of global regulatory coherence creates uncertainty in managing cross-border AI ethics. There is an urgent need for clear guidelines and regulatory oversight to ensure ethical compliance (Cath, 2018; Farah & Varela, 2023; Goh & Vinuesa, 2021; Girasa, 2020).

In academic and scientific research associated with AI in agriculture, ethical considerations extend to authorship, plagiarism, and overreliance on AI writing tools (Aithal & Aithal, 2023; Ajiye & Omokhabi, 2025; Casal & Kessler, 2023; Aljuaid, 2024; Espino et al., 2024; Fedoriv et al., 2024). The integrity of scientific contributions must be maintained through responsible AI use in writing and data interpretation (Abd-Elsalam & Abdel-Momen, 2023; AlSamhori & Alnaimat, 2024; Chetwynd, 2024; Dinçer, 2024; Eberlin, 2024; Ersöz & Engin, 2024; Aslam & Nisar, 2024; BaHammam, 2023).

Additionally, trust in AI systems is deeply tied to ethical deployment. Trust is cultivated through transparency, community engagement, and participatory design that includes the voices of farmers and agricultural stakeholders (Alexander et al., 2024; Gardezi et al., 2024). A human-centered approach to AI development can enhance ethical alignment and acceptance within farming communities.

In conclusion, the ethical integration of AI in agriculture requires a multidimensional approach—combining regulatory frameworks, technological transparency, equitable access, environmental stewardship, and data governance. Ethical challenges must be anticipated and managed through interdisciplinary collaboration and stakeholder involvement to harness AI's potential without compromising human and ecological values.

5. KNOWLEDGE TRANSFER AND THE ROLE OF LANGUAGE

The transmission of knowledge has always been intimately tied to language, serving not only as a communicative medium but as a cognitive scaffold for reasoning, innovation, and collaboration. In the realm of artificial intelligence (AI), especially within scientific writing and agriculture, language assumes an even more pivotal role—becoming the channel through which AI-driven insights are disseminated, shared, and ethically interpreted. This intersection of knowledge, language, and AI unveils a complex yet promising frontier in modern science and global agricultural practices.

5.1 Language as the Bridge of Scientific Intelligence

Scientific writing stands at the heart of academic and agricultural innovation. It is through structured, precise language that research findings are validated, shared, and replicated. AI has introduced a transformative shift in this process. Tools like ChatGPT and other large language models (LLMs) are increasingly employed in drafting, summarizing, and reviewing scientific manuscripts (Abd-Elsalam & Abdel-Momen, 2023; AlSamhori & Alnaimat, 2024; Ajiye & Omokhabi, 2025). This automation of linguistic functions accelerates knowledge creation while raising questions about authorship, originality, and ethical boundaries (Casal & Kessler, 2023; Chetwynd, 2024; Ersöz & Engin, 2024).

In agricultural domains, AI tools facilitate not only technical data analysis but also multilingual translation, contextualization of local knowledge, and dissemination of agronomic best practices (Ahmad et al., 2024; Chen et al., 2024). Through natural language processing (NLP), farmers in rural or linguistically marginalized regions can access advisory services in their native dialects, thereby enabling more inclusive knowledge transfer (Aggarwal et al., 2024; Aderibigbe et al., 2023).

5.2 Language, Trust, and Ethical Use

Language is also essential in building trust—between AI developers, users, and stakeholders—especially in sectors like agriculture where traditional knowledge meets algorithmic decision-making. Researchers argue that trust in AI applications depends significantly on the clarity, transparency, and cultural relevance of linguistic interactions (Alexander et al., 2024; Gardezi et al., 2024). Poorly communicated AI outputs can lead to mistrust, misinformation, and misuse, particularly in low-resource or high-risk agricultural environments (Ali et al., 2024; Ali et al., 2024).

Educational institutions and research organizations must therefore develop guidelines that ensure responsible communication when AI is involved. This includes accurate documentation of AI assistance in scientific writing and avoiding overreliance on generated content (BaHammam, 2023; Dinçer, 2024; Fedoriv et al., 2024). Ethical AI usage demands that linguistic outputs are not only technically sound but aligned with disciplinary standards and human values (Eberlin, 2024; Alahdab, 2024; Aslam & Nisar, 2024).

5.3 Knowledge Transfer through AI-Supported Language Systems

AI systems are now capable of learning from vast repositories of agricultural and environmental data and presenting that information in context-sensitive language. This functionality is pivotal for real-time decision-making, policy planning, and community outreach (Adanma & Ogunbiyi, 2024; Goh & Vinuesa, 2021). For instance, AI can translate satellite imagery or IoT-sensor outputs into human-readable advisories that are immediately actionable by farmers (Bhat & Huang, 2021; Bhangar & Shahriyar, 2023; Gavai et al., 2025).

In scientific communities, AI-driven knowledge transfer fosters interdisciplinary collaboration by making domain-specific texts more accessible across fields (Aithal & Aithal, 2023). This democratization of language and expertise is especially crucial in developing nations where research literacy varies significantly (Aderibigbe et al., 2023; Ahmed et al., 2024).

Furthermore, federated learning platforms now allow for decentralized knowledge acquisition while maintaining linguistic privacy, addressing both the need for data sovereignty and the integrity of localized narratives (Dembani et al., 2025; Devare et al., 2023).

The process of transferring knowledge through AI in agriculture involves multiple stages, from data collection to localized communication. The following flowchart outlines a typical AI-assisted knowledge dissemination pipeline.

Figure 4. Pipeline for AI-supported knowledge transfer in agriculture

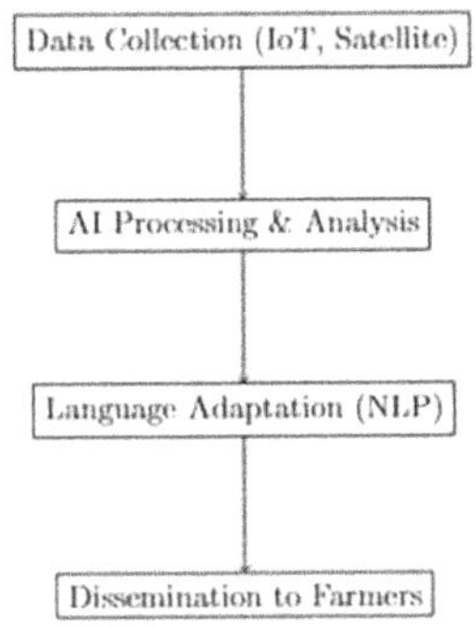

5.4 The Language-Law Nexus in Knowledge Systems

The role of language extends into legal and regulatory frameworks where terminologies shape rights, obligations, and responsibilities in AI governance (Benabed & Tudoran, 2023; Farah & Varela, 2023; Cath, 2018). Legal definitions of authorship, plagiarism, and data usage increasingly hinge on how AI-generated texts are interpreted and presented in linguistic form.

This is particularly evident in discussions around academic publishing ethics and intellectual property rights, where AI's role in drafting scientific texts challenges traditional authorship norms (Espino et al., 2024; Aljuaid, 2024; Dinçer, 2024). Language thus becomes a double-edged sword—capable of enabling innovation but also of obfuscating responsibility if not governed properly.

5.5 Linguistic Equity and the Democratization of AI Knowledge

A key ethical imperative is ensuring linguistic inclusivity in AI-driven knowledge systems. Many AI tools are primarily trained on English-language datasets, creating disparities in accessibility and comprehension for non-English-speaking populations (Alghamdy, 2023). This imbalance risks marginalizing valuable indigenous knowledge systems and reinforcing epistemic inequalities in global agriculture (Araújo et al., 2021; Denhere & Shao, 2024).

Efforts to incorporate linguistic diversity into AI models not only expand the reach of agricultural intelligence but also honor cultural contexts and traditional wisdom (Dara et al., 2022; Chen et al., 2024). This broader linguistic representation is crucial for sustainable and ethical AI deployment in food systems worldwide (Ali et al., 2024; Gardezi et al., 2024).

6. LANGUAGE, INCLUSIVITY, AND EQUITY IN POLICY IMPLEMENTATION

The intersection of language, inclusivity, and equity is a pivotal axis in the formulation and execution of artificial intelligence (AI) policies, especially within the domains of scientific research, agricultural innovation, and educational access. Language not only shapes communication but also determines accessibility and power structures in AI-driven decision-making environments. As AI technologies increasingly influence policy formulation in agriculture, education, and environmental sustainability, there is a growing imperative to ensure that these policies are inclusive, linguistically equitable, and attuned to the diverse sociocultural realities they affect.

AI policy in agriculture intersects crucially with language, legal frameworks, and technological infrastructure. The following Venn diagram conceptualizes how these three domains overlap and interact.

Figure 5. Intersection of language, law, and technology in AI policy

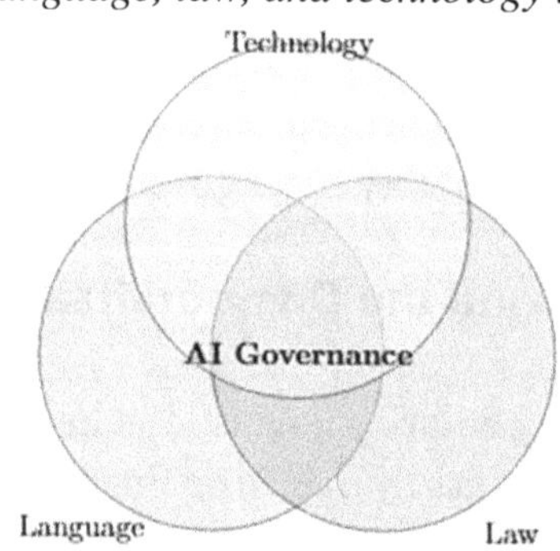

6.1 Linguistic Accessibility in AI-Driven Scientific Writing and Research

Scientific and academic communities have witnessed a growing dependence on AI tools such as large language models (LLMs) and generative AI for writing and content creation. While these tools offer remarkable assistance in enhancing scientific communication, they also risk reinforcing linguistic hegemonies. English remains the dominant language in scientific discourse, which marginalizes non-native speakers and limits global equity in knowledge production and dissemination (Aljuaid, 2024; Casal & Kessler, 2023). This linguistic centralization can exclude capable researchers from the Global South, creating epistemic injustices in both academia and agriculture (Abd-Elsalam & Abdel-Momen, 2023).

In higher education, tools such as ChatGPT have transformed writing instruction by assisting students in structuring ideas and enhancing coherence. However, concerns remain regarding over-reliance, ethical boundaries, and unequal access to such tools (Aithal & Aithal, 2023; Alahdab, 2024; Ersöz & Engin, 2024). Inclusivity demands that AI-based academic aids support diverse language abilities and cognitive styles, avoiding the propagation of Western-centric models of reasoning and expression (Fedoriv, Shuhai, & Pirozhenko, 2024).

6.2 Equity in Agricultural and Environmental Policy Implementation

In agriculture and environmental policy, AI applications often reflect systemic biases rooted in data sources, algorithmic assumptions, and deployment strategies. Policies driven by AI-based precision agriculture or agri-environmental modeling frequently lack the sensitivity to local linguistic and cultural contexts (Chen et al., 2024; Ali et al., 2024; Bhat & Huang, 2021). This not only limits the uptake of technologies in low-resource settings but also perpetuates forms of digital colonialism that replicate historical inequities (Aderibigbe et al., 2023; Aggarwal, Bansal, & Goel, 2024).

Moreover, implementation of AI solutions in climate technology and conservation efforts must consider the languages and knowledge systems of indigenous and rural communities. AI policies that fail to integrate these dimensions risk alienating stakeholders and generating resistance to technological adoption (Adanma & Ogunbiyi, 2024; Denhere & Shao, 2024; Goh & Vinuesa, 2021). To counteract this, inclusive policymaking must engage participatory frameworks that center local voices and vernacular languages.

6.3 Equity in Data Governance and Digital Infrastructure

Data governance policies, especially those involving AI, should account for the disparities in access to digital infrastructure and computational resources. Equity in AI policy must encompass equitable access to datasets, platforms, and model outputs, especially in contexts such as farming in the Global South (Araújo et al., 2021; Devare et al., 2023). Agricultural data privacy and federated learning frameworks need to be co-designed with stakeholders to ensure language inclusivity and respect for socio-technical differences (Dembani et al., 2025; Gavai et al., 2025).

Ethical AI governance must also consider how language mediates the inclusion of minority groups in AI policymaking processes. Initiatives advocating responsible AI in agriculture underscore the need to build trust among farmers and researchers by communicating clearly, respectfully, and multilingually (Alexander, Yarborough, & Smith, 2024; Gardezi et al., 2024). The same applies in agritourism and smart agriculture, where language inclusivity becomes essential for equitable user engagement (Ali et al., 2024; Bhangar & Shahriyar, 2023).

6.4 Policy Recommendations for Linguistic and Equity Integration

To implement equitable AI policy across agriculture, education, and scientific research, several recommendations emerge:

1. **Multilingual AI Interfaces:** AI systems must support multilingual capabilities to democratize access across regions and sectors (Alghamdy, 2023; Aslam & Nisar, 2024).
2. **Community-Centered Co-design:** AI-based agricultural and environmental solutions should be co-developed with local communities in their languages to ensure relevance and ownership (Dara, Hazrati Fard, & Kaur, 2022).
3. **Equity-Focused Data Ethics:** Agricultural data governance frameworks should embed principles of linguistic justice and equity, ensuring inclusive access to AI-generated insights (Gardezi et al., 2024; Gavai et al., 2025).
4. **Ethical Writing Tools:** AI tools in academic writing must be designed to support equity in authorship, reflecting sensitivity to educational and linguistic diversity (Espino et al., 2024; Chetwynd, 2024; Ajiye & Omokhabi, 2025).
5. **Global Governance Standards:** International legal and regulatory frameworks should incorporate equity indicators, including language inclusivity, in AI certification and auditing processes (Benabed & Tudoran, 2023; Girasa, 2020; Farah & Varela, 2023).

By embracing language as a core element of equity, AI policy frameworks can move beyond abstract principles and become truly inclusive instruments that respond to the plural realities of stakeholders across regions, disciplines, and linguistic boundaries.

7. BEST PRACTICES AND RECOMMENDATIONS

The integration of Artificial Intelligence (AI) into scientific writing and agricultural innovation holds tremendous potential. However, realizing this potential requires thoughtful adherence to ethical, technical, educational, and legal best practices. Below is a comprehensive outline of key recommendations derived from current literature.

7.1. Promoting Ethical AI Usage in Scientific Writing and Research

AI tools such as ChatGPT offer unprecedented assistance in scientific writing, but they raise significant concerns regarding authenticity, plagiarism, and authorship (Abd-Elsalam & Abdel-Momen, 2023; Casal & Kessler, 2023; Ajiye & Omokhabi, 2025). Institutions should develop clear guidelines on acceptable AI use, emphasizing transparency, acknowledgment of AI contributions, and human oversight (Chetwynd, 2024; Alahdab, 2024; Aljuaid, 2024).

Researchers must be trained in the ethical use of AI tools, which includes understanding their limitations and potential biases (Dinçer, 2024; Ersöz & Engin, 2024). Aslam and Nisar (2024) recommend implementing peer-review mechanisms to evaluate AI-assisted manuscripts for integrity.

7.2. Fostering Trust Through Responsible AI Development

Trust is foundational for AI adoption in agriculture and academic contexts. Gardezi et al. (2024) and Alexander et al. (2024) emphasize that trust-building requires participatory design, explainability, and continuous dialogue with stakeholders. Similarly, BaHammam (2023) highlights the importance of balancing innovation with research integrity.

Developers and policymakers should implement transparent auditing mechanisms and uphold responsible innovation principles (Cath, 2018; Farah & Varela, 2023). AlSamhori and Alnaimat (2024) advise that trust can also be supported by promoting interdisciplinary collaborations between ethicists, technologists, and educators.

7.3. Ensuring Data Privacy and Governance in Agriculture

The protection and governance of agricultural data remain central to responsible AI deployment (Devare et al., 2023; Dembani et al., 2025; Gavai et al., 2025). Platforms leveraging federated learning and decentralized data-sharing models should be prioritized to reduce risks of data breaches and misuse (Ali et al., 2024; Chen et al., 2024).

Moreover, governments and institutions should standardize data ethics policies in alignment with international legal norms (Benabed & Tudoran, 2023; Girasa, 2020; Goh & Vinuesa, 2021).

7.4. Bridging Technological and Capacity Gaps in Developing Regions

Adopting AI in agriculture and academia demands capacity building, especially in developing countries. Challenges such as lack of infrastructure, technical know-how, and funding persist (Aderibigbe et al., 2023; Ahmad et al., 2024; Ahmed et al., 2024). Recommendations include investing in digital infrastructure, training programs, and public-private partnerships to support equitable AI adoption (Aggarwal et al., 2024; Ali et al., 2024).

Denhere and Shao (2024) argue that contextualized solutions, culturally relevant tools, and localized innovation ecosystems are essential for sustainable development.

7.5. Integrating AI Literacy in Education and Research

Educational institutions should embed AI literacy across curricula to enable future researchers and professionals to engage responsibly with AI tools (Aithal & Aithal, 2023; Alghamdy, 2023). Training should cover ethical considerations, data handling, and algorithmic bias.

As highlighted by Espino et al. (2024), academic policies must distinguish between acceptable assistive use and unethical reliance. Encouraging critical engagement with AI-generated content helps preserve academic rigor.

7.6. Advancing Interdisciplinary Research and Standards

To harmonize AI's role across sectors, coordinated efforts in interdisciplinary research, ethical standard-setting, and regulatory foresight are needed (Chen et al., 2024; Bhat & Huang, 2021; Granjeiro et al., 2024). Institutions must support cross-sectoral studies that explore the synergy between AI, agriculture, and law.

Dara et al. (2022) advocate for adaptive ethical frameworks that evolve with technological advancements, while Espino et al. (2024) recommend continuous community dialogue to refine usage norms.

7.7. Encouraging Innovation While Preventing Misuse

Policymakers and stakeholders must encourage innovation without compromising social values. For example, Bahrini et al. (2023) caution against blind reliance on AI, suggesting proactive governance strategies to monitor misuse.

Academic publishers and institutions should implement AI disclosure policies, ensuring that the use of tools like ChatGPT is transparent and appropriately cited (Eberlin, 2024; Dinçer, 2024; Aljuaid, 2024).

7.8. Building Inclusive and Sustainable AI Systems in Agriculture

Sustainable AI integration in agriculture should prioritize environmental responsibility and social inclusion (Adanma & Ogunbiyi, 2024; Bhangar & Shahriyar, 2023). AI models must be designed to optimize resource use, enhance biodiversity, and support smallholder farmers.

Araújo et al. (2021) and Chen et al. (2024) emphasize the importance of feedback loops, stakeholder input, and transparent impact assessments to ensure sustainability. Additionally, inclusive policies should support gender equity and marginalized communities.

7.9 Summary

These best practices and recommendations are essential to ensure that the integration of artificial intelligence in scientific writing and agriculture is ethical, equitable, and impactful. By aligning with these principles and drawing upon global scholarship, stakeholders can unlock AI's full potential while mitigating associated risks.

8. CONCLUSION

Artificial intelligence (AI) continues to transform the landscape of scientific writing and agriculture, offering unprecedented opportunities for innovation, efficiency, and inclusivity. From enhancing crop prediction and yield optimization to enabling precision agriculture and democratizing academic research, AI technologies are at the forefront of digital transformation across sectors (Ahmad et al., 2024; Chen et al., 2024; Ali et al., 2024).

In scientific writing, AI-driven tools such as large language models (LLMs) and assistive applications have begun reshaping how researchers draft, review, and publish scientific content. While these tools offer time-saving benefits and improve linguistic clarity, their misuse also raises concerns around plagiarism, data integrity, authorship ethics, and academic misconduct (Ajiye & Omokhabi, 2025; Alahdab, 2024; Casal & Kessler, 2023). Ensuring ethical and responsible use of AI in academic contexts necessitates comprehensive policy frameworks, institutional guidelines, and user education (Aljuaid, 2024; AlSamhori & Alnaimat, 2024; Dinçer, 2024).

In agriculture, AI is enabling the shift to Agriculture 4.0, characterized by data-driven decision-making, automation, and real-time monitoring of crops and resources (Araújo et al., 2021; Bhat & Huang, 2021; Aggarwal et al., 2024). The role of AI in enhancing food security, particularly in developing countries, is evident through its ability to address inefficiencies, reduce environmental degradation, and empower smallholder farmers (Ahmad et al., 2024; Aderibigbe et al., 2023; Gardezi et al., 2024). Nonetheless, this promise comes with the responsibility to manage cyber threats, ensure equitable access, and address ethical dilemmas (Adanma & Ogunbiyi, 2024; Ali et al., 2024; Dembani et al., 2025).

Trust, transparency, and regulation are essential pillars for sustaining AI's positive impact. Calls for global regulatory frameworks that balance innovation with accountability are growing, highlighting the need to navigate ethical complexities while maximizing benefits (Benabed & Tudoran, 2023; Cath, 2018; Goh & Vinuesa, 2021; Girasa, 2020). The agricultural and academic sectors must also adopt best practices such as federated learning for data privacy, inclusive governance models, and multi-stakeholder engagement strategies (Devare et al., 2023; Gavai et al., 2025; Alexander et al., 2024).

Ultimately, the intersection of AI, scientific writing, and agriculture presents a unique language-law-technology nexus—one that necessitates a holistic approach to policy, ethics, and innovation. Institutions, governments, and individuals alike must collaborate to ensure that AI advances knowledge creation and agricultural resilience without compromising core human values of integrity, inclusivity, and sustainability (Chetwynd, 2024; Espino et al., 2024; Fedoriv et al., 2024; Eberlin, 2024).

As we move forward, the key lies not just in harnessing AI's computational capabilities but in aligning them with principles of ethical stewardship and social good. Only then can we ensure that AI serves as a true partner in both the academic and agricultural domains—bridging gaps, elevating standards, and paving the way for a more informed, productive, and equitable future.

REFERENCES

Abd-Elsalam, K. A., & Abdel-Momen, S. M. (2023). Artificial intelligence's development and challenges in scientific writing. *Egyptian Journal of Agricultural Research, 101*(3), 714–717. DOI: 10.21608/ejar.2023.220363.1414

Adanma, U. M., & Ogunbiyi, E. O., (2024). Artificial intelligence in environmental conservation: Evaluating cyber risks and opportunities for sustainable practices. *Computer Science & IT Research Journal, 5*(5), 1178–1209. DOI: 10.51594/csitrj.v5i5.1156

Aderibigbe, A. O., Ohenhen, P. E., Nwaobia, N. K., Gidiagba, J. O., & Ani, E. C. (2023). Artificial intelligence in developing countries: Bridging the gap between potential and implementation. *Computer Science & IT Research Journal, 4*(3), 185–199. DOI: 10.51594/csitrj.v4i3.629

Aggarwal, S., Bansal, S., & Goel, R. (2024). Ai In Agriculture: A Looming Challenge, A Gleaming Opportunity. *International Journal of Engineering Science and Humanities, 14*(Special Issue 1), 43-52.

Ahmad, A., Liew, A. X., Venturini, F., Kalogeras, A., Candiani, A., Di Benedetto, G., Ajibola, S., Cartujo, P., Romero, P., Lykoudi, A., De Grandis, M. M., Xouris, C., Lo Bianco, R., Doddy, I., Elegbede, I., D'Urso Labate, G. F., García del Moral, L. F., & Martos, V. (2024). AI can empower agriculture for global food security: Challenges and prospects in developing nations. *Frontiers in Artificial Intelligence, 7*, 1328530. DOI: 10.3389/frai.2024.1328530 PMID: 38726306

Ahmed, M. N., Singh, A. P., Hussain, M. R., Rasool, M. A., Khan, I. M., & Dildar, M. S. (2024, July). Enhancing Crop Production using Artificial Intelligence in Agricultural Revolution. In *2024 IEEE 7th International Conference on Advanced Technologies* [ATSIP]. *Signal and Image Processing : an International Journal, 1*, 432–437.

Aithal, P. S., & Aithal, S. (2023). Application of ChatGPT in higher education and research–A futuristic analysis. [IJAEML]. *International Journal of Applied Engineering and Management Letters, 7*(3), 168–194. DOI: 10.47992/IJAEML.2581.7000.0193

Ajiye, O. T., & Omokhabi, A. A. (2025). THE POTENTIAL AND ETHICAL ISSUES OF ARTIFICIAL INTELLIGENCE IN IMPROVING ACADEMIC WRITING. *ShodhAI: Journal of Artificial Intelligence, 2*(1), 1–9. DOI: 10.29121/shodhai.v2.i1.2025.24

Alahdab, F. (2024). Potential impact of large language models on academic writing. *BMJ Evidence-Based Medicine*, *29*(3), 201–202. DOI: 10.1136/bmjebm-2023-112429 PMID: 37620013

Alexander, C. S., Yarborough, M., & Smith, A. (2024). Who is responsible for 'responsible AI'?: Navigating challenges to build trust in AI agriculture and food system technology. *Precision Agriculture*, *25*(1), 146–185. DOI: 10.1007/s11119-023-10063-3

Alghamdy, R. Z. (2023). Pedagogical and ethical implications of artificial intelligence in EFL context: A review study. *English Language Teaching*, *16*(10), 87–98. DOI: 10.5539/elt.v16n10p87

Ali, A., Anderson, L., Venturini, F., Athanasios, K., Candiani, A., Di Benedetto, G., ... & Martos, V. (2024). AI can empower agriculture for global food security: challenges and prospects in developing nations.

Ali, G., Mijwil, M. M., Buruga, B. A., Abotaleb, M., & Adamopoulos, I. (2024). A survey on artificial intelligence in cybersecurity for smart agriculture: State-of-the-art, cyber threats, artificial intelligence applications, and ethical concerns. *Mesopotamian Journal of Computer Science*, *2024*, 53–103. DOI: 10.58496/MJCSC/2024/007

Aljuaid, H. (2024). The impact of artificial intelligence tools on academic writing instruction in higher education: A systematic review. *Arab World English Journal (AWEJ) Special Issue on ChatGPT*.

AlSamhori, A. F., & Alnaimat, F. (2024). Artificial intelligence in writing and research: Ethical implications and best practices. *Central Asian Journal of Medical Hypotheses and Ethics = Central'noaziatskij Zurnal Medicinskich Gipotez i Etiki = Medicinalyk Gipoteza Men Ètikanyn Orta Aziâlyk Zurnaly*, *5*(4), 259–268. DOI: 10.47316/cajmhe.2024.5.4.02

Araújo, S. O., Peres, R. S., Barata, J., Lidon, F., & Ramalho, J. C. (2021). Characterising the agriculture 4.0 landscape—Emerging trends, challenges and opportunities. *Agronomy (Basel)*, *11*(4), 667. DOI: 10.3390/agronomy11040667

Aslam, M. S., & Nisar, S. (2024). Ethical Considerations for Artificial Intelligence Tools in Academic Research and Manuscript Preparation: A Web Content Analysis. In *Digital Transformation in Higher Education, Part B: Cases, Examples and Good Practices* (pp. 155-196). Emerald Publishing Limited. DOI: 10.1108/978-1-83608-424-220241007

BaHammam, A. S. (2023). Balancing innovation and integrity: The role of AI in research and scientific writing. *Nature and Science of Sleep*, •••, 1153–1156. PMID: 38170140

Bahrini, A., Khamoshifar, M., Abbasimehr, H., Riggs, R. J., Esmaeili, M., Majdabadkohne, R. M., & Pasehvar, M. (2023, April). ChatGPT: Applications, opportunities, and threats. In *2023 Systems and Information Engineering Design Symposium (SIEDS)* (pp. 274-279). IEEE. DOI: 10.1109/SIEDS58326.2023.10137850

Benabed, A., & Tudoran, L. (2023). Artificial intelligence towards international regulations, frameworks and laws in the world of globalization: Implications and challenges. *Persp. L. Pub. Admin.*, *12*, 268.

Bhangar, N. A., & Shahriyar, A. K. (2023). Iot and ai for next-generation farming: Opportunities, challenges, and outlook. *International Journal of Sustainable Infrastructure for Cities and Societies*, *8*(2), 14–26.

Bhat, S. A., & Huang, N. F. (2021). Big data and ai revolution in precision agriculture: Survey and challenges. *IEEE Access : Practical Innovations, Open Solutions*, *9*, 110209–110222. DOI: 10.1109/ACCESS.2021.3102227

Casal, J. E., & Kessler, M. (2023). Can linguists distinguish between ChatGPT/AI and human writing?: A study of research ethics and academic publishing. *Research Methods in Applied Linguistics*, *2*(3), 100068. DOI: 10.1016/j.rmal.2023.100068

Cath, C. (2018). Governing artificial intelligence: Ethical, legal and technical opportunities and challenges. *Philosophical Transactions. Series A, Mathematical, Physical, and Engineering Sciences*, *376*(2133), 20180080. DOI: 10.1098/rsta.2018.0080 PMID: 30322996

Chen, T., Lv, L., Wang, D., Zhang, J., Yang, Y., Zhao, Z., & Tao, D. (2024). Empowering agrifood system with artificial intelligence: A survey of the progress, challenges and opportunities. *ACM Computing Surveys*, *57*(2), 1–37.

Chetwynd, E. (2024). Ethical use of artificial intelligence for scientific writing: Current trends. *Journal of Human Lactation*, *40*(2), 211–215. DOI: 10.1177/08903344241235160 PMID: 38482810

Dara, R., Hazrati Fard, S. M., & Kaur, J. (2022). Recommendations for ethical and responsible use of artificial intelligence in digital agriculture. *Frontiers in Artificial Intelligence*, *5*, 884192. DOI: 10.3389/frai.2022.884192 PMID: 35968036

Dembani, R., Karvelas, I., Akbar, N. A., Rizou, S., Tegolo, D., & Fountas, S. (2025). Agricultural data privacy and federated learning: A review of challenges and opportunities. *Computers and Electronics in Agriculture, 232*, 110048. DOI: 10.1016/j.compag.2025.110048

Denhere, V., & Shao, D. (2024). Artificial Intelligence in Agritourism: Utilitarian Analysis of Opportunities, Challenges, and Ethical Considerations in the African Context. *Agritourism in Africa*, 17-36.

Devare, M., Arnaud, E., Antezana, E., & King, B. (2023). Governing agricultural data: Challenges and recommendations. *Towards Responsible Plant Data Linkage: Data Challenges for Agricultural Research and Development, 201.*

Dinçer, S. (2024). The use and ethical implications of artificial intelligence in scientific research and academic writing. *Educational Research & Implementation, 1*(2), 139–144. DOI: 10.14527/edure.2024.10

Eberlin, M. N. (2024). The Art of Scientific Writing and Ethical Use of Artificial Intelligence. *Journal of the Brazilian Chemical Society, 35*(1), e-20230121.

Ersöz, A. R., & Engin, M. (2024). Exploring Ethical Dilemmas in the Use of Artificial Intelligence in Academic Writing: Perspectives of Researchers. *Journal of Uludag University Faculty of Education, 37*(3), 1190–1208. DOI: 10.19171/uefad.1514323

Espino, A. R. C., Esto, M. R. A., Manalo, C. G. S., Santiago, C. S., & Pragacha, R. N. (2024, June). Ethical Implications of Using Assistive Writing Tools in the Academe: A Literature Review. In *International Conference on Frontiers of Intelligent Computing: Theory and Applications* (pp. 133-145). Singapore: Springer Nature Singapore.

Farah, P. D., & Varela, J. C. (2023). Science, Technology, Society, and Law. In *Science, Technology, Policy and International Law* (pp. 1-19). Routledge.

Fedoriv, Y., Shuhai, A., & Pirozhenko, I. (2024). Foundations of Ethical Use of AI in EFL Academic Writing.

Gardezi, M., Joshi, B., Rizzo, D. M., Ryan, M., Prutzer, E., Brugler, S., & Dadkhah, A. (2024). Artificial intelligence in farming: Challenges and opportunities for building trust. *Agronomy Journal, 116*(3), 1217–1228. DOI: 10.1002/agj2.21353

Gavai, A. K., Bouzembrak, Y., Xhani, D., Sedrakyan, G., Meuwissen, M. P., Souza, R. G. S., ... & van Hillegersberg, J. (2025). Agricultural data Privacy: Emerging platforms & strategies. *Food and Humanity*, 100542.

Girasa, R. (2020). *Artificial intelligence as a disruptive technology: Economic transformation and government regulation*. Springer Nature. DOI: 10.1007/978-3-030-35975-1

Goh, H. H., & Vinuesa, R. (2021). Regulating artificial-intelligence applications to achieve the sustainable development goals. *Discover Sustainability*, *2*(1), 1–6. DOI: 10.1007/s43621-021-00064-5 PMID: 35425914

Granjeiro, J. M., Cury, A. A. D. B., Cury, J. A., Bueno, M., Sousa-Neto, M. D., & Estrela, C. (2025). The Future of Scientific Writing: AI Tools, Benefits, and Ethical Implications. *Brazilian Dental Journal*, *36*, e25–e6471. DOI: 10.1590/0103-644020256471 PMID: 40197923

Groumpos, P. P. (2023, July). A critical historic overview of artificial intelligence: Issues, challenges, opportunities, and threats. *Artificial Intelligence and Applications (Commerce, Calif.)*, *1*(4), 181–197. DOI: 10.47852/bonviewAIA3202689

Guleria, A., Krishan, K., Sharma, V., & Kanchan, T. (2023). ChatGPT: Ethical concerns and challenges in academics and research. *Journal of Infection in Developing Countries*, *17*(09), 1292–1299. DOI: 10.3855/jidc.18738 PMID: 37824352

Gupta, D. K., Pagani, A., Zamboni, P., & Singh, A. K. (2024). AI-powered revolution in plant sciences: Advancements, applications, and challenges for sustainable agriculture and food security. *Exploration of Foods and Foodomics*, *2*(5), 443–459. DOI: 10.37349/eff.2024.00045

Harati, K. (2024). ChatGPT and AI-Powered Writing Tools: Unveiling Risks and Ethical Challenges in Scientific Writing. *Journal of Research in Medical Sciences : the Official Journal of Isfahan University of Medical Sciences*, *4*(1), 1–6.

He, H., Gray, J., Cangelosi, A., Meng, Q., McGinnity, T. M., & Mehnen, J. (2021). The challenges and opportunities of human-centered AI for trustworthy robots and autonomous systems. *IEEE Transactions on Cognitive and Developmental Systems*, *14*(4), 1398–1412. DOI: 10.1109/TCDS.2021.3132282

Holzinger, A., Weippl, E., Tjoa, A. M., & Kieseberg, P. (2021, August). Digital transformation for sustainable development goals (sdgs)-a security, safety and privacy perspective on ai. In *International cross-domain conference for machine learning and knowledge extraction* (pp. 1-20). Cham: Springer International Publishing.

Jerhamre, E., Carlberg, C. J. C., & van Zoest, V. (2022). Exploring the susceptibility of smart farming: Identified opportunities and challenges. *Smart Agricultural Technology*, *2*, 2. DOI: 10.1016/j.atech.2021.100026

Kanyepe, J., Chibaro, M., Morima, M., & Moeti-Lysson, J. (2025). AI-Powered Agricultural Supply Chains: Applications, Challenges, and Opportunities. *Integrating Agriculture, Green Marketing Strategies, and Artificial Intelligence*, 33-64.

Kapoor, P. (2025). Harvesting Ethics: Forging Responsible Paths in AI and ML for the Agri-Food Industry. In *Food and Industry 5.0: Transforming the Food System for a Sustainable Future* (pp. 305–315). Springer Nature Switzerland. DOI: 10.1007/978-3-031-76758-6_19

Kaushik, K., Khan, A., Kumari, A., Sharma, I., & Dubey, R. (2024). Ethical considerations in AI-based cybersecurity. In *Next-generation cybersecurity: AI, ML, and Blockchain* (pp. 437–470). Springer Nature Singapore. DOI: 10.1007/978-981-97-1249-6_19

Khalifa, M., & Albadawy, M. (2024). Using artificial intelligence in academic writing and research: An essential productivity tool. *Computer Methods and Programs in Biomedicine Update*, *5*, 100145. DOI: 10.1016/j.cmpbup.2024.100145

Khup, V. K., & Bantugan, B. (2025). Exploring the Impact and Ethical Implications of Integrating AI-Powered Writing Tools in Junior High School English Instruction: Enhancing Creativity, Proficiency, and Academic Outcomes. *International Journal of Research and Innovation in Social Science*, *9*(IIIS, 3s), 361–378. DOI: 10.47772/IJRISS.2025.903SEDU0022

Kirov, B. (2023, September). Artificial Intelligence in Creation of Scientific Written Works: Weighing the Benefits and Ethical Dilemmas-Should We Use It? In *2023 International Scientific Conference on Computer Science (COMSCI)* (pp. 1-5). IEEE. DOI: 10.1109/COMSCI59259.2023.10315821

Kochupillai, M., Kahl, M., Schmitt, M., Taubenböck, H., & Zhu, X. X. (2022). Earth observation and artificial intelligence: Understanding emerging ethical issues and opportunities. *IEEE Geoscience and Remote Sensing Magazine*, *10*(4), 90–124. DOI: 10.1109/MGRS.2022.3208357

Kochupillai, M., & Köninger, J. (2023). Creating a digital marketplace for agrobiodiversity and plant genetic sequence data: Legal and ethical considerations of an ai and blockchain based solution. *Towards Responsible Plant Data Linkage: Data Challenges for Agricultural Research and Development*, 223.

Leong, Y. M., Lim, E. H., Subri, N. F. B., & Jalil, N. B. A. (2023, September). Transforming agriculture: Navigating the challenges and embracing the opportunities of artificial intelligence of things. In *2023 IEEE International Conference on Agrosystem Engineering, Technology & Applications (AGRETA)* (pp. 142-147). IEEE. DOI: 10.1109/AGRETA57740.2023.10262747

Li, J., Zong, H., Wu, E., Wu, R., Peng, Z., Zhao, J., Yang, L., Xie, H., & Shen, B. (2024). Exploring the potential of artificial intelligence to enhance the writing of english academic papers by non-native english-speaking medical students-the educational application of ChatGPT. *BMC Medical Education*, *24*(1), 736. DOI: 10.1186/s12909-024-05738-y PMID: 38982429

Liu, Y., Kong, W., & Merve, K. (2025). ChatGPT applications in academic writing: A review of potential, limitations, and ethical challenges. *Arquivos Brasileiros de Oftalmologia*, *88*(3), e2024–e0269. DOI: 10.5935/0004-2749.2024-0269 PMID: 39879415

Lund, B. D., Wang, T., Mannuru, N. R., Nie, B., Shimray, S., & Wang, Z. (2023). ChatGPT and a new academic reality: Artificial Intelligence-written research papers and the ethics of the large language models in scholarly publishing. *Journal of the Association for Information Science and Technology*, *74*(5), 570–581. DOI: 10.1002/asi.24750

Malhotra, K., & Firdaus, M. (2022). Application of artificial intelligence in IoT security for crop yield prediction. *ResearchBerg Review of Science and Technology*, *2*(1), 136–157.

Manning, L., Brewer, S., Craigon, P. J., Frey, J., Gutierrez, A., Jacobs, N., Kanza, S., Munday, S., Sacks, J., & Pearson, S. (2022). Artificial intelligence and ethics within the food sector: Developing a common language for technology adoption across the supply chain. *Trends in Food Science & Technology*, *125*, 33–42. DOI: 10.1016/j.tifs.2022.04.025

Mark, R. (2019). Ethics of using AI and big data in agriculture: The case of a large agriculture multinational. *The ORBIT Journal*, *2*(2), 1–27. DOI: 10.29297/orbit.v2i2.109

Miao, J., Thongprayoon, C., Suppadungsuk, S., Garcia Valencia, O. A., Qureshi, F., & Cheungpasitporn, W. (2023). Ethical dilemmas in using AI for academic writing and an example framework for peer review in nephrology academia: A narrative review. *Clinics and Practice*, *14*(1), 89–105. DOI: 10.3390/clinpract14010008 PMID: 38248432

Molligan, J., & Pérez-López, E. (2024). Artificial intelligence in academia: Opportunities, challenges, and ethical considerations. *Biochemistry and Cell Biology*, *103*, 1–3. DOI: 10.1139/bcb-2024-0216 PMID: 39611424

Nam, B. H., & Bai, Q. (2023). ChatGPT and its ethical implications for STEM research and higher education: A media discourse analysis. *International Journal of STEM Education*, *10*(1), 66. DOI: 10.1186/s40594-023-00452-5

Neupane, S., Mitra, S., Fernandez, I. A., Saha, S., Mittal, S., Chen, J., Pillai, N., & Rahimi, S. (2024). Security considerations in ai-robotics: A survey of current methods, challenges, and opportunities. *IEEE Access : Practical Innovations, Open Solutions, 12*, 22072–22097. DOI: 10.1109/ACCESS.2024.3363657

Nurchurifiani, E., Maximilian, A., Ajeng, G. D., Wiratno, P., Hastomo, T., & Wicaksono, A. (2025). Leveraging AI-Powered Tools in Academic Writing and Research: Insights from English Faculty Members in Indonesia. *International Journal of Information and Education Technology (IJIET), 15*(2), 312–322. DOI: 10.18178/ijiet.2025.15.2.2244

Ocampo, T. S. C., Silva, T. P., Alencar-Palha, C., Haiter-Neto, F., & Oliveira, M. L. (2023). ChatGPT and scientific writing: A reflection on the ethical boundaries. *Imaging Science in Dentistry, 53*(2), 175. DOI: 10.5624/isd.20230085 PMID: 37405199

Omodan, B. I., & Marongwe, N. (2024). The role of artificial intelligence in decolonising academic writing for inclusive knowledge production. *Interdisciplinary Journal of Education Research, 6*(s1), 1–14. DOI: 10.38140/ijer-2024.vol6.s1.06

Otieno, M. (2023). An extensive survey of smart agriculture technologies: Current security posture. *World J. Adv. Res. Rev, 18*(3), 1207–1231. DOI: 10.30574/wjarr.2023.18.3.1241

Pandey, D. K., & Mishra, R. (2024). *Towards sustainable agriculture: Harnessing AI for global food security*. Artificial Intelligence in Agriculture.

Pedro, F., Subosa, M., Rivas, A., & Valverde, P. (2019). Artificial intelligence in education: Challenges and opportunities for sustainable development.

Peng, S. Y., Lin, C. F., & Streinz, T. (Eds.). (2021). *Artificial intelligence and international Economic law*. Cambridge University Press. DOI: 10.1017/9781108954006

Perkins, M. (2023). Academic Integrity considerations of AI Large Language Models in the post-pandemic era: ChatGPT and beyond. *Journal of University Teaching & Learning Practice, 20*(2), 1–24. DOI: 10.53761/1.20.02.07

Salvagno, M., Taccone, F. S., & Gerli, A. G. (2023). Can artificial intelligence help for scientific writing? *Critical Care, 27*(1), 75. DOI: 10.1186/s13054-023-04380-2 PMID: 36841840

Senoo, E. E. K., Anggraini, L., Kumi, J. A., Luna, B. K., Akansah, E., Sulyman, H. A., & Aritsugi, M. (2024). IoT solutions with artificial intelligence technologies for precision agriculture: Definitions, applications, challenges, and opportunities. *Electronics (Basel), 13*(10), 1894. DOI: 10.3390/electronics13101894

Shafik, W., Tufail, A., De Silva, C. L., Haji, R. A. A., & Apong, M. (2025). The Role, Application, and Impact of Artificial Intelligence in the Agriculture Industry. In *Future Tech Startups and Innovation in the Age of AI* (pp. 36–60). CRC Press.

Shofiah, N., Putera, Z. F., & Solichah, N. (2023, December). Challenges and opportunities in the use of artificial intelligence in education for academic writing: A scoping review. In *Conference Psychology and Flourishing Humanity (PFH 2023)* (pp. 174-193). Atlantis Press. DOI: 10.2991/978-2-38476-188-3_20

Sood, A., Sharma, R. K., & Bhardwaj, A. K. (2022). Artificial intelligence research in agriculture: A review. *Online Information Review*, *46*(6), 1054–1075. DOI: 10.1108/OIR-10-2020-0448

Sparrow, R., & Howard, M. (2021). Robots in agriculture: prospects, impacts, ethics, and policy. *precision agriculture, 22*, 818-833.

Sparrow, R., Howard, M., & Degeling, C. (2021). Managing the risks of artificial intelligence in agriculture. *NJAS: Impact in Agricultural and Life Sciences*, *93*(1), 172–196. DOI: 10.1080/27685241.2021.2008777

Subaveerapandiyan, A., Kalbande, D., & Ahmad, N. (2025). Perceptions of effectiveness and ethical use of AI tools in academic writing: A study Among PhD scholars in India. *Information Development*, •••, 02666669251314840. DOI: 10.1177/02666669251314840

Tai, A. M. Y., Meyer, M., Varidel, M., Prodan, A., Vogel, M., Iorfino, F., & Krausz, R. M. (2023). Exploring the potential and limitations of ChatGPT for academic peer-reviewed writing: Addressing linguistic injustice and ethical concerns. *Journal of Academic Language and Learning*, *17*(1), T16–T30.

Tasa-Fuster, V. (2024). The Legal Rationales of the Leading Technological Models: The Challenges of Regulating Linguistic and Gender Biases. In *Gendered Technology in Translation and Interpreting* (pp. 27-65). Routledge.

Turner, J. (2018). *Robot rules: Regulating artificial intelligence*. Springer.

Tzachor, A., Devare, M., King, B., Avin, S., & Ó hÉigeartaigh, S. (2022). Responsible artificial intelligence in agriculture requires systemic understanding of risks and externalities. *Nature Machine Intelligence*, *4*(2), 104–109. DOI: 10.1038/s42256-022-00440-4

Uddin, M., Chowdhury, A., & Kabir, M. A. (2024). Legal and ethical aspects of deploying artificial intelligence in climate-smart agriculture. *AI & Society*, *39*(1), 221–234. DOI: 10.1007/s00146-022-01421-2

Ugwu, N. F., Igbinlade, A. S., Ochiaka, R. E., Ezeani, U. D., Okorie, N. C., Opele, J. K., Onayinka, T. S., Iroegbu, O., Onyekwere, O. K., Adams, A. B., Aigbona, P., & Ojobola, F. B. (2024). Clarifying Ethical Dilemmas in Using Artificial Intelligence in Research Writing: A Rapid Review. *Higher Learning Research Communications*, *14*(2), 29–47. DOI: 10.18870/hlrc.v142.1549

Uplaonkar, S. S., Veershetty, R., Bahar, Z., & Sangeeta, G. (2024). The role of productive AI: A supporter or challenger in the future of agricultural librarianship. *IJAR*, *10*(4), 46–53.

Wei, H., Xu, W., Kang, B., Eisner, R., Muleke, A., Rodriguez, D., deVoil, P., Sadras, V., Monjardino, M., & Harrison, M. T. (2024). Irrigation with artificial intelligence: Problems, premises, promises. *Human-Centric Intelligent Systems*, *4*(2), 187–205. DOI: 10.1007/s44230-024-00072-4

Williamson, H. F., Brettschneider, J., Caccamo, M., Davey, R. P., Goble, C., Kersey, P. J., May, S., Morris, R. J., Ostler, R., Pridmore, T., Rawlings, C., Studholme, D., Tsaftaris, S. A., & Leonelli, S. (2023). Data management challenges for artificial intelligence in plant and agricultural research. *F1000 Research*, *10*, 324. DOI: 10.12688/f1000research.52204.2 PMID: 36873457

Wiwanitmkit, S., & Wiwanitkit, V. (2024). Artificial Intelligence, Academic Publishing, Scientific Writing, Peer Review, and Ethics. *Brazilian Journal of Cardiovascular Surgery*, *39*(4), e20230377. DOI: 10.21470/1678-9741-2023-0377 PMID: 39038191

Ya'u, M. S., & Mohammed, M. S. (2025). AI-Assisted Writing and Academic Literacy: Investigating the Dual Impact of Language Models on Writing Proficiency and Ethical Concerns in Nigerian Higher Education. *International Journal of Education and Literacy Studies*, *13*(2), 593–604. DOI: 10.7575/aiac.ijels.v.13n.2p.593

Zangana, H. M., Amelia, P., Mustafa, F. M., & Li, S. (2025). The Role of English Language and AI in Scientific Writing: Ethical and Academic Implications. In Zangana, H., & Omar, M. (Eds.), *Ensuring Secure and Ethical STM Research in the AI Era* (pp. 191–218). IGI Global Scientific Publishing., DOI: 10.4018/979-8-3373-4252-8.ch005

Zangana, H. M., Luckyardi, S., Mustafa, F. M., & Li, S. (2025). Enhancing Agricultural Cybersecurity: Leveraging Deep Learning and Large Language Models for Smart Farming Protection. In Zangana, H., Al-Karaki, J., & Omar, M. (Eds.), *Revolutionizing Cybersecurity With Deep Learning and Large Language Models* (pp. 307–338). IGI Global Scientific Publishing., DOI: 10.4018/979-8-3373-3296-3.ch010

Zangana, H. M., Luckyardi, S., Mustafa, F. M., & Li, S. (2025). Ethical and Secure AI Applications in Agricultural Research: Challenges and Opportunities. In Zangana, H., & Omar, M. (Eds.), *Ensuring Secure and Ethical STM Research in the AI Era* (pp. 43–76). IGI Global Scientific Publishing., DOI: 10.4018/979-8-3373-4252-8.ch002

Zohouri, M., Sabzali, M., & Golmohammadi, A. (2024). Ethical considerations of ChatGPT-assisted article writing. *Synesis (ISSN 1984-6754), 16*(1), 94-113.

Chapter 12
Policy Implications of Gene Editing and Biotechnology Regulation

Rebet Keith Jones
https://orcid.org/0009-0008-0487-1301
Capitol Technology University, USA

ABSTRACT

Gene editing and biotechnology represent transformative advancements with profound potential to reshape medicine, agriculture, and environmental management. However, their rapid development poses significant regulatory and ethical challenges that require comprehensive policy frameworks. This chapter explores the policy implications surrounding gene editing technologies, such as CRISPR, highlighting the balance between fostering innovation and ensuring public safety, ethical standards, and equitable access. It discusses regulatory approaches adopted worldwide, the role of international cooperation, and the socio-political dynamics influencing governance. By examining current legislative landscapes and emerging best practices, the chapter aims to inform policymakers, legal scholars, and industry stakeholders about effective governance models that align with ethical imperatives and technological progress.

1. INTRODUCTION

In the rapidly evolving landscape of the 21st century, artificial intelligence (AI), environmental sustainability, and advanced healthcare technologies are shaping global societal and legal frameworks. The convergence of these domains demands a multidisciplinary approach that integrates regulatory oversight, ethical consider-

DOI: 10.4018/979-8-3373-4862-9.ch012

Copyright © 2025, IGI Global Scientific Publishing. Copying or distributing in print or electronic forms without written permission of IGI Global Scientific Publishing is prohibited.

ations, technological innovation, and socio-economic realities. This chapter aims to explore the complex regulatory responses that govern AI in healthcare and medical diagnostics, with a focus on the broader implications for sustainability and environmental law.

AI technologies, particularly generative AI and machine learning, are revolutionizing diverse sectors including finance (Ali & Aysan, 2024, 2025; Ali, Zafar, & Aysan, 2024), healthcare (Mennella, Maniscalco, De Pietro, & Esposito, 2024; Sheliemina, 2024), and environmental management (Arya & Rastogi, 2024; Emon et al., 2025). Their transformative potential is accompanied by significant ethical and legal challenges such as data privacy, algorithmic bias, and accountability (Shukla & Taneja, 2024; Veluru, 2024). The deployment of AI in medical diagnostics, for instance, has introduced new regulatory complexities that require careful governance frameworks to ensure patient safety and efficacy (Larson et al., 2021; Naili, Mangkunegara, Purwono, & Baballe, 2025; Pesapane et al., 2021).

Simultaneously, the urgency of the climate crisis underscores the critical role of legal mechanisms in promoting sustainability and environmental protection (Akindele & Chabinga, 2024; Ali, 2024; Aloamaka, 2024). International environmental law has evolved to address issues ranging from renewable energy deployment (Jafarizadeh et al., 2024; Oduro, Uzougbo, & Ugwu, 2024) to biodiversity protection (Singh & Kaunert, 2025; Saikia, 2024). These efforts often intersect with technological advances such as AI-driven climate monitoring and green technology (Emon et al., 2025; Eswaran & Eswaran, 2025), requiring integrated policy models that balance innovation and regulation (Schünemann et al., 2024).

Governance of emerging technologies such as genome editing and AI-enhanced cybersecurity further complicates this landscape. Regulatory frameworks must grapple with ethical issues surrounding biotechnology (Bartkowski, Theesfeld, Pirscher, & Timaeus, 2018; Brookes & Smyth, 2024; Friedrichs et al., 2019) and AI-driven warfare (Batabyal, 2024; Al-Sinani & Mitchell, 2024). At the same time, the digital transformation of firms demands human-centric approaches to AI adoption, emphasizing responsible innovation (Fenwick, Molnar, & Frangos, 2024; Rashid & Kausik, 2024).

Recent regulatory initiatives, such as the EU Artificial Intelligence Act (Butt, 2024) and international efforts toward just climate transitions (Chowdhury, 2024), exemplify the challenges of crafting laws that are both flexible enough to accommodate rapid technological change and robust enough to protect societal interests. The legal complexities of AI in healthcare are highlighted by considerations of patient rights, safety, and the right to science (Ho, 2023; Terry, 2019; Verma, Rao, Eluri, & Sharma, 2020).

This chapter will systematically address these intertwined themes, offering a comprehensive review of regulatory responses to AI in healthcare and diagnostics while contextualizing them within global sustainability efforts. It will highlight the ethical, legal, and technological challenges, drawing on cutting-edge research and policy analysis (Daniel, 2024; Darvishi, Liu, & Lim, 2022; Luan et al., 2024; Filetti, Fenza, & Gallo, 2024). Ultimately, the chapter aims to propose emerging best practices and governance models that can guide policymakers, industry stakeholders, and researchers toward a responsible, sustainable, and equitable technological future.

2. SCIENTIFIC AND TECHNOLOGICAL BACKGROUND

The rapid evolution of scientific and technological advancements has ushered in transformative shifts across multiple domains including artificial intelligence (AI), climate change mitigation technologies, gene editing, healthcare diagnostics, and environmental sustainability. Understanding these innovations' scientific underpinnings and technological trajectories is essential to navigating the complex regulatory, ethical, and socio-economic landscapes they engender.

2.1 Advances in Artificial Intelligence and Machine Learning

Artificial intelligence has emerged as a pivotal technology influencing diverse sectors from finance and healthcare to environmental monitoring and cybersecurity. Recent research highlights the expanding role of generative AI models, emphasizing their ethical and multi-domain applications. Ali and Aysan (2024, 2025) demonstrate through machine learning structural topic modeling how generative AI not only revolutionizes finance but also poses complex ethical challenges that require cross-disciplinary frameworks for governance. Rashid and Kausik (2024) provide a comprehensive overview of AI's transformative impact worldwide, further underscoring the urgency for balanced regulatory oversight.

Within cybersecurity, AI-driven approaches such as ethical hacking are gaining traction to preempt vulnerabilities and enhance system defenses. Al-Sinani et al. (2024, 2025) illustrate experimental advancements leveraging Linux-based AI tools to elevate ethical hacking, promoting a proactive cybersecurity stance.

AI's integration with human resource management also represents a paradigm shift towards human-centric adoption of digital transformation, as detailed by Fenwick, Molnar, and Frangos (2024). Furthermore, AI's role in enhancing phishing detection in e-commerce platforms through semantic web technologies reflects its potential for securing digital economies (Gaurav et al., 2024).

Simultaneously, advances in quantum machine learning suggest a convergence of AI with quantum computing and semiconductor technologies, opening novel frontiers for computational capabilities (Campus, 2024; Eswaran & Eswaran, 2025).

However, concerns regarding data privacy and the misuse of AI remain paramount. Veluru (2024) and Shafik (2024) emphasize the importance of responsible AI deployment on large datasets to prevent unethical practices and security breaches, while Trotsyuk et al. (2024) call for frameworks to mitigate AI misuse in biomedical research, reflecting the growing need for regulatory safeguards in rapidly evolving technological domains.

2.2 AI in Healthcare and Medical Diagnostics

Healthcare has witnessed significant AI integration, particularly in diagnostics and patient care, with AI-based medical devices increasingly subjected to complex regulatory scrutiny. Pesapane et al. (2018, 2021) provide critical insights into the ethical and regulatory frameworks governing AI in radiology and broader healthcare contexts across global jurisdictions including the EU, US, China, and Russia.

Mennella et al. (2024) discuss the narrative challenges of ethical and regulatory compliance in deploying AI health technologies, while Naili et al. (2025) address the legal implications specifically concerning AI diagnostic tools. These works align with Ho's (2023) advocacy for embedding the human right to science within regulatory governance to ensure equitable and ethical AI deployment in healthcare.

Moreover, Sheliemina (2024) outlines the opportunities and risks AI poses in medical diagnostics, underscoring the balance between innovation and patient safety. The complexity of regulatory frameworks is further examined by Larson et al. (2021), highlighting recommendations for AI algorithm evaluation in diagnostic imaging.

2.3 Climate Change Technologies and Environmental Sustainability

Parallel to AI advances, scientific innovation in climate and environmental technologies forms a critical part of global sustainability strategies. Akindele and Chabinga (2024) explore Nigeria's engagement with international environmental law as a model for climate change and sustainability efforts, while Ali (2024) frames the political and governance challenges in aligning net-zero policies with environmental goals.

Renewable energy innovations and their legal-economic implications are elaborated by Jafarizadeh et al. (2024) and Oduro, Uzougbo, and Ugwu (2024), who identify regulatory barriers and strategies to promote sustainable energy expansion. Saikia (2024) and Sakapaji et al. (2024) emphasize ecologically informed approaches and indigenous socioecological resilience, respectively, advocating for integrative frameworks that respect environmental and cultural sustainability.

International legal developments in climate governance are comprehensively addressed by Aloamaka (2024) and Chowdhury (2024), who stress the complexities of climate discourse and the necessity of just climate policies. Singh and Kaunert (2025) further analyze biodiversity protection within evolving legal landscapes, tying environmental sustainability to community resilience and SDG attainment.

Within business ecosystems, Soomro, Suhrab, and Abbasi (2025) investigate governmental roles in navigating green regulations, highlighting compliance challenges and opportunities for fostering eco-friendly corporate practices.

2.4 Gene Editing and Biotechnology Innovations

Cutting-edge biotechnologies, particularly genome editing via CRISPR/Cas systems, introduce profound scientific opportunities and regulatory dilemmas. Bartkowski et al. (2018) and Brookes and Smyth (2024) discuss the economic, ethical, and risk-appropriate regulatory approaches essential for responsible gene editing.

Global regulatory perspectives are further enriched by Friedrichs et al. (2019) and Shukla-Jones, Friedrichs, and Winickoff (2018), who map regulatory regimes across agriculture and biotechnology sectors. Garden and Winickoff (2018) and Monast (2018) provide foundational policy analyses underscoring governance challenges in the rapidly evolving biotech landscape.

Li, Liu, and Chen (2019) highlight the persistent gap between technological application and policy adaptation, a crucial factor for effective governance. This is echoed in ongoing debates over genome editing's role in advanced therapies and societal impact (Garden & Winickoff, 2018).

2.5 Research Methodologies and Scholarly Trends in AI and Science

The scientific method itself is evolving under AI's influence. Leontidis (2024) reviews how AI reshapes scientific research's nature and methodologies, facilitating more efficient and expansive inquiry. Luan et al. (2024) demonstrate AI's utility in scientometric analyses to support large-scale scholarly reviews, exemplifying how AI can augment social science research.

Filetti, Fenza, and Gallo (2024) provide guidance on leveraging AI tools for research design and scholarly writing, indicating AI's growing role in knowledge dissemination.

Furthermore, computational social science techniques such as topic modeling offer powerful means for qualitative data exploration and threat identification in digital spaces (Rodriguez & Storer, 2020; San Biagio et al., 2023).

2.6 Regulatory Frameworks and Legal Challenges

The intersection of emerging technologies with law and policy is a dynamic and critical area of inquiry. Butt (2024) provides an analytical study of the EU's pioneering AI Act, a benchmark for global AI regulation efforts. Patra (2025) explores the legal landscape surrounding sustainable Industry 4.0, emphasizing the need for updated regulatory frameworks that accommodate technological innovations without stifling progress.

Verma et al. (2020) and Terry (2019) address public health AI regulation challenges, focusing on systemic and ethical concerns. Pesapane et al. (2021) offer comparative analysis of international AI healthcare regulations, emphasizing new scenarios catalyzed by the COVID-19 pandemic.

Ethical AI considerations and data privacy remain at the forefront of regulatory discourse, as elaborated by Shukla and Taneja (2024) and Verma and Rohit (2024), who advocate for frameworks that balance innovation with human rights protection.

2.7 Emerging Technologies and Future Outlook

Emerging technologies such as AI-powered drones in smart cities (Maguluri, Arularasan, & Boopathi, 2023), and AI chatbot integration in STEM education (Jamro & Jamro, 2023), reflect the broadening horizon of AI applications.

The green technology revolution, integrating AI with sustainable innovations, is poised to address societal challenges while navigating regulatory and ethical complexities (Emon et al., 2025).

Taken together, these scientific and technological developments form a complex and interwoven backdrop requiring nuanced understanding and multidisciplinary governance approaches to harness their full potential responsibly and ethically.

The convergence of artificial intelligence and biotechnology creates ripple effects across multiple sectors including healthcare, climate, agriculture, and finance. The following flowchart outlines how these technologies intersect with key application areas.

Figure 1. Cross-sector impacts of AI and biotechnology

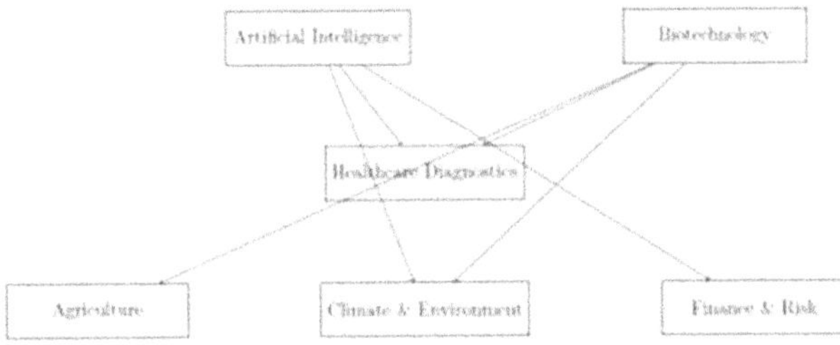

3. REGULATORY LANDSCAPE

The regulatory landscape governing artificial intelligence (AI), especially in healthcare and medical diagnostics, is complex and rapidly evolving, shaped by diverse international, national, and sector-specific frameworks. These regulations aim to ensure the ethical use, safety, accountability, and transparency of AI technologies while fostering innovation and public trust (Mennella et al., 2024; Pesapane et al., 2021). At the intersection of AI with healthcare, environment, finance, and security, regulatory bodies face unprecedented challenges due to AI's dynamic capabilities, risks of misuse, and ethical dilemmas (Ali, H., & Aysan, 2025; Batabyal, 2024).

3.1. Global and Sector-Specific Regulatory Frameworks

Internationally, the governance of AI in healthcare and other critical sectors is often guided by broad principles emphasizing human rights, privacy, and safety. The EU Artificial Intelligence Act represents one of the pioneering legislative efforts providing a risk-based regulatory framework that classifies AI applications according to their potential harm, enforcing stricter compliance on high-risk AI systems such as diagnostic tools in healthcare (Butt, 2024; Pesapane et al., 2018). Similarly, the United States employs a more sectoral regulatory approach, with agencies like the FDA overseeing AI-based medical devices, ensuring clinical efficacy and safety (Larson et al., 2021; Pesapane et al., 2021).

At the crossroads of AI and healthcare, ethical and legal standards are being adapted to manage issues of bias, accountability, and informed consent (Mennella et al., 2024; Naili et al., 2025). Moreover, AI's deployment in diagnostics demands transparency in algorithmic decision-making, aligning with principles underscored by the human right to science, which requires equitable access and regulatory oversight (Ho, 2023).

AI applications in healthcare, especially diagnostics, follow a lifecycle that requires regulatory engagement at each stage. The flowchart below maps this lifecycle, highlighting regulatory checkpoints.

Figure 2. Lifecycle of AI Tools in medical diagnostics

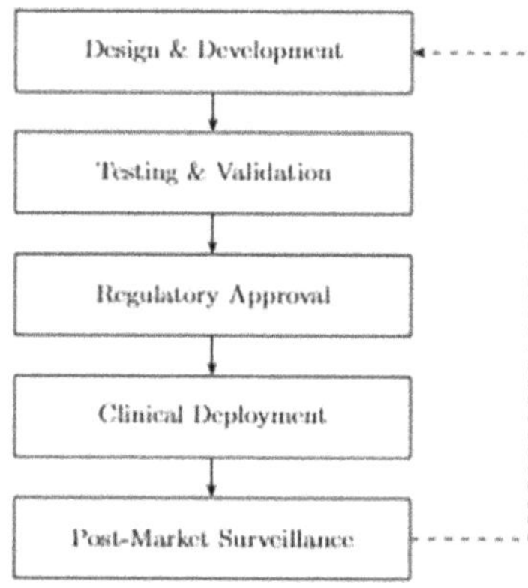

3.2. Environmental and Climate Regulation Nexus with AI

The regulatory landscape extends beyond healthcare, intersecting with climate technologies and environmental sustainability. Governments and international bodies are developing legal instruments to oversee AI applications that monitor, predict, and mitigate climate change impacts (Akindele & Chabinga, 2024; Ali, 2024; Saikia, 2024). Regulatory efforts focus on balancing innovation with sustainability goals, often through frameworks encouraging renewable energy adoption and environmental protection laws (Jafarizadeh et al., 2024; Oduro et al., 2024; Singh & Kaunert, 2025).

Navigating these regulatory frameworks is critical as AI-enabled technologies advance in green tech, renewable energy storage, and biodiversity protection, where legal clarity can catalyze or hinder innovation (Emon et al., 2025; Soomro et al., 2025; Sakapaji et al., 2024). In this domain, legal scholars highlight the need for adaptive, risk-appropriate regulations that keep pace with rapid technological change while safeguarding ecological systems (Brookes & Smyth, 2024; Aloamaka, 2024).

3.3. Ethical and Legal Challenges in AI-Driven Domains

The AI regulatory landscape is deeply entwined with ethical considerations, particularly in the use of AI for sensitive applications such as warfare, finance, and medical diagnostics (Batabyal, 2024; Ali, H., & Aysan, 2025). Ethical hacking experiments leveraging AI to strengthen cybersecurity, particularly in Linux environments, illustrate the ongoing challenges of balancing security benefits with potential misuse (Al-Sinani et al., 2024, 2025).

In healthcare, AI's regulatory challenges also encompass data privacy, consent, and bias mitigation (Mennella et al., 2024; Shukla & Taneja, 2024). Data governance policies, including safeguarding sensitive patient information in AI systems such as ChatGPT-powered diagnostics, are crucial to maintaining trust (Shafik, 2024). The need to regulate the lifecycle of AI applications, from development through deployment, is echoed in calls for comprehensive ethical frameworks addressing the entire AI value chain (Trotsyuk et al., 2024; Veluru, 2024).

3.4. Legal Frameworks Governing Biotechnology and Genome Editing

The regulation of genome editing technologies, often coupled with AI for advanced analysis and applications, demonstrates a convergence of ethical, social, and legal issues. International governance attempts to reconcile the transformative potential of CRISPR/Cas and other gene-editing tools with concerns over safety, equity, and socio-economic impacts (Bartkowski et al., 2018; Friedrichs et al., 2019; Li et al., 2019). The OECD and other bodies have issued working papers emphasizing governance structures to manage gene editing across agriculture and healthcare sectors (Garden & Winickoff, 2018; Shukla-Jones et al., 2018; Monast, 2018).

Risk-appropriate regulatory models seek to enable innovation while preventing misuse or unintended consequences, necessitating dynamic legal instruments that can respond to emergent scientific developments (Brookes & Smyth, 2024; Batabyal, 2024). The interface of AI and genome editing underscores the increasing complexity of the regulatory landscape, requiring interdisciplinary cooperation and international harmonization (Daniel, 2024; Larsson et al., 2021).

3.5. Industry 4.0, AI Integration, and Regulatory Challenges

The rise of Industry 4.0 introduces further regulatory considerations, especially regarding AI's integration into manufacturing, supply chains, and smart technologies (Patra, 2025; Karim et al., 2023). Legal frameworks are evolving to address issues of intellectual property, data sovereignty, and compliance in increasingly automated and interconnected industrial ecosystems (Maguluri et al., 2023). Governments and industries are challenged to develop sustainable regulatory pathways that foster innovation while addressing cybersecurity risks and ethical AI deployment (Fenwick et al., 2024; Rashid & Kausik, 2024).

3.6. Emerging Legal Models and Future Directions

Current trends highlight a shift towards adaptive, multi-level governance models combining top-down regulations with bottom-up standards and best practices. These approaches emphasize transparency, stakeholder engagement, and continuous risk assessment (Schünemann et al., 2024; Verma et al., 2020). AI's rapid evolution requires frameworks that are flexible yet robust, integrating human-centric principles and addressing the societal implications of AI technology (Larson et al., 2021; Mennella et al., 2024).

Researchers advocate for the incorporation of AI ethics directly into legal frameworks to anticipate future challenges such as algorithmic bias, accountability, and misuse prevention (Ali, H., & Aysan, 2024; Trotsyuk et al., 2024; Veluru, 2024). Cross-domain analyses and machine learning techniques assist regulators in forecasting trends and identifying emerging risks, thereby informing proactive governance (Ali, H., Zafar, & Aysan, 2024; Luan et al., 2024).

4. ETHICAL AND SOCIAL CONSIDERATIONS

The rapid advancement and integration of Artificial Intelligence (AI), especially generative AI and AI-driven diagnostic tools, in critical sectors such as healthcare, finance, environment, and governance have raised complex ethical and social questions. These considerations must be addressed to ensure that AI technologies promote equity, transparency, and sustainability while mitigating potential harms (Ali, 2025; Mennella et al., 2024). This section explores the multi-dimensional ethical and social challenges associated with AI deployment, focusing on fairness, accountability, privacy, environmental impact, and governance.

4.1 Fairness, Bias, and Equity

One of the foremost ethical concerns in AI applications, particularly in healthcare and finance, is the risk of bias and unfair discrimination (Ali, H., & Aysan, 2025). AI systems trained on incomplete or biased datasets can perpetuate or exacerbate existing social inequalities, adversely affecting marginalized populations. For instance, in medical diagnostics, biased AI algorithms may lead to inaccurate diagnoses or unequal access to treatment, raising significant ethical issues regarding patient safety and justice (Mennella et al., 2024; Naili et al., 2025). Moreover, gender and racial biases embedded in data can affect AI's predictive safety solutions and impact women's empowerment negatively if unaddressed (Pimpalkar et al., 2024).

Addressing these challenges requires integrating fairness-aware machine learning models and promoting transparency about data provenance and algorithmic decision-making (Ali, H., Zafar, & Aysan, 2024; Shukla & Taneja, 2024). Ethical AI frameworks must include rigorous auditing processes and stakeholder involvement to ensure equitable outcomes (Fenwick et al., 2024).

Ethical considerations in AI and biotechnology frequently overlap. Issues such as fairness, accountability, and transparency are central to both domains. The diagram below illustrates shared and unique ethical concerns.

Figure 3. Overlapping ethical challenges in AI and biotechnology

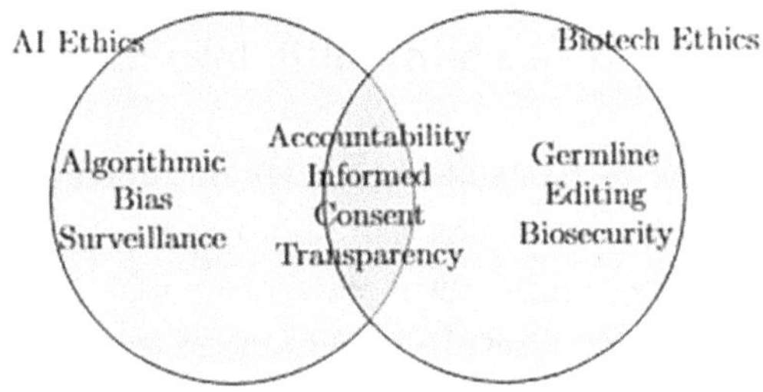

4.2 Accountability and Governance

AI's autonomous decision-making capabilities complicate traditional notions of accountability. Determining liability when AI systems cause harm or errors is legally and ethically challenging, especially in high-stakes domains such as medical diagnostics and warfare (Batabyal, 2024; Pesapane et al., 2021). There is a growing consensus on the need for comprehensive regulatory frameworks that clarify responsibilities among AI developers, deployers, and users (Butt, 2024; Larsson et al., 2021).

International cooperation and harmonization of AI regulations are crucial, as cross-border data flows and AI deployments transcend national jurisdictions (Akindele & Chabinga, 2024; Aloamaka, 2024). Additionally, mechanisms for ethical oversight, such as independent review boards and AI ethics committees, can foster trust and ensure adherence to societal values (Ho, 2023; Trotsyuk et al., 2024).

4.3 Privacy and Data Security

Privacy concerns are paramount in AI systems, particularly those handling sensitive personal data in healthcare and finance sectors. Generative AI and large language models pose unique risks regarding unauthorized data use, inadvertent disclosure, and data breaches (Shafik, 2024; Ali, H., & Aysan, 2024). Safeguarding customer and patient information demands robust encryption, anonymization, and strict access controls (Veluru, 2024; Shukla & Taneja, 2024).

Data privacy is also intertwined with broader social trust in AI technologies. Transparent communication about data practices and adherence to data protection laws are essential to mitigate public apprehension and foster acceptance (Verma, Rao, Eluri, & Sharma, 2020; Naili et al., 2025).

4.4 Environmental and Sustainability Implications

The ethical dimension of AI extends to its environmental footprint and role in sustainability. AI-driven technologies can significantly contribute to combating climate change through optimized resource management, smart agriculture, and renewable energy systems (Emon et al., 2025; Arya & Rastogi, 2024). However, the high computational demands of AI models and associated energy consumption raise concerns about environmental degradation (Daniel, 2024; Jafarizadeh et al., 2024).

Regulatory and policy responses must balance AI's potential for environmental benefits with mandates for energy-efficient AI development and deployment (Ali, 2024; Oduro, Uzougbo, & Ugwu, 2024). Moreover, equitable access to AI-enabled green technologies is necessary to avoid deepening global inequalities, especially in developing regions (Soomro, Suhrab, & Abbasi, 2025; Singh & Kaunert, 2025).

4.5 Social Impact and Public Trust

AI's increasing influence reshapes societal norms, employment landscapes, and human interactions. Automation and AI-driven decision-making could exacerbate job displacement and economic disparities without adequate social policies (Rashid & Kausik, 2024; Fenwick, Molnar, & Frangos, 2024). Ethical AI frameworks should include considerations for workforce reskilling, inclusivity, and human-centric design to preserve dignity and agency (Jamro & Jamro, 2023).

Public trust is critical for successful AI adoption. Transparent governance, explainability of AI systems, and ethical communication strategies are vital to address fears related to AI misuse and surveillance (San Biagio et al., 2023; Leontidis, 2024). This is particularly important in sensitive areas such as healthcare diagnostics, where patient autonomy and informed consent must be upheld (Mennella et al., 2024; Sheliemina, 2024).

4.6 Emerging Ethical Challenges and Future Directions

Emerging AI technologies such as AI-enhanced ethical hacking and quantum machine learning introduce novel ethical dilemmas around dual-use, misuse, and security vulnerabilities (Al-Sinani & Mitchell, 2024; Campus, 2024; Eswaran & Eswaran, 2025). Proactive risk mitigation frameworks and international legal instruments are essential to address these challenges (Veluru, 2024; Trotsyuk et al., 2024).

Gene editing, often intersecting with AI in biotechnology, poses additional ethical questions about governance, social acceptability, and long-term impacts on biodiversity and human health (Bartkowski et al., 2018; Brookes & Smyth, 2024; Garden & Winickoff, 2018; Li, Liu, & Chen, 2019). Sustainable and responsible innovation pathways must be developed to balance scientific progress with societal values and environmental stewardship (Monast, 2018; Shukla-Jones, Friedrichs, & Winickoff, 2018).

5. POLICY CHALLENGES

The rapid evolution of artificial intelligence (AI), climate technologies, and biotechnologies presents significant policy challenges that require nuanced regulatory approaches to balance innovation, ethical considerations, and sustainability goals. These challenges span multiple domains including environmental law, healthcare, finance, and data privacy, and demand a multidimensional governance framework.

5.1 Complexity of Regulatory Environments

Emerging technologies such as AI and gene editing operate in regulatory landscapes that are often fragmented and lag behind technological advancements. Scholars note that existing laws and policies frequently struggle to address the speed and scale of innovation (Darvishi, Liu, & Lim, 2022; Butt, 2024). For instance, genome editing technologies pose unique risks and ethical questions, yet regulatory approaches vary widely across jurisdictions (Brookes & Smyth, 2024; Friedrichs et al., 2019; Li, Liu, & Chen, 2019). Similarly, AI applications in healthcare and finance demand specialized oversight to ensure safety, privacy, and ethical use (Mennella et al., 2024; Pesapane et al., 2021; Ali, H., & Aysan, A. F., 2024).

5.2 Environmental and Climate Policy Challenges

In the environmental domain, aligning national and international policies to combat climate change remains a formidable challenge. Developing countries like Nigeria face complex legal and sustainability hurdles while trying to meet international environmental commitments (Akindele & Chabinga, 2024; Saikia, 2024). The path to net zero policies requires integration of political will, governance reforms, and robust legal frameworks (Ali, A., 2024). Moreover, renewable energy expansion encounters regulatory barriers that stifle innovation, demanding coordinated legal strategies (Jafarizadeh et al., 2024; Oduro, Uzougbo, & Ugwu, 2024). Indigenous socioecological systems also highlight the need for policies that support resilience and sustainability while respecting traditional knowledge (Sakapaji et al., 2024).

5.3 Ethical and Legal Implications in AI and Biotechnology

Ethical governance is central to addressing the policy challenges posed by AI and biotechnologies. AI-enhanced systems, such as those used in ethical hacking or medical diagnostics, require clear ethical frameworks to mitigate risks of misuse and bias (Al-Sinani & Mitchell, 2024; Al-Sinani et al., 2025; Naili et al., 2025). The dual-use nature of these technologies complicates regulatory oversight, as they can both advance societal benefits and exacerbate ethical dilemmas (Batabyal, 2024; Trotsyuk et al., 2024). The regulation of AI as a medical device introduces specific challenges in balancing innovation with patient safety and privacy (Larson et al., 2021; Pesapane et al., 2018).

5.4 Data Privacy and Security Concerns

AI systems generate and process vast amounts of personal data, heightening risks related to privacy and cybersecurity. Ensuring data protection in AI platforms such as ChatGPT and others demands stringent policy safeguards and transparent governance models (Shafik, 2024; Shukla & Taneja, 2024). Furthermore, the integration of AI in critical infrastructures such as smart cities and drones raises novel security concerns that traditional regulatory frameworks are ill-equipped to address (Maguluri, Arularasan, & Boopathi, 2023).

5.5 Cross-Domain Policy Integration and Coordination

One of the overarching policy challenges is the need for interdisciplinary and cross-sector coordination. Complex systems modeling and agent-based approaches have been proposed to better inform policy advice and design adaptive regulations

(Schünemann et al., 2024). In the finance sector, the ethical implications of generative AI require multi-level governance that integrates academic, industry, and grey literature insights to create coherent policies (Ali, H., & Aysan, 2025; Ali, H., Zafar, & Aysan, 2024).

Policy challenges across AI, biotech, and climate vary in frequency and urgency. The bar chart below ranks common policy challenges based on frequency of discussion in recent scholarly literature.

Figure 4. Frequency of policy challenges across domains

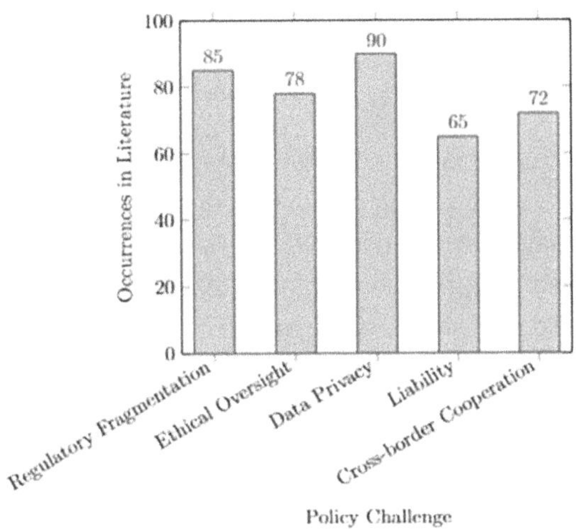

5.6 Socioeconomic and Human Rights Dimensions

Policies must also consider the broader socioeconomic impacts of emerging technologies, including implications for vulnerable populations and human rights. The implementation of the human right to science in AI governance frameworks underscores the importance of equitable access and ethical oversight in healthcare innovation (Ho, 2023). Women's empowerment through AI-driven safety solutions highlights the intersection of technology with social justice goals (Pimpalkar et al., 2024). In contrast, failures in regulation can exacerbate inequities and erode public trust (Fenwick, Molnar, & Frangos, 2024; Verma et al., 2020).

5.7 Policy Challenges in Sustainable Industry and Climate Action

The transition to Industry 4.0 and green technologies presents regulatory challenges tied to sustainability and innovation governance (Patra, 2025; Emon et al., 2025). Governments must balance incentivizing eco-friendly business practices while enforcing compliance, often in contexts where institutional capacities are limited (Soomro, Suhrab, & Abbasi, 2025). Biodiversity protection within climate policy trajectories calls for integrated legal frameworks that align conservation with development goals (Singh & Kaunert, 2025).

5.8 Summary

Overall, the policy challenges in regulating AI, biotechnology, and climate technologies are multifaceted, requiring innovative legal frameworks, ethical oversight, and inclusive governance mechanisms. Addressing these challenges necessitates global cooperation, interdisciplinary research, and continuous adaptation of policies to emerging risks and opportunities (Campus, 2024; Daniel, 2024; Leontidis, 2024).

6. INTERNATIONAL COORDINATION AND GOVERNANCE

The rapid advancement of artificial intelligence (AI) and related technologies, especially in critical sectors such as healthcare and medical diagnostics, necessitates robust international coordination and governance frameworks. These frameworks must address the ethical, legal, technical, and environmental challenges posed by AI while ensuring that innovation aligns with sustainable development and human rights standards globally.

6.1 The Need for Global Governance Structures

Global governance of AI and emerging technologies in healthcare involves aligning diverse regulatory approaches, ethical norms, and technical standards to mitigate risks such as data misuse, privacy breaches, and systemic biases (Mennella et al., 2024; Naili et al., 2025). Given AI's transboundary nature, no single nation can manage its impacts independently. Effective governance requires multilateral cooperation, transparent policymaking, and harmonization of regulations to foster trust, safety, and equitable access (Pesapane et al., 2021; Ho, 2023).

In the environmental domain, international governance plays a pivotal role in addressing climate change and sustainability, illustrating the critical need for cross-border policy alignment (Akindele & Chabinga, 2024; Ali, 2024; Aloamaka, 2024). These lessons inform AI governance models, as climate initiatives reveal both the complexities and opportunities of coordinating policy across nations, sectors, and socio-economic contexts (Singh & Kaunert, 2025; Saikia, 2024).

6.2 Existing Frameworks and Their Limitations

Several international initiatives and agreements provide foundational elements for AI governance, yet often struggle with enforcement and adaptability. The European Union's AI Act, for example, establishes risk-based regulatory mechanisms but faces challenges in global applicability and rapid technology evolution (Butt, 2024; Pesapane et al., 2018). Similarly, regulatory approaches to genome editing technologies underscore tensions between innovation and precaution, emphasizing the need for globally coherent yet locally adaptable policies (Brookes & Smyth, 2024; Friedrichs et al., 2019; Garden & Winickoff, 2018).

These regulatory challenges are compounded in sectors like healthcare diagnostics, where AI tools cross national borders through data sharing and cloud platforms (Larson et al., 2021; Mennella et al., 2024). Additionally, emerging technologies such as quantum machine learning introduce novel governance demands, merging AI with next-generation computing capabilities (Campus, 2024; Eswaran & Eswaran, 2025).

6.3 Ethical and Human Rights Considerations

International governance must embed ethical principles and human rights protections, especially the right to science and health, in AI regulatory frameworks (Ho, 2023; Batabyal, 2024). Cross-domain ethical analyses reveal challenges in balancing AI's benefits against risks of discrimination, opacity, and misuse (Ali & Aysan, 2025; Trotsyuk et al., 2024; Veluru, 2024). This requires establishing global standards for transparency, accountability, and equitable benefit-sharing while safeguarding data privacy and security (Shukla & Taneja, 2024; Shafik, 2024; Verma et al., 2020).

The international community also grapples with governance of AI-driven warfare and dual-use technologies, which complicate regulatory coherence and trust-building efforts (Batabyal, 2024; Al-Sinani & Mitchell, 2024; Al-Sinani et al., 2025).

6.4 Multi-Level Coordination and Stakeholder Engagement

Effective international governance involves multi-level coordination that includes governments, intergovernmental organizations, industry, academia, and civil society (Fenwick et al., 2024; Luan et al., 2024). Collaborative platforms facilitate sharing best practices, harmonizing standards, and addressing emerging threats, such as cyber risks in AI-powered systems and ethical hacking initiatives (Maguluri et al., 2023; Al-Sinani & Mitchell, 2024).

Incorporating perspectives from developing countries is essential for inclusive governance that respects diverse socio-ecological systems and development goals (Akindele & Chabinga, 2024; Sakapaji et al., 2024; Soomro et al., 2025). For example, Nigeria's leadership in environmental law highlights the significance of national context in shaping international commitments (Akindele & Chabinga, 2024).

6.5 Towards Harmonized Legal and Regulatory Approaches

Legal scholars emphasize the necessity of harmonizing laws to facilitate innovation while minimizing regulatory fragmentation that impedes global cooperation (Darvishi et al., 2022; Patra, 2025; Oduro et al., 2024). The evolving landscape of AI regulation calls for flexible, adaptive governance models that can integrate scientific advances and socio-political realities, informed by system dynamics and complex policy modeling (Schünemann et al., 2024; Daniel, 2024).

Examples from gene editing governance demonstrate how international treaties, soft law mechanisms, and multi-stakeholder dialogues contribute to crafting workable rules balancing risk and progress (Monast, 2018; Shukla-Jones et al., 2018; Li et al., 2019).

Governance of emerging technologies requires coordination across levels—from local implementation to global standards. The following model illustrates a layered governance framework.

Figure 5. Multi-level governance framework for emerging technologies

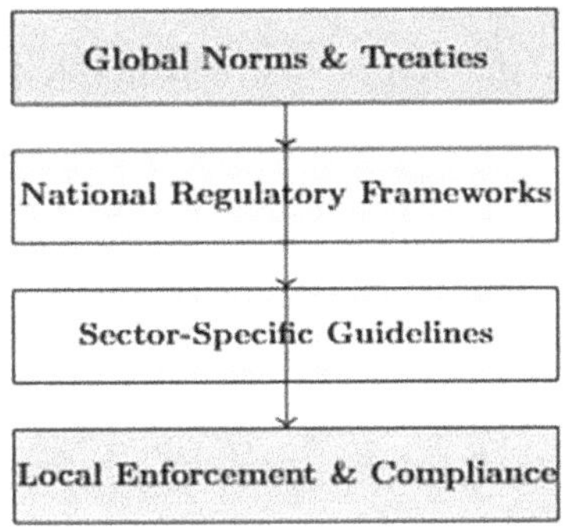

6.6 Promoting Responsible Innovation and Sustainability

Sustainable AI innovation must align with global climate goals and biodiversity protection, reflecting the interconnectedness of technology, environment, and society (Emon et al., 2025; Singh & Kaunert, 2025). International coordination also underpins efforts to green AI technologies, encouraging compliance with eco-friendly standards and leveraging governmental support for sustainable industry practices (Soomro et al., 2025; Jafarizadeh et al., 2024).

Moreover, governance frameworks increasingly incorporate ethical AI for healthcare diagnostics that protect patient safety and data integrity while enabling scientific progress (Mennella et al., 2024; Naili et al., 2025; Pesapane et al., 2021).

6.7 Summary

In sum, international coordination and governance remain fundamental to the responsible development and deployment of AI in healthcare and other sectors. Building resilient, ethical, and harmonized regulatory frameworks requires ongoing global dialogue, inclusive policy design, and mechanisms that keep pace with rapid technological change. Drawing on multidisciplinary insights from climate law, AI ethics, and governance science offers valuable pathways toward sustainable and equitable AI futures.

7. EMERGING POLICY MODELS AND BEST PRACTICES

The rapid evolution and integration of artificial intelligence (AI), climate technologies, and biotechnology have necessitated the development of innovative policy models and best practices to address ethical, legal, and regulatory challenges across diverse domains. This section explores the emerging frameworks and strategies that aim to balance innovation with governance, promote sustainability, and safeguard human rights and security.

7.1 Adaptive and Multi-Stakeholder Governance Models

Emerging policy models emphasize adaptive governance mechanisms that engage multiple stakeholders, including governments, industry players, academia, civil society, and international organizations, to ensure more inclusive and responsive regulation. Schünemann et al. (2024) advocate for complex system policy modeling approaches—such as systems thinking, system dynamics, and agent-based modeling—that can simulate and predict policy impacts in multifaceted environments, allowing for flexible and iterative policymaking.

Such models are essential for addressing the dynamic challenges posed by AI in healthcare, environmental sustainability, and biotechnologies, where rapid technological advancement outpaces traditional regulatory frameworks (Mennella et al., 2024; Daniel, 2024). Adaptive governance is particularly crucial in the context of climate change, where international cooperation and continuous policy adjustments are required to align with evolving scientific insights and geopolitical realities (Akindele & Chabinga, 2024; Ali, 2024).

7.2 Risk-Appropriate and Proportionate Regulation

A best practice gaining prominence is the adoption of risk-appropriate regulatory approaches that calibrate oversight based on the level of potential harm and uncertainty associated with new technologies. Brookes and Smyth (2024) argue that risk-appropriate regulations for gene-editing technologies foster innovation while protecting public safety and ethical standards. Similarly, Larsson et al. (2021) emphasize regulatory frameworks that are sufficiently rigorous to ensure safety in AI-based diagnostic tools but flexible enough to accelerate beneficial innovation.

This approach has been reflected in the European Union's AI Act, which Butt (2024) describes as a pioneering effort to introduce a tiered regulatory scheme based on risk categories, balancing innovation facilitation with ethical and safety considerations. Tailored regulation also applies to AI-enabled cybersecurity and ethical hacking, where Al-Sinani et al. (2025) highlight the necessity for frameworks that evolve alongside threat landscapes to ensure effective protection without stifling research.

7.3 Ethical AI and Responsible Innovation

The integration of ethical principles in AI and related technologies is central to emerging best practices. Ali and Aysan (2025) provide a cross-domain analysis that underscores the necessity for ethical frameworks that address transparency, fairness, privacy, and accountability in generative AI systems. Responsible AI deployment in healthcare and finance necessitates strict adherence to these principles to maintain public trust and prevent misuse (Mennella et al., 2024; Ali, H., Zafar, & Aysan, 2024).

Veluru (2024) and Shukla and Taneja (2024) further highlight the importance of embedding ethical considerations into data privacy and security policies, particularly given the vast amounts of sensitive data processed by AI systems. This is critical for applications such as AI-driven diagnostics (Naili et al., 2025) and AI-powered safety solutions for women (Pimpalkar et al., 2024), where data misuse could result in significant harm.

7.4 Integrating Environmental and Climate Policies

Emerging policy models also prioritize sustainability and climate resilience by integrating environmental concerns within technological innovation frameworks. Ali (2024) stresses the alignment of net-zero policies with governance structures to drive meaningful environmental sustainability. Complementing this, Akindele and Chabinga (2024) discuss Nigeria's role in international environmental law, emphasizing the need for legal instruments that support climate adaptation and sustainable resource management.

Furthermore, innovations in renewable energy, green technologies, and circular economy models require legal strategies that lower regulatory barriers and promote green innovation, as detailed by Oduro et al. (2024) and Emon et al. (2025). These strategies often rely on government incentives, public-private partnerships, and robust compliance mechanisms to foster sustainable industrial transformation (Soomro, Suhrab, & Abbasi, 2025; Singh & Kaunert, 2025).

7.5 International Harmonization and Cross-Border Cooperation

Due to the transnational nature of AI, biotechnology, and environmental challenges, emerging best practices advocate for international harmonization of standards and regulatory cooperation. Aloamaka (2024) and Saikia (2024) underscore the importance of navigating international legal frameworks to ensure equitable and effective governance of climate and environmental technologies.

Monast (2018) and Shukla-Jones, Friedrichs, and Winickoff (2018) similarly highlight that gene-editing governance benefits significantly from harmonized policies that mitigate risks of regulatory arbitrage and enable responsible innovation globally. Such international coordination also applies to AI governance in healthcare, where Pesapane et al. (2021) and Ho (2023) advocate for common standards that protect patient safety while promoting innovation.

7.6 Leveraging Technology for Regulatory Effectiveness

Advances in AI and quantum machine learning present opportunities to enhance regulatory oversight and enforcement. Campus (2024) and Eswaran and Eswaran (2025) discuss how AI-driven analytic tools and quantum technologies can improve data-driven policy formulation, risk assessment, and compliance monitoring. These capabilities support the development of proactive regulatory models that anticipate emerging risks and optimize resource allocation.

In cybersecurity, Gaurav et al. (2024) demonstrate how AI-based semantic web approaches can detect phishing threats, illustrating how technological innovation can also strengthen regulatory compliance and consumer protection. Similarly, Al-Sinani and Mitchell (2024) show how AI can advance ethical hacking practices, reinforcing the security of complex systems.

7.7 Emphasizing Transparency, Accountability, and Public Engagement

A recurrent theme in emerging policy models is the emphasis on transparency, accountability, and public engagement. Fenwick, Molnar, and Frangos (2024) stress the shift toward human-centric AI adoption that involves clear communication and workforce inclusion to bridge the gap between technology deployment and social acceptance.

Open dialogue and participatory approaches are crucial for building societal trust, especially in sensitive domains such as healthcare AI (Mennella et al., 2024) and environmental policy (Chowdhury, 2024). Rashid and Kausik (2024) advocate for governance models that incorporate continuous stakeholder feedback and independent oversight to ensure ethical compliance and social legitimacy.

7.8 Policy Innovation for Future Challenges

Finally, policymakers are increasingly adopting innovative frameworks that combine foresight, scenario planning, and structural topic modeling to navigate uncertainty and complex future landscapes. Ali and Aysan (2024) use machine learning to decode the future trajectories of generative AI, providing a blueprint for anticipatory regulation.

Similarly, Schünemann et al. (2024) argue that policy advice informed by advanced modeling can better prepare governance systems for unexpected disruptions and multi-dimensional challenges. This forward-looking stance is necessary to balance innovation incentives with precautionary measures amid rapid technological change.

7.9 Summary

Emerging policy models and best practices reflect a paradigm shift from reactive, rigid regulations to dynamic, inclusive, and risk-sensitive governance frameworks. By integrating ethical principles, leveraging technological advances, promoting sustainability, and fostering international cooperation, these approaches aim to responsibly guide the development and deployment of AI, biotechnology, and climate technologies. As the technological landscape evolves, continuous adaptation, stakeholder engagement, and evidence-based policymaking will be essential to meet future challenges and harness opportunities.

8. FUTURE DIRECTIONS AND RECOMMENDATIONS

As artificial intelligence (AI), environmental sustainability, and regulatory landscapes continue to evolve, future pathways must strategically address technological innovation, ethical governance, legal frameworks, and societal impacts. This section outlines critical future directions and recommendations across these intersecting domains, drawing on recent scholarship to guide policymakers, industry stakeholders, and researchers.

8.1. Strengthening Integrated Regulatory Frameworks for AI and Sustainability

The convergence of AI technologies with environmental sustainability efforts necessitates cohesive and adaptive regulatory frameworks. Current frameworks remain fragmented, often lagging behind rapid technological advancements, particularly in AI applications within healthcare, climate technologies, and industry (Mennella et al., 2024; Pesapane et al., 2021; Oduro et al., 2024). Future regulatory efforts should emphasize flexibility to accommodate emerging innovations such as generative AI, quantum machine learning, and AI-driven diagnostics while ensuring public safety and ethical compliance (Ali, H., & Aysan, 2024; Campus, 2024; Naili et al., 2025).

Policymakers are encouraged to adopt risk-appropriate regulations that balance innovation with precaution, particularly for sensitive domains like gene editing and AI-enabled medical devices (Brookes & Smyth, 2024; Friedrichs et al., 2019; Pesapane et al., 2018). Additionally, cross-jurisdictional cooperation is essential to harmonize standards, as international disparities can hinder sustainable development and technology diffusion (Akindele & Chabinga, 2024; Aloamaka, 2024).

8.2. Enhancing Ethical and Human-Centric AI Development

Ethical challenges inherent in AI deployment—privacy, bias, transparency, and potential misuse—remain paramount concerns. The integration of AI in healthcare, finance, and security sectors demands frameworks that prioritize human rights, ethical decision-making, and data governance (Ali, H., & Aysan, 2025; Ho, 2023; Shukla & Taneja, 2024). Emerging approaches such as AI-enhanced ethical hacking demonstrate promising avenues to strengthen cybersecurity defenses while adhering to ethical norms (Al-Sinani & Mitchell, 2024; Al-Sinani et al., 2025).

Future research and policy must promote explainability and accountability mechanisms in AI systems to build trust and reduce risks of misuse or unintended harm (Veluru, 2024; Trotsyuk et al., 2024). Human resource management strategies also play a pivotal role in facilitating smooth digital transformations through human-centric AI adoption (Fenwick et al., 2024).

8.3. Promoting Sustainability through AI-Driven Environmental Solutions

AI's potential in addressing climate change, renewable energy, and biodiversity conservation is increasingly recognized (Emon et al., 2025; Singh & Kaunert, 2025). However, challenges such as regulatory barriers to renewable energy expansion and the resilience of socioecological systems demand holistic policy and technological responses (Jafarizadeh et al., 2024; Sakapaji et al., 2024; Oduro et al., 2024).

Governments and businesses should foster green technology innovation ecosystems by implementing clear incentives, compliance support, and public-private partnerships aimed at net-zero targets (Ali, 2024; Soomro et al., 2025). Leveraging AI to enhance monitoring and management in agriculture, forestry, and border protection can further enable sustainable resource management (Arya & Rastogi, 2024).

8.4. Facilitating Interdisciplinary Research and Data Integration

Future advancements rely on interdisciplinary collaboration, combining AI, law, ethics, environmental science, and economics to develop comprehensive solutions (Darvishi et al., 2022; Luan et al., 2024). Enhanced data analytics capabilities, including machine learning-driven topic modeling and semantic web approaches, are vital for synthesizing large, heterogeneous data sources (Ali, H., Zafar, & Aysan, 2024; Rodriguez & Storer, 2020; Gaurav et al., 2024).

Support for open-access data sets and responsible data sharing frameworks will accelerate innovation while safeguarding privacy and intellectual property rights (Shuja et al., 2021; Shafik, 2024; Patra, 2025).

8.5. Addressing Social Equity and Inclusiveness in AI and Sustainability Policies

Ensuring that AI and sustainability innovations benefit diverse populations requires intentional policy design focused on inclusiveness and equity (Pimpalkar et al., 2024; Singh & Kaunert, 2025). For instance, women's empowerment through AI-enabled safety and predictive analytics can contribute to safer communities and workplace environments (Pimpalkar et al., 2024).

Further, indigenous socioecological systems should be integrated into resilience planning and regulatory designs to preserve cultural and environmental heritage (Sakapaji et al., 2024).

8.6. Building Robust Governance for Emerging Technologies

The rapid development of gene-editing, AI-driven warfare technologies, and quantum computing demands preemptive governance strategies to mitigate ethical, legal, and security risks (Batabyal, 2024; Garden & Winickoff, 2018; Eswaran & Eswaran, 2025). Collaborative international frameworks, continuous monitoring, and public engagement are necessary to navigate the complex terrain of technological governance (Monast, 2018; Shukla-Jones et al., 2018).

Special attention should be given to the evolving role of AI in warfare and cybersecurity, ensuring compliance with international laws and human rights standards (Batabyal, 2024; Maguluri et al., 2023).

8.7 Summary

Future directions in AI, environmental sustainability, and regulatory policy must embrace an integrated, ethical, and adaptive approach to keep pace with accelerating technological innovation. By fostering interdisciplinary collaboration, strengthening human-centric governance, and promoting inclusive sustainability, stakeholders can better navigate the complex challenges of the 21st century. Policymakers, industry leaders, and researchers are urged to operationalize these recommendations to advance equitable, secure, and sustainable futures.

9. CONCLUSION

The rapid evolution of artificial intelligence, generative technologies, and sustainable innovations presents unprecedented opportunities alongside significant regulatory, ethical, and societal challenges. This chapter has explored the multifaceted landscape of AI applications in healthcare, environmental sustainability, finance, and legal frameworks, emphasizing the pressing need for adaptive, risk-appropriate, and ethically grounded regulatory strategies.

As AI technologies advance, their integration into critical sectors such as medical diagnostics, environmental monitoring, and financial systems demands rigorous governance to safeguard human rights, data privacy, and societal welfare (Mennella et al., 2024; Pesapane et al., 2021; Ali, 2024). The growing complexity of AI-driven systems also necessitates transparent and explainable models to foster trust and accountability, particularly when these technologies influence life-altering decisions (Ali, H., & Aysan, A. F., 2025; Larson et al., 2021).

Simultaneously, addressing climate change and sustainability goals through AI and green technologies calls for harmonized international legal frameworks and collaborative governance approaches. The interplay between innovation and regulation must balance fostering technological progress while minimizing risks such as ecological degradation or socio-economic inequities (Akindele & Chabinga, 2024; Saikia, 2024; Singh & Kaunert, 2025). The implementation of just and effective policies remains critical to overcoming barriers and enabling a resilient transition to net-zero economies (Ali, 2024; Chowdhury, 2024).

Furthermore, the ethical deployment of AI, particularly in sensitive domains like warfare, healthcare, and data security, remains an ongoing concern. Research underscores the necessity of embedding human-centric values and ethics within AI development and deployment processes to prevent misuse, discrimination, and unintended consequences (Batabyal, 2024; Veluru, 2024; Shukla & Taneja, 2024).

Looking ahead, the convergence of AI with emerging fields such as quantum computing, genome editing, and biosensors promises transformative impacts but also introduces novel regulatory challenges that demand proactive, interdisciplinary approaches (Campus, 2024; Brookes & Smyth, 2024; Arya & Rastogi, 2024). The path forward lies in fostering robust collaboration among policymakers, technologists, ethicists, and civil society to co-create regulatory ecosystems that are flexible, inclusive, and forward-looking (Darvishi et al., 2022; Schünemann et al., 2024).

In conclusion, navigating the complex terrain of AI and sustainability regulation requires a balanced, nuanced understanding of technological potential and human values. By learning from diverse jurisdictions, embracing adaptive governance models, and prioritizing transparency and ethics, stakeholders can harness the benefits of innovation while safeguarding societal well-being and environmental integrity for future generations.

REFERENCES

Akindele, A., & Chabinga, R. (2024). Navigating Climate Change and Sustainability Solutions: Nigeria's Role in International Environmental Law. *African Journal of Climate Change and Resource Sustainability*, *3*(1), 331–344. DOI: 10.37284/ajccrs.3.1.2188

Al-Sinani, H. S., & Mitchell, C. J. (2024). AI-enhanced ethical hacking: A Linux-focused experiment. *arXiv preprint arXiv:2410.05105.*

Al-Sinani, H. S., Sahli, N., Mitchell, C. J., & Al-Siyabi, M. (2025). Advancing ethical hacking with AI: A Linux-based experimental study. *Proceedings of ITASEC and SERICS, Bologna, Italy (Feb 2025),* https://www. chrismitchell. net/Papers/aehwaa. pdf

Ali, A. (2024). Navigating Road for Net Zero Policies to Aligning Policy, Politics, and Governance for Environmental Sustainability. In *Transition Towards a Sustainable Future: Net Zero Policies and Environmental Sustainability* (pp. 205–230). Springer Nature Singapore. DOI: 10.1007/978-981-97-5756-5_10

Ali, H., & Aysan, A. F. (2024). Decoding Future of Generative AI in Finance: A Machine Learning Exploration of Academic and Grey Corpus. *Available atSSRN* 4787211. DOI: 10.2139/ssrn.4787211

Ali, H., & Aysan, A. F. (2025). Ethical dimensions of generative AI: A cross-domain analysis using machine learning structural topic modeling. *International Journal of Ethics and Systems*, *41*(1), 3–34. DOI: 10.1108/IJOES-04-2024-0112

Ali, H., Zafar, M. B., & Aysan, A. F. (2024). Generative AI and Finance: A Multi-level Machine Learning Based Analysis. *Available atSSRN* 5129013.

Aloamaka, P. C. (2024). Navigating the Climate Crisis: Exploring International Law's Evolution and Application. *GLS Law Journal*, *6*(1), 48–58. DOI: 10.69974/glslawjournal.v6i1.127

Arya, L., & Rastogi, R. (2024). Study on Aerial Monitoring System in Agriculture, Forestry, Defense, and Border Protection Using Artificial Intelligence (AI). In *Agriculture and Aquaculture Applications of Biosensors and Bioelectronics* (pp. 392-407). IGI Global Scientific Publishing.

Bartkowski, B., Theesfeld, I., Pirscher, F., & Timaeus, J. (2018). Snipping around for food: Economic, ethical and policy implications of CRISPR/Cas genome editing. *Geoforum*, *96*, 172–180. DOI: 10.1016/j.geoforum.2018.07.017

Batabyal, G. S. (2024). Ethics, laws on war and artificial intelligence-driven warfare. In *Artificial intelligence, ethics and the future of warfare* (pp. 187–215). Routledge India. DOI: 10.4324/9781003421849-9

Brookes, G., & Smyth, S. J. (2024). Risk-appropriate regulations for gene-editing technologies. *GM Crops and Food: Biotechnology in Agriculture and the Food Chain, 15*(1), 1–14. DOI: 10.1080/21645698.2023.2293510 PMID: 38215017

Butt, J. (2024). Analytical study of the world's first EU Artificial Intelligence (AI) Act. *International Journal of Research Publication and Reviews, 5*(3), 7343–7364. DOI: 10.55248/gengpi.5.0324.0914

Campus, M. T. (2024). Quantum Machine Learning, Leveraging Al, and. *Integration of AI, Quantum Computing, and Semiconductor Technology*, 57.

Chowdhury, S. (2024). Towards a Just Climate: Navigating Complexities and Challenges in Climate Change Discourse and Action. *Issue 2 Int'l JL Mgmt. &. Human., 7*, 1807.

Daniel, J. (2024). *Environmental Law: Navigating Legal Pathways for a Sustainable Future*. Pencil.

Darvishi, K., Liu, L., & Lim, S. (2022). Navigating the Nexus: Legal and Economic Implications of Emerging Tech-nologies. *Law and Economics, 16*(3), 172–186. DOI: 10.35335/laweco.v16i3.59

Eisenberg, D. (2024). *Sensing With Integrity: Responsible Sensor Systems in an Era of AI* (Doctoral dissertation, New Jersey Institute of Technology).

Emon, M. M. H., Khan, T., Rahman, M. A., Hamid, A. B. A., & Yaakub, N. I. (2025). GreenTech revolution: Navigating challenges and seizing opportunities. In *AI and green technology applications in society* (pp. 63–90). IGI Global Scientific Publishing.

Eswaran, U., & Eswaran, V. (2025). Quantum Machine Learning, Leveraging AI, and Semiconductor Technology. In *Integration of AI, Quantum Computing, and Semiconductor Technology* (pp. 57-78). IGI Global.

Fenwick, A., Molnar, G., & Frangos, P. (2024). The critical role of HRM in AI-driven digital transformation: A paradigm shift to enable firms to move from AI implementation to human-centric adoption. *Discover Artificial Intelligence, 4*(1), 34. DOI: 10.1007/s44163-024-00125-4

Filetti, S., Fenza, G., & Gallo, A. (2024). Research design and writing of scholarly articles: New artificial intelligence tools available for researchers. *Endocrine, 85*(3), 1104–1116. DOI: 10.1007/s12020-024-03977-z PMID: 39085566

Flannery, J., Ajayi, S. O., & Oyegoke, A. S. (2021). Alcohol and substance misuse in the construction industry. *International Journal of Occupational Safety and Ergonomics, 27*(2), 472–487. DOI: 10.1080/10803548.2019.1601376 PMID: 30935301

Friedrichs, S., Takasu, Y., Kearns, P., Dagallier, B., Oshima, R., Schofield, J., & Moreddu, C. (2019). An overview of regulatory approaches to genome editing in agriculture. *Biotechnology Research and Innovation, 3*(2), 208–220. DOI: 10.1016/j.biori.2019.07.001

Garden, H., & Winickoff, D. (2018). Gene editing for advanced therapies GOVERNANCE, POLICY AND SOCIETY. *OECD Science, Technology and Industry Working Papers, 2018*(12), 0_1-46.

Gaurav, A., Chui, K. T., Arya, V., Attar, R. W., Bansal, S., Alhomoud, A., & Psannis, K. (2024). Optimized AI-Driven Semantic Web Approach for Enhancing Phishing Detection in E-Commerce Platforms. [IJSWIS]. *International Journal on Semantic Web and Information Systems, 20*(1), 1–13. DOI: 10.4018/IJSWIS.359767

Ho, C. W. (2023). Implementing the human right to science in the regulatory governance of artificial intelligence in healthcare. *Journal of Law and the Biosciences, 10*(2), lsad026. DOI: 10.1093/jlb/lsad026 PMID: 37854168

Jafarizadeh, H., Yamini, E., Zolfaghari, S. M., Esmaeilion, F., Assad, M. E. H., & Soltani, M. (2024). Navigating challenges in large-scale renewable energy storage: Barriers, solutions, and innovations. *Energy Reports, 12*, 2179–2192. DOI: 10.1016/j.egyr.2024.08.019

Jamro, M. Y., & Jamro, F. A. (2023). AI Matters: Chatbot Integration in Holistic STEM Education.

Karim, R., Galar, D., & Kumar, U. (2023). *AI factory: theories, applications and case studies*. CRC Press. DOI: 10.1201/9781003208686

Larson, D. B., Harvey, H., Rubin, D. L., Irani, N., Tse, J. R., & Langlotz, C. P. (2021). Regulatory frameworks for development and evaluation of artificial intelligence–based diagnostic imaging algorithms: Summary and recommendations. *Journal of the American College of Radiology, 18*(3), 413–424. DOI: 10.1016/j.jacr.2020.09.060 PMID: 33096088

Leontidis, G. (2024). Science in the age of ai: How artificial intelligence is changing the nature and method of scientific research.

Li, G., Liu, Y. G., & Chen, Y. (2019). Genome-editing technologies: The gap between application and policy. *Science China. Life Sciences*, *62*(11), 1534–1538. DOI: 10.1007/s11427-019-1566-1 PMID: 31686319

Luan, H., Perron, B. E., Victor, B. G., Wan, G., Niu, Y., & Xiao, X. (2024). Using artificial intelligence to support scientometric analysis of scholarly literature: A case example of research on mainland China's left-behind children. *Journal of the Society for Social Work and Research*, *15*(3), 435–457. DOI: 10.1086/731613

Maennig, W. (2014). Inefficiency of the anti-doping system: Cost reduction proposals. *Substance Use & Misuse*, *49*(9), 1201–1205. DOI: 10.3109/10826084.2014.912065 PMID: 24832718

Maguluri, L. P., Arularasan, A. N., & Boopathi, S. (2023). Assessing security concerns for ai-based drones in smart cities. In *Effective AI, Blockchain, and E-Governance Applications for Knowledge Discovery and Management* (pp. 27-47). IGI Global Scientific Publishing. DOI: 10.4018/978-1-6684-9151-5.ch002

Mennella, C., Maniscalco, U., De Pietro, G., & Esposito, M. (2024). Ethical and regulatory challenges of AI technologies in healthcare: A narrative review. *Heliyon*, *10*(4), e26297. DOI: 10.1016/j.heliyon.2024.e26297 PMID: 38384518

Monast, J. J. (2018). Editing nature: Reconceptualizing biotechnology governance. *BCL Rev.*, *59*, 2377.

Naili, Y. T., Mangkunegara, I. S., Purwono, P., & Baballe, M. A. (2025). Regulatory challenges in ai-based diagnostics: Legal implications of ai use in medical diagnostics. In *BIO Web of Conferences* (Vol. 152, p. 01034). EDP Sciences.

Oduro, P., Uzougbo, N. S., & Ugwu, M. C. (2024). Renewable energy expansion: Legal strategies for overcoming regulatory barriers and promoting innovation. *International Journal of Applied Research in Social Sciences*, *6*(5), 927–944. DOI: 10.51594/ijarss.v6i5.1145

Patra, S. P. (2025). Navigating the legal landscape of sustainable Industry 4.0. *Industry 4.0 for Manufacturing Systems: Concepts, Technologies, and Applications*, 109.

Pesapane, F., Bracchi, D. A., Mulligan, J. F., Linnikov, A., Maslennikov, O., Lanzavecchia, M. B., Tantrige, P., Stasolla, A., Biondetti, P., Giuggioli, P. F., Cassano, E., & Carrafiello, G. (2021). Legal and regulatory framework for AI solutions in healthcare in EU, US, China, and Russia: New scenarios after a pandemic. *Radiation*, *1*(4), 261–276. DOI: 10.3390/radiation1040022

Pesapane, F., Volonté, C., Codari, M., & Sardanelli, F. (2018). Artificial intelligence as a medical device in radiology: Ethical and regulatory issues in Europe and the United States. *Insights Into Imaging*, *9*(5), 745–753. DOI: 10.1007/s13244-018-0645-y PMID: 30112675

Pimpalkar, A. P., Wankhade, N. R., Chole, V., & Golhar, Y. (2024). Women's Empowerment Through AI: Discovering Data Analytics for Predictive Safety Solutions and Future Trends. In *AI Tools and Applications for Women's Safety* (pp. 304-326). IGI Global Scientific Publishing.

Rashid, A. B., & Kausik, A. K. (2024). AI revolutionizing industries worldwide: A comprehensive overview of its diverse applications. *Hybrid Advances*, 100277.

Rodriguez, M. Y., & Storer, H. (2020). A computational social science perspective on qualitative data exploration: Using topic models for the descriptive analysis of social media data. *Journal of Technology in Human Services*, *38*(1), 54–86. DOI: 10.1080/15228835.2019.1616350

Saikia, B. (2024). Ecologically-Informed approaches: International mechanisms for navigating environmental challenges and ensuring sustainability in the oil and gas exploration and production industry. *Proceedings of the International Academy of Ecology and Environmental Sciences*, *14*(2), 60.

Sakapaji, S. C., García Molinos, J., Parilova, V., Gavrilyeva, T., & Yakovleva, N. (2024). Navigating legal and regulatory frameworks to achieve the resilience and sustainability of indigenous socioecological systems. *Resources*, *13*(4), 56. DOI: 10.3390/resources13040056

San Biagio, M., Cipolla, M., La Mattina, E., & Morreale, V. (2023, December). A Topic Clustering Method to Identify Online Threats against Soft Targets. In *2023 International Conference on Computational Science and Computational Intelligence (CSCI)* (pp. 727-733). IEEE. DOI: 10.1109/CSCI62032.2023.00124

Schünemann, C., Johanning, S., Reger, E., Herold, H., & Bruckner, T. (2024). Complex system policy modelling approaches for policy advice–comparing systems thinking, system dynamics and agent-based modelling. *Political Research Exchange : an ECPR Journal*, *6*(1), 2387438. DOI: 10.1080/2474736X.2024.2387438

Shafik, W. (2024). Data privacy and security safeguarding customer information in ChatGPT systems. In *Revolutionizing the Service Industry Wth OpenAI Models* (pp. 52–86). IGI Global. DOI: 10.4018/979-8-3693-1239-1.ch003

Sheliemina, N. (2024). The use of artificial intelligence in medical diagnostics: Opportunities, prospects and risks. *Health Economics and Management Review, 5*(2), 104–124. DOI: 10.61093/hem.2024.2-07

Shuja, J., Alanazi, E., Alasmary, W., & Alashaikh, A. (2021). COVID-19 open source data sets: A comprehensive survey. *Applied Intelligence, 51*(3), 1296–1325. DOI: 10.1007/s10489-020-01862-6 PMID: 34764552

Shukla, R. P., & Taneja, S. (2024). Ethical considerations and data privacy in artificial intelligence. In *Integrating generative AI in education to achieve sustainable development goals* (pp. 86–97). IGI Global. DOI: 10.4018/979-8-3693-2440-0.ch005

Shukla-Jones, A., Friedrichs, S., & Winickoff, D. E. (2018). Gene editing in an international context: Scientific, economic and social issues across sectors. *OECD science, technology and industry working papers, 2018*(4), 0_1-51.

Singh, B., & Kaunert, C. (2025). Navigating the Terrain of Sustainability Trajectories of Environment: Biodiversity Protection and Legal Landscapes. In *Community Resilience and Climate Change Challenges: Pursuit of Sustainable Development Goals (SDGs)* (pp. 355-374). IGI Global Scientific Publishing.

Soomro, J. A., Suhrab, M., & Abbasi, B. A. (2025). Navigating Green Regulations in the Business Ecosystem: Government Support, Compliance, and Obstacles in the Context of Pakistan. In *Government Influences on Eco-Friendly Practices in Business* (pp. 55-86). IGI Global.

Terry, N. (2019). Of regulating healthcare AI and robots. *Yale JL & Tech., 21*, 133.

Trotsyuk, A. A., Waeiss, Q., Bhatia, R. T., Aponte, B. J., Heffernan, I. M., Madgavkar, D., Felder, R. M., Lehmann, L. S., Palmer, M. J., Greely, H., Wald, R., Goetz, L., Trengove, M., Vandersluis, R., Lin, H., Cho, M. K., Altman, R. B., Endy, D., Relman, D. A., & Magnus, D. (2024). Toward a framework for risk mitigation of potential misuse of artificial intelligence in biomedical research. *Nature Machine Intelligence, 6*(12), 1–8. DOI: 10.1038/s42256-024-00926-3

Veluru, C. S. (2024). Responsible Artificial Intelligence on Large Scale Data to Prevent Misuse, Unethical Challenges and Security Breaches. *Journal of Artificial Intelligence & Cloud Computing. SRC/JAICC-349. DOI: doi. org/(3), 331*, 2-6.DOI: 10.47363/JAICC/2024

Verma, A., Rao, K., Eluri, V., & Sharma, Y. (2020). Regulating AI in public health: systems challenges and perspectives. *ORF Occasional Paper, 261.*

Verma, M., & Rohit, K. (2024). Ethical AI Shaping Scholarly Communication: Challenges and Opportunities.

Voigt, B., & Münichsdorfer, A. (2019). Regulation of genome editing in plant biotechnology: European Union. *Regulation of Genome Editing in Plant Biotechnology: A Comparative Analysis of Regulatory Frameworks of Selected Countries and the EU*, 137-238.

Vyawahare, H., Khandelwal, S., & Rathod, S. (2024). Artificial Intelligence in Detecting and Preventing Online Harassment. In *AI Tools and Applications for Women's Safety* (pp. 14–35). IGI Global Scientific Publishing. DOI: 10.4018/979-8-3693-1435-7.ch002

Wang, Q. (2024). Maritime law enforcement concerning offshore energy platforms: Navigating international law constraints and challenges. *Marine Policy*, *170*, 106370. DOI: 10.1016/j.marpol.2024.106370

Wolt, J. D. (2017). Safety, security, and policy considerations for plant genome editing. *Progress in Molecular Biology and Translational Science*, *149*, 215–241. DOI: 10.1016/bs.pmbts.2017.03.005 PMID: 28712498

Wolt, J. D., & Wolf, C. (2018). Policy and governance perspectives for regulation of genome edited crops in the United States. *Frontiers in Plant Science*, *9*, 1606. DOI: 10.3389/fpls.2018.01606 PMID: 30467510

World Health Organization. (2023). *Regulatory considerations on artificial intelligence for health*. World Health Organization.

Zreik, M. (2024). Harnessing AI for entrepreneurial idea generation: Navigating the new frontier. In *Generating Entrepreneurial Ideas With AI* (pp. 1–18). IGI Global Scientific Publishing. DOI: 10.4018/979-8-3693-3498-0.ch001

Compilation of References

Abbott, K. W. (2011). An international framework agreement on scientific and technological innovation and regulation. *The Growing Gap between Emerging Technologies and Legal-Ethical Oversight: The Pacing Problem*, 127-156.

Abd-Elsalam, K. A., & Abdel-Momen, S. M. (2023). Artificial intelligence's development and challenges in scientific writing. *Egyptian Journal of Agricultural Research, 101*(3), 714–717. DOI: 10.21608/ejar.2023.220363.1414

Adanma, U. M., & Ogunbiyi, E. O. (2024). Artificial intelligence in environmental conservation: Evaluating cyber risks and opportunities for sustainable practices. *Computer Science & IT Research Journal, 5*(5), 1178–1209. DOI: 10.51594/csitrj.v5i5.1156

Aderibigbe, A. O., Ohenhen, P. E., Nwaobia, N. K., Gidiagba, J. O., & Ani, E. C. (2023). Artificial intelligence in developing countries: Bridging the gap between potential and implementation. *Computer Science & IT Research Journal, 4*(3), 185–199. DOI: 10.51594/csitrj.v4i3.629

Aggarwal, S., Bansal, S., & Goel, R. (2024). Ai In Agriculture: A Looming Challenge, A Gleaming Opportunity. *International Journal of Engineering Science and Humanities, 14*(Special Issue 1), 43-52.

Ahmad, A., Liew, A. X., Venturini, F., Kalogeras, A., Candiani, A., Di Benedetto, G., Ajibola, S., Cartujo, P., Romero, P., Lykoudi, A., De Grandis, M. M., Xouris, C., Lo Bianco, R., Doddy, I., Elegbede, I., D'Urso Labate, G. F., García del Moral, L. F., & Martos, V. (2024). AI can empower agriculture for global food security: Challenges and prospects in developing nations. *Frontiers in Artificial Intelligence, 7*, 1328530. DOI: 10.3389/frai.2024.1328530 PMID: 38726306

Ahmed, M. N., Singh, A. P., Hussain, M. R., Rasool, M. A., Khan, I. M., & Dildar, M. S. (2024, July). Enhancing Crop Production using Artificial Intelligence in Agricultural Revolution. In *2024 IEEE 7th International Conference on Advanced Technologies* [ATSIP]. *Signal and Image Processing : an International Journal, 1*, 432–437.

Aithal, P. S., & Aithal, S. (2023). Application of ChatGPT in higher education and research–A futuristic analysis. [IJAEML]. *International Journal of Applied Engineering and Management Letters*, *7*(3), 168–194. DOI: 10.47992/IJAEML.2581.7000.0193

Ajiye, O. T., & Omokhabi, A. A. (2025). THE POTENTIAL AND ETHICAL ISSUES OF ARTIFICIAL INTELLIGENCE IN IMPROVING ACADEMIC WRITING. *ShodhAI: Journal of Artificial Intelligence*, *2*(1), 1–9. DOI: 10.29121/shodhai.v2.i1.2025.24

Akindele, A., & Chabinga, R. (2024). Navigating Climate Change and Sustainability Solutions: Nigeria's Role in International Environmental Law. *African Journal of Climate Change and Resource Sustainability*, *3*(1), 331–344. DOI: 10.37284/ajccrs.3.1.2188

Akuthota, V., Kasula, R., & Sumona, S. T. (2023). *Vulnerability detection and monitoring using LLM*. IEEE. https://ieeexplore.ieee.org/abstract/document/10456393/

Alahdab, F. (2024). Potential impact of large language models on academic writing. *BMJ Evidence-Based Medicine*, *29*(3), 201–202. DOI: 10.1136/bmjebm-2023-112429 PMID: 37620013

Alexander, C. S., Yarborough, M., & Smith, A. (2024). Who is responsible for 'responsible AI'?: Navigating challenges to build trust in AI agriculture and food system technology. *Precision Agriculture*, *25*(1), 146–185. DOI: 10.1007/s11119-023-10063-3

Alghamdy, R. Z. (2023). Pedagogical and ethical implications of artificial intelligence in EFL context: A review study. *English Language Teaching*, *16*(10), 87–98. DOI: 10.5539/elt.v16n10p87

Ali, A., Anderson, L., Venturini, F., Athanasios, K., Candiani, A., Di Benedetto, G., ... & Martos, V. (2024). AI can empower agriculture for global food security: challenges and prospects in developing nations.

Ali, A. (2024). Navigating Road for Net Zero Policies to Aligning Policy, Politics, and Governance for Environmental Sustainability. In *Transition Towards a Sustainable Future: Net Zero Policies and Environmental Sustainability* (pp. 205–230). Springer Nature Singapore. DOI: 10.1007/978-981-97-5756-5_10

Ali, B., Gregory, M. A., & Li, S. (2023). Trust-aware task load balancing in multi-access edge computing based on blockchain and a Zero Trust security capability framework. *Transactions on Emerging Telecommunications Technologies, 34*(12), 34. DOI: 10.1002/ett.4845

Ali, G., Mijwil, M. M., Buruga, B. A., Abotaleb, M., & Adamopoulos, I. (2024). A survey on artificial intelligence in cybersecurity for smart agriculture: State-of-the-art, cyber threats, artificial intelligence applications, and ethical concerns. *Mesopotamian Journal of Computer Science, 2024*, 53–103. DOI: 10.58496/MJCSC/2024/007

Ali, H., & Aysan, A. F. (2024). Decoding Future of Generative AI in Finance: A Machine Learning Exploration of Academic and Grey Corpus. *Available atSSRN* 4787211. DOI: 10.2139/ssrn.4787211

Ali, H., & Aysan, A. F. (2025). Ethical dimensions of generative AI: A cross-domain analysis using machine learning structural topic modeling. *International Journal of Ethics and Systems, 41*(1), 3–34. DOI: 10.1108/IJOES-04-2024-0112

Ali, H., Zafar, M. B., & Aysan, A. F. (2024). Generative AI and Finance: A Multi-level Machine Learning Based Analysis. *Available atSSRN* 5129013.

Aljuaid, H. (2024). The impact of artificial intelligence tools on academic writing instruction in higher education: A systematic review. *Arab World English Journal (AWEJ) Special Issue on ChatGPT.*

Aloamaka, P. C. (2024). Navigating the Climate Crisis: Exploring International Law's Evolution and Application. *GLS Law Journal, 6*(1), 48–58. DOI: 10.69974/glslawjournal.v6i1.127

AlSamhori, A. F., & Alnaimat, F. (2024). Artificial intelligence in writing and research: Ethical implications and best practices. *Central Asian Journal of Medical Hypotheses and Ethics = Central'noaziatskij Zurnal Medicinskich Gipotez i Etiki = Medicinalyk Gipoteza Men Ètikanyn Orta Aziâlyk Zurnaly, 5*(4), 259–268. DOI: 10.47316/cajmhe.2024.5.4.02

Al-Sherman, N., & Aldabousi, A. M. (2024). The Complementary Penalties Enforced to Combat Corporate Crimes in UAE Law. *Pakistan Journal of Criminology, 16*(3).

Al-Sinani, H. S., & Mitchell, C. J. (2024). AI-enhanced ethical hacking: A Linux-focused experiment. *arXiv preprint arXiv:2410.05105.*

Al-Sinani, H. S., Sahli, N., Mitchell, C. J., & Al-Siyabi, M. (2025). Advancing ethical hacking with AI: A Linux-based experimental study. *Proceedings of ITASEC and SERICS, Bologna, Italy (Feb 2025),* https://www. chrismitchell. net/Papers/aehwaa. pdf

Amani, B. (2007). *Merchants missionaries: Patenting life, competing international obligations and the proselytization of a Realistic Utopia.*

Amaral, C., Paiva, M., Rodrigues, A. R., Veiga, F., & Bell, V. (2024). Global regulatory challenges for medical devices: Impact on innovation and market access. *Applied Sciences (Basel, Switzerland), 14*(20), 9304. DOI: 10.3390/app14209304

Araújo, S. O., Peres, R. S., Barata, J., Lidon, F., & Ramalho, J. C. (2021). Characterising the agriculture 4.0 landscape—Emerging trends, challenges and opportunities. *Agronomy (Basel), 11*(4), 667. DOI: 10.3390/agronomy11040667

Arya, L., & Rastogi, R. (2024). Study on Aerial Monitoring System in Agriculture, Forestry, Defense, and Border Protection Using Artificial Intelligence (AI). In *Agriculture and Aquaculture Applications of Biosensors and Bioelectronics* (pp. 392-407). IGI Global Scientific Publishing.

Asad, A. (2021). From bureaucratic-centralism management to school based management: managing human resources in the management of education program. *Indonesian Research Journal in Education| IRJE|, 5*(1), 201–225.

Asiri, E. A. S., Bin-Hady, W., & Sahari, Y. (2024). Assessing the Degree of Compliance with the Ethical Principles of the'Translator's Professional Guide'amongst Translators in Saudi Arabia. *Jurnal Arbitrer, 11*(2), 109–122. DOI: 10.25077/ar.11.2.109-122.2024

Aslam, M. S., & Nisar, S. (2024). Ethical Considerations for Artificial Intelligence Tools in Academic Research and Manuscript Preparation: A Web Content Analysis. In *Digital Transformation in Higher Education, Part B: Cases, Examples and Good Practices* (pp. 155-196). Emerald Publishing Limited. DOI: 10.1108/978-1-83608-424-220241007

Awa, H. O., Etim, W., & Ogbonda, E. (2024). Stakeholders, stakeholder theory and corporate social responsibility (CSR). *International Journal of Corporate Social Responsibility, 9*(1), 11. DOI: 10.1186/s40991-024-00094-y

AWS. (2024). Phased approach to Zero Trust. *Amazon Web Services.* Retrieved fromh ttps://docs.aws.amazon.com/prescriptive-guidance/latest/strategy-zero-trust - a rchitecture/phased-migration.html

Backman, S. (2023). *Making sense of large-scale cyber incidents: International cybersecurity beyond threat-based security perspectives. Department of Economic History and I nternational Relations*. Stockholm University.

BaHammam, A. S. (2023). Balancing innovation and integrity: The role of AI in research and scientific writing. *Nature and Science of Sleep*, •••, 1153–1156. PMID: 38170140

Bahrini, A., Khamoshifar, M., Abbasimehr, H., Riggs, R. J., Esmaeili, M., Majdabadkohne, R. M., & Pasehvar, M. (2023, April). ChatGPT: Applications, opportunities, and threats. In *2023 Systems and Information Engineering Design Symposium (SIEDS)* (pp. 274-279). IEEE. DOI: 10.1109/SIEDS58326.2023.10137850

Bain, L. E., Tchuisseu-Kwangoua, L. A., Adeagbo, O., Nkfusai, N. C., Amu, H., Saah, F. I., & Kombe, F. (2022). Fostering research integrity in sub-Saharan Africa: Challenges, opportunities, and recommendations. *The Pan African Medical Journal*, *43*(1). Advance online publication. DOI: 10.11604/pamj.2022.43.182.37804 PMID: 36923394

Banta, N. M. (2019). Electronic wills and digital assets: Reassessing formality in the digital age. *Baylor Law Review*, *71*, 547.

Bartkowski, B., Theesfeld, I., Pirscher, F., & Timaeus, J. (2018). Snipping around for food: Economic, ethical and policy implications of CRISPR/Cas genome editing. *Geoforum*, *96*, 172–180. DOI: 10.1016/j.geoforum.2018.07.017

Batabyal, G. S. (2024). Ethics, laws on war and artificial intelligence-driven warfare. In *Artificial intelligence, ethics and the future of warfare* (pp. 187–215). Routledge India. DOI: 10.4324/9781003421849-9

Benabed, A., & Tudoran, L. (2023). Artificial intelligence towards international regulations, frameworks and laws in the world of globalization: Implications and challenges. *Persp. L. Pub. Admin.*, *12*, 268.

Bhangar, N. A., & Shahriyar, A. K. (2023). Iot and ai for next-generation farming: Opportunities, challenges, and outlook. *International Journal of Sustainable Infrastructure for Cities and Societies*, *8*(2), 14–26.

Bharwani, S., & Mathews, D. (2012). Risk identification and analysis in the hospitality industry: Practitioners' perspectives from India. *Worldwide Hospitality and Tourism Themes*, *4*(5), 410–427. DOI: 10.1108/17554211211277851

Bhat, S. A., & Huang, N. F. (2021). Big data and ai revolution in precision agriculture: Survey and challenges. *IEEE Access : Practical Innovations, Open Solutions*, *9*, 110209–110222. DOI: 10.1109/ACCESS.2021.3102227

Bhusa, G., & Shrestha, B. (2024). *The role of PASTA in addressing future trends in regulatory compliance: Emerging cyber threats. International Journal of Innovative Science and Research Technology*. IJISRT.

BigScience Workshop. (2022). *BLOOM: A 176B-Parameter Open-Access Multilingual Language Model.* https://huggingface.co/bigscience/bloom

Borta, H. G., Alemu, A., Shute, T., Zewdie, B., Fantaw, D., Shimelis, B., ... & Tamiru, M. T. (2024). Narcotic Drugs and Psychotropic Substances Control System in Ethiopia: A National Survey.

Bousri, M. M. S. (2019). *A comparative analysis of legal and institutional framework for arbitration: Comoros and Uganda* (Doctoral dissertation, School of law).

Bradley, C. A. (2021). Reassessing the Legislative Veto: The Statutory President, Foreign Affairs, and Congressional Workarounds. *The Journal of Legal Analysis*, *13*(1), 439–501. DOI: 10.1093/jla/laab008

Brookes, G., & Smyth, S. J. (2024). Risk-appropriate regulations for gene-editing technologies. *GM Crops and Food: Biotechnology in Agriculture and the Food Chain*, *15*(1), 1–14. DOI: 10.1080/21645698.2023.2293510 PMID: 38215017

Brown, T., et al. (2020). *Language models are few-shot learners.* NeurIPS.

Bush, M., & Mashatan, A. (2022). From Zero to One Hundred. *ACM Queue; Tomorrow's Computing Today*, *20*(4), 80–106. DOI: 10.1145/3561799

Butt, J. (2024). Analytical study of the world's first EU Artificial Intelligence (AI) Act. *International Journal of Research Publication and Reviews*, *5*(3), 7343–7364. DOI: 10.55248/gengpi.5.0324.0914

Calvert, M. J., Marston, E., Samuels, M., Rivera, S. C., Torlinska, B., Oliver, K., Denniston, A. K., & Hoare, S. (2021). Advancing UK regulatory science and innovation in healthcare. *Journal of the Royal Society of Medicine*, *114*(1), 5–11. DOI: 10.1177/0141076820961776 PMID: 33043790

Campus, M. T. (2024). Quantum Machine Learning, Leveraging Al, and. *Integration of AI, Quantum Computing, and Semiconductor Technology*, 57.

Casal, J. E., & Kessler, M. (2023). Can linguists distinguish between ChatGPT/AI and human writing?: A study of research ethics and academic publishing. *Research Methods in Applied Linguistics*, *2*(3), 100068. DOI: 10.1016/j.rmal.2023.100068

Cath, C. (2018). Governing artificial intelligence: Ethical, legal and technical opportunities and challenges. *Philosophical Transactions. Series A, Mathematical, Physical, and Engineering Sciences, 376*(2133), 20180080. DOI: 10.1098/rsta.2018.0080 PMID: 30322996

Cauchon, N. S., Oghamian, S., Hassanpour, S., & Abernathy, M. (2019). Innovation in chemistry, manufacturing, and controls—A regulatory perspective from industry. *Journal of Pharmaceutical Sciences, 108*(7), 2207–2237. DOI: 10.1016/j.xphs.2019.02.007 PMID: 30794794

Cavalerie, L., Wardeh, M., Lebrasseur, O., Nanyingi, M., McIntyre, K. M., Kaba, M., Asrat, D., Christley, R., Pinchbeck, G., Baylis, M., & Mor, S. M. (2021). One hundred years of zoonoses research in the Horn of Africa: A scoping review. *PLoS Neglected Tropical Diseases, 15*(7), e0009607. DOI: 10.1371/journal.pntd.0009607 PMID: 34270551

Cazac, O. (2012). Towards a comprehensive concept of termination of contracts. *Revista Moldovenească de Drept Internaţional şi Relaţii Internaţionale, 25*(3), 75-92.

Chatterjee, S., Chaudhuri, R., Kumar, A., Wang, C. L., & Gupta, S. (2023). Impacts of consumer cognitive process to ascertain online fake review: A cognitive dissonance theory approach. *Journal of Business Research, 154*, 113370. DOI: 10.1016/j.jbusres.2022.113370

Chen, S., & Song, Q. (2005). Perimeter-based defense against high bandwidth DDoS attacks. *IEEE Transactions on Parallel and Distributed Systems, 16*(6), 526–537. DOI: 10.1109/TPDS.2005.74

Chen, T., Lv, L., Wang, D., Zhang, J., Yang, Y., Zhao, Z., & Tao, D. (2024). Empowering agrifood system with artificial intelligence: A survey of the progress, challenges and opportunities. *ACM Computing Surveys, 57*(2), 1–37.

Chetwynd, E. (2024). Ethical use of artificial intelligence for scientific writing: Current trends. *Journal of Human Lactation, 40*(2), 211–215. DOI: 10.1177/08903344241235160 PMID: 38482810

Chowdhury, S. (2024). Towards a Just Climate: Navigating Complexities and Challenges in Climate Change Discourse and Action. *Issue 2 Int'l JL Mgmt. &. Human., 7*, 1807.

Cisco. (n.d.). *Zero trust outcomes report*. Cisco. https://www.cisco.com/c/en/us/products/security/zero-trust-outcomes-report.html

Colangelo, M. (2017). Reverse payment patent settlements in the pharmaceutical sector under EU and US competition laws: a comparative analysis. *World competition, 40*(3).

Conway, N., & Chisholm, O. (2024). Building a Competency Framework to Integrate Inter-disciplinary Precision Medicine Capabilities into the Medical Technology and Pharmaceutical Industry. *Therapeutic Innovation & Regulatory Science*, *58*(3), 567–577. DOI: 10.1007/s43441-024-00626-5 PMID: 38491262

Cooper, S. E. (2018). *The End of an Era? Social Housing and Social Property in a Post-subsidy World* (Doctoral dissertation, University of Illinois Chicago).

Cooper, S., & Zell, S. (2023). *Staying on Board: Non-profit housing provider board capacity in a changing context*. Institute of Urban Studies, The University of Winnipeg.

CrowdStrike. (2024). *CrowdStrike 2024 Global Threat Report | CrowdStrike*. Crowdstrike.com. https://www.crowdstrike.com/en-us/global-threat-report/

Daah, C., Qureshi, A., Awan, I., & Konur, S. (2024). Enhancing zero trust models in the f inancial industry through blockchain integration: A proposed framework. *Electronics (Basel)*, *13*(5), 865. DOI: 10.3390/electronics13050865

Daniel, J. (2024). *Environmental Law: Navigating Legal Pathways for a Sustainable Future*. Pencil.

Dara, R., Hazrati Fard, S. M., & Kaur, J. (2022). Recommendations for ethical and responsible use of artificial intelligence in digital agriculture. *Frontiers in Artificial Intelligence*, *5*, 884192. DOI: 10.3389/frai.2022.884192 PMID: 35968036

Darvishi, K., Liu, L., & Lim, S. (2022). Navigating the Nexus: Legal and Economic Implications of Emerging Tech-nologies. *Law and Economics*, *16*(3), 172–186. DOI: 10.35335/laweco.v16i3.59

Dehaini, K. Y. (2021). *Contracts Termination: Main Contract vs Subcontract Back-to-Back Practices* (Doctoral dissertation).

Dembani, R., Karvelas, I., Akbar, N. A., Rizou, S., Tegolo, D., & Fountas, S. (2025). Agricultural data privacy and federated learning: A review of challenges and opportunities. *Computers and Electronics in Agriculture*, *232*, 110048. DOI: 10.1016/j.compag.2025.110048

Dempsey, K., Chawla, N., Johnson, L., Johnston, R., Jones, A., Orebaugh, A., Scholl, M., & Stine, K. (2011). Information security continuous monitoring (ISCM) for federal i nformation systems and organizations (NIST Special Publication 800-137). National Institute of Standards and Technology. https://csrc.nist.gov/publications/detail/sp/800- 137/final

Denhere, V., & Shao, D. (2024). Artificial Intelligence in Agritourism: Utilitarian Analysis of Opportunities, Challenges, and Ethical Considerations in the African Context. *Agritourism in Africa*, 17-36.

Devare, M., Arnaud, E., Antezana, E., & King, B. (2023). Governing agricultural data: Challenges and recommendations. *Towards Responsible Plant Data Linkage: Data Challenges for Agricultural Research and Development, 201.*

Devlin, J., Chang, M. W., Lee, K., & Toutanova, K. (2018). *BERT: Pre-training of deep bidirectional transformers for language understanding*. arXiv:1810.04805.

Diaz Rivera, J. J., Muhammad, A., & Song, W. (2024). Securing digital identity in the zero trust architecture: A blockchain approach to privacy-focused multi-factor authentication. *IEEE Open Journal of the Communications Society, 5*, 2792-2814. https://DOI: <ALIGNMENT.qj></ALIGNMENT>10.1109/OJCOMS.2024.3250511

Dinçer, S. (2024). The use and ethical implications of artificial intelligence in scientific research and academic writing. *Educational Research & Implementation, 1*(2), 139–144. DOI: 10.14527/edure.2024.10

Drexl, J., Conde, B., & Kim, D. (2025). Position Statement of the Max Planck Institute for Innovation and Competition of 25 April 2025 in the framework of the revision of the Technology Transfer Block Exemption Regulation and the accompanying Guidelines. *Max Planck Institute for Innovation & Competition Research Paper*, (25-10).

Durrett, D. M. (2022, January 28). *(Zero) Trust but Verify*. Stamus Networks. Retrieved from https://www.stamus-networks.com/blog/zero-trust-but-verify

Du, X., Zheng, G., Wang, K., Feng, J., Deng, W., & Liu, M. (2024). *Vul-RAG: Enhancing LLM-based vulnerability detection via knowledge-level RAG*. https://arxiv.org/abs/2406.11147

Eberlin, M. N. (2024). The Art of Scientific Writing and Ethical Use of Artificial Intelligence. *Journal of the Brazilian Chemical Society*, *35*(1), e-20230121.

Eisenberg, D. (2024). *Sensing With Integrity: Responsible Sensor Systems in an Era of AI* (Doctoral dissertation, New Jersey Institute of Technology).

Eitrem, A., Meidell, A., & Modell, S. (2024). The use of institutional theory in social and environmental accounting research: A critical review. *Accounting and Business Research*, *54*(7), 775–810. DOI: 10.1080/00014788.2024.2328934

Emerson, R. W. (2025). Franchise Noncompetes: Their Legal Effect, Practical Impact, and Superior Alternatives. *The Journal of Corporation Law*, *50*(3).

Emon, M. M. H., Khan, T., Rahman, M. A., Hamid, A. B. A., & Yaakub, N. I. (2025). GreenTech revolution: Navigating challenges and seizing opportunities. In *AI and green technology applications in society* (pp. 63–90). IGI Global Scientific Publishing.

Ersöz, A. R., & Engin, M. (2024). Exploring Ethical Dilemmas in the Use of Artificial Intelligence in Academic Writing: Perspectives of Researchers. *Journal of Uludag University Faculty of Education, 37*(3), 1190–1208. DOI: 10.19171/uefad.1514323

Espenlaub, S., Goergen, M., Khurshed, A., & Remenar, M. (2013). Do directors trade after IPO lockup expiry? In *Handbook of Research on IPOs* (pp. 275–294). Edward Elgar Publishing. DOI: 10.4337/9781781955376.00024

Espino, A. R. C., Esto, M. R. A., Manalo, C. G. S., Santiago, C. S., & Pragacha, R. N. (2024, June). Ethical Implications of Using Assistive Writing Tools in the Academe: A Literature Review. In *International Conference on Frontiers of Intelligent Computing: Theory and Applications* (pp. 133-145). Singapore: Springer Nature Singapore.

Estreicher, S., & Hirsch, J. M. (2013). Comparative Wrongful Dismissal Law: Reassessing American Exceptionalism. *SSRN, 92*, 343. DOI: 10.2139/ssrn.2238776

Eswaran, U., & Eswaran, V. (2025). Quantum Machine Learning, Leveraging AI, and Semiconductor Technology. In *Integration of AI, Quantum Computing, and Semiconductor Technology* (pp. 57-78). IGI Global.

Farah, P. D., & Varela, J. C. (2023). Science, Technology, Society, and Law. In *Science, Technology, Policy and International Law* (pp. 1-19). Routledge.

Federici, F., Martintoni, D., & Senni, V. (2023). A zero-trust architecture for remote access in industrial IoT infrastructures. *Electronics, 12*(3), 566. h t t p s://DOI: 10.3390/electronics12030566

Fedoriv, Y., Shuhai, A., & Pirozhenko, I. (2024). Foundations of Ethical Use of AI in EFL Academic Writing.

Fenwick, A., Molnar, G., & Frangos, P. (2024). The critical role of HRM in AI-driven digital transformation: A paradigm shift to enable firms to move from AI implementation to human-centric adoption. *Discover Artificial Intelligence, 4*(1), 34. DOI: 10.1007/s44163-024-00125-4

Filetti, S., Fenza, G., & Gallo, A. (2024). Research design and writing of scholarly articles: New artificial intelligence tools available for researchers. *Endocrine, 85*(3), 1104–1116. DOI: 10.1007/s12020-024-03977-z PMID: 39085566

Fischer, A., Fuhry, B., Kußmaul, J., Janneck, J., Kerschbaum, F., & Bodden, E. (2022). C omputation on encrypted data using dataflow authentication. *ACM Transactions on Privacy and Security, 25*(3), 1–36. DOI: 10.1145/3513005

Flannery, J., Ajayi, S. O., & Oyegoke, A. S. (2021). Alcohol and substance misuse in the construction industry. *International Journal of Occupational Safety and Ergonomics, 27*(2), 472–487. DOI: 10.1080/10803548.2019.1601376 PMID: 30935301

Forrester. (n.d.). *Building a Zero Trust roadmap: A practical guide*. Forrester. ht t ps://www.forrester.com/blogs/building-a-zero-trust-roadmap-a-practical-guide/

Friedrichs, S., Takasu, Y., Kearns, P., Dagallier, B., Oshima, R., Schofield, J., & Moreddu, C. (2019). An overview of regulatory approaches to genome editing in agriculture. *Biotechnology Research and Innovation, 3*(2), 208–220. DOI: 10.1016/j.biori.2019.07.001

Gai, K., She, Y., Zhu, L., Choo, K. R., & Wan, Z. (2022). A blockchain-based access control scheme for zero trust cross-organizational data sharing. *ACM Transactions on Internet Technology, 23*(3), 1–25. DOI: 10.1145/3511899

Gajbhiye, B., Jain, S., & Goel, O. (2023). *Defense in depth strategies for Zero Trust security models*. Darpan International Research Analysis.

Garden, H., & Winickoff, D. (2018). Gene editing for advanced therapies GOVERNANCE, POLICY AND SOCIETY. *OECD Science, Technology and Industry Working Papers, 2018*(12), 0_1-46.

Gardezi, M., Joshi, B., Rizzo, D. M., Ryan, M., Prutzer, E., Brugler, S., & Dadkhah, A. (2024). Artificial intelligence in farming: Challenges and opportunities for building trust. *Agronomy Journal, 116*(3), 1217–1228. DOI: 10.1002/agj2.21353

Gartner. (2024, April 22). Gartner survey reveals 63 percent of organizations worldwide have implemented a Zero Trust strategy. Gartner. ht t p s : / /www.gartner.com/en/newsroom/press-releases/2024-04-22-gartner-survey-reveals-63-_percent-of-organizations-worldwide-have-implemented-a-zero-trust-strategy

Gaurav, A., Chui, K. T., Arya, V., Attar, R. W., Bansal, S., Alhomoud, A., & Psannis, K. (2024). Optimized AI-Driven Semantic Web Approach for Enhancing Phishing Detection in E-Commerce Platforms. [IJSWIS]. *International Journal on Semantic Web and Information Systems, 20*(1), 1–13. DOI: 10.4018/IJSWIS.359767

Gavai, A. K., Bouzembrak, Y., Xhani, D., Sedrakyan, G., Meuwissen, M. P., Souza, R. G. S., ... & van Hillegersberg, J. (2025). Agricultural data Privacy: Emerging platforms & strategies. *Food and Humanity*, 100542.

Gavou, T. P., Iliya, J., Ihuoma, E. C., & Gusen, J. N. (2024). *Cyber security enhancement in Nigeria: A case study of six states in the North Central (Middle Belt) of Nigeria. American Journal of Humanities and Social*

Ghaffarian, S. M., & Shahriari, H. R. (2017). Software Vulnerability Analysis and Discovery Using Machine-Learning and Data-Mining Techniques. *ACM Computing Surveys*, *50*(4), 1–36. DOI: 10.1145/3092566

Ghanad, A. (2023). An overview of quantitative research methods. *International Journal of Multidisciplinary Research and Analysis*, *6*(08), 3794–3803. DOI: 10.47191/ijmra/v6-i8-52

Ghasemshirazi, S., Shirvani, G., & Alipour, M. A. (2023). Zero trust: Applications, challenges, and opportunities. *arXiv Preprint.* https://arxiv.org/pdf/2309.03582v1

Gholami, S., & Omar, M. (2023). Does Synthetic Data Make Large Language Models More Efficient? *arXiv preprint arXiv:2310.07830.*

Gholami, S., & Omar, M. (2024). Can a student large language model perform as well as its teacher? In *Innovations, Securities, and Case Studies Across Healthcare, Business, and Technology* (pp. 122-139). IGI Global. DOI: 10.4018/979-8-3693-1906-2.ch007

Girasa, R. (2020). *Artificial intelligence as a disruptive technology: Economic transformation and government regulation.* Springer Nature. DOI: 10.1007/978-3-030-35975-1

Goh, H. H., & Vinuesa, R. (2021). Regulating artificial-intelligence applications to achieve the sustainable development goals. *Discover Sustainability*, *2*(1), 1–6. DOI: 10.1007/s43621-021-00064-5 PMID: 35425914

Google Research. (2024). GEMINI-pro 1.0: Leveraging Large Language Models for Code Analysis. Google. https://gemini.google.com/

Goyal, K. (2017). *Overlapping of Intellectual Property Rights: An analysis with reference to conflict vis-à-vis Design, Trademark, Copyright and Patent.* College of Legal Studies, UPES Dehradun.

Granjeiro, J. M., Cury, A. A. D. B., Cury, J. A., Bueno, M., Sousa-Neto, M. D., & Estrela, C. (2025). The Future of Scientific Writing: AI Tools, Benefits, and Ethical Implications. *Brazilian Dental Journal*, *36*, e25–e6471. DOI: 10.1590/0103-644020256471 PMID: 40197923

Grosskopf, O. (2011). Dividing the surplus upon termination: The case of relational contracts. *American Business Law Journal*, *48*(1), 1–26. DOI: 10.1111/j.1744-1714.2010.01110.x

Groumpos, P. P. (2023, July). A critical historic overview of artificial intelligence: Issues, challenges, opportunities, and threats. *Artificial Intelligence and Applications (Commerce, Calif.)*, *1*(4), 181–197. DOI: 10.47852/bonviewAIA3202689

Guerra-Bretaña, R. M., & Flórez-Rendón, A. L. (2018). Impact of regulations on innovation in the field of medical devices. *Research on Biomedical Engineering*, *34*(4), 356–367. DOI: 10.1590/2446-4740.180054

Guha, N., Nyarko, J., Ho, D., Ré, C., Chilton, A., Chohlas-Wood, A., & Li, Z. (2023). Legalbench: A collaboratively built benchmark for measuring legal reasoning in large language models. *SSRN*, *36*, 44123–44279. DOI: 10.2139/ssrn.4583531

Guleria, A., Krishan, K., Sharma, V., & Kanchan, T. (2023). ChatGPT: Ethical concerns and challenges in academics and research. *Journal of Infection in Developing Countries*, *17*(09), 1292–1299. DOI: 10.3855/jidc.18738 PMID: 37824352

Guo, Y., Patsakis, C., Hu, Q., Tang, Q., & Casino, F. (2024). *Outside the comfort zone: Analysing LLM capabilities in software vulnerability detection*. https://link.springer.com/chapter/10.1007/978-3-031-70879-4_14

Gupta, D. K., Pagani, A., Zamboni, P., & Singh, A. K. (2024). AI-powered revolution in plant sciences: Advancements, applications, and challenges for sustainable agriculture and food security. *Exploration of Foods and Foodomics*, *2*(5), 443–459. DOI: 10.37349/eff.2024.00045

Hamza, Y. A., & Omar, M. D. (2013). Cloud computing security: Abuse and nefarious use of cloud computing. *International Journal of Computer Engineering Research*, *3*(6), 22–27.

Han, Y., Fan, L. L., & Xue, Y. (2024). A sustainable balance between innovation and risk: How the "right to science" affects China's medical biotechnology regulatory policy. *Computational and Structural Biotechnology Journal*, *24*, 306–313. DOI: 10.1016/j.csbj.2024.04.027 PMID: 38681134

Harati, K. (2024). ChatGPT and AI-Powered Writing Tools: Unveiling Risks and Ethical Challenges in Scientific Writing. *Journal of Research in Medical Sciences : the Official Journal of Isfahan University of Medical Sciences*, *4*(1), 1–6.

He, H., Gray, J., Cangelosi, A., Meng, Q., McGinnity, T. M., & Mehnen, J. (2021). The challenges and opportunities of human-centered AI for trustworthy robots and autonomous systems. *IEEE Transactions on Cognitive and Developmental Systems*, *14*(4), 1398–1412. DOI: 10.1109/TCDS.2021.3132282

Hejazi, S. S., Hosseini, M., Ebadi, A., & Alavi Majd, H. (2022). Development and psychometric properties evaluation of caregiver burden questionnaire in family caregivers of hemodialysis patients. *BMC Nursing*, *21*(1), 246. DOI: 10.1186/s12912-022-01025-7 PMID: 36064396

Hines, P. A., Guy, R. H., Brand, A., Humphreys, A. J., & Papaluca-Amati, M. (2020). Regulatory science and innovation Programme for Europe (ReScIPE): A proposed model. *British Journal of Clinical Pharmacology*, *86*(12), 2530–2534. DOI: 10.1111/bcp.14099 PMID: 31426120

Ho, C. W. (2023). Implementing the human right to science in the regulatory governance of artificial intelligence in healthcare. *Journal of Law and the Biosciences*, *10*(2), lsad026. DOI: 10.1093/jlb/lsad026 PMID: 37854168

Hodge, P. S. (2017). Judicial development of the law of contract in the United Kingdom. *Geo. Wash. L. Rev.*, *85*, 1587.

Holmen-Jensen, P. R., & Åsmoen, O. (2024). Navigating the Patent Cliff.

Holzinger, A., Weippl, E., Tjoa, A. M., & Kieseberg, P. (2021, August). Digital transformation for sustainable development goals (sdgs)-a security, safety and privacy perspective on ai. In *International cross-domain conference for machine learning and knowledge extraction* (pp. 1-20). Cham: Springer International Publishing.

Howard. (2024, May 24). From perimeter to zero trust: The evolution of cyber defense. *FS.com*.https://community.fs.com/article/from-perimeter-to-zero-trust-the-evolution-of-cyber- defense.html

Huff, A. J., Burrell, D. N., Nobles, C., Richardson, K., Wright, J. B., Burton, S. L., Jones, A. J., Springs, D., Omar, M., & Brown-Jackson, K. L. (2023). Management Practices for Mitigating Cybersecurity Threats to Biotechnology Companies, Laboratories, and Healthcare Research Organizations. In *Applied Research Approaches to Technology, Healthcare, and Business* (pp. 1-12). IGI Global.

Hughes, C., & Turner, T. (2023). *Software transparency: Supply chain security in an era of a software-driven society*. Wiley.

IBM. (2024). *Cost of a Data Breach 2024*. IBM; IBM. https://www.ibm.com/reports/data-breach

Ishwara, P., & Mekonnen, N. (2024). Ethical decision-making dynamics: Insights from professional accountants. *Cogent Business & Management*, *11*(1).

Ismail, M., & Abd El-Gawad, A. F. (2023). *Revisiting Zero-Trust security for Internet of Things*. Sustainable Machine Intelligence Journal. DOI: 10.61185/SMIJ.2023.33106

Jafarizadeh, H., Yamini, E., Zolfaghari, S. M., Esmaeilion, F., Assad, M. E. H., & Soltani, M. (2024). Navigating challenges in large-scale renewable energy storage: Barriers, solutions, and innovations. *Energy Reports*, *12*, 2179–2192. DOI: 10.1016/j.egyr.2024.08.019

Jamro, M. Y., & Jamro, F. A. (2023). AI Matters: Chatbot Integration in Holistic STEM Education.

Jerhamre, E., Carlberg, C. J. C., & van Zoest, V. (2022). Exploring the susceptibility of smart farming: Identified opportunities and challenges. *Smart Agricultural Technology*, *2*, 2. DOI: 10.1016/j.atech.2021.100026

Jones, R., Omar, M., Mohammed, D., Nobles, C., & Dawson, M. (2023). Harnessing the Speed and Accuracy of Machine Learning to Advance Cybersecurity. In *2023 Congress in Computer Science, Computer Engineering, & Applied Computing (CSCE)* (pp. 418-421). IEEE. DOI: 10.1109/CSCE60160.2023.00074

Jones, R., & Omar, M. (2024). Revolutionizing Cybersecurity: The GPT-2 Enhanced Attack Detection and Defense (GEADD) Method for Zero-Day Threats. *International Journal of Informatics* [INJIISCOM]. *Information System and Computer Engineering*, *5*(2), 178–191.

Kang, H., Liu, G., Wang, Q., & Liu, J. (2023). Theory and application of zero trust security: A brief survey. *Entropy (Basel, Switzerland)*, *25*(12), 1595. DOI: 10.3390/e25121595 PMID: 38136475

Kanyepe, J., Chibaro, M., Morima, M., & Moeti-Lysson, J. (2025). AI-Powered Agricultural Supply Chains: Applications, Challenges, and Opportunities. *Integrating Agriculture, Green Marketing Strategies, and Artificial Intelligence*, 33-64.

Kapoor, P. (2025). Harvesting Ethics: Forging Responsible Paths in AI and ML for the Agri-Food Industry. In *Food and Industry 5.0: Transforming the Food System for a Sustainable Future* (pp. 305–315). Springer Nature Switzerland. DOI: 10.1007/978-3-031-76758-6_19

Kappel, K. (2024). Navigating Zero Trust security in the remote work era: Guidance for o rganizations. *KPMG*. Retrieved from_https://kpmg.com/us/en/media/news/navigating- zero-trust-security-in-the-remote-work-era-2024.html

Karanam, R. (2024). Zero Trust architecture in DevSecOps: Enhancing security in cloud-native environments. *International Journal for Research in Applied Science and Engineering Technology*, *12*(8), 1071–1077. DOI: 10.22214/ijraset.2024.64045

Karim, R., Galar, D., & Kumar, U. (2023). *AI factory: theories, applications and case studies*. CRC Press. DOI: 10.1201/9781003208686

Kaur, J., Hasan, S. N., Orthi, S. M., Miah, M. A., Goffer, M. A., Barikdar, C. R., & Hassan, J. (2024). Advanced cyber threats and cybersecurity innovation: Strategic approaches and emerging solutions. *Journal of Computer Science and Technology Studies*.

Kaushik, K., Khan, A., Kumari, A., Sharma, I., & Dubey, R. (2024). Ethical considerations in AI-based cybersecurity. In *Next-generation cybersecurity: AI, ML, and Blockchain* (pp. 437–470). Springer Nature Singapore. DOI: 10.1007/978-981-97-1249-6_19

Khalifa, M., & Albadawy, M. (2024). Using artificial intelligence in academic writing and research: An essential productivity tool. *Computer Methods and Programs in Biomedicine Update*, *5*, 100145. DOI: 10.1016/j.cmpbup.2024.100145

Khare, A., Dutta, S., Li, Z., Solko-Breslin, A., & Alur, R. (2023). *Understanding the effectiveness of large language models in detecting security vulnerabilities*. arXiv. https://arxiv.org/abs/2311.16169

Khup, V. K., & Bantugan, B. (2025). Exploring the Impact and Ethical Implications of Integrating AI-Powered Writing Tools in Junior High School English Instruction: Enhancing Creativity, Proficiency, and Academic Outcomes. *International Journal of Research and Innovation in Social Science*, *9*(IIIS, 3s), 361–378. DOI: 10.47772/IJRISS.2025.903SEDU0022

Kindervag, J., & Balaouras, S. (2010). No more chewy centers: Introducing the zero trust model of information security. *Forrester Research, 3*.

Kirov, B. (2023, September). Artificial Intelligence in Creation of Scientific Written Works: Weighing the Benefits and Ethical Dilemmas-Should We Use It? In *2023 International Scientific Conference on Computer Science (COMSCI)* (pp. 1-5). IEEE. DOI: 10.1109/COMSCI59259.2023.10315821

Kochupillai, M., & Köninger, J. (2023). Creating a digital marketplace for agrobiodiversity and plant genetic sequence data: Legal and ethical considerations of an ai and blockchain based solution. *Towards Responsible Plant Data Linkage: Data Challenges for Agricultural Research and Development*, 223.

Kochupillai, M., Kahl, M., Schmitt, M., Taubenböck, H., & Zhu, X. X. (2022). Earth observation and artificial intelligence: Understanding emerging ethical issues and opportunities. *IEEE Geoscience and Remote Sensing Magazine*, *10*(4), 90–124. DOI: 10.1109/MGRS.2022.3208357

Kyriazos, T., & Poga-Kyriazou, M. (2023). Applied psychometrics: Estimator considerations in commonly encountered conditions in CFA, SEM, and EFA practice. *Psychology (Irvine, Calif.)*, *14*(5), 799–828. DOI: 10.4236/psych.2023.145043

Larson, D. B., Harvey, H., Rubin, D. L., Irani, N., Tse, J. R., & Langlotz, C. P. (2021). Regulatory frameworks for development and evaluation of artificial intelligence–based diagnostic imaging algorithms: Summary and recommendations. *Journal of the American College of Radiology*, *18*(3), 413–424. DOI: 10.1016/j.jacr.2020.09.060 PMID: 33096088

Leong, Y. M., Lim, E. H., Subri, N. F. B., & Jalil, N. B. A. (2023, September). Transforming agriculture: Navigating the challenges and embracing the opportunities of artificial intelligence of things. In *2023 IEEE International Conference on Agrosystem Engineering, Technology & Applications (AGRETA)* (pp. 142-147). IEEE. DOI: 10.1109/AGRETA57740.2023.10262747

Leontidis, G. (2024). Science in the age of ai: How artificial intelligence is changing the nature and method of scientific research.

Lewis, M.. (2020). *BART: Denoising sequence-to-sequence pre-training for natural language generation*. ACL.

Liang, Z., Lai, Y., Li, M., Shi, J., Lei, C. I., Hu, H., & Ung, C. O. L. (2021). Applying regulatory science in traditional chinese medicines for improving public safety and facilitating innovation in China: A scoping review and regulatory implications. *Chinese Medicine*, *16*(1), 1–16. DOI: 10.1186/s13020-021-00433-2 PMID: 33593397

Lievevrouw, E., Marelli, L., & Van Hoyweghen, I. (2021). The FDA's standard-making process for medical digital health technologies: Co-producing technological and organizational innovation. *Biosocieties*, *17*(3), 549–576. DOI: 10.1057/s41292-021-00232-w PMID: 34002115

Li, G., Liu, Y. G., & Chen, Y. (2019). Genome-editing technologies: The gap between application and policy. *Science China. Life Sciences*, *62*(11), 1534–1538. DOI: 10.1007/s11427-019-1566-1 PMID: 31686319

Li, J., Zong, H., Wu, E., Wu, R., Peng, Z., Zhao, J., Yang, L., Xie, H., & Shen, B. (2024). Exploring the potential of artificial intelligence to enhance the writing of english academic papers by non-native english-speaking medical students-the educational application of ChatGPT. *BMC Medical Education*, *24*(1), 736. DOI: 10.1186/s12909-024-05738-y PMID: 38982429

Lim, D. (2013). Patent misuse and antitrust: Rebirth or false dawn. *Michigan Telecommunications and Technology Law Review*, *20*, 299.

Liu, Z., Yang, Z., & Liao, Q. (2024). *Exploration on prompting LLM with code-specific information for vulnerability detection*. https://ieeexplore.ieee.org/abstract/document/10664399/

Liu, C., Tan, R., Wu, Y., Feng, Y., Jin, Z., Zhang, F., Liu, Y., & Liu, Q. (2024). Dissecting zero trust: Research landscape and its i mplementation in IoT. *Cybersecurity*, *7*(1), 20. DOI: 10.1186/s42400-024-00212-0

Liu, Y.. (2019). *RoBERTa: A robustly optimized BERT pretraining approach*. arXiv:1907.11692

Liu, Y., Kong, W., & Merve, K. (2025). ChatGPT applications in academic writing: A review of potential, limitations, and ethical challenges. *Arquivos Brasileiros de Oftalmologia*, *88*(3), e2024–e0269. DOI: 10.5935/0004-2749.2024-0269 PMID: 39879415

Li, Y.. (2024). *Attention is all you need for LLM-based code vulnerability localization*. https://arxiv.org/abs/2410.15288

Li, Z., Dutta, S., & Naik, M. (2024). *LLM-assisted static analysis for detecting security vulnerabilities*. https://arxiv.org/abs/2405.17238

Lu, G., Ju, X., Chen, X., Pei, W., & Cai, Z. (2024). *GRACE: Empowering LLM-based software vulnerability detection with graph structure and in-context learning*. https://www.sciencedirect.com/science/article/pii/S0164121224000748

Lu, S., Liu, D., Wang, D., & Xu, L. (2021). CodeXGLUE: A Machine Learning Benchmark Dataset for Code Understanding and Generation. *arXiv preprint arXiv:2102.04664*. https://arxiv.org/abs/2102.04664

Luan, H., Perron, B. E., Victor, B. G., Wan, G., Niu, Y., & Xiao, X. (2024). Using artificial intelligence to support scientometric analysis of scholarly literature: A case example of research on mainland China's left-behind children. *Journal of the Society for Social Work and Research*, *15*(3), 435–457. DOI: 10.1086/731613

Lund, B. D., Wang, T., Mannuru, N. R., Nie, B., Shimray, S., & Wang, Z. (2023). ChatGPT and a new academic reality: Artificial Intelligence-written research papers and the ethics of the large language models in scholarly publishing. *Journal of the Association for Information Science and Technology*, *74*(5), 570–581. DOI: 10.1002/asi.24750

MacNeil, M., Koch, M., Kuspinar, A., Juzwishin, D., Lehoux, P., & Stolee, P. (2019). Enabling health technology innovation in Canada: Barriers and facilitators in policy and regulatory processes. *Health Policy (Amsterdam)*, *123*(2), 203–214. DOI: 10.1016/j.healthpol.2018.09.018 PMID: 30352755

Maennig, W. (2014). Inefficiency of the anti-doping system: Cost reduction proposals. *Substance Use & Misuse*, *49*(9), 1201–1205. DOI: 10.3109/10826084.2014.912065 PMID: 24832718

Maguluri, L. P., Arularasan, A. N., & Boopathi, S. (2023). Assessing security concerns for ai-based drones in smart cities. In *Effective AI, Blockchain, and E-Governance Applications for Knowledge Discovery and Management* (pp. 27-47). IGI Global Scientific Publishing. DOI: 10.4018/978-1-6684-9151-5.ch002

Malhotra, K., & Firdaus, M. (2022). Application of artificial intelligence in IoT security for crop yield prediction. *ResearchBerg Review of Science and Technology*, *2*(1), 136–157.

Malik, V. (2024). Securing AI-native application workloads with zero trust: Preventing LLM attacks and poisoning. *Cloud Security Alliance*. Retrieved from https://cloudsecurityalliance.org/blog/2024/05/23/securing-ai-native-application-workloads-with-zero-trust-preventing-llm-attacks-and-poisoning

Manganelli, A. G. (2019). Reverse payments and risk of bankruptcy under private information. *International Journal of the Economics of Business*, *26*(3), 411–429. DOI: 10.1080/13571516.2019.1613146

Manning, L., Brewer, S., Craigon, P. J., Frey, J., Gutierrez, A., Jacobs, N., Kanza, S., Munday, S., Sacks, J., & Pearson, S. (2022). Artificial intelligence and ethics within the food sector: Developing a common language for technology adoption across the supply chain. *Trends in Food Science & Technology*, *125*, 33–42. DOI: 10.1016/j.tifs.2022.04.025

Mao, Q., Li, Z., Hu, X., Liu, K., Xia, X., & Sun, J. (2024). *Towards effectively detecting and explaining vulnerabilities using large language models*. arXiv. https://arxiv.org/html/2406.09701v2

Maresova, P. (2022). Impact of Regulatory Changes on Innovations in the Medical Device Industry: Comment on" Clinical Decision Support and New Regulatory Frameworks for Medical Devices: Are We Ready for It?-A Viewpoint Paper. *International Journal of Health Policy and Management*, *12*, 7262. DOI: 10.34172/ijhpm.2022.7262 PMID: 35942961

Margalit, Y., Levy, O., & Loike, J. (2014). The new frontier of advanced reproductive technology: Reevaluating modern legal parenthood. *Harvard Journal of Law & Gender*, *37*, 107.

Mark, R. (2019). Ethics of using AI and big data in agriculture: The case of a large agriculture multinational. *The ORBIT Journal*, *2*(2), 1–27. DOI: 10.29297/orbit.v2i2.109

Ma, X., Li, R., Lu, Z., Lu, J., & Dong, M. (2011). Specifying and enforcing the principle of least privilege in role-based access control. *Concurrency and Computation*, *23*(2), 203–215. DOI: 10.1002/cpe.1731

McBratney, A. (2004). Post-WTO China: Competition and Technology Transfer Laws in the 'New' Socialist Market Economy. *Asia Pacific Law Review*, *12*(1), 1–30. DOI: 10.1080/18758444.2004.11788126

Mennella, C., Maniscalco, U., De Pietro, G., & Esposito, M. (2024). Ethical and regulatory challenges of AI technologies in healthcare: A narrative review. *Heliyon*, *10*(4), e26297. DOI: 10.1016/j.heliyon.2024.e26297 PMID: 38384518

Mhia-Alddin, D. A., & Hussein, A. M. (2025). AI-Powered Contract Security: Managing Expiry, Compliance, and Risk Mitigation Through Deep Learning and LLMs. In *Revolutionizing Cybersecurity With Deep Learning and Large Language Models* (pp. 37-64). IGI Global Scientific Publishing.

Mhia-Alddin, D. A., & Hussein, A. M. (2025). Contract Expiry in AI-Driven STM Research: Legal Challenges, Risks, and Regulatory Considerations. In *Ensuring Secure and Ethical STM Research in the AI Era* (pp. 77-110). IGI Global Scientific Publishing.

Miao, J., Thongprayoon, C., Suppadungsuk, S., Garcia Valencia, O. A., Qureshi, F., & Cheungpasitporn, W. (2023). Ethical dilemmas in using AI for academic writing and an example framework for peer review in nephrology academia: A narrative review. *Clinics and Practice*, *14*(1), 89–105. DOI: 10.3390/clinpract14010008 PMID: 38248432

Microsoft. (n.d.). *Illustration of the Zero Trust model* [Illustration]. Retrieved from https://www.microsoft.com/en-us/security/business/zero-trust

Miracle, N. O. (2024). The importance of network security in protecting sensitive data and information. *International Journal of Research and Innovation in Applied Science*.

Mistral, A. I. (2023). *Mistral 7B Model Card*. https://mistral.ai

Mohammed, D., Omar, M., & Nguyen, V. (2018). Wireless sensor network security: Approaches to detecting and avoiding wormhole attacks. *Journal of Research in Business. Economics and Management*, *10*(2), 1860–1864.

Molligan, J., & Pérez-López, E. (2024). Artificial intelligence in academia: Opportunities, challenges, and ethical considerations. *Biochemistry and Cell Biology*, *103*, 1–3. DOI: 10.1139/bcb-2024-0216 PMID: 39611424

Monast, J. J. (2018). Editing nature: Reconceptualizing biotechnology governance. *BCL Rev.*, *59*, 2377.

Munton, J., Stewart, A., McCrystal, S., Hardy, T., & Orifici, A. (2021). Submission to the Senate Education and Employment Legislation Committee Inquiry in the Fair Work Amendment (Supporting Australia's Jobs and Economic Recovery) Bill 2020.

Munton, J., Stewart, A., McCrystal, S., Hardy, T., & Orifici, A. (2021). The (Omni) bus that Broke Down: Changes to Casual Employment and the Remnants of the Coalition's Industrial Relations Agenda. *Australian Journal of Labour Law*.

Naili, Y. T., Mangkunegara, I. S., Purwono, P., & Baballe, M. A. (2025). Regulatory challenges in ai-based diagnostics: Legal implications of ai use in medical diagnostics. In *BIO Web of Conferences* (Vol. 152, p. 01034). EDP Sciences.

Nam, B. H., & Bai, Q. (2023). ChatGPT and its ethical implications for STEM research and higher education: A media discourse analysis. *International Journal of STEM Education*, *10*(1), 66. DOI: 10.1186/s40594-023-00452-5

Narayana, S. A., Pati, R. K., & Padhi, S. S. (2019). Market dynamics and reverse logistics for sustainability in the Indian Pharmaceuticals industry. *Journal of Cleaner Production*, *208*, 968–987. DOI: 10.1016/j.jclepro.2018.10.171

National Academies of Sciences, Engineering, and Medicine. (2023). A Governance Framework for Aligning Innovation in Health and Medicine with Equity. In *Toward Equitable Innovation in Health and Medicine: A Framework*. National Academies Press (US).

Neupane, S., Mitra, S., Fernandez, I. A., Saha, S., Mittal, S., Chen, J., Pillai, N., & Rahimi, S. (2024). Security considerations in ai-robotics: A survey of current methods, challenges, and opportunities. *IEEE Access : Practical Innovations, Open Solutions*, *12*, 22072–22097. DOI: 10.1109/ACCESS.2024.3363657

Nguyen, V., Mohammed, D., Omar, M., & Banisakher, M. (2018). The Effects of the FCC Net Neutrality Repeal on Security and Privacy. [IJHIoT]. *International Journal of Hyperconnectivity and the Internet of Things*, *2*(2), 21–29. DOI: 10.4018/IJHIoT.2018070102

Nicolai, M., Richmond, N., & Morrow, T. (2022). *Industry best practices for Zero Trust a rchitecture*. Software Engineering Institute. Retrieved from https://resources.sei.cmu.edu/asset_files/WhitePaper/2022_019_001_890272.pdf

Nurchurifiani, E., Maximilian, A., Ajeng, G. D., Wiratno, P., Hastomo, T., & Wicaksono, A. (2025). Leveraging AI-Powered Tools in Academic Writing and Research: Insights from English Faculty Members in Indonesia. *International Journal of Information and Education Technology (IJIET)*, *15*(2), 312–322. DOI: 10.18178/ijiet.2025.15.2.2244

Nvidia. (2024). Llama-3: Enhanced Code Analysis Capabilities in Compact Models. Nvidia. https://build.nvidia.com/nvidia/llama-3_1-nemotron-70b-instruct

Ocampo, T. S. C., Silva, T. P., Alencar-Palha, C., Haiter-Neto, F., & Oliveira, M. L. (2023). ChatGPT and scientific writing: A reflection on the ethical boundaries. *Imaging Science in Dentistry*, *53*(2), 175. DOI: 10.5624/isd.20230085 PMID: 37405199

Oduro, P., Uzougbo, N. S., & Ugwu, M. C. (2024). Renewable energy expansion: Legal strategies for overcoming regulatory barriers and promoting innovation. *International Journal of Applied Research in Social Sciences*, *6*(5), 927–944. DOI: 10.51594/ijarss.v6i5.1145

Oh, S., Choi, C. Y., & Lee, J. H. (2020). Regulatory reform for fostering an innovation ecosystem.

Okta. (2023). *SOZT report*. Okta. https://www.okta.com/sites/default/files/2023- 0 9 /SOZT_Report.pdf

Omar, M. (2021). New insights into database security: An effective and integrated approach for applying access control mechanisms and cryptographic concepts in Microsoft Access environments.

Omar, M. (2022). *Machine Learning for Cybersecurity: Innovative Deep Learning Solutions*. Springer Brief. https://link.springer.com/book/978303115

Omar, M. (2024). From Attack to Defense: Strengthening DNN Text Classification Against Adversarial Examples. In *Innovations, Securities, and Case Studies Across Healthcare, Business, and Technology* (pp. 174-195). IGI Global.

Omar, M. (2024). Revolutionizing Malware Detection: A Paradigm Shift Through Optimized Convolutional Neural Networks. In *Innovations, Securities, and Case Studies Across Healthcare, Business, and Technology* (pp. 196-220). IGI Global. DOI: 10.4018/979-8-3693-1906-2.ch011

Omar, M., Zangana, H. M., Al-Karaki, J. N., & Mohammed, D. (2024). Harnessing LLMs for IoT malware detection: A comparative analysis of BERT and GPT-2. In *2024 8th International Symposium on Multidisciplinary Studies and Innovative Technologies (ISMSIT)* (pp. 1-6). Ankara, Turkiye. https://doi.org/DOI: 10.1109/ISMSIT63511.2024.10757249

Omar, M., & Zangana, H. (Eds.). (2025). *Digital Forensics in the Age of AI*. IGI Global., DOI: 10.4018/979-8-3373-0857-9

Omar, M., & Zangana, H. M. (Eds.). (2024). *Redefining Security With Cyber AI*. IGI Global., DOI: 10.4018/979-8-3693-6517-5

Omar, M., & Zangana, H. M. (Eds.). (2025). *Application of Large Language Models (LLMs) for Software Vulnerability Detection*. IGI Global., DOI: 10.4018/979-8-3693-9311-6

Omar, M., Zangana, H. M., & Mohammed, D. (Eds.). (2025). *Integrating Artificial Intelligence in Cybersecurity and Forensic Practices*. IGI Global., DOI: 10.4018/979-8-3373-0588-2

Omodan, B. I., & Marongwe, N. (2024). The role of artificial intelligence in decolonising academic writing for inclusive knowledge production. *Interdisciplinary Journal of Education Research*, *6*(s1), 1–14. DOI: 10.38140/ijer-2024.vol6.s1.06

Open, A. I. (2023). GPT-3.5: Bridging the Gap Between GPT-3 and GPT-4. OpenAI. https://platform.openai.com/docs/models/gpt-3-5

Open, A. I. (2024). GPT-4 Technical Report. OpenAI. https://www.openai.com/research/gpt-4

Osei-Tutu, J. J. (2001). Trips and domestic control: implications for developing countries.

Otieno, M. (2023). An extensive survey of smart agriculture technologies: Current security posture. *World J. Adv. Res. Rev*, *18*(3), 1207–1231. DOI: 10.30574/wjarr.2023.18.3.1241

Pai, Y. (2018). Patent Injunction Heuristics in India. *Pai, Yogesh, Patent Injunction Heuristics in India in Rafal Sikorski (Ed.) Patent Law Injunctions, Kluwer Law International BV (2019).*

Pakshad, P. (2025). *TextualPromptsLLM-s-* [Source code]. GitHub. https://github.com/ppakshad/TextualPromptsLLM-s-

Pandey, D. K., & Mishra, R. (2024). *Towards sustainable agriculture: Harnessing AI for global food security*. Artificial Intelligence in Agriculture.

Patra, S. P. (2025). Navigating the legal landscape of sustainable Industry 4.0. *Industry 4.0 for Manufacturing Systems: Concepts, Technologies, and Applications*, 109.

Pedro, F., Subosa, M., Rivas, A., & Valverde, P. (2019). Artificial intelligence in education: Challenges and opportunities for sustainable development.

Pendle, N. (2021). Competing authorities and norms of restraint: Governing community-embedded armed groups in South Sudan. *International Interactions*, *47*(5), 873–897. DOI: 10.1080/03050629.2021.1918126

Peng, S. Y., Lin, C. F., & Streinz, T. (Eds.). (2021). *Artificial intelligence and international Economic law*. Cambridge University Press. DOI: 10.1017/9781108954006

Perkins, M. (2023). Academic Integrity considerations of AI Large Language Models in the post-pandemic era: ChatGPT and beyond. *Journal of University Teaching & Learning Practice*, *20*(2), 1–24. DOI: 10.53761/1.20.02.07

Pesapane, F., Bracchi, D. A., Mulligan, J. F., Linnikov, A., Maslennikov, O., Lanzavecchia, M. B., Tantrige, P., Stasolla, A., Biondetti, P., Giuggioli, P. F., Cassano, E., & Carrafiello, G. (2021). Legal and regulatory framework for AI solutions in healthcare in EU, US, China, and Russia: New scenarios after a pandemic. *Radiation*, *1*(4), 261–276. DOI: 10.3390/radiation1040022

Pesapane, F., Volonté, C., Codari, M., & Sardanelli, F. (2018). Artificial intelligence as a medical device in radiology: Ethical and regulatory issues in Europe and the United States. *Insights Into Imaging*, *9*(5), 745–753. DOI: 10.1007/s13244-018-0645-y PMID: 30112675

Peter, L., Hajek, L., Maresova, P., Augustynek, M., & Penhaker, M. (2020). Medical devices: Regulation, risk classification, and open innovation. *Journal of Open Innovation*, *6*(2), 42. DOI: 10.3390/joitmc6020042

Pimpalkar, A. P., Wankhade, N. R., Chole, V., & Golhar, Y. (2024). Women's Empowerment Through AI: Discovering Data Analytics for Predictive Safety Solutions and Future Trends. In *AI Tools and Applications for Women's Safety* (pp. 304-326). IGI Global Scientific Publishing.

Pomeroy, S. (2017). *Discussion paper: Envisioning a modernized social and affordable housing sector in Canada*. Carleton University Centre for Urban Research and Education.

Ponemon Institute. (2025). Costs and Consequences of Gaps in Vulnerability Response: A global report. ServiceNow. https://www.servicenow.com/lpayr/ponemon-vulnerability-survey.html

Raffel, C.. (2020). *Exploring the limits of transfer learning with a unified text-to-text transformer*. JMLR.

Rais, R., Morillo, C., Gilman, E., & Barth, D. (2024). *Zero Trust Networks: Building Secure Systems in Untrusted Networks*. O'Reilly Media, Incorporated.

Rashid, A. B., & Kausik, A. K. (2024). AI revolutionizing industries worldwide: A comprehensive overview of its diverse applications. *Hybrid Advances*, 100277.

Read, A., Botha, R., & Jamaloodien, K. (2023). COVID-19 vaccination procurement and contract management in a South African context. *Journal of Strategic Contracting and Negotiation*, *7*(1-2), 33–43. DOI: 10.1177/20555636231198053

Rodríguez, D. C., Balaji, L. N., Chamdimba, E., Kafumba, J., Koon, A. D., Mazalale, J., Mkombe, D., Munywoki, J., Mwase-Vuma, T., & Namakula, J. (2023). Political economy analysis of subnational health management in Kenya, Malawi and Uganda. *Health Policy andPlanning, 38*(5), 631–647.

Rodriguez, M. Y., & Storer, H. (2020). A computational social science perspective on qualitative data exploration: Using topic models for the descriptive analysis of social media data. *Journal of Technology in Human Services*, *38*(1), 54–86. DOI: 10.1080/15228835.2019.1616350

Rosenblatt, M., Boutin, M. M., & Nussbaum, S. R. (2016). Innovation in medicine and device development, regulatory review, and use of clinical advances. *Journal of the American Medical Association*, *316*(16), 1671–1672. DOI: 10.1001/jama.2016.12486 PMID: 27669080

Saikia, B. (2024). Ecologically-Informed approaches: International mechanisms for navigating environmental challenges and ensuring sustainability in the oil and gas exploration and production industry. *Proceedings of the International Academy of Ecology and Environmental Sciences*, *14*(2), 60.

Sakapaji, S. C., García Molinos, J., Parilova, V., Gavrilyeva, T., & Yakovleva, N. (2024). Navigating legal and regulatory frameworks to achieve the resilience and sustainability of indigenous socioecological systems. *Resources, 13*(4), 56. DOI: 10.3390/resources13040056

Salvagno, M., Taccone, F. S., & Gerli, A. G. (2023). Can artificial intelligence help for scientific writing? *Critical Care, 27*(1), 75. DOI: 10.1186/s13054-023-04380-2 PMID: 36841840

Samsuri, A., Zakaria, Z., Manaf, K. H., & Ismail, I. (2017). Key enablers in a production sharing contract operatorship transfer exercise. *Journal of Advanced Review on Scientific Research, 36*(1), 1–13.

San Biagio, M., Cipolla, M., La Mattina, E., & Morreale, V. (2023, December). A Topic Clustering Method to Identify Online Threats against Soft Targets. In *2023 International Conference on Computational Science and Computational Intelligence (CSCI)* (pp. 727-733). IEEE. DOI: 10.1109/CSCI62032.2023.00124

Schnichels, D., & Sule, S. (2010). The pharmaceutical sector inquiry and its impact on competition law enforcement. *Journal of European competition law & practice, 1*(2), 93-111.

Schünemann, C., Johanning, S., Reger, E., Herold, H., & Bruckner, T. (2024). Complex system policy modelling approaches for policy advice–comparing systems thinking, system dynamics and agent-based modelling. *Political Research Exchange : an ECPR Journal, 6*(1), 2387438. DOI: 10.1080/2474736X.2024.2387438

Scott, I. (2021). Context and innovation in traditional bureaucracies: A Hong Kong study. *Public Administration and Development, 41*(1), 12–22. DOI: 10.1002/pad.1899

Seaman, J. (2020). *PCI DSS: An integrated data security standard guide*. Apress. DOI: 10.1007/978-1-4842-5808-8

Senoo, E. E. K., Anggraini, L., Kumi, J. A., Luna, B. K., Akansah, E., Sulyman, H. A., & Aritsugi, M. (2024). IoT solutions with artificial intelligence technologies for precision agriculture: Definitions, applications, challenges, and opportunities. *Electronics (Basel), 13*(10), 1894. DOI: 10.3390/electronics13101894

Sethi, N. (2019). Regulating for uncertainty: Bridging blurred boundaries in medical innovation, research and treatment. *Law, Innovation and Technology, 11*(1), 112–133. DOI: 10.1080/17579961.2019.1573400 PMID: 31057671

Shafik, W. (2024). Data privacy and security safeguarding customer information in ChatGPT systems. In *Revolutionizing the Service Industry Wth OpenAI Models* (pp. 52–86). IGI Global. DOI: 10.4018/979-8-3693-1239-1.ch003

Shafik, W., Tufail, A., De Silva, C. L., Haji, R. A. A., & Apong, M. (2025). The Role, Application, and Impact of Artificial Intelligence in the Agriculture Industry. In *Future Tech Startups and Innovation in the Age of AI* (pp. 36–60). CRC Press.

Shao, M., & Ding, Y. (2024). *FVD-DPM: Fine-grained Vulnerability Detection via Conditional Diffusion Probabilistic Models*. USENIX Security Symposium. https://www.usenix.org/conference/usenixsecurity24/presentation/shao

Shaw, P. (2023, March 16). Zero trust. *Defense Acquisition University*. https://www.dau.edu/sites/default/files/Migrate/EventAttachments/885/DAU%20Zero%20Trust%20Shaw%20%2020230316.pdf

Sheikhi, F., Fakher, L., & Chekani, D. (2024, February). Depression Detection on e-Risk 2017 using Long Short-term Memory Models. In 2024 20th CSI International Symposium on Artificial Intelligence and Signal Processing (AISP) (pp. 1-6). IEEE.

Sheliemina, N. (2024). The use of artificial intelligence in medical diagnostics: Opportunities, prospects and risks. *Health Economics and Management Review*, *5*(2), 104–124. DOI: 10.61093/hem.2024.2-07

Sheng, Z., Chen, Z., Gu, S., Huang, H., & Gu, G. (2025). *Large Language Models in Software Security: A Survey of Vulnerability Detection Techniques and Insights*. arXiv. https://arxiv.org/abs/2502.07049

Shereen, E., Ristea, D., Vyas, S., & McFadden, S. (2024). *SoK: On Closing the Applicability Gap in Automated Vulnerability Detection*. arXiv. https://arxiv.org/abs/2412.11194

Shofiah, N., Putera, Z. F., & Solichah, N. (2023, December). Challenges and opportunities in the use of artificial intelligence in education for academic writing: A scoping review. In *Conference Psychology and Flourishing Humanity (PFH 2023)* (pp. 174-193). Atlantis Press. DOI: 10.2991/978-2-38476-188-3_20

Shoraka, S. (2006). *World trade dispute resolution and developing countries: Taking a development approach to fair adjudication in the context of WTO law*. London School of Economics and Political Science.

Shuja, J., Alanazi, E., Alasmary, W., & Alashaikh, A. (2021). COVID-19 open source data sets: A comprehensive survey. *Applied Intelligence*, *51*(3), 1296–1325. DOI: 10.1007/s10489-020-01862-6 PMID: 34764552

Shukla-Jones, A., Friedrichs, S., & Winickoff, D. E. (2018). Gene editing in an international context: Scientific, economic and social issues across sectors. *OECD science, technology and industry working papers, 2018*(4), 0_1-51.

Shukla, R. P., & Taneja, S. (2024). Ethical considerations and data privacy in artificial intelligence. In *Integrating generative AI in education to achieve sustainable development goals* (pp. 86–97). IGI Global. DOI: 10.4018/979-8-3693-2440-0.ch005

Siew-Kuan, E. (2012). Evolving landscape of patent remedies in a changing marketplace. *Singapore Academy of Law Journal, 24*, 634-668.

Singh, B., & Kaunert, C. (2025). Navigating the Terrain of Sustainability Trajectories of Environment: Biodiversity Protection and Legal Landscapes. In *Community Resilience and Climate Change Challenges: Pursuit of Sustainable Development Goals (SDGs)* (pp. 355-374). IGI Global Scientific Publishing.

Sood, A., Sharma, R. K., & Bhardwaj, A. K. (2022). Artificial intelligence research in agriculture: A review. *Online Information Review, 46*(6), 1054–1075. DOI: 10.1108/OIR-10-2020-0448

Soomro, J. A., Suhrab, M., & Abbasi, B. A. (2025). Navigating Green Regulations in the Business Ecosystem: Government Support, Compliance, and Obstacles in the Context of Pakistan. In *Government Influences on Eco-Friendly Practices in Business* (pp. 55-86). IGI Global.

Sparrow, R., & Howard, M. (2021). Robots in agriculture: prospects, impacts, ethics, and policy. *precision agriculture, 22*, 818-833.

Sparrow, R., Howard, M., & Degeling, C. (2021). Managing the risks of artificial intelligence in agriculture. *NJAS: Impact in Agricultural and Life Sciences, 93*(1), 172–196. DOI: 10.1080/27685241.2021.2008777

Spindler, P., Bach, K. F., Schmiegelow, M., Bedlington, N., & Eichler, H. G. (2016). Innovation of medical products: The evolution of regulatory science, research, and education. *Therapeutic Innovation & Regulatory Science, 50*(1), 44–48. DOI: 10.1177/2168479015599810 PMID: 30236007

Statista. (2024). *Zero trust adoption stage among companies worldwide*. Statista. h t tps://www.statista.com/statistics/1422664/zero-trust-adoption-stage-companies/

Subaveerapandiyan, A., Kalbande, D., & Ahmad, N. (2025). Perceptions of effectiveness and ethical use of AI tools in academic writing: A study Among PhD scholars in India. *Information Development*, •••, 02666669251314840. DOI: 10.1177/02666669251314840

Sullivan, C. (2015). Interim dilapidations. *Journal of Building Survey. Appraisal & Valuation, 3*(4), 323–334. DOI: 10.69554/UTKA7017

Sullivan, C. A. (2016). Tending the Garden: Restricting Competition via" Garden Leave. *Berkeley Journal of Employment and Labor Law*, •••, 293–325.

Swirnoff, A. H., & Becker, D. M. (2010). Judicial developments in the US Hatch-Waxman infringement safe harbor. *Expert Opinion on Therapeutic Patents*, *20*(4), 451–458. DOI: 10.1517/13543771003604737 PMID: 20302449

Tai, A. M. Y., Meyer, M., Varidel, M., Prodan, A., Vogel, M., Iorfino, F., & Krausz, R. M. (2023). Exploring the potential and limitations of ChatGPT for academic peer-reviewed writing: Addressing linguistic injustice and ethical concerns. *Journal of Academic Language and Learning*, *17*(1), T16–T30.

Tanwar, R., & Agarwal, P. K. (2024). Analysis of the determinants of service quality in the multimodal public transport system of Bhopal city using structural equation modelling (SEM) and factor analysis. *Expert Systems with Applications*, *256*, 124931. DOI: 10.1016/j.eswa.2024.124931

Tasa-Fuster, V. (2024). The Legal Rationales of the Leading Technological Models: The Challenges of Regulating Linguistic and Gender Biases. In *Gendered Technology in Translation and Interpreting* (pp. 27-65). Routledge.

Technology Innovation Institute. (2024). Falcon-180B: Advanced Large Language Models for Open-Source Applications. TII. https://falconllm.tii.ae/falcon-models .html

Terry, N. (2019). Of regulating healthcare AI and robots. *Yale JL & Tech.*, *21*, 133.

Tihanyi, N., Ferrag, M. A., Jain, R., Bisztray, T., & Debbah, M. (2024, September). *CyberMetric: A benchmark dataset based on retrieval-augmented generation for evaluating LLMs in cybersecurity knowledge*. In *2024 IEEE International Conference on Cyber Security and Resilience (CSR)* (pp. 296–302). IEEE. DOI: 10.1109/ CSR61664.2024.10679494

Tóth, R., Bisztray, T., & Erdődi, L. (2024). *LLMs in web development: Evaluating LLM-generated PHP code*. https://link.springer.com/chapter/10.1007/978-3-031 -68738-9_34

Touvron, H.. (2023). *LLaMA: Open and efficient foundation language models*. Meta AI.

Trotsyuk, A. A., Waeiss, Q., Bhatia, R. T., Aponte, B. J., Heffernan, I. M., Madgavkar, D., Felder, R. M., Lehmann, L. S., Palmer, M. J., Greely, H., Wald, R., Goetz, L., Trengove, M., Vandersluis, R., Lin, H., Cho, M. K., Altman, R. B., Endy, D., Relman, D. A., & Magnus, D. (2024). Toward a framework for risk mitigation of potential misuse of artificial intelligence in biomedical research. *Nature Machine Intelligence*, *6*(12), 1–8. DOI: 10.1038/s42256-024-00926-3

Turner, J. (2018). *Robot rules: Regulating artificial intelligence*. Springer.

Tzachor, A., Devare, M., King, B., Avin, S., & Ó hÉigeartaigh, S. (2022). Responsible artificial intelligence in agriculture requires systemic understanding of risks and externalities. *Nature Machine Intelligence*, *4*(2), 104–109. DOI: 10.1038/s42256-022-00440-4

Uddin, M., Chowdhury, A., & Kabir, M. A. (2024). Legal and ethical aspects of deploying artificial intelligence in climate-smart agriculture. *AI & Society*, *39*(1), 221–234. DOI: 10.1007/s00146-022-01421-2

Ugwu, N. F., Igbinlade, A. S., Ochiaka, R. E., Ezeani, U. D., Okorie, N. C., Opele, J. K., Onayinka, T. S., Iroegbu, O., Onyekwere, O. K., Adams, A. B., Aigbona, P., & Ojobola, F. B. (2024). Clarifying Ethical Dilemmas in Using Artificial Intelligence in Research Writing: A Rapid Review. *Higher Learning Research Communications*, *14*(2), 29–47. DOI: 10.18870/hlrc.v142.1549

Uplaonkar, S. S., Veershetty, R., Bahar, Z., & Sangeeta, G. (2024). The role of productive AI: A supporter or challenger in the future of agricultural librarianship. *IJAR*, *10*(4), 46–53.

Uwaoma, C. (2023). *The challenges and processes of achieving optimal implementation of Zero Trust Architecture in the workplace*. SIGMIS-CPR. DOI: 10.1145/3579168.3632735

Veluru, C. S. (2024). Responsible Artificial Intelligence on Large Scale Data to Prevent Misuse, Unethical Challenges and Security Breaches. *Journal of Artificial Intelligence & Cloud Computing. SRC/JAICC-349. DOI: doi. org/(3), 331*, 2-6.DOI: 10.47363/JAICC/2024

Verma, A., Rao, K., Eluri, V., & Sharma, Y. (2020). Regulating AI in public health: systems challenges and perspectives. *ORF Occasional Paper, 261.*

Verma, M., & Rohit, K. (2024). Ethical AI Shaping Scholarly Communication: Challenges and Opportunities.

Voigt, B., & Münichsdorfer, A. (2019). Regulation of genome editing in plant biotechnology: European Union. *Regulation of Genome Editing in Plant Biotechnology: A Comparative Analysis of Regulatory Frameworks of Selected Countries and the EU*, 137-238.

Vyawahare, H., Khandelwal, S., & Rathod, S. (2024). Artificial Intelligence in Detecting and Preventing Online Harassment. In *AI Tools and Applications for Women's Safety* (pp. 14–35). IGI Global Scientific Publishing. DOI: 10.4018/979-8-3693-1435-7.ch002

Wang, W., Sadjadi, S. M., Rishe, N., & Mahara, A. (2024). Applying transparent shaping for Zero Trust Architecture implementation in AWS: A case study. *arXiv preprint a rXiv:2405.01412v2.* https://arxiv.org/pdf/2405.01412v2

Wang, J., Huang, Z., Liu, H., Yang, N., & Xiao, Y. (2023). *DefectHunter: A novel LLM-driven boosted-conformer-based code vulnerability detection mechanism.* https://arxiv.org/abs/2309.15324

Wang, Q. (2024). Maritime law enforcement concerning offshore energy platforms: Navigating international law constraints and challenges. *Marine Policy*, *170*, 106370. DOI: 10.1016/j.marpol.2024.106370

Wei, H., Xu, W., Kang, B., Eisner, R., Muleke, A., Rodriguez, D., deVoil, P., Sadras, V., Monjardino, M., & Harrison, M. T. (2024). Irrigation with artificial intelligence: Problems, premises, promises. *Human-Centric Intelligent Systems*, *4*(2), 187–205. DOI: 10.1007/s44230-024-00072-4

Whitman, M. E., & Mattord, H. J. (2019). Management of information security (6th ed.). C engage Learning.

Wiersma, M., Kerridge, I., & Lipworth, W. (2023). Clinical innovation ethics frameworks: A systematic narrative review. *Health Policy (Amsterdam)*, *129*, 104706. DOI: 10.1016/j.healthpol.2023.104706 PMID: 36639310

Williamson, H. F., Brettschneider, J., Caccamo, M., Davey, R. P., Goble, C., Kersey, P. J., May, S., Morris, R. J., Ostler, R., Pridmore, T., Rawlings, C., Studholme, D., Tsaftaris, S. A., & Leonelli, S. (2023). Data management challenges for artificial intelligence in plant and agricultural research. *F1000 Research*, *10*, 324. DOI: 10.12688/f1000research.52204.2 PMID: 36873457

Wiwanitmkit, S., & Wiwanitkit, V. (2024). Artificial Intelligence, Academic Publishing, Scientific Writing, Peer Review, and Ethics. *Brazilian Journal of Cardiovascular Surgery*, *39*(4), e20230377. DOI: 10.21470/1678-9741-2023-0377 PMID: 39038191

Wolt, J. D. (2017). Safety, security, and policy considerations for plant genome editing. *Progress in Molecular Biology and Translational Science*, *149*, 215–241. DOI: 10.1016/bs.pmbts.2017.03.005 PMID: 28712498

Wolt, J. D., & Wolf, C. (2018). Policy and governance perspectives for regulation of genome edited crops in the United States. *Frontiers in Plant Science*, *9*, 1606. DOI: 10.3389/fpls.2018.01606 PMID: 30467510

Woodcock, R. (2019). Using Price Regulation Instead of Competition to Reduce Prices after Patents Expire. *Available atSSRN* 3466473. DOI: 10.2139/ssrn.3466473

World Economic Forum. (2022). The Zero Trust model in cybersecurity: Towards understanding and deployment. h t t p s : / / w ww3.weforum.org/docs/WEF_The_Zero_Trust_Model_in_Cybersecurity_2022.pdf

World Economic Forum. (2024). Cybersecurity rules saw big changes in 2024. *World Economic Forum*. Retrieved from https://www.weforum.org/agenda/2024/10/cybersecurity- r egulation-changes-nis2-eu-2024/

World Health Organization. (2023). *Regulatory considerations on artificial intelligence for health*. World Health Organization.

Wright, J., Dawson, M. E.Jr, & Omar, M. (2012). Cyber security and mobile threats: The need for antivirus applications for smartphones. *Journal of Information Systems Technology and Planning*, *5*(14), 40–60.

Ya'u, M. S., & Mohammed, M. S. (2025). AI-Assisted Writing and Academic Literacy: Investigating the Dual Impact of Language Models on Writing Proficiency and Ethical Concerns in Nigerian Higher Education. *International Journal of Education and Literacy Studies*, *13*(2), 593–604. DOI: 10.7575/aiac.ijels.v.13n.2p.593

Yalli, J. (n.d.). *A comprehensive review of security challenges and countermeasures in IoT architectural systems. SSRN*. https://doi.org/DOI: 10.2139/ssrn.4752445

Yin, X., Ni, C., & Wang, S. (2024). *Multitask-based evaluation of open-source LLM on software vulnerability*. https://ieeexplore.ieee.org/abstract/document/10706805/

Zangana, H. M. (2015). A New Skin Color Based Face Detection Algorithm by Combining Three Color Model Algorithms. *IOSR J. Comput. Eng*, *17*, 06-125.

Zangana, H. M. (2017). A new algorithm for shape detection. *IOSR Journal of Computer Engineering (IOSR-JCE)*, *19*(3), 71-76.

Zangana, H. M. (2018). Developing Data Warehouse for Student Information System (IIUM as a Case Study). *International Organization of Scientific Research*, *20*(1), 09-14.

Zangana, H. M. (2018). Implementing a System for Recognizing Optical Characters.

Zangana, H. M. (2019). Issues of Data Management in the Library: A Case Study.

Zangana, H. M. (2019). ITD Data Quality Maturity (A Case Study). *International Journal Of Engineering And Computer Science, 8*(10).

Zangana, H. M. (2022). Improving The Web Services for Remittance Company: Express Remit as a Case Study. *Academic Journal of Nawroz University (AJNU), 11*(3).

Zangana, H. M. (2024). Exploring Blockchain-Based Timestamping Tools: A Comprehensive Review. *Redefining Security With Cyber AI*, 92-110.

Zangana, H. M. (2024). Exploring the Landscape of Website Vulnerability Scanners: A Comprehensive Review and Comparative Analysis. *Redefining Security With Cyber AI*, 111-129.

Zangana, H. M., Mustafa, F. M., Mohammed, A. K., & Omar, M. (2025). The Role of Change Control Boards in Ensuring Cybersecurity Compliance for IT Infrastructure. *JITCE (Journal of Information Technology and Computer Engineering), 9*(1). Retrieved from https://jitce.fti.unand.ac.id/index.php/JITCE/article/view/303

Zangana, H. M., Omar, M., Al-Karaki, J. N., & Mohammed, D. (2024). Comprehensive Review and Analysis of Network Firewall Rule Analyzers: Enhancing Security Posture and Efficiency. *Redefining Security With Cyber AI*, 15-36.

Zangana, H. M. (2017). Library Data Quality Maturity (IIUM as a Case Study). *IOSR Journal of Computer Engineering, 19*(March), 29. DOI: 10.9790/0661-1902033844

Zangana, H. M. (2017). Watermarking System Using LSB. *IOSR Journal of Computer Engineering, 19*(3), 75–79. DOI: 10.9790/0661-1903027579

Zangana, H. M. (2018). Design an information management system for a pharmacy. *International Journal of Advanced Research in Computer and Communication Engineering, 7*(10), 52–55. DOI: 10.17148/IJARCCE.2018.71012

Zangana, H. M. (2020). Mobile Device Integration in IIUM Service. *International Journal (Toronto, Ont.), 8*(5).

Zangana, H. M. (2021). The Global Finical Crisis from an Islamic Point Of View. *Qubahan Academic Journal, 1*(2), 55–59. DOI: 10.48161/qaj.v1n2a39

Zangana, H. M. (2022). Creating a Community-Based Disaster Management System. *Academic Journal of Nawroz University, 11*(4), 234–244. DOI: 10.25007/ajnu.v11n4a1485

Zangana, H. M. (2022). Implementing New Interactive Video Learning System for IIUM. *Academic Journal of Nawroz University, 11*(2), 23–29. DOI: 10.25007/ajnu.v11n2a1281

Zangana, H. M., & Abdulazeez, A. M. (2023). Developed Clustering Algorithms for Engineering Applications: A Review. *International Journal of Informatics* [IN-JIISCOM]. *Information System and Computer Engineering, 4*(2), 147–169.

Zangana, H. M., & Al-Shaikhli, I. F. (2013). A new algorithm for human face detection using skin color tone. *IOSR Journal of Computer Engineering, 11*(6), 31–38. DOI: 10.9790/0661-1163138

Zangana, H. M., Bazeed, S. M. S., Ali, N. Y., & Abdullah, D. T. (2024). Navigating Project Change: A Comprehensive Review of Change Management Strategies and Practices. *Indonesian Journal of Education and Social Sciences, 3*(2), 166–179. DOI: 10.56916/ijess.v3i2.735

Zangana, H. M., Mohammed, A. K., Sallow, A. B., & Sallow, Z. B. (2024). Cybernetic Deception: Unraveling the Layers of Email Phishing Threats. [INJURATECH]. *International Journal of Research and Applied Technology, 4*(1), 35–47.

Zangana, H. M., & Mustafa, F. M. (2024). From Classical to Deep Learning: A Systematic Review of Image Denoising Techniques. *Jurnal Ilmiah Computer Science, 3*(1), 50–65. DOI: 10.58602/jics.v3i1.36

Zangana, H. M., & Mustafa, F. M. (2024). Hybrid Image Denoising Using Wavelet Transform and Deep Learning. *EAI Endorsed Transactions on AI and Robotics, 3*. Advance online publication. DOI: 10.4108/airo.7486

Zangana, H. M., & Mustafa, F. M. (2024). Review of Hybrid Denoising Approaches in Face Recognition: Bridging Wavelet Transform and Deep Learning. *The Indonesian Journal of Computer Science, 13*(4). Advance online publication. DOI: 10.33022/ijcs.v13i4.4209

Zangana, H. M., & Mustafa, F. M. (2024). Surveying the Landscape: A Comprehensive Review of Object Detection Algorithms and Advancements. *Jurnal Ilmiah Computer Science, 3*(1), 1–15. DOI: 10.58602/jics.v3i1.29

Zangana, H. M., & Mustafa, F. M. (2025). A Novel Hybrid Wavelet-GAN Image Denoising System. In Bhatti, U., Aamir, M., Gulzar, Y., & Ullah Bazai, S. (Eds.), *Modern Intelligent Techniques for Image Processing* (pp. 409–424). IGI Global Scientific Publishing., DOI: 10.4018/979-8-3693-9045-0.ch017

Zangana, H. M., Mustafa, F. M., & Omar, M. (2024). A Hybrid Approach for Robust Object Detection: Integrating Template Matching and Faster R-CNN. *EAI Endorsed Transactions on AI and Robotics, 3*. Advance online publication. DOI: 10.4108/airo.6858

Zangana, H. M., & Omar, M. (2020). Threats, Attacks, and Mitigations of Smartphone Security. *Academic Journal of Nawroz University, 9*(4), 324–332. DOI: 10.25007/ajnu.v9n4a989

Zangana, H. M., & Omar, M. (2025). The Role of Leadership in Advancing Inclusive Health Technologies. In Burrell, D., & Nguyen, C. (Eds.), *New Horizons in Leadership: Inclusive Explorations in Health, Technology, and Education* (pp. 203–220). IGI Global Scientific Publishing., DOI: 10.4018/979-8-3693-6437-6.ch009

Zangana, H. M., Sallow, Z. B., & Omar, M. (2025). The Human Factor in Cybersecurity: Addressing the Risks of Insider Threats. *Jurnal Ilmiah Computer Science, 3*(2), 76–85. DOI: 10.58602/jics.v3i2.37

Zangana, H., Al-Karaki, J., & Omar, M. (Eds.). (2025). *Revolutionizing Cybersecurity With Deep Learning and Large Language Models*. IGI Global., DOI: 10.4018/979-8-3373-3296-3

Zangana, H., & Omar, M. (Eds.). (2025). *Ensuring Secure and Ethical STM Research in the AI Era*. IGI Global., DOI: 10.4018/979-8-3373-4252-8

Zangana, H., & Omar, M. (Eds.). (2025). *Leveraging Large Language Models for Quantum-Aware Cybersecurity*. IGI Global., DOI: 10.4018/979-8-3373-1102-9

Zhaksylyk, A., Zimba, O., Yessirkepov, M., & Kocyigit, B. F. (2023). Research integrity: Where we are and where we are heading. *Journal of Korean Medical Science, 38*(47), e405. DOI: 10.3346/jkms.2023.38.e405 PMID: 38050915

Zhou, K., & Gattinger, G. (2024). The evolving regulatory paradigm of AI in MedTech: A review of perspectives and where we are today. *Therapeutic Innovation & Regulatory Science, 58*(3), 456–464. DOI: 10.1007/s43441-024-00628-3 PMID: 38528278

Zhou, Y., Liu, S., Siow, J., Du, X., & Liu, Y. (2019). Devign: Effective vulnerability identification by learning comprehensive program semantics via graph neural networks. *Proceedings of the 2019 ACM SIGSAC Conference on Computer and Communications Security*, 877–892. DOI: 10.1145/3319535.3354211

Zohouri, M., Sabzali, M., & Golmohammadi, A. (2024). Ethical considerations of ChatGPT-assisted article writing. *Synesis (ISSN 1984-6754), 16*(1), 94-113.

Zreik, M. (2024). Harnessing AI for entrepreneurial idea generation: Navigating the new frontier. In *Generating Entrepreneurial Ideas With AI* (pp. 1–18). IGI Global Scientific Publishing. DOI: 10.4018/979-8-3693-3498-0.ch001

About the Contributors

Hewa Majeed Zangana is an Assistant Professor at Duhok Polytechnic University (DPU), Iraq, and a current PhD candidate in Information Technology Management (ITM) at the same institution. He has held numerous academic and administrative positions, including Assistant Professor at Ararat Private Technical Institute, Lecturer at DPU's Amedi Technical Institute and Nawroz University, and Acting Dean of the College of Computer and IT at Nawroz University. His administrative roles have included Director of the Curriculum Division at the Presidency of DPU, Manager of the Information Unit at DPU's Research Center, and Head of the Computer Science Department at Nawroz University. Dr. Zangana's research interests include network systems, information security, mobile and data communication, and intelligent systems. He has authored numerous articles in peer-reviewed journals, including Inform: Jurnal Ilmiah Bidang Teknologi Informasi dan Komunikasi, Indonesian Journal of Education and Social Science, TIJAB, INJIISCOM, IEEE, and AJNU. In addition to his journal contributions, he has published more than five academic books with IGI Global, several of which are indexed in Scopus and Web of Science (Clarivate). Beyond publishing, Dr. Zangana actively contributes to the academic community through editorial service. He serves as a reviewer for the Qubahan Academic Journal and the Scientific Journals of Nawroz University. He is also a member of several academic and scientific committees, including the Scientific Curriculum Development Committee, the Student Follow-up Program Committee, and the Committee for Drafting the Rules of Procedure for Consultative Offices.

***

Sajad Aqanasiri is currently a Master's student at the Faculty of Computer Science and Engineering, Shahid Beheshti University, Iran. His research focuses on smart contract security in blockchain systems, with particular interest in leveraging fault modeling and machine learning to detect vulnerabilities such as reentrancy attacks and cryptographic mismanagement. Through his work, he aims to enhance the reliability and resilience of decentralized technologies.

Hermano Jorge De Queiroz is an Associate Professor of Graduate Studies at the School of Graduate Business & Technology at Lindsey Wilson College in Columbia, Kentucky. and the former Chair of Undergraduate IT at the University of the Cumberlands. He holds a Ph.D. in Information Technology with a specialization in Information Systems Security from the University of the Cumberlands, as well as an M.Sc. in Information Systems Security from the same institution. Additionally, he earned an M.B.A. in Business Administration from Campbellsville University and a B.Sc. in Management Information Systems and Services from Anhanguera Educacional. Dr. De Queiroz is a dedicated researcher and expert in IT and educational systems, focusing on modern instruction techniques, information systems design, and online learning environments. He serves as a Subject Matter Expert for undergraduate and graduate courses and is proficient in curriculum development and program initiation. His research interests include data science, artificial intelligence, and information systems security. He is multilingual in Portuguese, English, and Spanish and actively engages in fostering academic and professional relationships across these linguistic communities. He has contributed to various educational initiatives, improving student outcomes and promoting academic excellence.

Angel Jones is an Adjunct Professor At the University of Virginia School of Continuing and Professional Studies. Dr. Angel began his 25-year cybersecurity career as a special agent with the U.S. Department of Homeland Security, Coast Guard, investigating cybercrime. His expertise has made him the go-to subject matter expert for complex cybersecurity and cyber breach investigation matters. Dr. Jones' experience includes serving as the Chief Information Security Officer for several global firms, proactively protecting organizations from dynamic cyber threats. Further, Dr. Jones holds several industry certifications, including the Certified Information Systems Security Professional (CISSP), Certified Information Security Manager (CISM), Certified Information Systems Auditor (CISA), Certified Chief Information Security Officer (CCISO), Certified in Risk and Information Systems Control (CRISC), Certified Ethical Hacker (CEH), EnCase Certified Examiner (EnCE), Digital Forensics Certified Practitioner (DFCP), AWS Certified Solutions Architect – Professional and AWS Certified Security - Specialty and Project Management Professional (PMP).

Firas Mahmood Mustafa holds a Ph.D. in Computer Engineering from Mosul University, Iraq. His academic journey began with a B.Sc. in Electrical Engineering (Electronics and Communication), graduating in the top quarter of his class. He earned an M.Sc. in Computer Engineering from Mosul University in 2000. Mustafa joined the Computer Science Department at AlHadba University in 2003 and completed his Ph.D. in 2007. From 2013 to 2017, he was with DPU University, and from 2017 to 2020, he chaired the CCE Department at Nawroz University. An active participant in Erasmus+ and IREX programs, he now teaches at DPU University, shaping future computer engineering professionals.

Puya Pakshad conducts research in the field of vulnerability/malware detection. With a solid educational foundation from his PhD studies in Information Technology, he leverages analytical skills to address complex security challenges.

Index

A

Accountability 3, 7, 8, 12, 13, 20, 22, 59, 60, 63, 64, 67, 68, 71, 72, 73, 75, 78, 81, 94, 97, 98, 100, 115, 160, 161, 162, 163, 169, 175, 179, 181, 184, 196, 197, 198, 201, 203, 204, 207, 208, 212, 226, 228, 230, 231, 234, 237, 238, 239, 242, 246, 247, 248, 252, 254, 271, 276, 277, 286, 287, 291, 293, 294, 304, 318, 323, 326, 327, 333, 337, 338, 340, 342
Adaptation 12, 17, 64, 74, 132, 194, 234, 262, 279, 289, 321, 332, 337, 339
Agricultural 32, 182, 193, 194, 195, 196, 197, 198, 199, 202, 204, 207, 209, 210, 211, 212, 213, 216, 217, 218, 221, 222, 223, 286, 287, 288, 289, 291, 292, 294, 295, 296, 298, 299, 300, 301, 302, 304, 305, 306, 309, 310, 311, 314, 315, 316
Agriculture 66, 74, 86, 161, 164, 180, 182, 183, 184, 186, 188, 194, 195, 196, 197, 198, 199, 200, 201, 203, 204, 205, 206, 207, 208, 209, 210, 211, 212, 213, 214, 215, 216, 217, 218, 219, 220, 221, 228, 249, 255, 285, 286, 287, 288, 289, 290, 291, 292, 293, 294, 295, 296, 297, 298, 299, 300, 301, 302, 303, 304, 306, 307, 308, 309, 310, 311, 312, 313, 314, 317, 321, 322, 325, 328, 340, 344, 345, 346
AI ethics 61, 164, 172, 176, 201, 241, 246, 294, 326, 327, 335
AI misuse 162, 163, 164, 165, 175, 176, 186, 235, 320, 328
Artificial Intelligence 6, 17, 21, 23, 26, 31, 33, 34, 59, 61, 64, 66, 67, 68, 71, 74, 78, 81, 85, 86, 87, 88, 89, 90, 116, 122, 134, 141, 143, 145, 159, 160, 162, 166, 169, 170, 172, 176, 180, 183, 186, 188, 189, 190, 191, 194, 195, 197, 200, 202, 205, 208, 212, 213, 214, 215, 216, 217, 218, 219, 220, 221, 222, 226, 227, 228, 230, 236, 242, 244, 247, 250, 253, 255, 256, 257, 258, 259, 260, 276, 285, 286, 287, 290, 291, 293, 295, 298, 301, 303, 304, 306, 307, 308, 309, 310, 311, 312, 313, 314, 315, 317, 318, 319, 322, 323, 326, 329, 332, 336, 339, 342, 344, 345, 346, 347, 348, 349, 350

B

Biotechnology 2, 3, 5, 6, 7, 9, 10, 11, 12, 13, 14, 15, 16, 17, 18, 19, 20, 21, 22, 23, 25, 27, 29, 237, 317, 318, 321, 322, 325, 327, 329, 330, 332, 336, 337, 339, 345, 346, 347, 350
Bureaucratic Barriers in Research Management 93, 100, 101, 102, 103, 104, 107, 108, 110, 111, 112, 114, 118

C

case studies 3, 6, 20, 28, 30, 81, 87, 147, 148, 159, 164, 165, 181, 189, 194, 225, 257, 346
Climate Change 94, 164, 171, 225, 227, 229, 233, 234, 251, 254, 255, 256, 259, 319, 320, 324, 328, 330, 333, 336, 340, 342, 344, 345, 349
Compliance 1, 3, 5, 8, 9, 12, 14, 16, 17, 20, 21, 22, 23, 33, 37, 38, 39, 44, 57, 71, 75, 84, 93, 94, 95, 96, 98, 99, 100, 101, 102, 103, 104, 105, 106, 107, 108, 110, 111, 112, 113, 114, 115, 116, 117, 118, 119, 139, 140, 141, 143, 144, 152, 156, 160, 164, 171, 181, 184, 186, 194, 198, 201, 207, 208, 228, 230, 231, 232, 237, 240, 241, 244, 247, 248, 249, 250, 251, 259, 261, 263, 264, 271, 272, 273, 275, 277, 278, 279, 280, 294, 320, 321, 323, 325, 332, 335, 337, 338, 340, 341, 349
Contract Law 35, 36, 37, 40, 41, 42, 43, 44, 51, 140, 142, 143, 146, 147

CRISPR 317, 321, 325, 344

D

Data governance 3, 8, 14, 15, 22, 24, 27, 71, 75, 79, 83, 163, 165, 195, 230, 231, 237, 240, 251, 285, 291, 293, 295, 300, 325, 340
Data protection 12, 14, 59, 63, 140, 150, 151, 163, 197, 198, 207, 230, 237, 240, 271, 272, 291, 328, 330

E

Environmental Law 226, 228, 233, 241, 243, 245, 246, 247, 251, 254, 255, 256, 318, 320, 329, 334, 337, 344, 345
ethical guidelines 96, 97, 103, 119, 159, 165, 172, 175, 176, 200, 208, 228, 229, 237, 239, 252
Ethics 17, 19, 22, 25, 31, 61, 64, 72, 83, 84, 86, 95, 96, 98, 103, 113, 114, 115, 119, 159, 162, 164, 172, 176, 186, 188, 194, 201, 205, 206, 208, 214, 215, 218, 219, 221, 222, 227, 241, 246, 247, 248, 249, 250, 253, 254, 255, 285, 286, 291, 294, 297, 300, 302, 304, 307, 308, 311, 312, 314, 315, 326, 327, 335, 341, 342, 343, 344, 345
Expiration 35, 36, 37, 38, 39, 40, 41, 42, 43, 44, 45, 46, 47, 48, 49, 50, 51, 52, 53, 54, 139, 140, 141, 142, 149, 150

G

Governance 1, 2, 3, 4, 5, 6, 7, 8, 12, 13, 14, 15, 16, 17, 18, 20, 22, 23, 24, 26, 27, 30, 60, 64, 65, 66, 67, 71, 73, 74, 75, 77, 78, 79, 80, 82, 83, 84, 85, 87, 88, 141, 160, 161, 162, 163, 165, 181, 183, 186, 187, 189, 194, 195, 197, 198, 200, 201, 202, 204, 205, 207, 208, 209, 226, 227, 229, 230, 231, 233, 234, 235, 236, 237, 238, 240, 244, 245, 246, 247, 248, 249, 250, 251, 252, 253, 254, 255, 257, 261, 271, 272, 274, 277, 279, 285, 286, 287, 289, 291, 292, 293, 294, 295, 297, 300, 302, 303, 304, 317, 318, 319, 320, 321, 322, 323, 325, 326, 327, 328, 329, 330, 331, 332, 333, 334, 335, 336, 337, 338, 339, 340, 341, 342, 343, 344, 346, 347, 350

H

Healthcare 2, 3, 4, 5, 6, 8, 9, 11, 13, 14, 16, 17, 18, 19, 20, 21, 22, 23, 27, 28, 29, 30, 59, 60, 61, 62, 63, 64, 65, 67, 69, 70, 71, 72, 73, 74, 75, 76, 77, 78, 79, 80, 81, 82, 83, 84, 85, 87, 88, 89, 140, 160, 162, 164, 166, 167, 168, 169, 175, 181, 183, 186, 196, 226, 227, 230, 231, 232, 235, 236, 237, 238, 239, 240, 241, 242, 243, 244, 245, 246, 247, 249, 250, 253, 254, 257, 258, 259, 264, 317, 318, 319, 320, 322, 323, 324, 325, 326, 328, 329, 331, 332, 333, 335, 336, 337, 338, 339, 340, 342, 346, 347, 349

I

Innovation 1, 2, 3, 4, 5, 6, 7, 8, 9, 11, 12, 13, 14, 15, 16, 17, 18, 19, 20, 21, 22, 23, 24, 25, 26, 27, 28, 29, 30, 31, 34, 38, 44, 56, 59, 60, 63, 64, 67, 71, 74, 78, 80, 81, 82, 85, 96, 118, 128, 136, 155, 160, 161, 173, 176, 181, 183, 185, 187, 194, 195, 197, 198, 199, 202, 205, 206, 207, 208, 209, 212, 215, 218, 221, 225, 226, 228, 229, 230, 231, 232, 233, 234, 236, 238, 239, 241, 242, 243, 244, 247, 248, 249, 250, 251, 252, 253, 254, 258, 279, 282, 286, 287, 289, 291, 292, 294, 295, 297, 298, 301, 302, 303, 304, 308, 311, 314, 317, 318, 320, 322, 323, 324, 325, 329, 330, 331, 332, 333, 334, 335, 336, 337, 338, 339, 340, 341, 342, 343, 346, 347
Intellectual Property 12, 38, 43, 49, 56, 73, 98, 140, 141, 143, 144, 147, 149, 155, 163, 170, 172, 177, 225, 240, 242,

252, 291, 293, 297, 325, 341

K

Knowledge transfer 26, 150, 285, 286, 295, 296

L

Language 3, 6, 8, 10, 16, 17, 23, 26, 28, 31, 32, 33, 34, 35, 38, 49, 50, 52, 56, 57, 62, 121, 122, 123, 124, 125, 128, 129, 132, 133, 134, 135, 136, 143, 147, 156, 173, 193, 194, 195, 196, 197, 200, 201, 202, 207, 214, 219, 220, 221, 222, 285, 286, 287, 288, 295, 296, 297, 298, 299, 300, 301, 304, 307, 312, 313, 314, 315, 328
Large Language Models 3, 6, 8, 10, 16, 17, 23, 26, 28, 31, 32, 33, 34, 38, 56, 57, 121, 122, 123, 124, 125, 128, 129, 132, 133, 134, 135, 136, 143, 156, 194, 214, 219, 220, 222, 286, 295, 299, 304, 307, 312, 313, 315, 328
Law 31, 35, 36, 37, 38, 39, 40, 41, 42, 43, 44, 45, 46, 47, 48, 49, 50, 51, 53, 54, 55, 56, 57, 58, 61, 73, 82, 87, 139, 140, 141, 142, 143, 144, 146, 147, 148, 153, 155, 156, 157, 181, 195, 196, 199, 200, 201, 216, 220, 226, 228, 230, 233, 234, 235, 241, 242, 243, 244, 245, 246, 247, 249, 251, 254, 255, 256, 257, 260, 272, 287, 292, 297, 303, 304, 309, 313, 318, 320, 322, 329, 334, 335, 337, 341, 344, 345, 346, 350
Legal Interpretation 64, 194, 196, 197, 200, 241
Legal Obligations 36, 47, 140, 237
Legislation 1, 57, 72, 74, 147, 156, 176
Liability 41, 42, 45, 50, 59, 60, 65, 73, 75, 143, 153, 197, 225, 227, 230, 237, 238, 240, 247, 327

M

Medical Devices 2, 5, 6, 7, 8, 10, 15, 20, 25, 28, 30, 31, 63, 68, 69, 70, 237, 320, 323, 340
mitigation strategies 179, 182, 211

P

Policy 2, 3, 5, 8, 9, 14, 19, 20, 21, 22, 23, 25, 26, 29, 30, 31, 39, 44, 60, 61, 63, 64, 68, 74, 77, 81, 85, 89, 94, 96, 118, 144, 146, 150, 151, 153, 160, 171, 173, 181, 183, 190, 194, 198, 199, 200, 201, 206, 208, 209, 211, 212, 216, 221, 226, 227, 234, 236, 238, 239, 245, 246, 247, 248, 249, 252, 254, 255, 259, 260, 276, 277, 285, 290, 291, 292, 296, 298, 299, 300, 301, 304, 309, 314, 317, 318, 319, 321, 322, 328, 329, 330, 331, 332, 333, 334, 335, 336, 337, 338, 339, 340, 341, 342, 344, 346, 347, 348, 350
Post-Expiry 39, 41, 43, 47, 139, 140, 141, 142, 143, 144, 146, 148, 149, 150, 151, 152, 153, 154
privacy 2, 3, 6, 12, 16, 19, 22, 24, 30, 34, 60, 62, 63, 65, 66, 70, 71, 75, 79, 82, 83, 85, 89, 160, 161, 162, 163, 170, 172, 179, 181, 182, 183, 184, 185, 186, 190, 195, 196, 198, 199, 201, 204, 205, 208, 209, 211, 212, 216, 217, 226, 231, 237, 241, 247, 248, 250, 251, 252, 254, 259, 269, 271, 272, 277, 278, 280, 281, 287, 289, 291, 293, 296, 300, 302, 304, 309, 310, 318, 320, 322, 323, 325, 326, 328, 329, 330, 332, 333, 337, 340, 341, 342, 348, 349

R

Regulation 2, 3, 4, 6, 7, 8, 9, 11, 12, 13, 14, 15, 16, 17, 18, 20, 22, 23, 26, 27, 28, 31, 39, 44, 56, 58, 61, 64, 66, 67, 68, 69, 70, 74, 75, 76, 81, 82, 84, 141, 142, 155, 157, 164, 165, 183, 194,

196, 198, 200, 201, 202, 217, 230, 235, 236, 243, 247, 249, 254, 271, 272, 291, 292, 304, 310, 317, 318, 322, 324, 325, 330, 331, 334, 336, 339, 342, 343, 350
regulations 4, 5, 6, 8, 12, 15, 19, 20, 21, 22, 25, 28, 39, 59, 60, 61, 65, 67, 70, 75, 94, 140, 147, 161, 163, 164, 170, 171, 181, 185, 200, 201, 207, 212, 215, 225, 230, 231, 238, 240, 250, 259, 263, 273, 277, 278, 291, 308, 321, 322, 323, 324, 326, 327, 330, 333, 336, 339, 340, 345, 349
Research Integrity Challenges 93, 94, 96, 99, 100, 101, 103, 104, 105, 107, 108, 110, 111, 112, 114, 119
Risk management 26, 38, 70, 139, 150, 154, 273

S

Safety 1, 2, 4, 5, 7, 8, 10, 11, 13, 15, 17, 18, 19, 20, 21, 23, 24, 25, 29, 59, 60, 61, 63, 64, 65, 66, 67, 68, 70, 73, 74, 75, 76, 78, 80, 83, 84, 85, 87, 88, 89, 161, 175, 182, 185, 189, 191, 209, 217, 226, 232, 247, 249, 250, 252, 253, 256, 258, 260, 289, 291, 294, 310, 317, 318, 320, 323, 325, 326, 327, 329, 330, 331, 333, 335, 336, 337, 338, 340, 341, 346, 348, 350
security 2, 3, 6, 7, 9, 12, 16, 19, 22, 23, 25, 26, 27, 28, 30, 31, 32, 33, 34, 57, 60, 63, 64, 65, 71, 74, 79, 84, 88, 89, 98, 121, 122, 123, 124, 125, 127, 128, 131, 134, 135, 136, 137, 156, 159, 160, 161, 163, 164, 177, 178, 179, 180, 182, 183, 184, 186, 189, 190, 194, 197, 204, 206, 210, 211, 212, 213, 214, 217, 219, 220, 237, 242, 249, 250, 251, 252, 254, 257, 259, 260, 261, 262, 263, 264, 265, 266, 267, 268, 269, 270, 271, 272, 273, 274, 275, 276, 277, 278, 279, 280, 281, 282, 283, 286, 287, 293, 304, 306, 307, 310, 312, 313, 320, 323, 325, 328, 329, 330, 333, 336, 337, 338, 340, 341, 342, 347, 348, 349, 350
Software Vulnerability Detection 12, 18, 19, 23, 25, 31, 32, 34, 122, 125, 129, 135
Standards 1, 3, 4, 5, 8, 11, 13, 15, 16, 17, 19, 22, 25, 34, 35, 36, 45, 60, 64, 71, 74, 76, 78, 79, 81, 82, 84, 85, 94, 95, 96, 97, 98, 99, 100, 101, 103, 105, 111, 113, 114, 115, 119, 132, 146, 148, 153, 165, 170, 171, 172, 175, 176, 181, 184, 186, 194, 197, 198, 199, 200, 201, 202, 207, 208, 210, 211, 225, 230, 231, 234, 237, 239, 240, 241, 244, 250, 251, 252, 272, 277, 280, 289, 290, 291, 292, 293, 296, 300, 303, 305, 317, 323, 326, 332, 333, 334, 335, 336, 337, 338, 340, 341
Sustainability 57, 156, 170, 171, 172, 182, 184, 194, 196, 197, 198, 199, 206, 212, 217, 226, 227, 233, 234, 236, 238, 239, 241, 243, 245, 246, 247, 248, 250, 251, 252, 253, 254, 255, 258, 259, 275, 285, 286, 287, 293, 294, 298, 303, 304, 310, 317, 318, 319, 320, 321, 324, 326, 328, 329, 330, 332, 333, 335, 336, 337, 339, 340, 341, 342, 343, 344, 348, 349

T

Technology 1, 2, 4, 5, 6, 7, 8, 11, 14, 16, 17, 21, 24, 28, 29, 30, 31, 32, 33, 34, 39, 44, 49, 56, 57, 59, 62, 68, 83, 86, 88, 116, 121, 128, 136, 141, 148, 155, 156, 159, 160, 178, 181, 182, 188, 190, 195, 196, 199, 200, 207, 210, 214, 216, 217, 218, 219, 220, 221, 225, 229, 233, 234, 236, 246, 247, 250, 251, 252, 256, 258, 261, 262, 268, 276, 277, 278, 280, 281, 282, 287, 299, 304, 307, 309, 310, 311, 312, 313, 314, 317, 318, 319, 322, 326, 331, 333, 335, 338, 340, 345, 346, 348, 349
Technology Transfer 39, 44, 56, 57, 155, 156, 199, 225, 229, 233
Termination 35, 36, 37, 38, 39, 40, 41, 42,

43, 44, 45, 46, 47, 48, 49, 50, 51, 52, 53, 54, 55, 56, 139, 140, 141, 142, 143, 144, 145, 146, 147, 150, 152, 153
Transparency 3, 7, 8, 12, 13, 22, 24, 27, 59, 60, 63, 64, 67, 68, 69, 70, 71, 72, 74, 75, 78, 79, 81, 83, 84, 85, 94, 97, 98, 100, 103, 105, 113, 116, 134, 149, 160, 161, 162, 163, 169, 170, 172, 175, 179, 181, 184, 185, 186, 195, 196, 198, 201, 202, 204, 205, 207, 208, 210, 212, 228, 231, 239, 241, 248, 250, 252, 254, 273, 285, 286, 287, 289, 291, 292, 293, 294, 295, 296, 301, 304, 323, 326, 327, 333, 337, 338, 340, 343

www.ingramcontent.com/pod-product-compliance
Lightning Source LLC
LaVergne TN
LVHW080607300926
849162LV00005B/1067
* 9 7 9 8 3 3 7 3 4 8 6 2 9 *